ISBN 978-0-282-25805-4
PIBN 10845711

English
Français
Deutsche
Italiano
Español
Português

www.forgottenbooks.com

Mythology Photography **Fiction**
Fishing Christianity **Art** Cooking
Essays Buddhism Freemasonry
Medicine **Biology** Music **Ancient
Egypt** Evolution Carpentry Physics
Dance Geology **Mathematics** Fitness
Shakespeare **Folklore** Yoga Marketing
Confidence Immortality Biographies
Poetry **Psychology** Witchcraft
Electronics Chemistry History **Law**
Accounting **Philosophy** Anthropology
Alchemy Drama Quantum Mechanics
Atheism Sexual Health **Ancient History**
Entrepreneurship Languages Sport
Paleontology Needlework Islam
Metaphysics Investment Archaeology
Parenting Statistics Criminology
Motivational

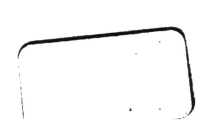

REPORT AND TRANSACTIONS

OF THE

DEVONSHIRE ASSOCIATION

FOR

THE ADVANCEMENT OF SCIENCE, LITERATURE, AND ART.

[DAWLISH, JULY, 1881.]

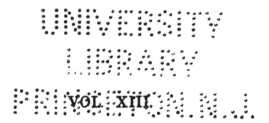

VOL. XIII.

PLYMOUTH:
W. BRENDON & SON, 26, GEORGE STREET.

1881.

The Editor is requested by the Council to make it known to the
Public, that the Committees and Authors alone are responsible for the
facts and opinions contained in their respective Reports and Papers.

It is hoped that Members will be so good as to send to the Editor,
the Rev. W. HARPLEY, Clayhanger Rectory, Tiverton, not later than
16th January, 1882, a list of any *errata* they may have detected in
the present volume.

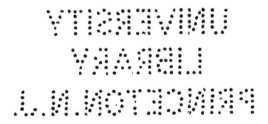

CONTENTS.

OFFICERS.

1881-82.

President.

Rev. Professor CHAPMAN, M.A.

Vice-Presidents.

H. W. DYKE ACLAND, Esq.,
M.A., M.D., F.R.S., ETC.
A. BAKER, Esq., M.D.
Rev. R. H. D. BARHAM, B.A.
W. F. COLLIER, Esq., J.P.
C. EALES, Esq., J.P.
Rev. O. MANLEY, B.A.

G. PYCROFT, Esq., M.R.C.S.
Mr. F. LEE.
Lieut.-Col. SAVILLE, J.P.
Mr. W. TAPPER.
C. J. WADE, Esq., J.P.
J. WHIDBORNE, Esq.

Hon. Treasurer.

E. VIVIAN, Esq., M.A., *Torquay.*

Hon. Local Treasurer.

A. de WINTER BAKER, Esq., L.R.C.P., M.R.C.S.

Hon. Secretary.

Rev. W. HARPLEY, M.A., F.C.P.S, *Clayhanger, Tiverton.*

Hon. Local Secretary.

J. S. WHIDBORNE, Esq.

Auditors of Accounts.

E. APPLETON, Esq., F.R.I.B.A.   C. WEEKS, Esq.

Council.

ACLAND, H. W. D.
AMERY, J. S.
AMERY, P. F. S.
APPLETON, E. A.
BAKER, A. de WINTER
BARNETT, C. G.
BATE, C. SPENCE.
CHAMPERNOWNE, A.
CHANTER, J. R.
CHAPMAN, C.
COLERIDGE, LORD.
COLLIER, Sir R. P.
COLLIER, W. F.
COTTON, R. W.
COTTON, W.
CROFT, O. W.
DAVIDSON, J. B.
DEVON, EARL OF
DOE, G.
DOWNES, W.
DYMOND, R.

EARLE, ARCHDEACON
ELWORTHY, F. T.
EXETER, BISHOP OF
FIRTH, F. H.
FRIEND, H.
FOX, S. B.
GAMLEN, W.
GERVIS, W. S.
GILL, H. S.
GREGORY, A.
HALL, T. M.
HAMILTON, A. H. A.
HARPLEY, W.
HAWKER, J. M.
HUNT, A. R.
HUTCHINSON, P. O.
JONES, WINSLOW
JORDAN, W. R. H.
KARKEEK, P. Q.
LAKE, W. C.
LEE, J. E.

MARTIN, J. M.
ORMEROD, G. W.
PARFITT, E.
PENGELLY, W.
PHILLIPS, J.
PYCROFT, G.
RISK, J. E.
ROWE, J. B.
SLADE-KING, E. J.
SLADE-KING, MRS.
TUCKER, R. C.
TUCKER, W. E.
USSHER, W. A. E.
VARWELL, P.
VIVIAN, E.
WHIDBORNE, J. S.
WINDEATT, E.
WINDEATT, T. W.
WORTH, R. N.
WORTHY, C.

TABLE SHOWING THE PLACES AND TIMES OF MEETING OF THE DEVONSHIRE ASSOCIATION,

With the Officers, Number of Members, and Number of Papers read, from its commencement.

PLACES, TIMES, &c.	PRESIDENTS.	VICE-PRESIDENTS.	TREASURERS.*	SECRETARIES.*
EXETER—August 14th, 15th, 1862. 69 Members 5 Papers	Sir John Bowring, LL.D., F.R.S.	The Mayor of Exeter (W. Kendall, Esq.) Sir L. Palk, Bart., M.P. A. H. A. Hamilton, Esq. T. Shapter, Esq., M.D.	W. Vicary, Esq., F.G.S.	C. Spence Bate, Esq., F.R.S. Rev. W. Harpley, M.A. H. S. Ellis, Esq., F.R.A.S.
PLYMOUTH—July 29th, 30th, 1863. 80 Members 10 Papers	C. Spence Bate, Esq., F.R.S. F.L.S.	Sir John Bowring, LL.D., F.R.S. The Mayor of Plymouth (W. Derry, Esq.) Sir W. Snow Harris, F.R.S. J. L. Colley, Esq.	W. Vicary, Esq., F.G.S. J. Debb, Esq.	Rev. W. Harpley, M.A. H. S. Ellis, Esq., F.R.A.S. J. B. Rowe, Esq., F.L.S.
TORQUAY—July 20th, 21st, 1864. 92 Members 16 Papers	E. Vivian, Esq., M.A.	C. Spence Bate, Esq., F.R.S., F.L.S. Chairman Torquay Local Board of Health (A. B. Sheppard, Esq.) Rev. R. H. Barnes, M.A. W. Pengelly, Esq., F.R.S., F.G.S.	W. Vicary, Esq., F.G.S.	Rev. W. Harpley, M.A. H. S. Ellis, Esq., F.R.A.S. E. Appleton, Esq.
TIVERTON—June 28th, 29th, 1865. 99 Members 14 Papers	O. G. B. Daubeny, M.D., LL.D., F.R.S., Professor of Botany, Oxford	E. Vivian, Esq., M.A. The Mayor of Tiverton (W. N. Row, Esq.) C. A. W. Troyte, Esq.	E. Vivian, Esq., M.A. J. G. Dickenson, Esq.	Rev. W. Harpley, M.A. H. S. Ellis, Esq., F.R.A.S. Rev. J. B. Hughes, M.A.
TAVISTOCK—August 8th, 9th, 1866. 132 Members 18 Papers	The Earl Russell, K.G., K.G.C., F.R.S., &c.	C. G. B. Daubeny, M.D., LL.D., F.R.S., &c. His Highness Rajah Brooke Sir J. Trelawny, Bart. J. Carpenter-Garnier, Esq. A. Russell, Esq., M.P. J. D. A. Samuda, Esq., M.P.	E. Vivian, Esq., M.A. E. Straker, Esq.	Rev. W. Harpley, M.A. H. S. Ellis, Esq., F.R.A.S. Rev. D. Griffith.
BARNSTAPLE—	W. Pengelly, Esq., F.R.S.,	The Earl Russell, K.G., K.G.C., F.R.S.,	E. Vivian, Esq., M.A.	Rev. W. Harpley, M.A. H. S. Ellis E. F.R.A.S.

Meeting	President	Members		
HONITON— July 28th to 30th, 1868. 178 Members 23 Papers	J. D. Coleridge, Esq., Q.C., M.A., M.P.	W. Pengelly, Esq., F.R.S., F.G.S. The Mayor of Honiton (D. Gould, Esq.) Right Hon. Sir J. T. Coleridge Sir J. Kennaway, Bart. W. R. Bayley, Esq. A. B. Cochrane, Esq., M.P. J. Goldsmid, Esq., M.P. C. Gordon, Esq. G. Neumann, Esq. Rev. Preb. Mackarness, M.A. W. Porter, Esq.	E. Vivian, Esq., M.A. *E. Wethey, Esq.*	Rev. W. Harpley, M.A. *Rev. R. Kirwan, M.A.* *Rev. H. K. Venn, M.A.*
DARTMOUTH— July 20th to 22nd, 1869. 246 Members 23 Papers	G. P. Bidder, Esq., C.E.	Sir J. D. Coleridge, Q.C., M.A., M.P. Sir H. P. Seale, Bart. W. Froude, Esq., M.A. C. S. Hayne, Esq. G. F. Luttrell, Esq. A. Ridgway, Esq. Rev. J. Tracey, M.A.	E. Vivian, Esq., M.A. *F. Ash, Esq.*	Rev. W. Harpley, M.A. *P. Hockin, Esq.*
DEVONPORT— July 20th to 22nd, 1870. 275 Members 22 Papers	J. A. Froude, Esq., M.A.	G. P. Bidder, Esq., C.E. The Mayor of Devonport (J. Rolston, Esq., M.D.) Vice-Adml. the Hon. J. R. Drummond, C.B. Rear-Admiral Stewart, C.B. G. Dansey, M.D. J. D. Lewis, Esq., M.P. J. May, Esq. A. Moore, Esq. I. C. Radford, Esq. J. W. W. Ryder, Esq. E. St. Aubyn, Esq. P. W. Swain, Esq. T. Woollcombe, Esq.	E. Vivian, Esq., M.A. *Rev. E. Roberts, M.A.*	Rev. W. Harpley, M.A. *G. T. Rolston, Esq.*

* Italics indicate *Local* officers.

TABLE SHOWING THE PLACES AND TIMES OF MEETING, ETC.—Continued.

PLACES, TIMES, &c.	PRESIDENTS.	VICE-PRESIDENTS.	TREASURERS.*	SECRETARIES.*
BIDEFORD— Aug. 15th to 17th, 1871. 283 Members 28 Papers	Rev. Canon C. Kingsley, M.A., F.L.S., F.G.S.	J. A. Froude, Esq., M.A. The Mayor of Bideford (J. How, Esq.) Rev. F. L. Bazeley J. B. Pine Coffin, Esq. Captain E. P. Charlewood, R.N. W. A. Deane, Esq. Rev. I. H. Gosset, M.A. General Sir E. Green Captain Molesworth, R.N. E. U. Vidal, Esq. N. Whitley, Esq. Captain Willett A. B. Wren, Esq.	E. Vivian, Esq., M.A. R. Simpkins, Esq.	Rev. W. Harpley, M.A. J. A. Parry, Esq.
EXETER— July 30 to Aug. 1, 1872. 294 Members 33 Papers	The Right Rev. Lord Bishop of Exeter	Rev. Canon C. Kingsley, M.A., F.L.S., F.G.S. The Mayor of Exeter (J. Harding, Esq.) The Sheriff (Horace G. Lloyd, Esq.) Sir L. Palk, Bart, M.P. Sir John Bowring, LL.D., F.R.S. Sir J. D. Coleridge, Q.C., M.A., M.P. R. A. Bowring, Esq., M.P. Rev. Precentor Cook, M.A. H. S. Ellis, Esq., F.R.A.S. Rev. Treasurer Hawker, M.A. J. Kennaway, Esq., M.P. R. Parfitt, Esq.	E. Vivian, Esq., M.A. W. Cotton, Esq.	Rev. W. Harpley, M.A. Rev. R. Kirwan, M.A., F.S.A. G. W. Ormerod, Esq., M.A., F.G.S. R. Parfitt, Esq.

	President	Committee	Treasurers	Secretaries
SIDMOUTH— July 22nd to 24th, 1873. 330 Members 26 Papers	The Right Hon. S. Cave, M.A., M.P.	The Right Rev. Lord Bishop of Exeter The Right Hon. and Rev. the Earl of Buckinghamshire The Hon. and Rev. the Lord Sidney Godolphin Osborne Sir J. Floyd, Bart. Sir J. H. Kennaway, Bart., M.P. Rev. H. G. J. Clements, M.A. W. R. Coleridge, Esq. C. J. Cornish, Esq. P. O. Hutchinson, Esq. J. Ingleby Mackenzie, Esq., M.B. W. Radford, M.D. R. N. Thornton, Esq.	E. Vivian, Esq., M.A. *Captain Roe, R.N.*	Rev. W. Harpley, M.A. *J. Ingleby Mackenzie, Esq., M.B.*
TEIGNMOUTH— July 28th to 30th, 1874. 327 Members 38 Papers	The Right Hon. the Earl of Devon	The Right Hon. S. Cave, M.A., M.P. J. G. Beavan, Esq. The Right Hon. Lord Clifford R. M. Dunn, Esq. E. Gulson, Esq. Rev. Treasurer Hawker, M.A. Rev. W. Laidley, M.A. W. C. Lake, Esq., M.D. J. A. Magrath, Esq., M.D. G. W. Ormerod, Esq., M.A., F.G.S. J. Parson, Esq. T. V. Wollaston, Esq., M.A., F.L.L. H. B. T. Wrey, Esq.	E. Vivian, Esq., M.A. *J. Whidborne, Esq.*	Rev. W. Harpley, M.A. *G. W. Ormerod, Esq., M.A., F.G.S.*

* Italics indicate *Local* officers.

TABLE SHOWING THE PLACES AND TIMES OF MEETING, ETC.—*Continued.*

PLACES, TIMES, &c.	PRESIDENTS.	VICE-PRESIDENTS.	TREASURERS.*	SECRETARIES.*
TORRINGTON— July 27th to 29th, 1875. 356 Members 29 Papers	R. J. King, Esq., M.A.	The Right Hon. The Earl of Devon The Mayor of Torrington (T. Jackson, Esq.) Rev. S. Buckland, M.A. W. Cann, Esq. The Right Hon. Lord Clinton Rev. F. T. Colby, B.D., F.S.A. W. A. Deane, Esq. W. H. Gamlen, Esq. H. S. Gill, Esq. J. G. Johnson, Esq., M.P. W. H. Halliday, Esq., M.A. Dr. A. Kingdon Rev. C. E. Palmer, M.A. W. E. Price, Esq. Hon. Mark Rolle J. C. Moore-Stevens, Esq. R. L. Tapley, Esq.	E. Vivian, Esq., M.A. *M. B. Loveband, Esq.*	Rev. W. Harpley, M.A. *Geo. Doe, Esq.*
ASHBURTON— July 25th to 27th, 1876. 400 Members 33 Papers	Rev. Treasurer Hawker, M.A.	R. J. King, Esq., M.A. The Portreeve of Ashburton (P. F. S. Amery, Esq.) Baldwin J. P. Bastard, Esq. A. Champernowne, Esq., M.A., F.G.S. R. Dymond, Esq, F.S.A. F. H. Firth, Esq. C. J. Follett, Esq. Rev. P. Jackson, M.A. R. Jardine, Esq. J. B. Paige-Browne, Esq., M.A. J. Robinson, Esq. Rev. W. H. Thornton, B.A. J. Tozer, Es .	E. Vivian, Esq., M.A. *W. S. Gervis, Esq., M.D.,* F.G.S.	Rev W. Harpley, M.A. *J. S. Amery, Esq.*

KINGSBRIDGE— July 31st to Aug. 2nd, 1877. 504 Members 33 Papers	Ven. Archdeacon Earle, M.A.	Rev. Treasurer Hawker, M.A. G. P. Bidder, Esq., C.E. L. B. Bowring, Esq., C.S.I. W. Cubitt, Esq. F. S. Cornish, Esq. J. Elliot, Esq. Rev. A. N. Hingston, M.A. Robert Hurrell, Esq. Rev. P. A. Ilbert, M.A. **Rev. W. D. Pittman, M.A.** **Rev. John Power, M.A.** **Rev. J. Sloane-Evans, M.A.**	E. Vivian, Esq., M.A. *B. Balkwill, Esq.*	Rev. W. Harpley, M.A. *J. S. Hurrell, Esq.*
PAIGNTON— July 30th to Aug. 1st, 1878. 471 Members 34 Papers	Sir Samuel White Baker, M.A., F.R.S., F.R.G.S.	Ven. Archdeacon Earle, M.A. J. H. Batten, Esq., F.R.G.S. R. S. S. Carey, Esq., J.P. A. H. Dendy, Esq., M.A. J. T. Goodridge, Esq., M.R.C.S. Rev. Preb. Hall, M.A. R. Mallock, Esq. C. H. Pridham, Esq., F.R.C.S. F. H. Spragge, Esq., J.P. Rev. T. R. R. Stebbing, M.A. Captain Synge, R.N. F. H. Trevithick, Esq.	E. Vivian, Esq., M.A. *A. Gregory, Esq.*	Rev. W. Harpley, M.A. *W. Edward Tucker, Esq.*

* Italics indicate *Local* officers.

TABLE SHOWING THE PLACES AND TIMES OF MEETING, ETC.—*Continued.*

PLACES, TIMES, &c.	PRESIDENTS.	VICE-PRESIDENTS.	TREASURERS.*	SECRETARIES.*
ILFRACOMBE— July 22nd to 24th, 1879. 457 Members 34 Papers	Sir R. P. Collier, M.A.	Sir. S. W. Baker, M.A., F.R.S., F.R.G.S. Rev. J. M. Chanter, M.A. J. R. Chanter, Esq. G. Doe, Esq. Rev. Treasurer Hawker, M.A. T. Hole, B.A., Esq. W. Huxtable, Esq. Chairman Ilfracombe Local Board of Health (R. Lake, Esq.) Rev. B. Price, M.A. J. Brooking Rowe, Esq., F.S.A., F.L.S. P. Stoneham, Esq., F.R.C.S. Rev. H. W. Toms, M.A.	E. Vivian, Esq., M.A. *C. G. Barnett, Esq.*	Rev. W. Harpley, M.A. *E. Slade-King, Esq. M.D.*
TOTNES— July 25th to 27th, 1880. 508 Members 41 Papers	H. W. Dyke Acland, M.A., M.D., LL.D., F.R.S., ETC.	Sir R. P. Collier, M.A. The Mayor of Totnes (J. Michelmore, Esq.) E. Appleton, Esq., F.R.I.B.A. A. Champernowne, Esq., M.A., F.G.S. J. W. Chaster, Esq., J.P. F. J. Cornish-Bowden, Esq., J.P. J. Fleming, Esq., J.P. T. C. Kellock, Esq. J. B. Paige-Browne, Esq., M.A. Rev. J. Powning, B.D. Rev. J. E. Risk, M.A. J. Roe, Esq. Rev. W. Watkins. R. H. Watson, Esq., J.P. T. W. Windeatt, Esq.	E. Vivian, Esq., M.A. *C. W. Croft, Esq.*	Rev. W. Harpley, M.A. *E. Windeatt, Esq.*

* Italics indicate *Local Officers.*

DAWLISH— July 26th to 28th, 1881. 483 Members 26 Papers	Rev. Professor Chapman, M.A.	H. W. Dyke Acland, M A., M.D., F.R.S., &c. A. Baker, Esq , M.D. Rev. R. H. D. Barham, B A. W. F. Collier, Esq , J.P. C. Eales, Esq., J.P. Rev. O. Manley, B.A. G. Pycroft, Esq., M R.C.S Mr. F. Lee (Chairman of the Local Board of Health), Lieut.-Col. Savile, J.P. Mr. W. Tapper. C. J. Wade, Esq., J.P. J. Whidborne, Esq.	E. Vivian, Esq., M.A. *A. de Winter Baker,* L.R.C.P., M.R.C.S.	Rev. W. Harpley, M.A. *J. S. Whidborne, Esq.*

* Italics indicate *Local* Officers.

RULES.

1. THE Association shall be styled the Devonshire Association for the advancement of Science, Literature, and Art.

2. The objects of the Association are—To give a stronger impulse and a more systematic direction to scientific enquiry in Devonshire; and to promote the intercourse of those who cultivate Science, Literature, or Art, in different parts of the county.

3. The Association shall consist of Members, Honorary Members, and Corresponding Members.

4. Every candidate for membership, on being nominated by a member to whom he is personally known, shall be admitted by the General Secretary, subject to the confirmation of the General Meeting of the Members.

5. Persons of eminence in Literature, Science, or Art, connected with the West of England, but not resident in Devonshire, may, at a General Meeting of the Members, be elected Honorary Members of the Association; and persons not resident in the county, who feel an interest in the Association, may be elected Corresponding Members.

6. Every *Member* shall pay an Annual Contribution of Half-a-guinea, or a Life Composition of Five Guineas.

7. Ladies only shall be admitted as Associates to an Annual Meeting, and shall pay the sum of Five Shillings each.

8. Every *Member* shall be entitled gratuitously to a lady's ticket.

9. The Association shall meet annually, at such a time in July and at such place as shall be decided on at the previous Annual Meeting.

10. A President, two or more Vice-Presidents, a General Treasurer, and one or more General Secretaries, shall be elected at each Annual Meeting.

11. The President shall not be eligible for re-election.

12. Each Annual Meeting shall appoint a local Treasurer and Secretary, who, with power to add to their number any Members of the Association, shall be a local Committee to assist in making such local arrangements as may be desirable.

13. In the intervals of the Annual Meetings, the affairs of the Association shall be managed by a Council, which shall consist exclusively of the following Members of the Association, excepting Honorary Members, and Corresponding Members :

(*a*) Those who fill, or have filled, or are elected to fill, the offices of President, General and Local Treasurers, General and Local Secretaries, and Secretaries of Committees appointed by the Council.

(*b*) Authors of Papers which have been printed *in extenso* in the Transactions of the Association.

14. The Council shall hold a meeting at Exeter in the month of January or February in each year, on such day as the General Secretary shall appoint, for the due management of the affairs of the Association, and the performing the duties of their office.

15. The General Secretary, or any four members of the Council, may call extraordinary meetings of their body, to be held at Exeter, for any purpose requiring their present determination, by notice under his or their hand or hands, addressed to every other member of the Council, at least ten clear days previously, specifying the purpose for which such extraordinary meeting is convened. No matter not so specified, and not incident thereto, shall be determined at any extraordinary meeting.

16. The General Treasurer and Secretary shall enter on their respective offices at the meeting at which they are elected ; but the President, Vice-Presidents, and Local Officers, not until the Annual Meeting next following.

17. With the exception of the Ex-Presidents only, every Councillor who has not attended any Meeting, or adjourned Meeting, of the Council during the period between the close

of any Annual General Meeting of the Members and the close of the next but two such Annual General Meetings, shall have forfeited his place as a Councillor, but it shall be competent for him to recover it by a fresh qualification.

18. The Council shall have power to fill any Official vacancy which may occur in the intervals of the Annual Meetings.

19. The Annual Contributions shall be payable in advance, and shall be due in each year on the day of the Annual Meeting.

20. The Treasurer shall receive all sums of money due to the Association; he shall pay all accounts due by the Association after they shall have been examined and approved; and he shall report to each meeting of the Council the balance he has in hand, and the names of such members as shall be in arrear, with the sums due respectively by each.

21. Whenever a Member shall have been three months in arrear in the payment of his Annual Contributions, the Treasurer shall apply to him for the same.

22. Whenever, at an Annual Meeting, a Member shall be two years in arrear in the payment of his Annual Contributions, the Council may, at its discretion, erase his name from the list of members.

23. The General Secretary shall, at least one month before each Annual Meeting, inform each member by circular of the place and date of the Meeting.

24. Members who do not, on or before the day of the Annual Meeting, give notice, in writing or personally, to the General Secretary of their intention to withdraw from the Association, shall be regarded as members for the ensuing year.

25. The Association shall, within three months after each Annual Meeting, publish its Transactions, including the Rules, a Financial Statement, a List of the Members, the Report of the Council, the President's Address, and such Papers, in abstract or *in extenso*, read at the Annual Meeting, as shall be decided by the Council.

26. The Association shall have the right at its discretion of printing *in extenso* in its Transactions all papers read at the Annual Meeting. The copyright of a paper read before any meeting of the Association, and the illustrations

of the same which have been provided at his expense, shall remain the property of the Author; but he shall not be at liberty to print it, or allow it to be printed elsewhere, either *in extenso* or in abstract amounting to as much as one-half of the length of the paper, before the first of November next after the paper is read.

27. The Authors of papers printed in the Transactions shall, within seven days after the Transactions are published, receive twenty-five private copies free of expense, and shall be allowed to have any further number printed at their own expense. All arrangements as to such extra copies to be made by the Authors with the printers to the Association.

28. If proofs of papers to be published in the Transactions be sent to Authors for correction, and are retained by them beyond four days for each sheet of proof, to be reckoned from the day marked thereon by the printers, but not including the time needful for transmission by post, such proofs shall be assumed to require no further correction.

29. Should the Author's corrections of the press in any paper published in the Transactions amount to a greater sum than in the proportion of twenty shillings per sheet, such excess shall be borne by the Author himself, and not by the Association.

30. Every *Member* shall, within three months after each Annual Meeting, receive gratuitously a copy of the Transactions.

31. The Accounts of the Association shall be audited annually, by Auditors appointed at each Annual Meeting, but who shall not be *ex officio* Members of the Council.

BYE-LAWS AND STANDING ORDERS.

1. IN the interests of the Association it is desirable that the President's Address in each year be printed previous to its delivery.

2. In the event of there being at an Annual Meeting more Papers than can be disposed of in one day, the reading of the residue shall be continued the day following.

3. The pagination of the Transactions shall be in Arabic numerals exclusively, and carried on consecutively, from the beginning to the end of each volume; and the Transactions of each year shall form a distinct and separate volume.

4. The General Secretary shall bring to each Annual Meeting of the Members a report of the number of copies in stock of each 'Part' of the Transactions, with the price per copy of each 'Part' specified; and such report shall be printed in the Transactions next after the Treasurer's financial statement.

5. The General Secretary shall prepare and bring to each Annual Meeting brief Obituary Notices of Members deceased during the previous year, and such notices shall be printed in the Transactions.

6. An amount not less than the sum of the Compositions of all existing Life-Members shall be kept at Interest in the names of the Treasurer and General Secretary.

7. The General Secretary shall, within one month of the close of each Annual Meeting of the Association, send to each Member newly elected at the said Meeting a copy of the following letter:—

Devonshire Association for the Advancement of Science, Literature, and Art.

SIR,—I have the pleasure of informing you that on the   of July,   you were elected a Member of the Association on the nomination of

The copy of the Transactions for the current year, which will be forwarded to you in due course, will contain the Laws of the Association. Meanwhile I beg to call your attention to the following statements:—

(1) Every Member pays an Annual Contribution of Half a Guinea, or a Life Composition of Five Guineas.

(2) The Annual Contributions are payable in advance, and are due in each year on the day of the Annual Meeting.

(3) Members who do not, on or before the day of the Annual Meeting, give notice in writing or personally to the General Secretary of their intention to withdraw from the Association are regarded as Members for the ensuing year.

The Treasurer's Address is—EDWARD VIVIAN, Esq., Woodfield, Torquay.—I remain, Sir, your faithful Servant,

Hon. Sec.

8. The reading of any Report or Paper shall not exceed twenty minutes, or such part of twenty minutes as shall be decided by the Council as soon as the Programme of Reports and Papers shall have been settled, and in any discussion which may arise, no speaker shall be allowed to speak more than ten minutes.

9. Papers to be read to the Annual Meetings of the Association must strictly relate to Devonshire, and, as well as all Reports intended to be printed in the Transactions of the Association, and prepared by Committees appointed by the Council, must, together with all drawings intended to be used in illustrating them in the said Transactions, reach the General Secretary's residence not later than the 24th day of June in each year. The General Secretary shall, not later than the 7th of the following July, return to the authors all such Papers as he may decide to be unsuitable to be printed in the said Transactions, and shall send the residue, together with the said Reports of Committees, to the Association's printers, who shall return the same so that they may reach the General Secretary's residence not later than on the 14th day of the said July, together with a statement of the number of pages each of them would occupy if printed in the said Transactions, as well as an estimate of the extra cost of the printing of such Tables, of any kind, as may form part of any of the said Papers and Reports; and the General Secretary shall lay the whole, as well as an estimate of the probable number of Annual Members of the Association for the year commencing on that day, before the first Council Meeting on the first day of the next ensuing Annual Meeting, when the Council shall select not a greater number of the Papers thus laid before them than will, with the other

documents to be printed in the said Transactions, make as many sheets of printed matter as can be paid for with 60 per cent. of the subscriptions, for the year, of the said probable number of Annual Members, exclusive of the extra cost of the printing of such aforesaid Tables, which have been approved and accepted by the Council, provided the aggregate of the said extra cost do not exceed 6 per cent. of the said subscriptions; exclusive also of the printers' charge for corrections of the press; and also exclusive of the cost of printing an Index, a list of Errata, and such Resolutions passed at the next Winter meeting of the Council, as may be directed to be so printed by the said Winter Meeting; and the number of Papers selected by the Council shall not be greater than will, with the Reports of Committees, make a total of 40 Reports and Papers.

10. Papers communicated by Members for Non-Members, and accepted by the Council, shall be placed in the Programme below those furnished by Members themselves.

11. Papers which have been accepted by the Council cannot be withdrawn without the consent of the Council.

12. The Council will do their best so to arrange Papers for reading as to suit the convenience of the authors; but the place of a Paper cannot be altered after the Programme has been settled by the Council.

13. Papers which have already been printed *in extenso* cannot be accepted, unless they form part of the literature of a question on which the Council has requested a Member or Committee to prepare a report.

14. Every meeting of the Council shall be convened by Circular, sent by the General Secretary to each Member of the Council, not less than ten days before the Meeting is held.

15. All Papers read to the Association which the Council shall decide to print *in extenso* in the Transactions, shall be sent to the printers, together with all drawings required in illustrating them, on the day next following the close of the Annual Meeting at which they were read.

16. All Papers read to the Association which the Council shall decide not to print *in extenso* in the Transactions, shall be returned to the authors not later than the day next following the close of the Annual Meeting at which they were read; and abstracts of such Papers to be printed in the

Transactions shall not exceed one-fourth of the length of the Paper itself, and must be sent to the General Secretary on or before the seventh day after the close of the Annual Meeting.

17. The Author of every Paper which the Council at any Annual Meeting shall decide to print in the Transactions shall be expected to pay for all such illustrations as in his judgment the said Paper may require; but the Council may, at their discretion, vote towards the expense of such illustrations any sum not exceeding the balance in hand as shown by the Treasurer's Report to the said Meeting, after deducting all Life Compositions, as well as all Annual Contributions received in advance of the year to which the said Report relates, which may be included in the said balance.

18. The printers shall do their utmost to print the Papers in the Transactions in the order in which they were read, and shall return every Manuscript to the author as soon as it is in type, *but not before.* They shall be returned *intact*, provided they are written on loose sheets and on one side of the paper only.

19. Excepting mere verbal alterations, no Paper which has been read to the Association shall be added to without the written approval and consent of the General Secretary; and no additions shall be made except in the form of notes or postscripts, or both.

20. In the intervals of the Annual Meetings, all Meetings of the Council shall be held at Exeter, unless some other place shall have been decided on at the previous Council Meeting.

21. When the Number of Copies on hand of any 'Part' of the Transactions is reduced to twenty, the price per copy shall be increased 25 per cent.; and when the number has been reduced to ten copies, the price shall be increased 50 per cent. on the original price.

22. The Association's Printers, but no other person, may reprint any Committee's Report printed in the Transactions of the Association, for any person, whether a Member of the said Committee, or of the Association, or neither, on receiving, in each case, a written permission to do so from the Honorary Secretary of the Association, but not otherwise; that the said printer shall pay to the said Secretary, for the Association, sixpence for every fifty copies of each half sheet of eight

pages of which the said Report consists; that any number of copies less than fifty, or between two exact multiples of fifty, shall be regarded as fifty; and any number of pages less than eight, or between two exact multiples of eight, shall be regarded as eight; that each copy of such Reprints shall have on its first page the words "Reprinted from the Transactions of the Devonshire Association for the Advancement of Science, Literature, and Art for —— with the consent of the Council of the Association," followed by the date of the year in which the said Report was printed in the said Transactions, but that, with the exception of printers' errors, and changes in the pagination which may be necessary or desirable, the said Reprint shall be in every other respect an exact copy of the said Report as printed in the said Transactions, without addition, or abridgment, or modification of any kind.

23. The General Secretary shall, within one month after each Annual General Meeting, inform the Hon. Local Treasurer and the Hon. Local Secretary, elected at the said Meeting, that, in making or sanctioning arrangements for the next Annual General Meeting, it is eminently desirable that they avoid and discourage everything calculated to diminish the attendance at the General and Council Meetings, or to disturb the said Meetings in any way.

24. The Bye-Laws and Standing Orders shall be printed after the "Rules" in the Transactions.

25. All resolutions appointing committees for special service for the Association shall be printed in the Transactions next before the President's Address.

REPORT OF THE COUNCIL,

As presented to the General Meeting, Dawlish, 1881.

THE Nineteenth Annual Meeting of the Association was held at Totnes, commencing on Tuesday, July 27th, and was eminently successful. Never has the Association been more hospitably received, both publicly and privately, than in this ancient borough and its locality. The number of Members enrolled, and papers read, exceeded that of any former occasion.

At 2 p.m. a Council Meeting was held, when the usual formal business was transacted. At the conclusion of this meeting the members were met by the Mayor and Corporation at the Gate House, and marched in procession, headed by the mace-bearers, through the Parish Church to the Guildhall, where an address of welcome was read by the Town Clerk, and the whole of the party were most hospitably entertained in the Council Chamber. A General Meeting was held at 4 p.m.; and in the evening, at 8 p.m., in the Assembly Rooms, Seven Stars Hotel, the President, Dr. W. H. Dyke Acland, who in the absence of the retiring President, Sir R. P. Collier, was introduced in befitting terms by the Rev. Treasurer Hawker, delivered his Introductory Address. The room was well filled, a large number of ladies being present.

On Wednesday, at 11 a.m., the reading and discussion of the following programme of Papers was commenced.

Fifth Report of the Committee on Devonshire Meteorology	*Dr. Lake.*
Fifth Report of the Committee on Scientific Memoranda	*W. Pengelly*, F.R.S., F.G.S., &c.
Fifth Report of the Committee on Devonshire Folk-Lore	*G. Doe.*
Fourth Report of the Committee on Devonshire Celebrities	*Rev. Treasurer Hawker*, M.A.
Second Report of the Committee on Works of Art in Devonshire . . .	*Rev. Treasurer Hawker*, M.A.
Second Report of the Committee on Barrows	*R. N. Worth*, F.G.S.

A Totnes Scholar—Edward Lye, M.A.	*E. Windeatt.*
The Fauna of Devon—*Aculeata*	*E. Parfitt.*
The Myth of Brutus the Trojan	*R. N. Worth*, F.G.S.
Notes on the early history of Dartmouth, with especial reference to its commerce, shipping, and seamen in the 14th century	*P. Q. Karkeek.*
Notes on Recent Notices of the Geology and Palæontology of Devonshire—Part VII.	*W. Pengelly*, F.R.S., F.G.S., &c.
The Font in Christ Church, Ilfracombe (communicated by the Rev. Treasurer Hawker, M.A.).	*Miss Price.*

In the evening the annual dinner of the Association was held at the Seymour Hotel, when an excellent repast was served up to a party of ladies and gentlemen numbering about 130. Dr. Acland presided.

There was afterwards a garden party on the Island, at the invitation of the Mayor and Local Committee, and although the weather proved somewhat unfavourable for such a gathering, still a large number of members attended, and thoroughly appreciated the order of proceedings. The Island groves were prettily illuminated with Chinese and other coloured lamps, and refreshments were unsparingly supplied to the company.

On Thursday, at 10 a.m., the reading of papers was resumed, and continued with unabated interest until the exceptionally long programme was exhausted at 3 p.m. A General Meeting and Council Meeting then followed, and brought to a close the formal business of the Meeting.

Through the kind invitation of the Mayor of Totnes, J. Michelmore, Esq., a number of Members and Associates had an enjoyable excursion to Berry Pomeroy Castle, the grand old ruins forming a feature of no inconsiderable interest. On the road from Totnes the remains of the ancient paved way attributed to the Romans, and evidently of great antiquity, were pointed out; and on arriving at the Castle the Mayor escorted the party to the chief features of interest, describing the many historic incidents with which the ancient fortress is associated. The party subsequently returned to Berry House, where they were most hospitably entertained by his Worship and the Mayoress. By the invitation of A. Champernowne, Esq., another party, numbering upwards of one hundred, availed themselves of the opportunity of visiting Dartington Hall, one of the most picturesque seats in the county; the walk or drive through the Park alone affording infinite pleasure to the admirers of lovely scenery. On arriving at the Hall the visitors were most cordially welcomed by Mr. and Mrs. Champernowne, who took delight in pointing out the various portions of historical interest, and entertained the party with unbounded hospitality.

On Friday, July 30th, there were excursions to the Moor and to Dartmouth. One party was conveyed in breaks and waggonettes to the Buckland Drives, New Bridge, Gallantry Bower, and Brook House, where Mr. Hamlyn of Buckfastleigh had kindly invited the excursionists to lunch. The Mine, with its recently erected ore dressing machinery, was inspected and explained by the local manager. The return journey was by Buckfast Abbey, under the joint guidance of the Mayor and Mr. Fabyan Amery. The party for Dartmouth started in a large boat drawn by a steam launch, and was conducted by Mr. Appleton and Mr. T. Windeatt. Heavy showers fell during the day, but the excursions in both directions were thoroughly enjoyed by all.

It having been decided that the next Annual Meeting should be held at Dawlish, the following were elected officers for that occasion:

President: Professor W. B. Hodgson, LL.D. Vice-Presidents: H. W. Dyke Acland, Esq., M.A., M.D., F.R.S., &c.; A. Baker, Esq., M.D.; Rev. R. H. D. Barham, B.A.; W. F. Collier, Esq., J.P.; C. Eales, Esq., J.P.; Rev. O. Manley, B.A.; G. Pycroft, Esq., M.R.C.S.; Mr. F. Lee (Chairman of the Local Board of Health); Lieut.-Col. Saville, J.P.; Mr. W. Tapper; C. J. Wade, Esq., J.P.; J. Whidborne, Esq. Hon. Treasurer: E. Vivian, Esq., M.A., *Torquay*. Hon. Local Treasurer: A. De Winter Baker, Esq., L.R.C.P., M.R.C.S. Hon. Secretary: Rev. W. Harpley, M.A., F.C.P.S., *Clayhanger, Tiverton*. Hon. Local Secretary: J. S. Whidborne, Esq.

Shortly afterwards, on August 24th, Dr. Hodgson, whose loss the Association cannot cease to deplore, died suddenly. Your Council were thus called upon to exercise the duties and privileges they enjoy under the 13th rule of the Association; accordingly, at their winter meeting they proceeded to fill the void caused by Dr. Hodgson's decease. Their choice fell upon the Rev. T. R. R. Stebbing, an old and valued member of the Association, who was duly elected. Again misfortune came. Early in April Mr. Stebbing announced the fact that his house had been destroyed by fire, and with it all his valuable notes and papers, the result of years of careful research and study. In consequence of this calamity he felt constrained to tender his resignation of the office of President, which was accepted. At a meeting of the Council on May the 10th, specially convened for the purpose, the Rev. Professor Chapman, who had kindly and courageously, at so late a period, consented to be put in nomination, was duly elected, and thus the Association will meet on this occasion under his presidency.

The Council have published the President's Address, together with Obituary Notices of members deceased during the year preceding, and the Reports and Papers read before the Association; also the Treasurer's Report, a List of Members, and the Rules, Standing Orders, and Bye-Laws; they have since added an Index, kindly prepared by Mr. P. O. Hutchinson.

A Copy of the *Transactions* and *Index* has been sent to each Member, and to the following Societies: The Royal Society, Linnæan Society, Geological Society, Anthropological Institute of Great Britain and Ireland, Royal Institution (Albemarle Street), The Society of Antiquaries, Devon and Exeter Institution (Exeter), Plymouth Institution, Torquay Natural History Society, Barnstaple Literary and Scientific Institution, Royal Institution of Cornwall (Truro), and the Library of the British Museum.

RECEIPTS.

		£	s.	d.
Balance in Treasurer's hand 24th July, 1880		47	3	5
Arrears of Annual Contributions 1878-9	0 10 6			
Ditto ditto 1879-80	5 15 6	6	6	0
Annual Contributions for 1880-1		198	9	9
Prepaid Annual Contributions for 1881-2	21 10 6			
Ditto ditto 1882-3	0 10 6	22	1	0
Ladies' Tickets sold at Totnes		1	5	0
Life Compositions		42	0	0
Sale of "Transactions," 4 copies for 1862		0	8	0
Ditto ditto 1863	2	0	4	0
Ditto ditto 1864	2	0	6	0
Ditto ditto 1865	1	0	2	6
Ditto ditto 1866	1	0	3	0
Ditto ditto 1867	2	0	12	0
Ditto ditto 1868	1	0	6	6
Ditto ditto 1869	2	1	4	0
Ditto ditto 1870	1	0	6	0
Ditto ditto 1871	1	0	6	6
Ditto ditto 1872	1	0	15	0
Ditto ditto 1873	1	0	6	0
Ditto ditto 1874	1	0	8	6
Ditto ditto 1875	2	1	0	0
Ditto ditto 1876	2	1	4	0
Ditto ditto 1877	2	0	12	0
Ditto ditto 1878	3	1	10	0
Interest on Deposit at Torquay Bank to June 30, 1881		9	14	0
		9	0	8
		£335	**19**	**1**

		£	s.	d.
Annual Contributions unpaid for 1879-80		8	8	0
Ditto ditto 1880-1		12	1	6
		£20	**9**	**6**

EXPENDITURE.

		£	s.	d.
Deposited at Interest in Torquay Bank		45	0	0
Brendon & Son for Printing "Transactions," vol. xii. (1880)	182 2 6			
Ditto Index to vol. xi. (1879)	2 17 6			
Ditto Cards, Circulars, &c.	4 8 6			
Ditto Postage and Carriage of Parcels	25 10 6			
Ditto Stationery	0 18 6	215	12	6
Mortimore Brothers for Printing Programmes		0	17	0
Torquay Directory Co. for Printing Receipt Forms		0	15	0
Insurance of "Transactions" in Stock to Midsummer, 1881		0	5	0
Hon. Gen. Treasurer for Petty Expenses		6	14	3
Hon. Gen. Secretary ditto		6	7	3
Advertising in 1880		5	3	2
Balance in Treasurer's hand 25th July, 1881		55	4	11
		£335	**19**	**1**

(Signed) EDWARD VIVIAN, Treasurer.

25th July, 1881.

We have compared the Books and Vouchers presented to us, and found them correct,

STATEMENT OF PROPERTY OF THE ASSOCIATION,

July 26th, 1881.

		£	s.	d.
Deposit at Interest in Torquay Bank (including Life Compositions of Sixty Members) . .		305	0	0
Balance in Treasurer's hand* (25th July, 1881) .		55	4	11
Arrears of Annual Contributions (valued at) . .		7	7	0
"Transactions" in Stock, 1862 .. 4 copies at 2s. 0d. .		0	8	0
,, ,, 1863 .. 97 ,, 2s. 0d. .		9	14	0
,, 1864 .. 108 ,, 3s. 0d. .		16	4	0
,, 1865 .. 105 ,, 2s. 6d. .		13	2	6
,, 1866 .. 82 ,, 3s. 0d. .		12	6	0
,, 1867 .. 79 ,, 6s. 0d. .		23	14	0
,, 1868 .. 53 ,, 6s. 6d. .		17	4	6
,, 1870 .. 30 ,, 6s. 0d. .		9	0	0
,, 1871 .. 30 ,, 6s. 6d. .		9	15	0
,, 1873 .. 37 ,, 6s. 0d. .		11	2	0
,, 1874 .. 40 ,, 8s. 6d. .		17	0	0
,, 1875 .. 19 ,, 10s. 0d. .		9	10	0
,, 1876 .. 22 ,, 12s. 0d. .		13	4	0
,, 1877 .. 23 ,, 6s. 0d. .		6	18	0
,, 1878 .. 8 ,, 12s. 0d. .		4	16	0
,, ,, 1879 .. 31 ,, 7s. 0d. .		10	17	0
,, ,, 1880 .. 26 ,, 10s. 0d. .		13	0	0
Due for "Transactions" sold . . .		0	0	0
		£565	6	11

(Signed)

W. HARPLEY,

Hon. Secretary.

" When the number of copies on hand of any Part of the 'Transactions' is reduced to twenty, the price per copy shall be increased 25 per cent.; and when the number has been reduced to ten copies, the price shall be increased 50 per cent."—*Standing Order, No. 21.*

The "Transactions" in Stock are insured against fire in the sum of £200. The vols. published in 1869 and 1872 are out of print.

* The balance in Treasurer's hand (£55 4s. 11d.) is indebted to Capital to the amount of £61 19s. (= Life Compositions, £42 + Prepaid Annual Contributions, £18 7s. 6d.)

SELECTED MINUTES OF COUNCIL, APPOINTING COMMITTEES.

Passed at the Meeting at Dawlish,

JULY, 1881.

---

14. That Dr. H. W. Dyke Acland, Mr. C. Spence Bate, Rev. Professor Chapman, Ven. Archdeacon Earle, Rev. W. Harpley, Rev. Treasurer Hawker, and Mr. W. Pengelly be a Committee for the purpose of considering at what place the Association shall hold its Meeting in 1883, who shall be invited to be the Officers at that Meeting, and who shall be invited to fill any official vacancies which may occur before the Annual Meeting in 1882; that Mr. Pengelly be the Secretary; and that they be requested to report to the next Winter Meeting of the Council.

15. That Mr. George Doe, Rev. W. Harpley, Mr. N. S. Heineken, Mr. H. S. Gill, Mr. E. Parfitt, and Mr. J. Brooking Rowe be a Committee for the purpose of noting the discovery or occurrence of such Facts in any department of scientific inquiry, and connected with Devonshire, as it may be desirable to place on permanent record, but which may not be of sufficient importance in themselves to form the subjects of separate papers; and that Mr. J. Brooking Rowe be the Secretary.

16. That Mr. P. F. S. Amery, Mr. George Doe, Mr. R. Dymond, Rev. W. Harpley, Mr. P. Q. Karkeek, and Mr. J. Brooking Rowe be a Committee for the purpose of collecting notes on Devonshire Folk-Lore; and that Mr. George Doe be the Secretary.

17. That Mr. R. W. Cotton, Mr. R. Dymond, Rev. Treasurer Hawker, Mr. P. Q. Karkeek, Sir J. H. Kennaway, Mr. E. Windeatt, and Mr. R. N. Worth be a Committee for the purpose of compiling a list of deceased Devonshire Celebrities, as well as an Index of the entire Bibliography having reference to them; that the list consist exclusively of Celebrities born in Devonshire; and that the Rev. Treasurer Hawker be the Secretary.

18. That Mr. R. Dymond, Mr. A. H. A. Hamilton, Mr. G. Pycroft, Rev. Treasurer Hawker, Mr. J. G. Templer, and Mr. R. N. Worth be a Committee to prepare a Report on the Public and Private Collections of Works of Art in Devonshire; and that Mr. Dymond be the Secretary.

19. That Mr. J. S. Amery, Mr. C. Spence Bate, Mr. W. F. Collier, Mr. J. Divett, Mr. R. Dymond, Mr. F. H. Firth, Rev. W. Harpley, Rev. Treasurer Hawker, Mr. W. Lavers, Mr. G. W. Ormerod, Mr. J. Brooking Rowe, and Rev. W. H. Thornton be a Committee for the purpose of collecting information on all matters connected with Public Rights on Dartmoor; that for the purposes of the said Committee "Dartmoor" shall be regarded as consisting inclusively and exclusively of the entire parishes of Ashburton, *Belstone*, Bovey Tracey, *Bridestowe*, Bridford, *Buck-fastleigh*, Buckland-in-the-Moor, Buckland Monachorum, *Chagford*, Cornwood, *Dean Prior*, Drewsteignton, *Gidleigh*, Harford, *Holne*, Islington, Lamerton, Lustleigh, *Lydford*, *Manaton*, Mary Tavy, *Meavy*, Moretonhampstead, *North Bovey*, Okehampton, *Peter Tavy*, *Sampford Spiney*, *Shaugh Prior*, *Sheepstor*, *Sourton*, *South Brent*, *South Tawton*, *Tavistock*, *Throwleigh*, Ugborough, *Walkhampton*, *Whitchurch*, and *Widecombe-in-the-Moor*; and that Mr. W. F. Collier be the Secretary.

N.B. Italics indicate Venville parishes.

20. That Mr. J. S. Amery, Mr. G. Doe, Mr. R. Dymond, Mr. F. T. Elworthy, Mr. F. H. Firth, Mr. P. O. Hutchinson, Mr. P. Q. Karkeek, and Dr. W. C. Lake be a Committee for the purpose of noting and recording the existing use of any Verbal Provincialisms in Devonshire, in either written or spoken language, not included in the lists published in the Transactions of the Association; that Mr. F. T. Elworthy be the Editor, and that Mr. F. H. Firth be the Secretary.

21. That Mr. J. S. Amery, Mr. J. B. Davidson, Mr. G. Doe, Mr. R. Dymond, Ven. Archdeacon Earle, Rev. W. Harpley, Mr. J. S. Hurrell, Mr. P. O. Hutchinson, Mr. J. Brooking Rowe, and Mr. R. N. Worth be a Committee for editing and annotating such parts of *Domesday Book* as relate to Devonshire; and that Mr. J. Brooking Rowe be the Secretary.

22. That Mr. C. Spence Bate, Mr. G. Doe, Mr. P. O. Hutchinson, Mr. E. Parfitt, Mr. J. Brooking Rowe, and Mr. R. N. Worth be a Committee to collect and record facts relating to Barrows in Devonshire, and to take steps, where possible, for their investigation; and that Mr. R. N. Worth be the Secretary.

23. That Mr. J. S. Amery, Mr. G. Doe, Mr. R. Dymond, Mr. G. W. Ormerod, Mr. J. Brooking Rowe, and Mr. E. Windeatt be a Committee to obtain information as to peculiar tenures of land, and as to customs of Manor Courts, in Devonshire; and that Mr. E. Windeatt be the Secretary.

24. That Mr. F. H. Firth, Rev. W. Harpley, Mr. H. Tozer, Mr. R. C. Tucker, and Rev. Preb. Smith be a Committee for the purpose of making the arrangements for the Association Dinner at Crediton in 1882; and that Mr. R. C. Tucker be the Secretary.

29. That Mr. T. H. Edmonds, Mr. H. S. Gill, Mr. E. E. Glyde, Mr. E. Parfitt, and Mr. P. F. S. Amery be a Committee to collect and tabulate trustworthy and comparable observations on the climate of Devon; and that Mr. P. F. S. Amery be the Secretary.

PRESIDENT'S ADDRESS.

LADIES AND GENTLEMEN,—I appear before you to-day in the honourable position of President of this Association—neither because, on my part, of any conscious fitness for the discharge of the duties pertaining to the office, nor because I see anything done in the past to merit your suffrages, but simply in obedience to the summons of those charged with the conduct of your affairs, whose judgment I am bound to respect even when it differs from my own. Had one of the calamities incidental to human life not fallen on a certain home, or had a valuable life been spared to enrich the world still further with vigorous thought and genial manners, you to-day would have been addressed by another voice, and I should have had the satisfaction of knowing that the Devonshire Association was maintaining, as heretofore, its well-earned reputation by means of the learning and wisdom of its Presidential Address. No doubt, under the shadow of an event which must cause sincere grief to many, you will extend to me a kind indulgence, as, in compliance with your wishes, at the eleventh hour, and at a season when, by reason of pressing ordinary duties, it is least possible for me to do justice to my theme, I endeavour to present for your consideration a few observations bearing, it is to be hoped, some obvious relation to the objects we all have in view on the present occasion.

We are familiar with the truth, illustrated in so many fields of Science, that it is by the combination of varied forces that definite results are brought about, which, later on, form a distinct factor in the world's development, to be used up with other elements in new combinations for still higher and more perfect issues. It seems to me that the founders of this Association were acting on this strictly scientific principle when they first sought to bring together the scattered elements of intellectual activity in the county of·

Devon, so that, by convergence and interblending, these might annually issue in a distinct contribution to the Advancement of Science, Literature, and Art, which in its turn should form a factor in a still wider development of Knowledge and Culture. To what extent this has been accomplished, a perusal of the published *Transactions* of the Association will indicate. Obviously many valuable fruits of Scientific and Literary toil have been conserved and rendered available for use in prosecuting further researches; and, without indulging in that local vanity which is the besetting sin of the provincial mind, may we not hope that, on the basis of population and average capacity of educated men, in addition to those who in special departments have already won honour for themselves and their county, there are yet in Devonshire many vigorous intellects naturally or by education fitted to render good service to mankind by scientific discovery, or wise presentation of historic truth, or works of Art? Moreover, if a Murchison was ultimately won over from the dubious joys associated with hunting and racing studs, to the pure pleasures and enduring honours of Science, by an incidental attendance on a scientific meeting, are we unreasonable in the supposition that, over and above the stimulus given to minds already intent on her aims, Science may throw her mighty spell around some of her erring children now unfortunately spending their intellectual substance, if not in riotous living, yet in things of no permanent advantage to themselves or their kind?

Public assemblies are symptoms of the state and tendency of public life; and so we may regard the annual gathering of this and kindred Associations as a sign of the ever-deepening and widening interest cherished in matters pertaining to the cultivation of Science, Literature, and Art, as also in these things themselves. Of course the interest is wider than the spheres filled by the real workers in these departments of toil, and relates to matters not strictly technical. As far as we know, the interest in scientific questions is, for strength and range, far in excess of any human experience in the past. When we reflect on the extreme antiquity and attested grandeur of certain kingdoms now in a state of decadence, or utterly gone, it becomes us to speak cautiously of our intellectual superiority; but the probability is that the world never was enriched with so many quiet investigators whose only desired recompense is the ascertainment of truth, and whose interest, while having a general outlook, is specially concentrated on their own department of research.

The ample subdivision of labour rendered necessary by the ever-widening range and complexity of investigations, and secured by the reduction of the interblended facts of observation and experience into well-defined Sciences, has given impetus to zeal, and ensured success to toil. Whether we think of the standard or the periodical literature devoted to the advancement of Science, we cannot fail to observe a contrast with the time when the issue of a scientific work, perhaps in the Latin tongue, was looked upon as a phenomenon, and when scientific terms and ideas were regarded by the public as out of all relation to the common life of the world. It is not to be doubted that much now offered to the public as Scientific Literature would fare ill if subjected to such criticisms as a severely scientific man, or one accustomed to rigorous exactitude of thought and presentation, might bestow upon it; and one who traces the effect on the mental life and general temper of defective, one-sided, representations of extremely difficult subjects, may well wish that the caterers for popular scientific interest would consider their responsibilities in this respect. But, be this as it may, there are inestimable advantages in this general awakening, and this endeavour to furnish the popular mind with such information as its condition of receptivity, and the nature of the subjects handled, render possible; and we are able to fall back on the consolation that, in the necessary struggle for existence between the vague notions and inflated vanity which, on the one side, are fed on defective Science, and the exact thought, reverence, and sobriety which, on the other, are nourished by pure truth, the fittest to survive will certainly survive.

The interest of the man of science in Science, and the scientific interest of the public, are, as I have intimated, to be kept distinct, and so, to some considerable extent, are the causes that create it. Among men of science of every age, from the early Greeks, with their defective induction, up to the most cautious observer under the conditions rendered possible by modern methods, there has been cherished an inexpressible delight in patient observation of facts, with the view of discovering their relation to other facts, and of ultimately formulating their laws. Science brings a pure and refreshing joy to all who sincerely woo her, and the clear light of her truthful eyes, to those who gaze upon it, is ample compensation for toil, and a stimulus to a more fervid zeal. But although the passion to know truth in Nature for the sake of what the truth is, irrespective of its bearing on the conveniences and comforts of life, is the real and primary spring of interest, other influences also, just now, tend to give it additional strength. Lord Bacon has said, "*Scientia et potentia humana in idem coincidunt, quia ignoratio causae destituit effectum. Natura enim non nisi parendo vincitur: et quod in contemplatione instar causae est, id in operatione instar regulae est.*" * Now, the enormous advances made of late years in the subjugation of Nature by interpretation and obedience; the mastery obtained over even what were deemed the most subtle and unmanageable of forces; the wider range of vision thus gradually opened to the scientific eye, with multiplied appliances for obtaining further conquests by yet more perfect obedience to Nature; the sense of the infinite complexity and subtlety, and yet underlying simplicity, of the processes by which the fabric of things is built up; the consciousness, when the spirit is oppressed with the disparity between the work to be done and the limits of individual strength, that other labourers are devoting their energies to sections of the wide field of research, and the recurrence of opportunities for workers in various departments to contribute the results of their toil towards an attainment of that unity of scientific thought after which the man of science yearns,— all these things tend to nourish the interest of the present time.

The influences that have combined to bring about the popular interest in scientific questions are also very varied. At the base we must recognize an effort of Nature. Man is born to know. "Πάντες ἄνθρωποι τοῦ εἰδέναι ὀρέγονται φύσει" is the first sentence in Aristotle's *Metaphysics*. Science considered as organized knowledge of what is, is the ideal goal of the developed intellectual man. In the untutored peasant, as truly as in the philosopher, there lies a sense more or less defined of that essential unity of Nature which it is the object of scientific investigation to trace. The potential science thus hidden in human nature is brought into what Aristotle would call its first ἐνεργέια by the improved general education of the people; and coincident with this, Literature in agreeable form has been made subservient to the exposition of certain scientific views which, by reason of their novelty and their vast suggestiveness, have special charm for a certain order of mind. The craving created by the fascinating presentation of specific doctrines for more accurate information has, in part, been provided for by the issue from the ablest pens of elementary works, giving succinctly and accurately the principles and scope of the

* *Aphorismi* 3.

various branches of scientific research, and thus there is being nourished in the more inquisitive and active minds of our population the pleasure inseparable from a wider view of life and its surroundings. Nor can we forget what reason the thrifty sons of commerce and the gay children of wealth and fashion have for turning a kindly face towards Science, seeing that by its conquests it tends to lessen the cost of production and render society more brilliant; while among the more sanguine and incautious, the recent triumphs of scientific research have a tendency to beget the vague notion that very soon perchance some startling revelations will be made, which shall revolutionize all our conceptions of life and its significance.

But although these considerations may account for the general interest of the present time, both in the case of the investigator and the public, they do not explain altogether the keenness of the zest with which the leading lines of research are followed, and their results looked for. It will be found on fuller enquiry that the one fact which affects so deeply the learned and the unlearned is this: That Man has become the object on which all scientific research of the present time is seen to converge. It is impossible but that even the calm spirit of the investigator in a special branch of Science should be somewhat stirred by the reflection that the path he is treading will lead him up to a position that may reflect some light on his own nature and origin; and of course the reading public cannot but lend a ready ear to any scientific oracle concerning themselves. This intense interest, arising from the importance of the object itself, waxes stronger because of the claim put forth for the supreme authority of Science, and the consequent homage men are disposed to pay to its decisions. Whether or not much that is reputed to be Science is in the strict sense of the term really so, or whether or not there is a sufficient discrimination between Science in the abstract and Science in process·of formation by fallible judgments, I do not stay to determine. Unquestionably ideal Science is infallible; for to know is to be above confutation. But the point we have to notice is this, that there is a disposition on the part of multitudes to invest the conclusions put forth in the name of Science with the deference and even undoubted authority properly due to Science *per se*. The actual and the ideal are apt to be regarded as one, and what belongs properly to abstract infallibility is unwittingly transferred to human fallibility. Such being the case, it is easy to see the reasonableness of the

intense interest with which ordinary readers await the conclusions of the scientific on the question of Man; and there
is certainly a naturalness in this when we consider the
circumstance that some writers, forgetting the caution proper
to the treatment of the most complicated of all subjects, have
ventured, in the name of Science, to affirm concerning the
nature and origin of Man, and in terms as bold and dogmatic
as could well be chosen, conclusions from which dissent is
impossible, except on pain of ostracism from the scientific
world.*

Under these circumstances it may not be inappropriate to
the present occasion if, without presuming to enter into
details, and apart from polemical purpose, I submit a few
observations bearing on the *present position of the scientific
question in relation to Man*. There is perhaps peculiar fitness
in this, inasmuch as Devonshire has contributed no mean
part towards the creation of the interest now generally felt
in the subject.

The world to-day is the outcome of what the world was in
days long gone by, and we cannot form a just estimate of its
nature except in its relation to the past. This continuity also
applies to our scientific views of the world. In the matter
of knowledge we are born to a great inheritance. However
much the present state of our scientific knowledge may, in
extent and accuracy, give passing occasion for a smile at the
modicum of defective truth enjoyed by our predecessors, we
ought not to forget that we owe our position of advantage
both to the successes and failures of the past. And especially
is it true that Science in its relation to man is a development,
and in order to discern and estimate its modern peculiarities
—to form a just judgment on its *differentia*—it must be
viewed in contrast with what passed as Science in former
times, and in fact laid the foundations of its present merits
and defects. In no age of mental activity has the scientific
position of Man been altogether lost sight of; for although
there have been long and dreary periods during which no
original thinker struck out new paths in the great quest, yet
even then the leaders of thought cherished and discussed in
some measure the forms of expression used and the conclusions-
arrived at by their more energetic ancestors.

Naturally we must turn to Greece, the fountain head for
the Western Nations of Science, Literature, and Art, and
where, above all countries, Man was, in respect to personal
form, the subject of Art; in respect to his emotions and aspira-

* *Vide* Haeckel's *History of Creation*, vol. i. p. 22, vol. ii. p. 347.

tions, the subject of Literature; and in respect to his nature
and origin, the subject of Science. But in so doing we must
be on our guard against disappointment; for it has happened,
through the inevitable defects of tradition as a channel of
transmission, and the loss of records subsequent to the era of
tradition, that we are furnished with the conclusions arrived
at by the early Greek investigators in far larger proportion
than is desirable, as compared with the processes of combined
induction and deduction on which those conclusions were
evidently based. There is, however, both in record and well-
tested tradition, enough to show that although these men,
venturing almost singly, and without the aid furnished by an
inheritance of accumulated knowledge, into the vast fields of
scientific truth, were so impressed by the vastness of the great
objective in its totality as to devote their chief strength to a
solution of its development, yet they were led on by the
logical necessities of their position to formulate some conception of the nature and origin of Man. By implication at
least the Ionics regarded him as generated by a very gradual
process out of the ἀρχάι, which, according to their respective
systems, formed the material ground of existence. Heraclitus
and Empedocles differed from the Ionics in the nature of the
primary substances they postulated, but not in the resolution
of Man into the ultimates of which all things were formed.
It was left to Anaxagoras to formulate the radical distinction
between the material particles and the νοῦς, the two factors,
by the interaction of which the universe of things was, by a
process of compounding σύγκρισις, generated out of the
original commingled mass of homogeneous infinitesimals.
The logic of his system required him, however, to regard the
moving cause in every distinct segregation of infinitesimals
as in some sense a part of the original νοῦς, and the superiority of Man lay in that part of the original νοῦς which
entered into his nature being allied with a superior organization. It is notorious, beyond the boundaries of scientific
knowledge, that Leukippus and Demokritus promulgated
that theory of atoms, which, after passing through the hands
of the Stoics, and being invested with special interest by
the poetic imagination of Lucretius, was revived in England
and France during the last century, to be hailed in modified
form with (may I not say) an enthusiasm rather alien to the
calm dignity of Science by many of our own time. There
was no hesitation on the part of Demokritus in working his
way from the primitive atoms, under the influence of the
mysterious ἀναγκή, through a series of gradations up to Man,

whose *differentia* from a star or a stone was that, in his case, the collocation of atoms was more complicated. It will have been noticed by all who have studied these old-time thinkers that, although they agree in placing Man at the highest point in a series of material changes, they do not appear to have devoted much attention to the transitions by which, from simplicity to combination, and from one combination to another, there appeared at last the form now bearing the name and endowed with the capacities of Man. So far as my reading and memory serve there is in Aristotle but one passage of obscure meaning, and in which he seems to doubt Spontaneous Origin, bearing on this subject;[*] and, with this exception, only two men ventured to point out a definite link in the long chain of antecedents from which, according to their views, Man must have arisen. Tradition says that Anaximines held Man to be a development from the frog. Diogenes Laertius explicitly states that Archelaus, a teacher of Socrates, went still further back, and found his origin in slime (ἰλύς), which, as a kind of milk, served the generative power of the heat of the earth.[†]

Up to this point then, with the exception of Anaxagoras, but not of the more idealistic Pythagoreans, a Monistic view of the Universe prevailed; for while admitting, and of necessity using, the popular distinction between Matter and Mind, and reasoning as though the phenomena of the two were sharply distinguished by characteristics indestructible and incommunicable, they nevertheless regarded the organism as a very high evolution of the ἀρχή which entered into all lower things, and that which bore the designation of Mind, as not a distinct substance, but either a concomitant inter-action of some form of the ἀρχή, or a resultant of the evolved combination which of itself made up the organism. In fact Mind was a name for the latest and highest evolution of the original ἀρχή.

The history of human speculation is a history of change, while the great facts of human experience and the primary convictions based thereon abide as of old. No scientific hypotheses appear to permanently shake men's faith in the fundamental convictions of the mind. The common belief of mankind, both in Greece and in the far East, had been, as it still is, distinctly Dualistic; and so deeply had this belief entered into all forms of thought and language that the Ionic and Demokritic Monists must have known something

---

[*] *De Generatione Animalium*, lib. iii. 11.
[†] περὶ βίων κ.τ.λ.   Ed. STEPHANUS, 1570, p. 55.

of the uneasiness of men who use words in a *non*-natural sense, when, with their belief in Monism, they were under the necessity of using language which, in its natural sense, was obviously a flat denial of it. Among the varied influences which contributed to invest the Platonic system with a charm for the wise and the unwise, and to cause the preceding Monistic systems to sink into obscurity, was undoubtedly this, that Plato, with an emphasis unmistakeable, and often with a reasoning hard to resist, asserted the essential distinction in ultimate substance of that in Man's Nature which entered into his organism, and that which constituted the thinking self. Popular and scientific thought once more became one; and perhaps the most important service Plato has rendered to posterity lies in the clearness and precision with which he has laid down the distinction between the Monistic and Dualistic conception of the Universe. Matter and Spirit to him were essentially distinct.

There is a modern phrase which in some quarters has found ready acceptance, to this effect, "Mind a function of Organism." An attempt has been made to show that Aristotle, dissenting from the Platonic Dualism, elaborated in his work entitled περὶ ψυχῆς, a doctrine which can be thus formulated. I am no lover of the vagueness and obscurity of meaning which obviously go with this phrase, and as a matter of argument should be disposed to abstain from contention till more precision of thought and expression be secured. But as touching a matter of historic fact, it may be worth while to point out that this interpretation of the views of the great philosopher of Stageira may have arisen from a tendency to import into the words of another ideas of our own; and, at all events, a more perfect acquaintance with the writings of Aristotle would have saved Mr. Lewes from the error of judgment. The views of Aristotle cannot be properly estimated without remembering how in his treatment of Man the logical conception is sometimes predominant over the physical history. It was his habit to regard Man as a σύνολον—a whole made up on the one side of the Material Cause, which in this case was some condition of Matter, and on the other of Form, τὸ τί ἦν εἶναι, or essential nature, which, without entering into the question of its substance physically considered, was, with Aristotle, that specific difference which lay at the base of the logical conception of the Species. It was the conjunction or implication of these two, brought about in the process of development by *Causa Efficiens*, that made up the total Man. The Material Cause,

in Aristotle's system, is a cause only so far as the Formal
Cause coincides with it in the production of the σύνολον, the
whole; and consequently the soul (ψυχή) is simply the
superior *differentia* of a certain generated organism. Here
also he brought in his famous distinction between the Potential and the Actual—τὸ ὄν δυνάμει, and τὸ ὄν ἐνεργείᾳ. The
soul is Potential (δυνάμει) in the organism, and when in the
process of development it, as Form, becomes implicated with
the organism so that at a certain point the material organism
may be said to assume its *differentia;* i.e. that which makes
it different from all else—then, at that point, the soul becomes Actual (ἐνεργείᾳ). Consequently he tells us it is vain
to ask whether the body and soul are one. As well ask
whether the wax and the impress are one, or whether Matter
formative of an object and the object formed are one. The
coexistence of the two, body and soul, make a live subject.
But in harmony with his doctrine of the production of higher
types on the completed subjects of the lower—which germin-
ally is the doctrine of formation of new species—he, instead
of speaking of Man as possessed of various faculties, represents him as being constituted of various souls, developing as
the complements the one of the other—the Nutritive, the
Sentient, the Movent, the Appetitive, the Imaginative, and
the Intelligent. Now no doubt if we accept his statement
that the coexistence, or rather implication, of body and soul
make up one live subject—that the soul is the *differentia* in
the development of organism—then, as the complement of
the body and in some sense potential (δυνάμει) in the material
out of which the organism arises, it can only be considered
as *logically* distinct, and necessarily ceases with the breaking
up of the body. But notwithstanding this it is remarkable
that Aristotle's Dualism in reference to Man is as pronounced
as well can be, and is thrown into bold relief by the representations to which I have just referred; for he states concerning the origin of νοῦς, the Intelligent soul in Man, that
it is superinduced on the Sentient and Imaginative soul from
the supernal region* where the unclouded contemplative
νοῦς, which is there free from association with the lower
forms of life, as here seen in material organisms, has its seat,
and becomes a cause of located νοῦς on earth; i.e. of νοῦς
implicated with other pre-existing powers in Man. You may
dispute his *data,* but you cannot dispute his Dualism.

It is a well-known fact that, between the decadence of
Greece and the period subsequent to the Elizabethan era, no

---

* *De Generatione An.,* iii. p. 736, Berlin Edition.

substantial advance was made in the scientific study of Man. The transitory influence of the Stoics in favour of the Atomic Monism was overborne by the predominance in Alexandria of a modified Platonism, which, on the fall of Alexandria as a seat of intellectual influence, was supplanted in the West, more especially, by a perverted Aristotelianism. But on the reawakening of the human intellect, the old question of Man's Nature again came into prominence, and for a while Dualism had to invent metaphysical solutions for some of its admitted difficulties. A common impression has prevailed, the justness of which I may notice further on, that to hold to a Dualistic view of Man's Nature involves more difficulties of conception than to accept the Monistic, whether it be that which unifies all in ultimate matter, or, as in the case of Berkeley, in the *non*-material. At all events, such a man as Descartes, holding, as he believed, on most indubitable grounds, the duality of Man's Nature, felt it incumbent on him to account, by a special hypothesis, for what was conceived to be the insuperable difficulty of a *non*-material substance acting on, or being acted on, by a substance essentially material; and therefore, to account for the observed apparent connection of the action of the one part of Man's Nature, on the other, Descartes adopted the doctrine of " Occasional Causes," which means that for every action of the spirit, which, according to him,* had its seat in the Pineal Gland, there is brought about by the concurrent action and assistance of God a regular and corresponding action in the matter of the body, and *vice versa*, from the same cause, there arises a synchronous action of the mind with the action of the body; that is to say, spirit and matter are the keys on which the Great First Cause produces notes respectively harmonious with those He produces on the other.

The contribution made by Leibnitz to the solution of the question of Man's Nature has not received of late years the attention which, in my judgment, its suggestiveness and its profound anticipation of some of our modern doctrines demand. Dissatisfied with the Dualism of Descartes, rejecting the absolute Monism of Spinoza, and assuming as *data* the fact that our truest knowledge of power or force is that given in our own consciousness, and that all compounds are ultimately resolvable into ultimates in which Monadal activity is the real essence, he came to the conclusion that the universe, when worked down to its elements, consists of Monads — centres of activity, invisible, devoid of the material quality of extension, diverse in degree of activity, and, while not

* *Traite des Passions*, 32.

acting by impact on one another, yet capable of acting each in relation to every other. The characteristic activity therefore of these Monads is not the mere blind mechanical force which is treated of in our modern dynamics, but an internal quality, which, existing in various degrees, accounts for, in gradation, the unconscious semi-dormant substances (which have capacity of sustaining relations), the lowest form of consciousness, the more distinct perception in brutes and the highest energy of all, reason in Man. According to this, then, the universe consists of varied systems or segregations of graduated centres of activity, each centre, though acting from within in relation to every other, being nevertheless perfect and self-contained. *"Elles ont en elles une certaine perfection"* (ἔχουσι τὸ ἐντελές); *"il y a une suffisance"* (αὐτάρκεια) *"qui les rend sources de leurs actions internes et pour ainsi dire des automates incorporeals."* *

This resolution of all things to Monads, endowed variously with the quality of activity, when received in relation to Man, necessitates that he be regarded as consisting of an aggregation of Monads of the various grades below conscious activity —forming the physical organism—*plus* Monads of the sentient grade acting in relation to the aggregated inferior kinds, *plus* the highest created Monad, whose activity manifested in the form of reason constitutes the enduring personality. It will be found on examination of details that this Monism approaches, in some of its postulates, very closely to that theory of a relative animation of all that bears the name of matter, which finds in our time very earnest advocates.† A reference to the words of Leibnitz ‡ will show that he uses the term *soul* not to indicate an essentially distinct substance, but to denote those Monads in which a more distinct perception is accompanied by memory, and solely for the sake of distinguishing their higher grade of activity.

In taking this very brief review of the progress of opinion with reference to Man, it will have been noticed how very much of what was accepted was the result of speculation, how little was known of Man's natural history, and what

---

* *Œuvres de Leibnitz*, Paris Ed. 1842. *La Monadologie*, 18.

† *Vide* Haeckel's *History of Creation*, vol. i. p. 23.

‡ *Si nous voulons appeler âme tout ce qui a perceptions et appetits dans le sens général que je viens d'expliquer, toutes les substances simples ou Monades créées pourraient être appelées âmes; mais, comme le sentiment est quelque chose de plus qu' une simple perception, je consens que le nom général de Monades et d'entéléchies suffise aux substances simples qui n'auront que cela, et qu' on appelle* ÂMES *seulement celles dont la perception est plus distincte et accompagnée de mémoire.* Monadologie, 19.

slight interest was awakened, beyond the limits of a small philosophical circle, in the discussions maintained and in the conclusions arrived at. A slight acquaintance with modern literature will suggest the contrast with the facts of the present time; and the question naturally arises, How has it come to pass that the position of Man in relation to the Order of Nature has now come so much to the front, and is discussed on all sides with such intense interest? Apart from the considerations which must always yield interest to the study of Man, and to which I have already alluded, the general answer is, I think, to be found in the circumstance that modern researches have, by a very natural process of enlargement and co-ordination, been observed to point in such a direction as to give occasion for the hypothesis of Evolution; and so wide is the reach of this hypothesis that it is both logically and physically impossible to exclude the nature and origin of Man from its application.

It is no new thing for a far-reaching hypothesis to be propounded as a solution of observed facts, as when the existence of luminiferous particles was assumed in days gone by to account for the phenomena of light, and the action of gravity to explain the movements of bodies towards one another. But the peculiarity of the hypothesis of Evolution in its effect on the public mind lies in the entire change it produces when applied to Man in our conceptions of his nature and origin. Men see themselves under the, shall I say light, or what? of this hypothesis as they never saw themselves before, and consequently the sensation produced is correspondingly profound. How this result has been brought to pass is familiar to all who have watched the development of modern Science, the tendency of which has been to put men in possession, by an analytic process, of the primitive condition of things out of which the harmonized Universe, as we now behold it, arose. As expounded by some, it professes to take the uninitiated by the hand, and lead them through strange and intricate paths up to the hypothetical starting-point of the varied changes which have culminated in what we now see and are. The geologist works continuously backwards to the time when the matter and forces now exposed to view in form of solid rock, fossil, sea, and soil, were, as such, non-existent, but only potential in a diffused indeterminate mass separated from other and probably similar masses of matter by the action of an incipient centripetal force. Others pushing research over a wider area, and stretching the scientific vision back to a still more remote period, direct attention to the probability of other worlds being composed of substantially the same elements that enter into the structure of our own, and being under the one comprehensive law of gravity, as also to the probability and, some would even say, the certainty that they all, in common with the matter now forming the earth, were existent at an inexpressibly remote period only in the form of a vast and highly attenuated Nebular Mass, within the mysterious folds of which all subsequent developments into starry worlds and organized bodies were potentially present in the most simple forms of Matter and Force. The conclusions thus pointed to by those who study great masses obedient to their respective laws seem to be justified by the analysis and synthesis of the chemist, who can show us how to resolve some of the most closely-knit compounds into their elements, and also produce solid bodies out of elemental forms; and an ambition dwells in some minds even to be able to demonstrate that the elementary substances hitherto regarded as simple are but the product, by some primitive and unknown process, of a modification of one element. Now, confining exclusive attention to these tendencies of departments of Science, without considering what of fact may be otherwise obtainable or what breaks there may be observable in the line of supposed continuity, it is easy to see how the scientific and the unscientific should lean alike toward the conclusion that the sum total of organized and unorganized bodies, liquids, and gases, is the simple outcome of the interaction from the beginning of ultimates of an exceedingly subtle character.

Very naturally at this point the enquiry would arise whether there is any reason for including Man in the sweep of these scientific tendencies, or whether, seeing that he is the being who makes the investigations and endeavours to form an intellectual transcript of Nature, he is not by necessity, at least as a thinking being, excluded. As a matter of fact events have moved on in such a direction that it has become impossible to avoid the discussion involved in the alternative just stated, whatever be the issue of it in relation either to the organism or the mind of Man. Since the time when Oken and Kant suggested the possibility of Man's organization being connected by a long process of development with inferior animals, great attention has been devoted to questions touching the antiquity of the human race, the anatomical and physiological relations of Man to the lower orders, and the place of Man in the zoological succession;

and as a consequence, it has been taught that, as truly as the geologist believes the solid rocks to be the steady and orderly outcome of the interaction of Matter and Force in differentiated existence when all was in a state of Nebulosity,—so Man, regarded as an organism superior to any other, is also the outcome of the interaction of differentiated Matter and Force, through a long line of more simple organisms, until at the point where living organism vanishes into an antecedent *non*-living condition of Matter, he is found to have his origin in the vast nebulous mass antedating the structure of the globe, which in its turn came forth from the interaction, through almost interminable ages, of the undifferentiated ultimates of Matter and Force.

Of course this refers to Man considered as an organism, in which certain mechanical and chemical forces have concurred in producing a definite structure with appropriate functions. But the logic of the principle of Evolution so far as gathered from considerations just now stated is imperious, and the question naturally arose whether Life, as distinguished from the peculiar structure known as physical organism, was also something evolved out of a prior condition of things. Mr. Darwin, with the caution and discrimination for which he is so distinguished, has not presumed to deal scientifically with so subtle and remote a question, being content to trace, as he believes, the connection of Man's living organism with the early forms of life on earth. But others, feeling the pressure of the logical definition of Evolution as the getting of all differentiation out of that in which there is no differentiation, but the most absolute simplicity, have made manifold experiments to ascertain whether, in its lowest form, Life can be produced out of that which is not Life by what is, I must say, most unscientifically called "spontaneous generation." Although researches in this direction have, on the admission of the greatest authorities, been utterly in vain, and although, as Haeckel candidly admits, failure here destroys the very principle of unbroken continuity which is involved in the conception of Evolution of all differentiations from one undifferentiated, yet he and others, with a daring more characteristic of the adventurer than of the calm man of science, have, in their desire to maintain a theoretic line of continuity without a single break from Man backwards to the original undifferentiated Matter and Force, by an extraordinary effort of the scientific imagination leapt at a single bound from the domain of organized Life right into that dim untraversed region where, before the faintest consciousness dawned in the

Universe, hard mechanical forces held undisputed sway among the particles of Matter; and, what is most of all remarkable in this brilliant feat is, they have supposed that by its performance the Evolution of Life from dead unorganized Matter and Force has been scientifically established.

But, note further, Man is more than organization animated by a Life which in its sensuous side bears affinity to other forms of Life. He is a Moral and Responsible being, conscious of a something which places him in a totally different category; and of course the logic of the doctrine of Evolution forces on the enquiry as to whether that which we call Mind in Man—that which really constitutes his Personality as a Moral and Responsible being—is not, also, the outcome of the interaction of the original undifferentiated Matter and Force. This enquiry has been pursued in a twofold direction. It has been the effort of some to show, from a comparison of Man's higher faculties with the gradations of reason said to be found in creatures beneath him, that, as his organism is relatively superior to their's, and is evolved by a gradual process from them, so the higher nature of Man, his Mind, is a concurrent Evolution from Mind as existing in lower forms—Mind being in fact a resultant of superior physical organization, and not a distinct entity. This line of thought appears to have found encouragement in the researches of the Physiologist, who by a variety of experiments and acute observations has pointed out that the fact and the varieties of consciousness are determined pre-eminently by the condition of the grey matter of the cortex, and that certain functions of thought and action are probably correlated to definite parts of the brain.

Thus I think it will be seen how it has come to pass that, in contrast with former times, the scientific investigations of our age, and the natural effect of the principles brought into prominence, should bring Man to the front, and create an interest hitherto unexampled. The broad issue raised by the line of thought to which I have referred is evidently this—whether Man in his totality of body and mind is simply the last link in a long chain of Evolution from an original condition of things in which undifferentiated Matter and Force were the sole existences; or whether there is in Man a nature essentially distinct from, although always in association with, an organism which, whatever its origin as a specific form among other specific forms on the globe, is, in some very definite sense, the result of the interaction of molecular and chemical forces. In saying this it will be observed that I am stating the question in its broadest issue.   It is *Monism* or *Dualism* in the most decisive . form—the *Monism* which consists of all that is human being the resultant of Matter and Force, as strictly as that the ocean is such a resultant, only that the human is in a later stage, and therefore the expression of greater complexities — the *Dualism* which claims for that which is said to constitute Personality a spiritual nature as distinct from the molecular intricacies which make up the rest of the man.   Whether what is known as Matter and Force are in nature primarily dissimilar, or are but two faces of one reality, it is not necessary for our purpose to determine.   Practically in this controversy, as a set-off against the spiritual nature of Mind, they are one.

In thus setting forth what is regarded as the broad issue of the controversy concerning Man I would guard against doing injustice to many of the great labourers in this field of Science.   There is a distinction to be drawn between the position taken by those who push the conception of Evolution, as a bare conception,* to its logical issue, and those who, without troubling themselves with logical consequences and bold speculations beyond the ascertained facts of Science, are content to work on in their respective departments and hold judgment in suspense as to the ulterior questions.   With respect to the actual conclusions arrived at in different fields of research it is not easy to speak with confidence, inasmuch as competent authorities are not fully agreed, while on the logic of Evolution as a bare conception, as I have said, many prefer not to speak.   On the question of the Antiquity of Man much light has been thrown by researches in Europe and America.   A vast accumulation of facts clearly points to times a long way beyond the first lines of history.   But while a few here and there think they find evidence of the existence of Man even in the Miocene period, others, less eager for age, are content to place him in the Pliocene, while others, having as they think due regard to all the facts of the case, think

---

* There can be no doubt but that Evolution as a conception means the getting out of the strictly undifferentiated all that is in the slightest degree differentiated.   It requires the *minimum* of original simplicity for all that is now complex.   Those who entertain this conception are perfectly logical in working back all that now is to a something entirely free from differentiation. But a conception of Evolution as a form of thought arrived at by a process of abstraction and generalization is one thing : the existence of a fact in Nature answering to it is another.   The fact that we have the conception does not warrant us to argue from its nature as a logical form to realities in the history of the Universe.   The schoolmen of the Middle Ages were guilty of this unscientific practice, and is there not danger of others getting into the snare ?

that they are within the limits warranted by a just induction in assigning the most ancient traces to the Post-Glacial epoch, or 7000 or 8000 years ago. Then, also, in respect to Man's natural history, it is well known that Mr. Darwin believes there is sufficient evidence for converting the hypothesis of the Evolution of Man from the first forms of life on earth, by a process of Natural Selection, into a fairly es'ablished fact of Science, while there are others who, admitting very wide degrees of variation in species, do, with all possible respect for his judgment, decidedly differ from him. The inchoate state of the whole question is perhaps seen also in this, that, while Mr. Wallace is regarded as joint propounder with Mr. Darwin of the theory of Evolution by Natural Selection, he excludes the higher nature of Man from its operation. In the department of Physiology of the Brain a considerable variety of interesting facts have been noted by Maudsley, Ferrier, Carpenter, Bastian, and others, but the conclusions arrived at as to the Monism or Dualism of Man's nature are by no means identical. It was owing to this acknowledged diversity of judgment in the interpretation of facts, combined with the result of independent research, that, before his lamented decease, and in the last production of his fertile pen, Agassiz expressed * his inability to accept the doctrine of Evolution as expounded by Darwin; and for the same reasons Virchow confronted Haeckel's proposition that Evolution should be taught as an accepted doctrine in the public schools of Germany, by the declaration † that the Evolution of Man was not yet proved.

The fact that so much energy of the scientific world is concentrated on this question cannot but arise from the presence in Nature of much that gives reasonableness at least to some form of a doctrine of Evolution. There is obviously so much in the structure of the earth, in the ascertained condition of the sun and stars, in the elaboration of complicated individual organisms from the most simple cellular conditions, in the incessant variations observable in animal and vegetable structures, in the graduated instincts and powers of observation in creatures below Man, and in the subtle character of matter when analysed into its simplest forms, to suggest a gradual process of world-building,—that it is conceivable enough how all this, when placed in a certain aspect, excluding other important considerations, and when combined with a philosophic yearning after unity, should incline

---

* Vide *Atlantic Monthly*, January, 1874.
† Vide *Freedom of Science in the Modern State*, p. 63.

many to interpret the special facts relating to the Antiquity of Man, his anatomical and physiological relation to lower orders, and the dependence of Thought on a certain condition of the grey substance of the brain, in such a way as to see in man the outcome of a long continued process of evolution, even from the most undifferentiated forms of Matter and Force. But, on the other hand, when we remember that scientific research is yet in its infancy; that although there are remarkable similarities of structure and function in graduated line between Man and inferior organisms, yet the theory proceeds on the tacit and unprovable assumption that if Evolution in this sense be not the law of the universe, such similarities would not or could not exist; that though many great variations have been known to take place under domestication, no one case of actual formation of a new species has yet been established; and that, considering the vast number of minute variations which, by hypothesis, must have occurred before definite permanent species were evolved, the traces of variation ought to be almost infinite in comparison with the traces of species which at last survived in the struggle for existence, whereas, to take one instance for illustration, the tailless ape, which is said to have been the form that gave rise in the Pleiocene or Pleistocene period to a higher grade, from which at last, by still further minute variations, Man came, still exists, while, strange to say, no single trace is found of the countless host of superior creatures which must have lived to fill up the enormous gap of 28½ inches of cranial capacity between it and the lowest man,—I say, when we remember such facts as these, it is not surprising that such men as I have named should hesitate to give their adhesion to so wide-reaching a conclusion.

Let it be borne in mind that I have distinguished between two forms of the doctrine of Evolution in relation to Man— that which is concerned with his organism, in so far as it is related to lower forms of life on the globe, connecting him, through his Pithecanthropic ancestors, with the earliest form of life, and the other, which not content to stop at the earliest form of life on earth, deduces Man in his entirety from the same undifferentiated Matter and Force which by interaction make up all else in the universe. So far as the former and more moderate view is concerned, it is obviously a question of evidence to be gathered from a careful study of the past history of the globe, and one can well afford to wait for further information; but the resolution of Man in all that makes him what he is intellectually, morally, and physically, into the simple interaction of molecular forces, so far transcends the sphere of observation, and, when closely examined, so puts speculation and mere conjecture in the place of scientific induction, and brings into doubt convictions hitherto regarded as lying at the base of all knowledge and practice, that many feel bound even to exclude its consideration from the circle of subjects strictly scientific.

It is important to note exactly what this extreme view of the nature and origin of Man really means and involves. It is Monism of the most absolute and uncompromising kind, since it is a denial of Mind as a real substance or nature distinct in essence from Matter under the action of Force. It is only a name for the product of two cunningly implicated factors, Matter and Force, or, in stricter phrase, the name given to a fleeting succession of such products. There is something harsh beyond all expression, and I will venture to say utterly unscientific, in the assertion of Voght that "thoughts bear the same relation to the brain as the gall to the liver," * and of Büchner, that "the same power which digests by means of the stomach thinks by means of the brain."† In all ages men have been accustomed to think and speak of their Personality, attaching to that term an idea more distinct and commanding than any other that enters into the sum of human knowledge. It is the Rational unity of our being amidst all the changes of our organism through a course of three-score years and ten, and from this, the only conception of our nature, *as datum*, we have been accustomed to think and speak of Personality beyond ourselves. But obviously if that which alone we call and know as Personality is simply the resultant of the action of molecular forces in the grey matter of the brain, and has no other reality; if it thus has no essential permanence as an identifiable seat of conscious power, but is, in its very nature, as much a transitory effect as is the form of a leaf or the waving of a fan, then of course we can have no reason for thinking of any Personality, human or more than human, than as being of the same kind. If we suppose any other Personality to be different from ours—a seat of conscious power, a real being, and not a resultant of molecular forces—then we use words for which we have no corresponding idea in the whole range of human knowledge, or else we arbitrarily create an idea of Personality different from what we know Personality to be. They are keen, far-seeing, and logically thoroughgoing men

* Lange's *Hist. Materialism*, vol. ii. p. 312.
† Vide *Matter and Force*, p. 125.

who, in getting rid of human Personality as a seat of conscious power, admit that they clear out from the universe all Personal Power.

Now I do not make these observations by way of reasoning from consequences in favour of a certain theory, but to exhibit the essential distinction between the two views concerning the Evolution of Man—the moderate and the extreme, and to indicate the real question pushed into the foreground in the name of Science. Whether the more moderate view of the Evolution of Man leads up logically to this other I do not stay to consider, nor to indicate how far Science and the logic of theoretical views really differ and are independent the one of the other. That such a position should be taken by some in reference to Man, and be urged on public attention with much emphasis, certainly explains the tension of the public mind on the question, and may be accepted as a justification for the few observations which, before I close, it is my desire to submit for your candid consideration.

It is important, in pushing our researches into the nature and origin of Man, that we be exceedingly sure in the principles on which we proceed. There are, of course, definite principles of physical Science on which scientific men are supposed to proceed in all their researches into the constitution of the physical universe; and it may be supposed that the adoption of these in their application to the questions involved in the existence of Man will suffice. But that does not at all follow, because to do so is to assume beforehand that this is purely a physical question, or that no considerations apply here which do not apply to every other subject of investigation. A moment's reflection ought to show that this is a *petitio principii* viewed as an argument, and a random method viewed as a procedure. It will be in the knowledge of some here, that a few years since Du Bois Raymond raised in Germany the question of the Limits of Natural Science; and at the present time there are profound thinkers who doubt whether it is at all possible to find a solution of the human problem by the observance of the rules of ordinary scientific procedure as applied to subjects indisputably physical. The same admission is tacitly and unwittingly made by those who as physicists declare that they will accept nothing but what can be demonstrably shown to exist by the appliances usually in vogue. Now in dealing with the question of Man, such persons should ask whether they can as certainly establish the causal connexion of molecular changes and the phenomena of consciousness, as they can of mo-

lecular changes and the phenomena confessedly physical;
whether these phenomena do not form a distinct class in the
universe as against all other phenomena; and whether, therefore, the problem does not need for its solution a wider range
of postulates than the ordinary problems of Science.

In this connexion there is forced on our notice the question
of our fundamental knowledge. Is it not often assumed that we
know the physical best, and even that only? Objective forms
and forces are supposed to be the most real, and some would
say the only *real things*. But I believe a more thorough
examination of the contents of human knowledge will reveal
the fact that our first, deepest, surest knowledge is not of the
objective *thing* or *being*, but of self as a real being. Indeed,
the very term "Physical," and the very conception of objective physical reality, imply as their necessary correlate the
non-physical subjective thing or being that knows. It appears to me that as the obverse of a coin necessitates the
existence of the reverse as an equal reality, so *the existence of
the physical thing or being* AS KNOWN implies, if language
means anything, and the whole fabric of knowledge is not a
delusion, *the existence of a non-physical thing or being* AS
KNOWING. Those who approach the question of Man from
the side of physical observation exclusively, may feel the
thrall of purely physical conceptions, and never be able to
get beyond them; but the corrective of this danger is to be
found in a concurrent approach from the subjective side,
which gives primary knowledge of self, and so furnishes the
other pole in the sphere of truth.

And now, having said this in reference to the principles
appropriate to the investigation, let me further say that we
may be quite fearless in our search after truth in relation to
this question of Man. A true man does not fear what comes
of finding truth. The very genius of Science is to ask what
is true, and to hold it fast at any cost. Here Morality and
Science are at one. The investigator should go forth with a
mind as untrammelled by fears as by preferences, keenly
alive to the presence around him of Truth in various guise.
Whatever consequences ensue they cannot but be right and
good if truth be found, although it is a sound maxim that we
may question our possession of truth when that we hold is
inconsistent with fundamental facts of our nature. The
history of knowledge shows us that hasty generalizations
have had a charm for the human spirit, but what ascendency
may be obtained by interpretations of the Universe which
are not in accord with actual fact, will and can be only

transitory. Things as they are will not be modified in the slightest by any human attempt to crystallize them into forms of conception which, because human, and therefore limited, are always disproportionate to the reality. If conclusions arrived at by a process of observation and judgment are valid, succeeding ages of intelligence will only lay more bare the solid foundations on which they repose; and should it happen that they clash with our wishes and traditional views of things, the inconvenience will be but temporary; our intellectual and emotional life will adjust itself to the order of Nature. No doubt erroneous judgments entertained, even though termed Scientific, exercise in their bearing on the mental and moral life a detrimental influence; for it is the teaching of history that error as to fact, and false judgment in any degree, disturb to the extent of the error or falsity the balance of the man, and render the development of his nature imperfect. Nevertheless, there is this compensating consideration suggested by a careful study of the past, that what is or seems wrong and disturbing in the course of a tedious development towards perfect knowledge is, in due time, so marvellously manipulated by an all-controlling Power and Wisdom as to be wrought up into varied combinations with more powerful agents for the realization of results obviously good. We may, therefore, with calm and fearless spirit, survey the efforts of all earnest workers in scientific fields, being assured that what is worthless will perish, or will mediately contribute to more cautious observation; and that any uneasiness which the transitory prevalence of strictly unscientific views may create will in the end render us more appreciative of the broader and more stable views into which the conflict of truth with error is sure to evolve.

But Man is a creature of many necessities, and cannot afford to allow his nature to be thrown out of balance by the sole exercise of any one class of emotions. Remembering that the area of knowledge is far wider than our keenest vision, that we necessarily see here and there only traces of the infinitely interwoven threads of fact and law, and that our discovery of what seems to be a hitherto concealed law tends to an emotional excitement dangerous in its influence on the judgment—it is clear that the fearlessness of the lover of truth should be accompanied by very much caution. We lay just claim to the designation *scientific* when a keen and wide observation of facts is conjoined with deliberateness and care in the arrangement and judgment of them. There is a fascination in a far-reaching hypothesis, inasmuch as, being a mental creation, it carries with it all the charm attaching to our own offspring.   The region of speculation so closely abuts on the usual lines of research that unless great care is used we may be freely traversing the one under the impression that we are within the limits of the other. Agassiz, not without reason I presume, expressed * his regret that many seemed disposed to deviate from the patient paths of research as though the purposes of Science were best promoted by hasty speculation.   A scientific formula indicating the position of Man as the highest point of Evolution from original undifferentiated Matter and Force practically becomes a formula for the entire Universe, since it postulates the two poles of existence, and the law of their connection. Considering how little we know of Matter itself, how almost interminable must have been the changes in its condition before forms known to us became cognizable, and not forgetting the fragmentary character of many of the facts which in relation to Man have actually come under observation—there is, at all events, some justification for the exercise of a cautious reserve in pronouncing a dogmatic judgment.

Whatever department of research you enter on it will be found that however certain facts may seem to point to the Evolution of Man, there are, as I have hinted, gaps and weaknesses which at least suggest a suspension of judgment. Thus, until great authorities are agreed as to the conditions under which human remains found their way into certain drifts and deposits, and also as to the time required for the formation in past ages of stalagmite and drifts, the question of less or more remote antiquity must remain to that degree a matter of debate; while it should be observed that if you decide the fossil men to belong to the Pliocene period, you thereby weaken the force of other evidence for Evolution, inasmuch as the fossil men said to be of that remote period are proved by comparison of the relics of them with known relics of the historic period, to have been not less men than multitudes now living on the earth.   Had more caution been shown in years gone by in reference to the deposits of the valley of the Somme, which had ascribed to them a very remote antiquity, Professor Huxley would have been saved the trouble of setting aside favourite conclusions by saying, at the Sheffield meeting of the British Association, "The question of time in this case could not be settled satisfactorily. Few persons except men of science were aware that there

* *Atlantic Monthly*, January, 1874.

had been enormous changes during the last five hundred years in the North of Europe. The volcanoes of Iceland had been continually active, great floods of lava had been poured forth, and the level of the coast had been most remarkably changed. Similar causes might have produced enormous changes in the valley of the Somme; therefore any arguments based as to time upon the appearance of the valley were not to be trusted." Then if we turn to another branch of the same question there is equal reason for extreme caution. For although there is an unquestionable correspondence between the anatomy and physiology of the Ape and Man, yet, as I have already pointed out, there is enough to create, at least, a judicious reserve, in the fact that between the lowest Man and highest Ape there exists the enormous difference of 28½ inches of cranial capacity, which, unless we deny the whole theory of Evolution by saying that this gap was overcome at a bound, necessarily implies a long succession of creatures superior to existing Apes and inferior to the lowest Man; and yet if these did exist we have not the slightest evidence of the fact either alive in the forest or fossil in the rocks, so that, contrary to the law of Natural Selection, the least fitted to survive have survived, and the most fitted to survive have perished in the struggle for existence. And, finally, turning to the Physiology of the Brain, there can be no doubt that, although recent investigations are by no means complete, yet a real dependence of mental phenomena on the structure of the brain is established, and Dr. Ferrier has certainly shown that in reference to certain movements there are functional centres in the brain. But when you reflect on the essential distinction between thought or consciousness and any known effect of molecular action, how the one cannot be expressed in the terms of the other, and is not convertible quantitatively or in any other way into the other, is there not a truly scientific spirit in hesitating to pronounce mental phenomena as being simply the outcome of molecular action, as truly as, though more subtlely than, are phenomena distinctly physical? I say, then, the area over which fact is to be found, and the extreme intricacy and delicacy of the questions involved in the scientific study of Man, necessitate a most cautious exercise of the judgment.

There is, however, another consideration I would urge as very important in our study of the nature and origin of Man, and it is this—that we ought not to suffer ourselves to be misled by the supposition of getting rid of difficulties, or, by the adoption of the extreme view of Evolution, of reducing the dif-

ficulties inherent in the subject, much less of obtaining for it
the demonstration which Physical Science demands.

The fact that a being attempts to solve the mystery of his
own existence is itself the most wonderful of phenomena,
and is suggestive of difficulty.   There is, if I mistake not, a
vague impression in scientific and unscientific circles that, by
assigning to Man a duality of nature; *i.e.* by speaking of him
as consisting of, on the one side, a very elaborate organism
in which molecular changes account for growth, movement,
form, and function; and on the other side, a *non*-material
entity, or being, a personal seat of power distinct from, though
associated with, molecular action, we affirm that of which we
can form no conception, for the existence of which we have
no satisfactory evidence, and which, if admitted to exist,
would destroy the equilibrium of the forces of nature.   That
is the supposed difficulty of the Dualistic view, whereas the
Monist who regards what is termed Mind as a mere name, a
symbol of the varied product of the interaction of the Matter
and Force which has built up all else, is supposed simply to
follow up his physical evidence, not going beyond it, and so
rests in conceptions familiar and verified.

Now, on the question of the possibility of conception of a
substantive part of Man's Nature, which is not physical, nor
a physical resultant, but a seat of knowledge and power; all
depends on what is meant by conception.   It is true we
largely think in figures derived from physical objects, and yet
I venture to affirm that some of our most important conceptions of things are never touched by any alloy of physical
extension, colour, or form.   A conception of an act of consciousness is familiar to all, and this is certainly free from
physical alloy.   A thinking process is also thinkable; we
conceive it as truly a reality as is the shooting of stars, and
yet under no form derivable from physical facts; for whatever element of time there may be in it is an element derived
from the succession of pure acts of consciousness.   No man,
I imagine, will deny the reality of an act of consciousness on
the ground that it is not thinkable under a physical image,
or some form recognized by Physical Science.   I say, then, no
scientific man, who is true to facts, and is guided in his judgment by every class of fact, can maintain that no conceptions
are valid except they be such as come within Physical Science
proper, or are under form of physical image, and that consequently we are only to believe in the existence of that which
we can conceive of under such a form.   Nor indeed is it
possible for the physical investigator to carry on his re-

searches, and at the same time be consistent with this erroneous opinion; for obviously he who resolves all Matter into centres of Force would at once destroy his own theory, since he would be obliged to confess that a centre of Force being without extension cannot exist, inasmuch as that is a thing of which we can form no conception. Moreover, the whole of our modern Science rests on the action around us of Force; but though we know of the presence of Force by changes wrought in the relative position of bodies and particles, I venture to say that no one can form a conception of it that answers to the reality, unless in the same way, and on the same principle of being an invisible cause of visible effects, that we form a conception of an invisible *non*-material nature of Man as the cause of Thought and Volition. The Duality of Man's Nature, then, is not set aside because of the difficulty of conceiving of something devoid of the properties of extension, colour, and form.

As to the evidence of the existence of such a nature, you do not get rid of difficulty by denial of evidence: for when the physiologist has completed his examination of the convolutions of the brain, and the molecular changes of the grey matter of the cortex, what does he find? He finds a certain physical structure and molecular movements—so far his Science goes, and no further—but he does not find Thought or Consciousness; he neither sees Thought nor the nexus between a molecular change of the grey matter and Thought. The conscious Thought does not come under his tests. If he in his darkness infers that Consciousness is exclusively the resultant of certain molecular movements, he tacitly admits that the chain of demonstration there comes to an end, and has to confront the enormous difficulty of getting out of molecular movements, by mere inference, that which, in its very nature, is *unique* in the universe, being utterly unlike all else obtainable from molecular changes. On the other hand, the difficulty in the evidence of the Monist is not nearly so formidable. For the most assured facts within the range of human knowledge are above all demonstration by physical processes—such as our own existence and personal identity. Moreover, the fact that an invisible and undetectable ether—a something never seen, never amenable to physical appliances—is assumed to exist in order to account for the phenomena of light, as a substitute for the old hypothesis of luminiferous particles, is certainly a justification for the assumption of an invisible, undetectable something, in excess of a correlated molecular arrangement, as the explanation of phenomena far more subtle and mysterious than are the physical facts involved in the phenomena of light. It is an admitted principle in Scientific Induction, that when you have a whole class of phenomena—separated by their peculiarities from all other phenomena—and which are not demonstrated to proceed from any given cause, you then are warranted in assuming as their cause the existence of something else; and therefore the Dualist, in ascribing the *unique* phenomena of Consciousness to a distinct non-physical cause, in correlation with a physical organ, on the ground that no physical cause can be shown to produce them, and that they are altogether dissimilar in qualities from all that is known to flow from physical causes, is acting strictly as a man of true Science, and, so far as evidence is concerned, is less encumbered with difficulty than is the Monist.

There is just one other point of difficulty to which I must allude, because it is felt by many scientific men to be almost insuperable. It is a postulate of modern Science that Force is one and indestructible; it admits of no increase, no diminution. The forms of its action are infinitely variable and varying, but it keeps up amidst the bodies and particles of Nature its self-contained equilibrium, or rather readjustment. If, then, in the nature of Man you admit Mind as something that is not Force and not Matter, or not the resultant of the interaction of these two, and which, by hypothesis, is a power that strikes in on the order of Nature, you practically introduce into the physical order another Force in the rear of that one Force which acts in and on the molecules—a Force too which is supposed to be inactive, except by fits of exertion. Now, obviously there is in this way of presenting the difficulty something rather embarrassing, when one overlooks a very subtle yet huge assumption. For you will observe that the objection to the Dualistic nature of Man proceeds on the supposition that Force, as known by the senses to act on and among particles of Matter, constitutes with that Matter the totality of Nature, and consequently all else that may be spoken of is to be conceived as outside Nature, and its supposed action as an impossible intrusion *ab extra*, which, of course, it is if Nature be complete without it. But here may it not be asked, Is not this the very question at issue? With justice the Dualist may say, "I cannot allow you, if you want to prove that there cannot be such a thing as Mind Power, which is neither Matter nor Force nor their effect, to assume at the outset that Matter and Force constitute the totality of Nature." If the phenomena of Consciousness as seen in Thought and Will are such as cannot, on the principles of Physical Science, be clearly proved to come from or to consist in molecular action, then, as we have seen, some other sufficient cause must be assumed, and this necessity existing, that other cause is thereby shown to be *in* Nature, and a complement to that Force which in like manner we know not in itself, but from its peculiar effects. As to the conceivability of a Mind Power distinct in kind from the Force which acts in Matter, and both co-existing with it and able to modify its action, this, I imagine, will not be found so great a difficulty as the conceivability of Force, while acting in Matter, transmuting itself into so marvellous and opposite a thing as Thought and conscious Volition, and yet, if the doctrine of Conservation of Force be true, remaining Force as really as before the transmutation. I submit this to the calm consideration of physical investigators, and would ask whether belief in a *non*-physical being as cause is not a scientific necessity.

The subject widens before our view; but I must be content with these few observations, and a word or two in conclusion. We shall do well to bear in mind what I have indicated; namely, that the two parts of this great question of the scientific position of Man are to be kept distinct in respect to the kind of evidence admissible to their successful treatment. There are, I admit, some very significant indications pointing to the possibility of the human organism being allied by descent with other inferior organisms, and, although I think there are at present more counter indications pointing in another direction, yet the question at issue is fairly one of further scientific evidence, and we may welcome any patient investigator who can furnish us with additional facts on which to frame our judgment. Should it be indisputably shown that the Great Author of all things has been pleased to exercise His creative energy in this way rather than any other, we shall not the less adore the Wisdom and the Power, and shall have no difficulty in modifying interpretations in another department of truth in harmony with modified interpretations of Nature. But in reference to the other part of this question, I do not see that we are to expect any further evidence in the domain of Physical Science; for no research of a physical kind can add to or alter our conception of what Consciousness is as a something *unique* in the world of things, since it has been the same in all ages, and in all stages of cultured and uncultured life, and, from the nature of the case, cannot be otherwise. Nor can research of a physical kind bridge the chasm which cuts off consciousness from the nature of molecular action, and from all known effects of that action, since the chasm remains as wide to the philosopher as to the peasant, and is not, from the nature of the case, a question of degree. Nor, further, can it ever destroy the necessary antithesis of material and *non*-material, since that lies at the base of all knowledge, and is the condition of all thinkable fact.

That a *non*-material being who finds himself in a Universe of material arrangements of varied complexity, amidst which he is to act his part, should be conditioned in the development of his true self by an organism of more or less complexity, and should not be able to act independently of its health or weakness—this is in perfect harmony with all we know of subordination of means to ends and of mutual dependence; and further, that in very diverse degree, from the dim sense of being barely alive experienced by the Amoebae up to the perfect animation of buoyant manhood, a Divine munificence should so scatter the blessing of conscious existence as to make almost every inch on the globe an abode of delight— the delight of life—this is a conception in which human reason and beneficence can rejoice. Shadows, no doubt, there are over human existence which rob Man of much that he would otherwise enjoy as part of the natural heritage of sentient beings, and by reason of the disorder of his moral nature he, alone of all creatures, may, in his impatience of limitation, often turn the measure of light obtained to the torment rather than to the solace of his own spirit. Nevertheless, if conscious of, and rejoicing in, the fact of our distinct personality, and inspired by faith in a grand and interminable existence, we are content to press on in the pathway of knowledge, and are careful to keep ourselves calm amidst conflicting opinions, and pure in heart amidst incitements to evil, then we have reason to believe, on the best of testimonies, that, instead of being burdened with a sense of spiritual orphanage in a vast arena where stern necessity remorselessly crushes alike our hopes and our fears, we shall, as the offspring of the Great Father of Spirits, attain to a fair measure of truth for the present education of our nature, shall enrich our posterity with enduring treasures of wisdom and goodness, and, by the help of Him who is the Light of the World, rise to an elevation from which, with undimmed eye, we may look onward with eager desire to our future inheritance of knowledge, of purity, and of restful joy in the Eternal Source of all Good.

Obituary Notices.

COMPILED BY THE REV. W. HARPLEY, M.A., HON. SECRETARY OF THE ASSOCIATION.

(Read at Dawlish, July, 1881.)

I.

W. CANN was a foundation member of the Association, and a Vice-President during the year 1875–6.

So long as his health permitted he was a constant attender of the meetings of the Association. He died at Exeter, December 7th, 1880, at the age of 82 years.

II.

CHARLES HUGH CLIFFORD, of Chudleigh, Baron, son of the 7th Baron, and Count of the Holy Roman Empire, was born 27th July, 1819, and died, after many months of patient suffering, on 5th August, 1880. He was educated at Stonyhurst and Prior Park, Bath; and finally studied for two years at Munich. He then travelled in India and the East for about two years. He succeeded to the title in February, 1858, having married Agnes Louisa Catherine, youngest daughter of William, Lord Petre, on September 30th, 1845.

Lord Clifford joined the Devonshire Association in 1873, and was a Vice-President at the Teignmouth meeting, when the Earl of Devon presided. That was the only time when Lord Clifford attended the meetings; but he always expressed a warm interest in the Association, and would have been present at the Ilfracombe meeting if it had been possible. Those who knew the late Lord Clifford well, knew what was not so generally known from his simple and retiring habits, that his intelligence and reading eminently qualified him to enter into the subjects dealt with by the Devonshire Association for the promotion of Science,

Literature, and Art. Its members felt a just pride in having his name amongst them.

And those, it may be permitted us to say, who had any opportunity of observing his inner life, could not, however they might differ from him, fail to see and admire the high religious tone which guided his daily conduct, and made all intercourse with him a privilege. For the great change, that came early to him, his family motto was eminently true, *semper paratus*.

III.

P. O. HINGSTON, of Kingsbridge, became a member of the Association on the occasion of its visit to that town in 1877. Few men were held in higher esteem or were better known in his locality than he was. By his unostentatious charity, simplicity of manners, and good-will towards all, he endeared himself to every one with whom he was brought into communication. His success was that of character over circumstances. Commencing as a clerk with the late Mr. W. Beer, he continued to rise higher by his conscientious devotion to duty, until he acquired a reputation that anyone might well aspire to obtain. No one in the locality was more trusted and more frequently applied to for advice, as well in public as in private matters ; indeed kindness may be said to have been the most prominent feature in his character. Unwilling at all times to give pain, he was ever ready to give advice, and bestow charity wherever it was needed, so that no one appealed to him in vain who was really in want. Mr. Hingston profitably filled many public appointments, and was identified from their foundation with the disposal of the most prominent of the local charities.

He died on the 26th March, 1881, at the comparatively early age of 54 years.

IV.

Dr. HODGSON was born at Edinburgh in 1815, and educated in the High School and University of that city, where he took his degree. From the first it was his intention to devote himself entirely to the work of education, and after having been engaged for some years as private tutor and in other capacities in his native town, he went to Liverpool in 1839. Here, at the age of 23, he was engaged as secretary to the Liverpool Institute, of which important establishment he subsequently became principal. In this position he directed three day schools and evening classes, which numbered more than 1,700 scholars. Besides the general direction which he gave to that exacting task, he also acted as head master of the High School, and there he first became known as a successful teacher and an eminent educational reformer. In 1846, in recognition of his labours in the cause of popular instruction, he had conferred on him the Edinburgh degree of LL.D. In 1847 he went to Manchester as principal of the Chorlton High School, and though his influence as a schoolmaster was extraordinary, yet it may be averred that during the four years in which he undertook this duty his services as a public man were even more remarkable ; for it was during this period that the Lancashire Public School Association was founded, a society now generally acknowledged as having given an impetus to the movement which resulted in the passing of the Elementary Education Act of 1870. This association was established in the vestry of Lloyd Street Chapel by five gentlemen—Dr. Hodgson, Mr. Jacob Bright, Mr. Samuel Lucas, Mr. A. Ireland, and Mr. Thomas Ballantyne. The outline of a plan of local education was there laid, and this, when it was fully developed, was unanimously adopted at a public meeting in the Mechanics' Institution. How sagacious Dr. Hodgson was at that time in council, and how eloquent on the platform, there are many who will remember. In this connection it may be stated that he had long been an intimate friend of Dr. Andrew Combe and other pioneers of popular instruction, and that Mr. Cobden was one of his most cordial colleagues in the movement then initiated at Manchester.

Dr. Hodgson went abroad in 1851, and remained some time on the Continent. He visited, in the course of his prolonged tour, France, Germany, Italy, and Switzerland ; and it is needless to state that during the years he spent there he lost no opportunity of making himself intimately acquainted with the theory and practice of education in those countries. In 1854 he returned to Edinburgh, and for several winters he was actively engaged in extending and improving the then existing system of instruction in schools. To his efforts was mainly due the introduction of economic and what were then called "sanitary" subjects. His friend, Dr. Combe, had long advocated the teaching of physiology in schools as the means of promoting physical health, and Dr. Hodgson was enabled to prove the efficacy of a theory which was then almost an entire novelty. When in 1859 the Royal Commission on primary schools was appointed, Dr. Hodgson's long and valuable services marked him out to the government of the

day as one of its members, and his special report on the
London district was appended to the Report presented by the
Commission to Parliament. Between 1863 and 1870 Dr.
Hodgson lived chiefly in London, and for five years he was
Examiner in Political Economy in the University of London.
He was elected in 1871 to the Chair of Commercial and
Political Economy and Mercantile Law in the University of
Edinburgh. The appointment was for seven years, and this
period having expired, he was appointed for another term.
His appointment excited the liveliest expectations, and a
most cordial welcome was given to him. These were more
than fulfilled, and the welcome accorded was repaid by a
devotion to public service seldom displayed by university
professors. But he did not confine his labours to the university. He sought to serve the citizens as well as the college.
As a practical educationist, his counsel and guidance were
freely placed at the disposal of the teachers' associations.
The most memorable and stimulative speeches delivered at
the meetings of the Educational Institute in Edinburgh were
undoubtedly those of which the Professor of Political Economy was the author. The Wate Institute and School of
Arts also found him a most helpful and willing friend, and
the advocacy of the interests of the People's College was to
him a congenial task. The ladies who so gallantly struggled
to open the doors of the Medical School to female students
likewise found in him a powerful and fearless champion.
He was not unwilling to fraternise with the people; for his
sympathies and convictions were essentially democratic; but
he never fraternised with the toiling masses without giving
them a word of encouragement, and seeking to elevate their
thoughts and aspirations. His labours as a member of the
Chamber of Commerce will not soon be forgotten. He worked
for the Chamber of Commerce as though it were a part of his
professional duty to serve it, and through it the public, and
his exertions were recognised by his elevation to the office of
President. About three years ago he was President of the
Co-operative Congress in Glasgow.

Throughout his career Dr. Hodgson had always been an
active member of the Liberal party. It is more than probable
that had he been spared much longer he would himself have
had an opportunity of serving his country in Parliament.

As an author and professor, Dr. Hodgson's fame had long
been secure. A series of eloquent and suggestive lectures,
which he delivered during his residence in Manchester, included not merely social and political, but metaphysical and

æsthetic subjects. All these were treated with no less lucidity than insight, and the remarkable power of illustration, which must have struck all who have read Dr. Hodgson's books, was invariably conspicuous in his lectures and speeches. The catalogue of his works includes a *Lecture on Education*, 1837; a translation of Bastial's, *What is Seen and what is not Seen; or, Political Economy in one Lesson*, 1852; *Classical Instruction: its Use and Abuse*, 1853; *The Conditions of Health and Wealth, educationally considered*, two lectures, 1860; *Remarks on Report of Public School Commissioners*, 1864; *Classical Instruction: Why, When, for Whom?* 1866; *Exaggerated Estimates of Reading and Writing as means of Education*, 1867; a translation of Count Cavour's *Ireland*, 1868; *What is Capital?* 1868; two lectures "*On the Edu-. cation of Girls and the Employment of Women of the Middle Classes*, 1869; lecture on the *True Scope of Economic Science*, 1870; lecture on *Competition*, 1870; and two lectures on *Turgot: his Life, Times, and Opinions*, 1870. To this list of his writings may be added many contributions to journalistic literature, including some admirable letters, signed "M.E.N.," which appeared in the *Manchester Examiner and Times*.

Dr. Hodgson's reading was as wide as his criticism was searching and his memory retentive. Few could vie with him in his familiarity with general literature. His mind was stored with the best that has been said or thought, not only by great Englishmen, but great men of every age and every land; and for purposes of illustration, the professor was ever ready to lay them aptly under contribution. In economics the extent of his reading was simply marvellous. Not a work remotely bordering on his subject but he knew it; not an attempt to throw new light upon a doubtful question but he had seen and appraised it; not an addition to the stock of economical fixed ideas but he had assimilated it; not an economist but he knew his theories and his crotchets, and could point out the fallacies into which he had fallen. Nor was this close acquaintance confined to English economists only. With French writers on the subject he was equally familiar, and Bastial and Saye were quoted as frequently and freely as McCulloch or Mill.

Dr. Hodgson joined this Association in 1867, and in the following year, at the meeting at Honiton, he read the paper mentioned above—"What is Capital?" This was his only contribution to the pages of the Transactions of the Association. The rule which limits the subjects to be treated strictly to Devonshire soon after came into operation, and, although he admitted this rule had been wisely framed, yet it shut him out, as he said, from the list of authors. He did not cease, however, to take a lively interest in the work of the Association, but attended several meetings, and took part in the discussions that arose. At the annual meeting last year he was unanimously elected to the office of President of the Association, and had his life been spared, he would have been here on this occasion to win fresh laurels, and increase, if that were possible, the high estimation in which he was held.

It is, of course, more difficult to refer to the private virtues and the delightful social qualities which endeared Dr. Hodgson to so large a circle of friends. Those who had known him longest, and most intimately, had the warmest regard for him. His nature was kindly and frank; he was generous, high-minded, and disinterested; and both as a public and a private man he took advantage of many opportunities for rendering assistance by counsel, and still more emphatic timely help to those who sought his advice. He was never more happy than in the midst of his friends at his delightful home, Bonaly Tower, on the slopes of the Pentland Hills, once the residence of Lord Cockburn; but, wherever he was, the charm of his conversation made him a welcome guest. With respect to his pupils in his class, he made it an especial object to acquaint himself personally with each of them, and to get nearer to them than could the professor at the head of the ordinary classes. The relation between Dr. Hodgson and his students was thus the more intimate one of friend with friend, than professor with student, and the regard which was entertained for him by them was warmer in kind than in perhaps any other instance, as there was in it something of filial affection in addition to the respect in which professors are usually held. It may, perhaps, be allowed to add one further word without risk of invading the sanctity of domestic life, and this merely to say that Dr. Hodgson was in the truest sense a religious and most reverent man; anyone who was intimate with him, and anyone who had been his guest, could not doubt of his feelings and belief. He married a daughter of Sir Joshua Walmsley, for some time member for Leicester.

He died suddenly at Brussels, on the night of Tuesday, the 24th of August, 1880, at the age of 65 years.

SIXTH REPORT OF THE COMMITTEE ON SCIENTIFIC MEMORANDA.

SIXTH REPORT *of the Committee, consisting of Mr. George Doe, Rev. W. Harpley, Mr. N. S. Heineken, Mr. H. S. Gill, Mr. E. Parfitt, and Mr. J. Brooking Rowe* (Secretary), *for the purpose of noting the discovery or occurrence of such facts, in any department of scientific inquiry, and connected with Devonshire, as it may be desirable to place on permanent record, but which may not be of sufficient importance in themselves to form the subjects of separate papers.*

Edited by J. BROOKING ROWE, F.S.A., &c., Hon. Secretary of the Committee.

(Read at Dawlish, July, 1881.)

FROM unknown causes, the facts brought to the knowledge of the Committee during the past year have been very much fewer than hitherto. As usual, the Report includes *Memoranda* of facts which have been discovered, or observed, or have become known to members of the Committee, during the twelve months ending 31st May, 1881.

I. ARCHÆOLOGICAL.

RUSH RINGS.

"Among the ancient title-deeds relating to the Long Bridge at Barnstaple, commencing 1303, is one dated 4th Edward IV. (1464, the earliest deed in English), which has a noticeable peculiarity worth recording. It purports to be a deed of award, whereby a tenement in Barnstaple is adjudged as belonging to several persons therein named for their lives, with the ultimate remainders: 'To the Wardyneys of ye long Brugge of the Town foresaid, and to their Heirs and Successors for ever, to the behove profite and mayntenaunce of the said Brugge. Sealed by John Pollard the Arbitrator, and also at his request for the preservation of the testimony of the document, sealed by John Denys, Gencier Boteler,

Simon Passlewe, Robert Pollard, John Wyggen, Richard Newcomb, and Walter Frost. Dated from Barnstaple, 1st May, 4th Edward IV.' Six of the seals are still attached to the document. The impressions are mostly monograms; but two of them have the singular addition of rush rings appended to and forming parts of the seals. These rings are of the same size and appearance as were commonly used by the peasantry in early times in plight of matrimonial troth, being formed of woven or plaited rushes, the ordinary size of a finger.

" The perfect rush ring of one of these seals still adheres to it, and was apparently placed on the wax while hot, and the seal then impressed through it.

" On the circular margin of the other seal the impression of the rush ring is as distinct as the impression of the seal itself—the rushes being decayed or broken away. This is the only document among the many thousands examined which has seals of this character.

" One of the Inspectors under the Historical Manuscripts Commission, J. Cordy Jeffreason, Esq., who visited Barnstaple some time since, and who has treated on the subject of ' rush rings ' in one of his valuable antiquarian works, made the present discovery, and was especially interested in it, as an instance had never before come under his notice. He suggested that the ring may have been the familiar symbol of perpetuity, thus used to heighten the solemnity of the ceremony, and indicate the perpetuity desired, for the testimony of the instrument and the gift to the bridge.

" Mr. Jeffreason writes me that since he left Barnstaple he has kept a sharp look-out for other instances of such seals; but only at Ipswich had he seen any to be grouped with the Barnstaple specimens; and even then there were only three among a collection of several thousand writings. Those he found were a deed of release of Edward III.'s reign, the seal gone, but a perfect rush ring hanging round the label, from which the seal had been broken; a deed of Henry VI.'s time, with a cluster of rush ring seals, some retaining the rush annulet, and all the others with marks showing that such circlets had been there; and another deed of Edward IV.'s time similarly sealed.

" It is singular that the only places in which this peculiar application of rush rings has hitherto been discovered should be two equally ancient burghs, placed at the extreme east and extreme west sides of England. It may be worth while to keep a look-out among ancient deeds for any similar instances of rush rings.

"Two somewhat analogous instances of appendages to seals are given in *Notes and Queries*, viz. :

"On a deed of sale of quit rents at Alnwick, in the year 1655, is the following testatum : 'Signed, sealed, and delivered, with one single twopence of lawful money of England put into the seale, in token of the possession, livery, and seisin of the out rend or quit rent of 5s. by yeare within named in presence of, &c.'—*N. and Q.*, 2nd Series, ii. 129.

"Stillingfleet, *Orig. Brit.*, iii. 13, referring to a monkish chronicle, says : 'He observes one particular custom of the Normans, that they were wont to put some of the hair of their heads or beard into the wax of their seals.'—*N. and Q.*, 1st Series, 317. (J. R. CHANTER.)"

"During the sinking of a well adjoining the site of the Priory at Plympton, in the month of August, 1880, a jetton or abbey-piece was found. It is almost identical with figure No. 24, plate ii., in Snelling's *View of Jettons*. Another, apparently an earlier form, with pellets and mullets, was also found, and a sixpence of Queen Elizabeth, 1573.

"A short time before finding the counters and coins mentioned above, a slab was discovered, buried face downwards, in the ground south of the refectory of the Priory. It is coffin-shaped, with incised floriated cross, probably early fourteenth-century work.

"These are in my possession, and full descriptions, with drawings, will, I hope, appear in my projected History of the Deanery of Plympton. (J. BROOKING ROWE.)"

II. BOTANICAL.

"The following list of shrubs and plants killed and injured during the past winter will show the severity of the weather in this usually mild climate :

Plants killed.

Veronica Andersoni, and several others that generally stand our winters in Devon.
Clianthus punicius.
Coronilla glauca.
Escallonia micrantha.
Escallonia rubra.
Myrtus ugnii.
Thuja orientalis.

Chinese Arbor-Vitæ. Large plants from twenty to thirty years old, completely killed. This is very general in this locality.
Thuja aurea. Generally killed.
Philesia buxifolia.
Cupressus macrocarpa. Small plants killed ; old plants very much injured.

Plants very much injured.

Laurel, common.   Bays.
Euonymus variegatus.   Ceanothus azureus.
Berberies, species.

Plants injured.

Rhododendrons.   Hydrangeas.
Aucuba Japonica.   Tea Roses.
Juniperus sabini.

                                    (E. PARFITT.) "

III. NUMISMATICAL.

" A seventeenth-century trade token was found in April
last at Halberton, near Tiverton, being the only one known
to have been issued there.

"Obverse, 'SIMON . HVSSEY . 1667 ;' and in the field (for
    device), The Cloth-workers' Arms.

"Reverse, 'OF . HALBERTON . IN . DEV.(on) = S. D. H.'

" It is well known by collectors that the second initial on
these tokens is that of the issuer's wife; and I have since
been informed by the vicar of Halberton that he found the
following entry in his church register: 'Simon Hussey and
Dorithy (*sic*) Osmond *was* married on the 6th da*ie* of July,
1659.' The vicar added that the name of Hussey still lingers
in Halberton and its neighbourhood.

" From the device it is obvious S. H. was engaged in cloth-
making, then the staple trade of the county; and doubtless
the token would be a great boon to his workmen and their
wives, as by it they could obtain of the village shopkeeper (no
small change less than a penny being in existence) the countless
daily necessaries of life, and the trader could always, as the
tokens accumulated, get them changed into silver by the issuer.

" Two other farthing tokens belonging to Plymouth have
been found since our last meeting.   One reads thus :
" Obv. 'MAXEMILLIAN . BOVSH.'   A trefoil.
" Rev. 'IN . PLYMOVTH . 1659.'   Three stars.
" This interesting token belongs to our member, Mr. R. N.
Worth, who bought it at a shop in London, and who suggests
it was issued by a foreigner, who at that period would have
to pay yearly fines to the Corporation of Plymouth, not being
a freeman, and yet in business.   The other is by—
" 'RICHARD . HAMLYN.'   A bunch of grapes.
" 'IN . PLYMOUTH . 1659. = R. P. H.'
" This coin belongs to a gentleman in Limerick, but for-
merly of Plymouth, from whence the description was also
kindly sent to me by Mr. R. N. Worth.

" When the Council of the Association met in Exeter, last February, one of our members showed me the following specimen. I tried to induce him to part with it, but the owner would not.

" Obverse, 'THO : POWELL . IN . GREAT.' The Mercers' Arms.

" Reverse, 'TORINGTON . MERCER . 71. = T. E. P.'

" Eight tokens were issued there, and five of them have only one R in the town. (H. S. GILL.) "

" A very thin copper coin, of Charles I. (Mionnet 4)—

" Obverse, two sceptres in saltier behind a crown.

" Leg. 'CAR . D . G . M . A . G . BRI.'

" Reverse, Irish harp, crowned.

" Leg. 'ET . H . I . B . R . E . X.'

" Found in Mill Street, Sidmouth, September 11th, 1880. (N. S. HEINEKEN.) "

" Small copper coin (Mionnet 3)—

" Ob. 'CAROLUS . D . G . MA . BRI.' round a crown, and two sceptres in saltier.

" Rev. A rose, crowned.

" Leg. 'F . R . A . E . T...R.'

" Found in October, in road near Cotmaton, 1880.

" Guinea of George III.; date 1785. In beautiful preservation, as if fresh from the mint. Found in a field under Willoughby Cottage, Peak Hill, Sidmouth, March 11th, 1881.

" Shilling of Elizabeth. Obverse and reverse nearly obliterated. Found at Cottington, Sidmouth, April 5th or 6th, 1881.

" French liard—

" Ob. Louis XIV., profile. Date 1655.

" Rev. 'LIARD DE FRANCE . A . 3 FLEURS DE LIS.'

" Found in the Western Field, Sidmouth, May, 1881. (P. O. HUTCHINSON.) "

IV. ZOOLOGICAL.

AVES.

" *Avocets at Kingsbridge.*—Mr. Henry Nicholls states, *Zoologist*, Nov., 1880, p. 486, that three Avocets (*recurvirostra avocetta*) were observed in the Kingsbridge Estuary October 2nd, all of which were eventually obtained. They were a male and two females. The largest was the male, which weighed 10½ ounces; its length was 17 inches, breadth 30 inches. One female weighed 9 ounces, and was 15¾ inches in length, and 29 inches in breadth.

"In December, 1880, a Little Bustard was killed near North Tawton; and later in the month a second specimen— like the first, a female—was obtained near Braunton.

"The sixteenth instance of the occurrence of White's Thrush (*Turdus varius*) is recorded by Mr. E. W. Holdsworth in the *Zoologist* for March, 1881, p. 108. It was killed at Dene Wood, near Ashburton, in January, 1881.

PISCES.

"*Eagle Ray off Plymouth.*—I obtained in May a specimen of the Eagle Ray (*Myliobatis aquila*), caught off Plymouth. The measurements taken when fresh were : Length from snout to root of tail, 9 inches; length of tail, 20 inches; breadth, 18 inches.

"*Maigre at Beer.*—A specimen of the Maigre (*Sciœna aquila*) was taken in August by the Beer fishermen in a pollack net, as recorded by Mr. W. S. M. D'Urban in the *Zoologist* for October. The measurements were: Length, 2 ft. 8¼ in.; girth over pectoral fins, 1 ft. 4¾ in. (J. BROOKING ROWE.) "

FIFTH REPORT OF COMMITTEE ON DEVONSHIRE CELEBRITIES.

FIFTH REPORT *of the Committee—consisting of Mr. R. Dymond, Mr. P. Q. Karkeek, Mr. R. N. Worth, Sir J. H. Kennaway (M.P.), Mr. Edward Windeatt, Mr. R. W. Cotton, and the Rev. Treasurer Hawker* (Secretary)—*to prepare Memoirs on Devonshire Celebrities.*

Edited by Rev. Treasurer HAWKER, M.A., Hon. Sec. of the Committee.

(Read at Dawlish, July, 1881.)

A LETTER, kindly inserted by the editor of the *Western Morning News* in the beginning of the year, brought much valuable information from various quarters respecting Devonshire Celebrities, and bibliographical notices of them. The thanks of the Committee are due to those who thus answered the appeal. All such information, whether entirely new or supplementary, adds greatly to the authority and usefulness of the Catalogue.

A story is told of Dr. Routh, the learned President of Magdalen College, Oxford, that, when he was asked, between ninety and a hundred years of age, what was the chief lesson of his long life, he pondered for some time and then said gravely, "To verify your quotations."

Your Committee hope that each year the additions and corrections made in their list, will help to facilitate the verification of statements about the Celebrities of Devon.

A small acquaintance with the grammar of assent, teaches one how soon a mistake or a misstatement is perpetuated by the indolent acceptance of the public. "They say," "it is always supposed," "there is no doubt," and the like expressions, have covered a vast number of inaccuracies, and caused an immense amount of unnecessary labour in unravelling past entanglements of History.

The Committee trust that by annual supervision and kind help from friends, their list of Devonshire Celebrities and their works, with any literary notices of them, may smooth the path of future enquirers. The County is one that will bear thorough searching, both as to quality and quantity.

The following additions, &c., are recommended :

Borough, Steven : *b* at Northam, Sept. 25th, 1525, *d* at Chatham, July 12th, 1584; navigator; discoverer of Northern Passage to Russia; one of the four masters of the navy, *temp.* Queen Elizabeth.
> *Trans. Devon. Assoc.* vol. xii. p. 332 ; R. W. Cotton.

Borough, William : *b* at Northam, 1536, *d* 1599 ; navigator; author of work on the variation of the compass, &c.; comptroller of the navy, *temp.* Queen Elizabeth.
> *Trans. Devon. Assoc.* vol. xii. p. 359 ; R. W. Cotton.

Carwithen, Rev. J. B. S., B.D. : *b* at Manaton (near Moreton Hampstead) April 10th, 1781, *d* at Sandhurst, 1832; Bampton Lecturer, 1809, subject, *A view of the Brahminical Religion in its confirmation of the truth of the Sacred History and its influence on the moral character;* (2.) *Letters to Rev. Daniel Wilson ; The History of the Church of England to the Restoration of the Church and Monarchy in* 1660.

Chidley (or Chudleigh) John : *b* at Chudleigh, *d* in the Straits of Magellan ; sailed from Plymouth in 1589 on a voyage round the world.

Coleridge, Rev. John : *b* at Crediton, Jan. 21st, 1719, *d* 1781, buried at Ottery St. Mary; father of Samuel Taylor Coleridge; Chaplain Priest, and Vicar of Ottery St. Mary, master of the Grammar School there; a great scholar; contributed to the *Gentleman's Magazine* learned papers between 1745 and 1780, bearing his name or initials; by his knowledge of Hebrew aided Dr. Kennicott in his works.
> *Gentleman's Magazine*, 1836.

Coleridge, James : *b* at Southmolton, Dec. 15th, 1760 ; a leading Magistrate for the County, and able administrator of its finances; an energetic organiser of Volunteers in the early part of the century, for which service he was eminently fitted by his training from 1775 to 1786 in the 8th regiment of infantry, where he attained the rank of captain; he held the rank of lieutenant-colonel in the East Devon Militia; he married Frances Duke Taylor, of Otterton.
> *Gentleman's Magazine*, 1836.

After notice of " Collins, Mortimer, &c.," add, "author of *Thoughts in my Garden, &c.*"

Dunn, Samuel : *b* at Crediton ; mathematician.

After notice of "Jewel," add, "author of *An Apology for the Church of England*, translated from the original Latin by Lady Bacon, daughter of Sir A. Cooke;" also, "Jewel's Birthplace."

Trans. Devon. Assoc. vol. xi. p. 256 ; J. M. Hawker.

Rennell, James, F.R.S.: *b* at Chudleigh, 1742, *d*   Geographer, author of *Geological System of Herodotus*.

Blewitt's *Panorama of Torquay*, 1832, p. 186.

Slade, William : *b*   *d* 1415 ; Abbot of Buckfastleigh ; theologian, artist, author of thirteen works.

Edinburgh Review, Oct., 1880, article " Boase's Annals of Exeter College. *Trans. Devon. Assoc.* vol. viii. p. 851; J. Brooking Rowe.

Towson, John Thomas : *b* at Devonport, 1804, *d* at Liverpool, Jan. 3rd, 1881 ; watchmaker ; eminent for science and discoveries in the art of navigation, particularly in regard to " Great Circle Sailing."

Athenæum, Jan. 8th, 1881, p. 59.

J. MANLEY HAWKER,

Chairman and Hon. Secretary.

FOURTH REPORT OF THE COMMITTEE ON DEVON-SHIRE VERBAL PROVINCIALISMS.

FOURTH REPORT *of the Committee—consisting of Mr. J. S. Amery, Mr. G. Doe, Mr. R. Dymond, Mr. F. T. Elworthy Mr. F. H. Firth* (Secretary), *Mr. P. O. Hutchinson, Mr. P. Q. Karkeek, and Dr. W. C. Lake—for the purpose of noting and recording the existing use of any Verbal Provincialisms in Devonshire, in either written or spoken language, not included in the lists published in the Transactions of the Association.*

Edited by F. T. ELWORTHY, Member of Council of the Philological Society.

(Read at Dawlish, July, 1881.)

I. EXPLANATORY.

YOUR Committee have, in the first place, to express their deep and unfeigned regret at the retirement of their old and valued friend, Mr. Pengelly, both from the work of the Committee and from the Editorship. They feel that the very cordial thanks of the Society at large are due to him for the warm interest and indefatigable labour which he has bestowed upon it; and they are deeply conscious that a loss has been sustained which cannot be replaced.

Last year your Committee had no report to offer, and were compelled to seek another Editor; probably as a consequence the interest in the work rather fell off, so that during the past year fewer members have contributed matter, and the report therefore contains fewer provincialisms. It is, however, the earnest hope of the Committee that its most valuable and important work may receive renewed and more vigorous help from the members of the Association, so that the immense advantage to be obtained from numbers of attentive observers may be fully realized.

Your Committee recommend the continued use of the Resolutions adopted and printed in their first report (see *Trans. Dev. Assoc.*, ix. 123–142), except that they advise the omission of paragraph F ("To avoid all attempts at derivation"), because it is desirable to encourage individual and extended investigation, and because by promoting speculation as to the origin of the provincialisms, whether it be valuable or not, a greater interest is created, and thereby more peculiarities are likely to be observed. It is only the habit of accurate observation that is needed to insure a very rich harvest among the spoken dialects of this county.

With the view of suggesting a more minute observation of the Devonshire speech, a few particulars are here subjoined, to which the attention of those willing to help is earnestly directed.

RESOLUTIONS.

1. That the members of this Committee be requested to observe the following regulations, with a view to uniformity of action :—

(A) To regard the following as Devonshire Provincialisms, if used by a speaker or writer within Devonshire, irrespective of their being, or not being, used elsewhere :—

(*a*) Every word not occurring in a good English dictionary of the present day.

(*b*) Every word which, though occurring in a good English dictionary of the present day, is used in a sense differing from any definition of the word given in such dictionary.

(*c*) Every provincial pronunciation of any word which is itself not a provincialism.

(*d*) Every provincial phrase or expression.

(*e*) Every provincial name of an animal, or vegetable, or other object.

(B) To state where and when each recorded provincialism was heard in speech, or seen in writing; and to accept nothing at second-hand.

(C) To state the sex, probable age and social status, and, if possible, the birth-place, residence, and occupation of the person using each recorded provincialism.

(D) To give the meaning of each recorded provincialism within a parenthesis immediately following the provincialism itself; and to illustrate the meaning by incorporating the word or phrase in the very sentence employed by the person who used the provincialism.

(E) To give, in all cases requiring it, some well-known word with which the recorded provincialism rhymes, so as to show its pronunciation; or, where this is not practicable, to give a word or words in which the power of the vowel or vowels is the same as in the provincialism.

(F) To state of each provincialism whether it has been noted by Halliwell, or Nares, or any other recognized compiler of provincial, obsolete, or obsolescent words.

(G) To write the communication respecting each recorded provincialism on a distinct and separate piece of paper, to write on one side of the paper only, and to sign and date each communication; the date to be that on which the recorded provincialism was heard or read.

(H) To make each communication as brief as possible, but not to sacrifice clearness to brevity.

(I) To draw the communications so as to correspond as nearly as possible with the following examples :—

"FLEECHES (= Large Flakes. Rhymes with *Breeches*). A servant girl, a native of Prawle, South Devon, residing at Torquay, and about 23 years of age, stated that the snow was 'falling in *fleeches*,' meaning in *large flakes*. She added that the *small* flakes were not *fleeches*.—19th March, 1877. XY."

"HALSE (= Hazel. The *al* having the same sound as in *Malice*, not as in *False*). A labouring man, a native of Ashburton, residing at Torquay, and about 55 years of age, stated in my hearing that he had put an' *alse* 'andle into his hammer; meaning a *hazel* handle (see *Halliwell* and *Williams*).—19th March, 1877. XY."

2. That the Report of the Committee to be presented to the next Annual General Meeting of the members of the Association shall include all suitable communications received by the Secretary not later than the 1st of June next, and that all communications received after that date shall be held over for another year.

3. That all meetings of the Committee shall be held at Exeter; that the Secretary shall convene them by separate notices to each member, posted not less than seven clear days before the dates of the meetings; and that two members shall be sufficient to form a quorum, with power to act.

4. That a meeting of the Committee shall be held not later than the 21st of June next, to receive and decide on a report to be prepared and brought up by the Secretary.

It is desirable to call the attention of observers more particularly to—

1. Pronunciation. To note more carefully—

(a) Vowel sounds, as in the various qualities :

Of *a* (as is found in *shall, gate, father, wall*).

Of *ay* (as in *day, pay, say, may, maid*, &c.), noting carefully whether it has the sound of *ā* long as in English *play*, or whether it has the broad sound of long *ĭ*, as in the Devonshire *ma-aid* (maid).

Of *e* (as in *pet, glebe, where*).

Of *i* (as in *pit, first, fight*).

Of *o* (as in *top, done, gone, bone*), noting carefully if there is any fracture approaching two syllables, as in the ordinary Devonshire *bō-ŭn* (bone), *pā-ir* (pair), &c.

Of *u* (as in *but, bull, church, use,* &c.).

(*b*) To note more carefully the consonants; *i.e.* if any are inserted, as in *finedest* for finest, *smalldest,* &c., or if any are omitted, as in *ving-er* for finger, the received pronunciation having two *g's, fing-ger,* and not one, as in *singer.* To note carefully what English words beginning with *f* or *s* are pronounced with *v* or *z.* Careful attention will show that the distinction between *f* and *v,* or between *s* and *z,* is as distinct in the dialect as in the literary language. Also to observe what words ending in *f* or *v* are peculiarly pronounced; *i.e.* whether *calf* is not pronounced *calv;* loaf, *loav;* sheaf, *sheav;* &c. Whether words ending in *f* drop or change them to other sounds, as in—*Bailiff:* is it pronounced *baily?* Plaintiff: is it *plainty?* Is not *self, zull?* Is not *handkerchief, hangkecher,* &c.? Do words ending in *v* make any change? Is *give* ever pronounced *gee?* Are *gave* and *given* the same as spoken by peasants? Are *have, serve, above, active, abusive,* and many others ending in *ive,* not changed? Is *r* before a short vowel not transposed? *i.e.* how are *red, run, Richard, riddance, great, front, grin,* and many others pronounced?

2. To observe more carefully grammatical peculiarities.

(*c*) How are plurals of nouns formed whenever they are not the same as in received English; for instance, what is the plural of *beast* or *priest?* Are any plurals now made in *en* or *n,* as *shoen, treen, housen?* Are any made by change of vowel, as in *man, men, tooth, teeth,* &c.? Are any plurals the same as in the singular, as in *sheep, deer, grouse,* &c.? Or if sometimes the words are changed, and sometimes not, under what circumstances do they remain unaltered or otherwise? For instance, "the frost will do good to the bud," is a common saying, and quite grammatical; yet *bud* is essentially in the plural number. So we say a "ten pound note," "a six foot wall," "a five bar gate." These phrases are all good English, and the nouns are all plural, though in each case the noun has another plural in *s, buds, pounds, feet, bars.* What is there in the dialect of the same kind?

(*d*) How is the genitive or possessive case formed? What circumstances would determine a speaker to say "*his head,*" or "*the head o' un;*" "*Jim's father,*" or "*the father of Jim*"?

(*e*) As to adjectives. How are the comparisons formed? Note every variation from literary English.

Are particular similes used with certain adjectives, such as "It was so dark's a bag"? Give all the words you hear used to express the absolute superlative, such as *bag* with *dark*, *vanity* with *light* (levis), &c.

Note all distinguishing adjectives; *i.e.* the cases in which *this, thik, thicky, thicky there, that, that there, they* (as in *they pigs*) are used. Is *them* (as in *them apples*) ever used?

(*f*) As to pronouns. Is there any variety in the first person sing. in the various cases of nom. acc. dat. in which it is used? Is the second person sing. used often? If so, in what way? How is the third person sing. used? Is the pronoun *it* often heard? and is the word always used as in literary English?

How are pronouns affected by the prepositions? *i.e.* do you hear *to, from, in, upon, of, with, I* or *me* (*i.e.* to *I*, or to *me*)? *he, her, him, it*, &c. (*i.e.* to *he* or to *him*)? *we* or *us*? *they* or *them*?

(*g*) As to verbs. Are to *see, grow, know, shear, swear, bear, begin, bleed, blow, breed, build, cleave, come, draw, drink, eat, fall, fling, fly, forsake, freeze, hang, meet, ring, run, see, shed, shoot, sing, sink, sling, spin, spring, sting, stink, strive, swim, swing, throw, weave, win, wring*, all, or any of them, conjugated as in literary English?

Are to *break, drive, speak, cleave, steal, tear, take, creep, raise*, not very differently conjugated from book English? Is the inflection *eth* much used? Is it used with all the persons, sing. and plur.? Is the full syllable sounded, as in *eateth?* or is it shortened, as in *eat'th*? Is the prefix to the past participle often used, as in "I've a-brokt my coat"?

CONTRIBUTIONS.

Each Contribution is placed within inverted commas, and whatever is not so placed is editorial.

The full address of each Contributor is given below, corresponding with his initials at the foot of his Contribution. It must be fully understood that each Contributor is alone responsible for the statements he makes:

F. T. E. = Mr. F. T. Elworthy, Foxdown, Wellington.
F. H. F. = Mr. F. H. Firth, Cator Court, Ashburton.
P. Q. K. = Mr. P. Q. Karkeek, 1, Matlock Terrace, Torquay.
W. C. L. = Dr. W. C. Lake, 2, West Cliff, Teignmouth.
G. H. W. = Mr. G. H. White, Glenthorn, St. Marychurch.

REFERENCES.

The following is a list of the authorities either quoted or who are referred to as illustrating the words contributed. A great number of others have been consulted, but those only are referred to who have something to the point.

Ash. Dictionary of the English Language. By John Ash, LL.D. 2 vols. London, 1775.

Arms. A Gaelic Dictionary. By R. A. Armstrong. London, 1825.

Blount. Glossographia; or, a Dictionary interpreting all such hard words, whether Hebrew, Greek, &c., as are now used in our refined English tongue. By T. B[lount]. 8°. London, 1656.

Bos. Anglo-Saxon and English Dictionary. By Rev. Joseph Bosworth, D.D. London, 1868.

Brit. Old Country and Farming Words. By James Britten. English Dialect Society, 1880.

Brit. and Hol. A Dictionary of English Plant Names. By James Britten and Robert Holland. English Dialect Society. Parts I. 1878, II. 1879.

Cotg. A Dictionary of the French and English Tongues. Compiled by Randle Cotgrave. London, 1632.

Crabb. Universal Technological Dictionary. By George Crabb. London, 1823.

Couch. Glossary of Words used in East Cornwall. By Thomas Q. Couch. English Dialect Society, 1880.

Court. Glossary of Words used in West Cornwall. By Miss M. A. Courtney. English Dialect Society, 1880.

Ex. Scold. An Exmoor Scolding and Courtship. Edited by F. T. Elworthy. English Dialect Society, 1879.

Ger. Gerard's Herbal. 1636.

Hal. A Dictionary of Archaic and Provincial Words. By James O. Halliwell. 2 vols. 8th Edition. London, 1874.

Hampole. Pricks of Conscience. Edited by Dr. R. Morris. Philological Society (Asher and Co.), 1863.

Earle. English Plant Names from the Tenth to the Fifteenth Century. By John Earle. Oxford, 1880.

John. Dictionary of the English Language. By Samuel Johnson. 4 vols. 9th Edition. London, 1805.

Jon. The Works of Ben Jonson. 1 vol. London (Moxon), 1838.

Lit. Dictionaire de la Langue Francais. Par E. Littré. 4 vols. Paris, 1863–69.

Nathan Hogg. Second Series of Nathan Hogg's Letters and Poems. London (J. R. Smith), 1866.

Pea. Glossary of Words used in Manley and Corringham. By Edward Peacock. English Dialect Society, 1877.

Pegge. An Alphabet of Kenticisms. By Samuel Pegge. English Dialect Society, 1876.

Jen. The Dialect of the West of England, particularly Somersetshire. By James Jennings. 2ud Edition. London (J. R. Smith), 1869.

Prior. Popular Names of British Plants. By R. C. A. Prior. 3rd Edition. London (F. Norgate), 1879.

Promp. Parv. Promptorium Parvulorum Sive Clericorum, Dictionarius Anglo-Latinus Princeps. Circa A.D. 1440. Edited by Albert Way. London (Camden Society), 1865.

Philosophical Transactions of the Royal Society. 1695.

Nares. A Glossary or Collection of Words, &c. New Edition. Edited by Halliwell and Wright. 2 vols. London (J. R. Smith), 1859.

Pul. Rustic Sketches. By G. P. R. Pulman. 3rd Edition. London (J. R. Smith), 1871.

O'Reilly. An Irish-English Dictionary. By Ed. O'Reilly. Dublin, 1821.

Richards. A Welsh and English Dictionary. By the late Rev. Thomas Richards. Trefriw, 1815.

Rob. of Glou. Reign of William the Conqueror. By Robert of Gloucester, A.D. 1298. Edited by Morris and Skeat. Clarendon Press, 1873.

Rob. Glossary of the Dialect of Mid-Yorkshire. By C. Clough Robinson. English Dialect Society, 1876.

Rogers. History of Naaman the Syrian, his Disease and Cure. By Dr. Samuel Rogers. London, 1632.

Sir Fer. Sir Ferumbras, Old Charlemagne Romance of A.D. 1380. Early English Text Society, Ex. Series, 1879.

Skeat. An Etymological Dictionary of the English Language. By Walter W. Skeat. Oxford (Clarendon Press), 1879.

Trevisa. Higden's Polychronicon, translated by John of Trevisa, A.D. 1387. Specimens of Early English. Edited by Morris and Skeat. Clarendon Press Series. Oxford, 1873.

Tusser. Fiue Hundred Pointes of Good Husbandrie. A.D. 1557. By Thomas Tusser. English Dialect Society, 1878.

Walters. An English-Welsh Dictionary. By John Walters. No place of publication. 1794.

Web. Webster's Unabridged Dictionary of the English Language. Revised by Goodrich and Porter. London. No date.

A, prefix to past participle. See a-paid, *Trans. Devon. Assoc.* ix. p. 117 (3).

The retention of this old inflection is one of the chief peculiarities of south-western provincialism. Sometimes in old writers it is written *a*, sometimes *i*, sometimes *y;* but as it was always a short syllable, it was the same sound, whatever vowel may have stood for it. In *Sir Fer.* it is found in all three forms—

l. 74, "In pauylons rich and wel *a* buld."

l. 307, "for traysoun þay had *i*do."

l. 875, "well *y*-armed wiþout faille."

In the *Ex. Scold.* the use of the prefix is almost the rule with every p. part. Had the author been more exact, and less literary, it is probable that it would have been quite the rule. He writes it throughout *a*. It would be easy to produce endless quotations from old authors, not distinctly Devonshire, which would show how universal the inflection once was, though now it may be said to have disappeared from literature, and to exist only as a spoken provincialism.

"AVORE = until. February 12th, 1879, at Plymouth, the conductor of an omnibus from the Royal Hotel said to me, 'Us can wait avore you be ready, sir.' F. T. E."

Ex. Scold., l. 108, "Avore zich Times as Neckle Halse comath about." See also ll. 122, 199, 261. In each instance the sense is distinctly *until*. Of course the commoner meaning is *before*, as given by *Hal., Jen., Pul.*, and others. But it is strange that all have overlooked the much more curious but frequent use of the word as above. It is in common use throughout the county.

"BATTERY = buttress. On February 14th, 1881, a shoemaker, about 30 years of age, born and now living in the parish of Culmstock, said to me of a wall which was leaning dangerously, 'I think he'd stand if was vor to put up a bit of a battery agin un.' F. T. E." See *Hal.* (Batter) *Web.*

"BAY = to keep back. A young man, about 28, on January 10th, 1880, a native of Thorverton, near Exeter, describing a flood that took place there about four or five years ago, said 'The water rose — feet in half an hour, and now you would have *to bay* back the stream to get a bucket-full.' P. Q. K."

This is now a common word throughout the West; but as a verb, it is most probably of modern use, and is therefore but another instance of the formation of verbs from nouns, which we see going on day by day.

Hal. and *Nares* have it as a noun only.

Promp. Parr. has " Bay, or wyth-stondynge," *obstaculum.*

Ash gives it as " v. t. not much used, from *bay*, a dam."

See *Web., John.,* who only quote Blount, " to enclose."

Pul. alone of modern glossarists gives the word as a verb. See *Hal., Nares.*

Cotg. has " Moile f., an arch, damme, or bay of planks, whereby the force of water is broken."

Crabb has " Bay (mech), or *pen*, a pond head, made very high, to keep in water for the supply of a mill. *Stat.* 27 *Eliz.*"

Skeat. has altogether overlooked the word in this sense.

Littré has the word only in the sense of the *bay* or *harbour ;* and in discussing the etymology, he quotes the dictum of Isidore (vi. cent.), " *Portum veteres a bajulandis mercibus vocabant baias ;*" and then adds, " Mais *bajulare* ne peut donner *baia.*" There is evidently much doubt about the word ; for though it looks so French, yet we find it in Irish.

O'Reilly, " Badh, an opening, a bay, a harbour."

Walters has " Bay [dam to stop water] argae i attal dwr." But there does not seem to be any word like *Badh* in Welsh.

Armstrong, " Badh, baidh, a harbour, a bay, a creek, an estuary ; sronbàidh, *stornoway,* literally *the nose of the bay.* From this last it would seem as if in Gaelic the word implied the *land* rather than the water. In any case, it.is not " a far cry " from enclosed water to that which encloses it.

" BEEN, with the present participle, used for the past tense. This form is very common in North Devon. Lynmouth, May 30th, 1881, an elderly boatman, or old ' Cap'n,' said to me, ' I've been shedding over two hundred pound,' meaning ' I have lost it.' F. T. E."

It is very usual to hear such phrases as " We've been killing a lot of fish in that water avore now." Such expressions by no means have a frequentative sense as they would elsewhere, but imply the simple past tense.

" BOLD-MAKING = accepting an invitation to take refreshment. September, 1878, a farmer, about 60, born and bred in Devon, called on me, and on being offered some refreshment, said, ' Thank 'ee, sir, if tid'n too bold making.' Very often, under similar circumstances, from labourers and others I have heard ' Thank 'ee for my bold making ;' *i.e.* for my boldness in accepting your hospitality. F. T. E."

"BONEN = made of bone. A young woman of 20–30, born and resident in Teignmouth, spoke of something she was in the habit of using as a *bonen* one. W. C. L."

This is another of the old inflections by which nouns become adjectives, still commonly retained in the West, but dying out of the literary language, and remaining only in *wooden, leathern*, perhaps *iron; i.e.* made of *ire*, and a few others.

"a stryde voide þer nas,
þat of þat ilke heþenene route al ful was euery plas."
Sir Fer. 1. 3221. (See *Hal.*)

"CAPOOCH. I heard a native of Torquay, who has never been out of the district, on May 29th, 1879, describe a dying child as, '*that child is going capooch.*' This bears a remarkable resemblance to the German *caput gehen*, which may be anglicized by the expression 'to come to grief.' P. Q. K."

Why may not this be the old word *caboche?*

Promp. Parv. translates it " in curvo."

Hal. "To bend." Hence, perhaps, to draw up the body, as in *articulo mortis.*

Mr. Mowat (Bursar, Pembroke College, Oxford) tells me he has often heard the word used in Devonshire in the sense of collapsing. He says that a boy blowing out a paper bag, and then making it burst with a bang, would be said to make the bag go "capooch."

According to *Littré*, capuce is a kind of cloth, cut to a point, and worn by *Capucins;* while other orders, *Benedictins, Bernardins*, &c., wear a *capuchon*, "sous son capuce."

Inasmuch as " Prendre le capuchon, se faire moine;" *i.e.* to become dead to the world, so its use as above by the Torquay native may refer to the covering with a *capuce*, or face-cloth (?).

"CLAVEL = clavel beam, the beam over the opening of a fireplace. March 5th, 1881, at Culmstock, a builder, a native of Sampford Peverell, about 60, in discussing details as to building a farm-house, asked me, 'Would you like to have a arch aturned, or a clavel?' He added, noticing that I was inclined to draw him out, 'You know, sir, we always calls em claa-ls, or else claa-l beams.' F. T. E."

Hal. is wrong. It does not mean a *mantel-piece.* It is as much the beam over the fire opening as the lintel is over the window opening.

Pul. makes the same mistake in his *Glossary*, though in

his introduction (p. v.) he seems to be quite aware of the real meaning.   Of course, if mantel-piece does not mean mantel-shelf, as it is generally understood, then both are right. (See *Wil.*)

Walter, " Mantle-tree [chimney-beam], Cladde." The word is no doubt Celtic.   *Th* or *dh* sounds, as in Welsh *dd,* would naturally be interchangeable with *v.*   (Comp. *thatches* for *vetches,* Pul.)   The *l,* which is very distinct, cannot be so easily accounted for; but for it, our dialect word would be modern Welsh. (See *Richards.*)

" Done, rhyming with 'cone.'   On the 16th August, 1879, a labourer, a native of Widecombe, about 60 years of age, said to me, ' Unless the hay be perfectly dry, a small matter of rain makes it *done.'*   F. H. F."

" Doss, rhymes with 'loss' = dose.   May 24th, 1881, a farmer, in the parish of Culmstock, said to me of the weather, ' 'Twas a beautiful rain ; but we shall very zoon lack another such doss.'   F. T. E."

" Eaver, rhymes with 'savour.'   In this county applied to a particular grass, of the *Bromus* family (Mollis ?) but known among seedsmen as ' Devon Eaver.'   The word is also applied generally in the West to all grass seeds other than clovers. March 5th, 1881, a labourer, about 40, at Culmstock, said to me that to *rive* the seed was 'to put it drue the *rivin* zeeve, vor to take out all the eaver,' meaning all the light grass seeds mixed with the clover.   It is very common among Devon farmers, in speaking of ' seeding out' a field, to say that nothing answers so well as ' the old-fashioned clover and eaver.'   F. T. E."

Hal. spells it *eever,* and calls it ray-grass. (See *Pul.*)

Court. " E-ver, a grass ; evergreen rye.   Eaver is the darnel principally found in red wheat."

Couch. "Eaver, in some parts pronounced hayver.   The grass *Lolium Perenne.*"

Haver (German ' hafer') usually means oats in other counties.   (See *John., Web., Robinson* (' havvers '), *Britten.*)

In Lincolnshire it means wild oats. (See *Peacock;* also *Brit.* and *Hol.*)

Prior says, " Haver means wild oats."

The name seems to be applied to grass in the western counties only.

"FRAIL = weak bodily. September 20th, 1879, widow of tradesman, about 60 years old, long resident in Teignmouth : 'I'm so dreadful *frail*, I can't *get up* and down stairs.' The use of this word, with this meaning, habitual at Teignmouth. W. C. L."

See *Ash. John., Web.,* &c., a purely French word.

Cotgrave, " Fraile, fraile, brittle, weake, easily broken."

"GUTTERING = draining. June 5th, 1881, a labourer, aged 45, native of Culmstock, said to me, 'I've a been guttering for —— down to Lane End.' F. T. E."

This word has become thoroughly technical in both Devon and Somerset. (See *Hal.*)

"HIGH-BY-DAY = in broad daylight. May 29th, 1881, a man over 70, at Lynmouth, speaking of foxes in the woods around, said, 'A little while ago they came down and car'd off some chicken all high-by-day.' Soon after he said, 'They be bold, sure enough, vor to car off poultry high-by-day.' F. T. E."

"HIRE-SAY, rhymes with 'wire.' December 3rd, 1880, a farmer's wife, native of Devon, and now living in the parish of Culmstock, age about 56, said to me in my own house, 'What I do zay is true, sure enough. Tid'n no hire-say; I yerd it my own zull.' Having some doubt, and to make quite sure, I led her on to repeat the word in two other sentences. F. T. E."

See *Hal., Jen.*—

" Twull do your heart good to hire et."—*Ex. Scold.* l. 444.

See also *Ibid,* ll. 31, 139, 566, 617.

" þan stode þus barouns of honour, and lokede þyderward out of þe tour, and al þys hyreþ and seeþ."—*Sir Fer.* l. 3794.

See *Bos.,* A.S. ' hiran,' to hear.

"HOLM = holly. March, 1881, a labourer, about 40 years of age, in my employ at Culmstock, said, ' We ant a cut down none of thick holm bush.' F. T. E."

The usual name in Devon and Somerset.

Promp. Parv. has " holme, or holy," *Ulmus, hussus.*

Parkinson gives "holm" as the name of the holly.

In the North it is called "hollin." It is said of St. Bernard, in the *Golden Legend,* that "he often made his pottage with leues of holm."

In Norfolk the holly is called "hulver." (See *Tusser*, p. 86, v. 23, and p. 105, v. 10. See *Wil., Jen., Hal., Web.*)
Ash says, "Holm is local for holly."

"HULK = seed or grain when mixed with the chaff; *i.e.* after being thrashed, but before it is winnowed. At Culmstock, February 12th, 1881, a farmer, about 56 years of age, said to me, 'We draws in the hulk into the barn, eens we do drash it, fear o' the rain.' F. T. E." See *Hal., Pegge.*

"LINHAY, rhymes with 'finny.' May, 1881, a builder, about 60, living at Sampford Peverell, said to me, 'I spose, sir, you'd like to have a bit of a tallet up over the linhay.' F. T. E."
(See *Hal., Wil., Jen., Pul.*) This is a thorough old west-country word. In the *Phil. Trans. of Roy. Soc.* for 1695, p. 30, is a letter from Mr. Zachary Mayne, concerning a spout of water that happened at Topsham, on the river between the sea and Exeter, in 1694. In it he says, "Backward in the court there was a linny that rested upon a wall."

"MAN-TIE = a very common weed. May 18th, 1881, a gardener, about 40, born and bred in Devonshire, said to me, 'About Exeter we always call it man-tie.' F. T. E."
In Somerset this is generally called "tacker-grass," though it is well known as above. (*Polygonum aviculare.*)

"MISK = mist. November 2nd, 1880, daughter of labourer, of 20 to 30, born and resident in Teignmouth, 'She could hardly find her way home, she felt in a *misk.*' This form not uncommon ; also misky for misty. W. C. L."
Common also in Somerset. (See *Wil.*)

"MONEY-IN-BOTH-POCKETS = the plant 'Honesty' (*Lunaria biennis*). July, 1876, a woman living at Tarr Steps (Somerset), but a native of East Anstey, told me that the plant (very common) was 'always called money-in-both-pockets in that country,' because the seeds are found on both sides of the division in the transparent seed-pod. F. T. E." (See *Britten.*)

"MUN, MIN = them. A farmer, born and bred near Crediton, but who came to live near me in Somerset, always used this form. He constantly used such phrases as, 'I know'd mun well enough,' said of boys stealing apples ; 'I gid mun all they asked;' ''Twas no good for mun to pretend.' The form is perfectly well known to all Devonshire men. F. T. E."

Ex. Scold. 1. 224, "Tha wut spudlee out the Yemors, and screedle over mun."

Nat. Hogg, p. 35—

> " Kinveyinces wiz stannin thare—
> ee korridges, I think, an pair—
> Ta teake min vur a ride."

This word is not to be confused with *min,* meaning *man,* as quoted by *Pul., Jen., Hal.*

Sir Fer.—

"By þat was araid duk Rolant! and saw hy men awayward schake." (1. 928.)

"þan spak Florippe þat burde brizt! to hymyn euerechone." (1. 2525.)

"hy men wondrede wal þe more! þat he therste hym profry to." (1. 291.)

In these examples we find it used in nom., acc., and dat.; and in the poem it is also used after *of, till, with.*

"NOTHING = not nearly. On March 2nd, 1881, the custodian of the Kent's Cavern, probably about 60, speaking of the Brixham Cave, said twice over, ' He idn nothing so large as this. F. T. E."

"To PECK = to measure with a peck. July, 1879, in Culmstock parish, I heard a middle-aged farmer say to a man in a barn, about some seed, ' Mind and peck it up careful like, ins might'n be no mistake. F. T. E."

"POACHED = to make pits with the hoof. On April 27th, 1881, I saw some sheep eating off young corn, and asked a native of St. Marychurch, about 50, if they did no harm, and he replied, 'Young corn is all the better for being well poached;' and, ' It is a good plan to turn in sheep to eat off and poach the young corn.' In reply to my question as to the meaning of poach, he explained that the pits or depressions caused by the hoofs of animals in soft land were called poached. I put the question to an agriculturist of good position, a native of Ilsham, near Torquay, about 35 or 40, what poached meant, and he said, ' When cattle walk over soft ground you will see that each hoof makes a pit; this pitting is called poaching.' I asked if the same expression applied to the footmarks of sheep in fields of young corn, and he replied in the affirmative. P. Q. K."

. See *Hal., Nares* (to poche), *Web., Britten.*

Johnson has "poachy," damp, marshy.

In Somerset "pawch" and "paunch." (See *Wil.*)

Cotg. has "poché," poched, thrust or digged out with the fingers; also blurred. *Cotg.* has also "poinçon," a bodkin. This rather agrees with the Somerset form, but in both the idea is *to punch*; *i.e.* to stab or pierce.

Promp. Parv. has "pownson," *puncto.*

" PROPERLY = completely. February 27th, 1880, a domestic servant, about 30, born in Torquay, resident since in Teignmouth, said, 'You must have it a little warm; you must not have it *properly cold.*' The use of this habitual in Teignmouth. W. C. L."

Cotg. has "propre," unto the purpose.

The meaning above is clearly, " Cold to the purpose." (See *Hal.*)

" REAR = to rouse. September 19th, 1880, a nurse, 60 to 70 years old, born and resident in Teignmouth, said, ' Her began to hollo; her *reared* the whole house.' W. C. L."

Cotg., " To rere," *eslever,* and " *eslever,*" to raise.

We have the same meaning in both modern French and English, as in the phrase, " to raise the whole neighbourhood," to raise a hue and cry. To reare and to raise were synonymous. We have the former in " to rear a monument."

Cotg. gives as the first meaning " *cabrer;*" *i.e.* to stand on the hind legs like a goat.

Hal. says, " To mock, or gibe." (Dev.)

" REXENS = rushes. June 5th, 1881, in the parish of Culmstock, a labourer, about 45 years of age, speaking of some land he had been 'guttering,' said, ' 'Twas urned all to ruin and rexens.' F. T. E." (See *Hal., Wil., Bos.*)

Earle, " Juncus " = risc (p. 14), risce (p. 31). " Juncus," vel scyrpus, resce. " Hec papirio " = resche-busk (p. 52). " Hic cirpus, hic junccus " = a rysche (p. 59). The change from the Saxon *sc* into *cs* is quite natural. Compare *ax; i.e. acs* from *asc.* The forms *rexen* and *raxen* are quite common throughout the South-west. A. S. " Risce," rixe.

" To RIDE = to be carried safely. June 3rd, 1881, the landlord of the Lyndale Hotel, native of Lynmouth, on placing a flower-pot with a plant in it in a certain position in the carriage, said, ' He 'll ride there, miss,' meaning that it would be carried safely. F. T. E."

The word means "to be carried," but implies nothing as to *safety* in ordinary English. (See *Web.*, *John.*) It is used constantly to imply *safe* carriage in Somerset.

"RIPPING = the act of stripping the bark from oak trees or coppice. May 24th, a labourer, about 45, said to me, 'I've a bin over to Holcombe (Rogus) ripping more 'n this vortnight.' F. T. E."
Oxon., " Barkin.'"

"TO RIVE, TO REIVE = to pass seed or grain through a particular sieve in the process of winnowing. March 5th, 1881, at Culmstock, a man of about 40, working in a barn, said to me, respecting some clover-seed, 'I 'an't a rīved a good much o' it not eet.'" (See *Hal.*)
Cotg., " Fendre," to cleave, slit, rive, divide ; hence used as above to separate (*i.e.* by sifting) the seed from the chaff. Cf. " rift."

"RIVING SIEVE = a sieve used in winnowing. March 5th, 1881, asking the man above what he meant by *riving*, he said, 'To put it drue the rīvin-zeeve, vor to take out all the eaver.' F. T. E."
The idea is to separate, as much as to cleave or split.
Promp. Parv. has " ryve, or rake." (*Rastrum.*)
Hampole, "And rogg þam in sonder and ryue." (l. 1230.)

"SAFFRON. August, 1880, a Devonshire farmer, living near Exeter, said to me of a certain farm, ''Tis a very purty little place ; he'd let so dear as saffron.' F. T. E."
Earle, " Hiccrocus," safurroun (p. 52), sapherone (p. 57), safryn (p. 64).
Promp. Parv., " Safrun." (*Crocum.*)
Its value or dearness is given by *Gerard*, p. 152 : " It is also such a speciall remedie for those that have consumption of the lungs, and are, as wee terme it, at deaths doore, and almost past breathing, that it bringeth breath again."

" SHORDS = pieces of broken earthenware. May 12th, 1879, a labourer, a native of Lydford, about 40 years of age, said to me, when moving some thin dense bits of stone with his shovel, 'They ring like shords.' F. H. F."
Cotg. 'Tais' = 'a potshard.' 'Tests' = 'a shard, or piece of a broken pot.' (See Job ii. 8 ; Isaiah xxx. 14 ; Ezekiel xxiii. 34.)

"SLOEN = adjectival form of sloe.   Summer of 1878, a
nurse, between 60 and 70 years old, born at Uffculme, long
resident in Teignmouth, said, 'Her eyes were not quite a sloen
black.'   W. C. L."

This form is most interesting, and quite agrees with the
usual adjectival inflection *en*, as in *bonen, holmen, cloamen,
oaken, stonen, glassen,* &c., but only remaining in standard
Eng. in a few words like *wooden, leathern, waxen*.   The *sloe* is
a common comparative of blackness.   "So black's a sloe" is
heard everywhere in the South.

Earle, "Nigra spina = slag þorn."
Prior, "Sloe," *Prunus spinosa.*

"SPINE-FIELD = pasture field.   May 24th, 1881, a farmer
at Culmstock said to me, 'You main the fust o' they two
spine-fields, don 'ee, sir?'   F. T. E."   (See *Hal., Pul., Wil.*)
The word seems peculiar to the West.

"SHROUDY = branchy, bushy, covered with branches.
February, 1881, at Culmstock, in giving orders for the
'making' of a hedge, I told the labourer (a Devonshire man)
to save all the sticks suitable for peas or kidney beans.   He
said, 'They be come now vor to use all shroudy sticks vor
kidney beans; and I'd so lay use shroudy sticks my zull as
ever I would trimmed ones.'   F. T. E."

Cotg. Abri = a couvert, shrowd, shelter, or shadie place.
Refuge = a shrowd, shelter.

Hence a shroudy tree is one with plenty of branches,
affording *shroud,* or shelter.

Web. "Affording shelter" [*rare*], *Milton.*

"TALLET = a loft over a stable or shed.   May, 1881, a
builder (see Clavel), said to me, 'I spose, sir, you'd like to
have a bit of a tallet up over the linhay.'   F. T. E."   (See
Hal., Jen., Wil.)

Pul. tries to explain its derivation, but not successfully.
The word is not known beyond the western counties; and
there can be scarcely a doubt of its being true Celtic.
Modern Welsh, "*Taflod,* a loft, commonly a hay loft" (see
Richards), must be the same word.

"TAME = prune (as a rose bush).   March 12th, 1881, a
lodging-house keeper, about 30 to 40, born and resident in
Teignmouth, 'I think you have *tamed* him enough, sir.'
W. C. L."

(See *Trans. Dev. Assoc.*, vol. xi., 115.) It is usual to say of a fast-growing shrub that it is *rude* growing; hence naturally to *prune* it is to tame it. (See *Hal., Pul., Wil.*)

"To = at. May, 1881, at Culmstock, a labourer, in reply to a question as to where some other men were, said, 'I zeed em playing to skittles.' F. T. E."

This form is the usual one throughout Devon and Somerset. To play *at* is modern English, and was no doubt midland in Chaucer's time; but in his day the idiom in Devonshire was as now (viz., to play *to*). This is seen by the following from *Sir Fer.* l. 2224: "þo þat willieþ to leue at hame! pleyeþ to þe eschekkere, and summe of hem to iew-de-dame! and summe to tablere."

"To = of, in the sense of 'living at.' Used throughout the county, as 'Mr. White *to* Loxbeer Barton.' F. T. E." Compare modern Dutch, as in "Stads-Bank van Leening *te* Amsterdam."—*Nineteenth Century*, June, 1881, p. 988. This very curious grammatical form, so universal in Devon and Somerset, is (I believe) unknown in other counties.

"To = to break. On 15th March, 1881, a 'hind,' about 28 years of age, living in Lydford, used the following expressions when scolding his dog for being too 'rough' with the sheep, 'Darn you, "Watch," you'n have yourn holders t'brock'd.' 'Watch,' the name of the dog; 'holders,' the canine teeth, the points of which are sometimes nipped off when a dog is too rough with the flock. F. H. F."

An interesting survival of Old English—

Judges ix. 53: 'And a certain woman cast a piece of a millstone upon Abimelech's head, and all to brake his skull' (or smashed)."

Cf. "Sone þay had hit al to-clatryd! þe peeces leye on þe grounde." *Sir Fer.* 897.

"And hure scheldes stronge and grete! þey were al to-hewe." *Sir Fer.* 676. So also—

"To-falle" (*i.e.* knocked to pieces). *Sir Fer.* 5011.

"To-flente" = flew in pieces. *Sir Fer.* 4940.

"To-rente" = torn to pieces. *Sir Fer.* 675.

"To-taar" = torn to pieces. *Sir Fer.* 4533.

"And hor vantwarde was to-broke. *Robt. of Gloucester*, 155.

"To-draw" = to rend. *Robt. of Gloucester*, 287.

See also Chaucer and Shakspeare.

" To TRY = to arbitrate, to act as umpire. December, 1879, a farmer of Alphington, in this county, with whom there was a misunderstanding, said to me, 'I be safe o' t, be tried by other farmer in the county,' meaning, 'I am sure of it, let it be decided by any farmer in the county. F. T. E."

The umpire at a wrestling match is always called the "trier." See *Web., Ash.*

" UN = him it. At Culmstock a shoemaker said of a wall, ' I think he 'd stand nif was vor to put up a bit of a battery agin un.' F. T. E." See *Hal., Jen.*

"Did you ever know un, goodman Clench?" JON. *Tale of a Tub*, act i. scene 2.

"Hotded tha yoe do, whan tha hadst a cort en by tha heend legs o' en?" *Ex. Scold.*, l. 208.

This form is not, as generally said to be, a corruption, but is the remains of the true old English pronoun, *Hin, hine, hen, hyn,* and is still found in the modern German *ihn.*

" To URN = to run. June 5th, 1881, a labourer, native of Culmstock, aged about 45, said to me of some land, ' 'Twas urned all to ruin and rexens.' F. T. E."

Bos. (A. S.) ' irnan,' *to run,* yrnan.

Ancren Riwle, p. 112, " þet ilke blodi swot of his blisfule bodie, þet te streames vrnen adun to þer eorþe."

Trevisa, p. 236, l. 21, "Basilius seiþ þat þe water þat eorneþ and passeþ." (See *Hal.*)

" WANDERING SAILORS = Ivy-leaved toad-flax (*Linaria Cymbalaria*). June 1st, 1881, an old resident fisherman at Lynmouth, said in reply to a question as to the name of a creeper on a wall, common in North Devon, but very profuse at Lynmouth, 'We always call it "Wandering Sailors." ' F. T. E."

" WINTER-PROUD. January 3rd, 1881, a farmer at St. Marychurch, native and life-long resident in Devon, said that with such a mild December the 'wheat was apt to get *winter-proud*, as we say in these parts' (meaning too forward in growth), and then to be injured by cold or frosts in spring. G. H. W."

(See *Hal.*) Comp. 'Proud-flesh,' said of a wound healing too quickly; *i.e.* young flesh growing so fast as to cover the sore beneath.

"WITCH-HALSE = witch elm (*Ulmus montana*). The common name in the neighbourhood of Lynton, where the tree is very abundant. F. T. E."

Hal. says witch-hazel is the mountain ash. This is wrong. (See *Prior, Web.*)

"WRASTLE, rhymes with 'castle' = to wrestle. This is the usual pronunciation throughout North Devon. In West Somerset it is often sounded much broader, so as almost to rhyme with 'jostle.' Many also in both Devon and Somerset sound the *w* = *vrastle, vrastling*. F. T. E."

Rogers, p. 332, "Such as have wrastled much with the Lord for a blessing."

See *Hal.*, " Wrastelynge."

Robt. of Gloucester, p. 5, l. 116—

"Ac he ouercom þe deuel and adoun him caste,
  To-gadere as hii wrastlede and bond is honden vaste."

"YANNING TIME = lambing time. On March 3rd, 1880, by a native of St. Marychurch, aged 25. P. Q. K."

See *Web., Hal., Bos.* (A. S. eácan), *Britten.*

Tusser, p. 73 v. 21—

"Eawes readie to yeane
  Craeus ground red cleane."

THIRD REPORT OF THE BARROW COMMITTEE.

THIRD REPORT *of the Committee—consisting of Mr. C. Spence Bate, Mr. G. Doe, Mr. P. O. Hutchinson, Mr. J. Brooking Rowe, and Mr. R. N. Worth (Secretary)—to collect and record facts relating to Barrows in Devonshire, exclusive of Dartmoor as defined in the twelfth minute (of 1880), and to take steps where possible for their investigation.*

Edited by R. N. WORTH, F.G.S., Hon. Secretary.

(Read at Dawlish, July, 1881.)

THE Barrow Committee are indebted to Mr. Francis Brent, of Plymouth, an old member of this Society, for an illustrated account of a singularly interesting discovery of an ancient grave—a kist-vaen with urn—associated with the remains of a kitchen-midden, beneath a house in one of the oldest parts of Plymouth.

The Rev. Treasurer Hawker has called the attention of the Committee to some Barrows at Berrynarbor, permission to examine which has been kindly given. It is hoped that the group may be explored when the harvest is over in the ensuing autumn, and the results duly recorded in the next report.

The Committee beg to recommend that in their reappointment the limitation of their operations with regard to Dartmoor be omitted. No adequate conclusions can be be formed by them concerning the Barrows of the county, if so large and peculiarly important an area is excluded from their investigation.

J. BROOKING ROWE, Chairman.
R. N. WORTH, Secretary.

June 17th, 1881.

DISCOVERY OF AN ANCIENT GRAVE IN STILLMAN STREET, PLYMOUTH.

DURING alterations made by the Messrs. Pitts upon premises in Stillman Street, Plymouth, preparatory to the erection of a new malt-house, an interesting discovery was made of a little grave, containing an urn which once held the ashes of the burnt body of one of the ancient inhabitants of Devonshire. The workmen in the course of their excavations came upon some shells, mostly of the oyster, periwinkle, cockle, and mussel, all very much decayed from age, so that a few only could be preserved, and probably part of an ancient refuse heap or kitchen-midden. The actual quantity was not large, but similar shells were scattered throughout the adjoining soil, showing that the heap had been disturbed in former years. Two flat stones were then found, which at first were taken to be the covering of an old drain, each about three feet long by fifteen inches wide and three thick. They were what is locally called dunstone—a hard, green, gritty, trap rock, which had been brought from a distance, and seemed to have been weathered before being used for this present purpose.

The stones were placed at a right angle to each other, thus forming a roof, the gable ends of which were crossed by two pieces of stone, each about a foot long, of similar description to the cover stones.

On raising the stones a large urn, composed of black ware, was discovered, placed in a small grave or cist, which was about eighteen inches deep, by two feet wide, and three feet in length; this had been excavated in the native rock, which was here a soft and brittle shale.

Unfortunately no one was on the spot to record what I have since learnt from the workmen employed; and soon the grave was cleared out, the urn destroyed, and the *débris* carted away to some ballast-heap, whence it has been taken on board ship and lost. When I first saw the grave it had been completely emptied, and the west side destroyed. The grave lay nearly north and south; the east and south ends had been built up of small slabs of dunstone, and were quite perpendicular, whilst the north end consisted of the native rock, sloping away at a considerable angle, and exceedingly decayed and shattered. It is not improbable that the north and west sides were originally as perpendicular as the rotten rock would admit, but that in excavating the soil the labourers had removed all the loose stuff, which was carted away with the rest, leaving the rock at the angle at which it had most readily broken.

From the few fragments of the urn which I was able to preserve, the drawing of the restored figure has been prepared. This may not be absolutely correct, but at all events it will enable us to form some idea of what this interesting urn was like, wherein were placed the ashes of the cremated body of one of Plymouth's ancient forefathers. That it once contained ashes cannot I think be doubted; the portions of the bottom still present a white appearance, which probably comes from the contact of the ashes with the clay. No human bones were, however, brought under my notice.

It is much to be regretted that further excavations could not be made, which might have led to additional discoveries, and perhaps more careful observations than could now be recorded, but the nature of the new building would not admit of this; much soil and soft rock were removed, but nothing of interest was discovered, although I visited the spot several times daily.   •

The urn itself, in its restored figure, presents a somewhat unusual form, and differs from that of most vessels found in kist-vaens, or barrows, in its larger diameter at the mouth (13 inches) in proportion to its height; it is also very thin. It was placed in the grave with the mouth upwards. A fragment of an urn, nearly allied to this, but smaller, was found by the Rev. Mr. Kirwan, July, 1868, in a large barrow on Broad Down, near Sidbury. A drawing of the fragments, as well as of the restored urn, are given in the *Transactions of the Devonshire Association* of this year. The barrow is No. 57 of Mr. Hutchinson's list in the Second Report of the Barrow Committee. Mr. Kirwan's urn was about half the size of the Stillman Street one.*

I am not aware that any grave similar to this has ever been recorded, and if not, this discovery may be considered as highly interesting. The Romano-British graves met with by Mr. Spence Bate on the hill at Fort Stamford, near Plymouth, were composed of slabs of stone, without roof cover, and contained many relics, but I think no cinerary urns, or other pottery, except what may be considered as food or water vessels. The barrows opened by Mr. Kirwan, near Sidmouth, rarely contained kist-vaens, but the urns were usually enclosed with flint stones. The barrows opened and explored in Cornwall did not contain similar cists; and

* Vide *Trans. Devon. Assoc.* vol. ii. p. 641; vol. xii. p. 134, and illustrations.

none opened elsewhere, as far as I am aware, contained cists with roof stones placed at right angles to each other, as have been found in this Plymouth grave. The early Roman

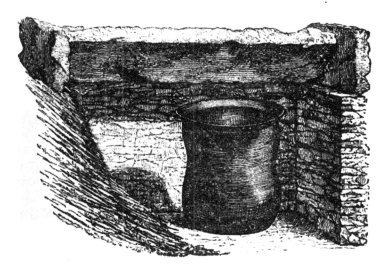

inhabitants of Britain, however, used tiled graves. One with eight roof tiles, placed in a similar manner to the Plymouth grave, and closed at each end with a tile in the same fashion, was found near York.[*] This contained no urn, but a layer of charcoal and burnt bones. Again, the Stillman Street urn is of somewhat finer ware than ordinary British, and seems to have been made on a potter's wheel, nor do the fragments show any sign of the lines or rude ornaments so common on British urns. It exhibits, however, every appearance of having been subjected to the funeral fire, and fragments of charcoal still adhere to the surface.

In all probability, then, we have here the grave of one who lived in Devon after the Romans had visited our county, and introduced their mode of burial.

FRANCIS BRENT.

* *Celt, Roman, and Saxon,* p. 308.

SECOND REPORT OF THE COMMITTEE
TO OBTAIN INFORMATION AS TO PECULIAR TENURES OF LAND,

AND AS TO CUSTOMS OF MANOR COURTS IN DEVONSHIRE, EXCLUSIVE OF DARTMOOR.

SECOND REPORT *of the Committee—consisting of Mr. R. Dymond, Mr. G. Doe, Mr. A. W. Hurrell, Mr. G. W. Ormerod, Mr. J. Brooking Rowe, and Mr. Edward Windeatt* (Secretary), *on Peculiar Tenures of Land in Devonshire.*

Edited by EDWARD WINDEATT, Honorary Secretary.

(Read at Dawlish, July, 1881.)

YOUR Committee have gleaned but little on which to report this year, but they would call especial attention to the reference to documents which have come to light relative to the manor courts and tenures of lands belonging to the Pomeroys, of Berry Castle, on which they hope to report fully next year.

Your Committee trust that the definition of Dartmoor will be so altered as to admit of their next year reporting on several manor courts of peculiar interest.

The contributor's name is appended to each note.

ROBERT DYMOND, Chairman.
EDWARD WINDEATT, Hon. Sec.

COURT ROLLS OF POMEROYS.

An account of some documents that have lately come to light relating to the manor courts and tenures of lands which belonged to the Pomeroys, of Berry Castle.

By far the largest number belong to the manor courts of Berry Pomeroy and Bridgetown Pomeroy. One of the oldest of these, dated 7 Henry IV. (1405–6), has, under the head Pannage, a long list of persons who owned pigs; opposite the names is the number of pigs kept, with the amount each person had to pay. Pannage was money paid to the lord of the manor for leave to feed cattle on the masts in the woods. In some cases presentments are made of cattle that have died of murrain. There were generally seventeen courts held in the year, being one every three weeks.

The documents relating to Berry and Bridgetown Pomeroy extend, though not continuously, from 3 Henry IV. to 27 Henry VIII.

There are six that relate to the manor of Great Totnes, and give the names of holders of lands under Totnes Castle for military service. One dates 22 Henry VII., and the others from 15 to 30 Henry VIII. The following are a few of the names :—

Lord de la Ware, for Hempston Cautelhoe, *alias* Broadhempston.

Lord Hastyngs, for Southpole and Scobehill.

Lady Cecilia, Marchioness of Dorset, for Wodeford.

Prioress of Corneworthy, for Tydworthy, Alleluy and Westcorneworthy.

Prior of Plympton, for Shaugh (?)

William Courtenay, miles, for Southuyshe and Galweton.

Edward Pomeroy, miles, for Sydenham, Wagshen, and Colaton.

Katherine Dudley, for Northbovy.

Antonius Worthe, for moiety of Wayshefyd.

Adrian Fortescue.

John Lord Fitzwaryn.

Oliver Wyse.

Six more relate to Stokeleigh Pomeroy, and date from the 9th to 34th Henry VI.

Four relate to Brixham, and one each to Fillegh, Lamerton, and Wear Gifford.

I hope in a future report to give some longer and fuller extracts from these interesting papers.   J. S. AMERY.

PECULIAR TENURE AT BICTON.

Soon after the Conquest, the king appointed one of his followers to the office of door-keeper to the jail for malefactors ; and for this service the said door-keeper received a grant of the lands of Bicton, lying between Budleigh and Colyton Rawleigh, in the county of Devon. In the Exeter Domesday, f. 472, and in the printed edition at p. 437, we have—Will'em[9] Portitor ht ɪ. mañs ꝗ uocatͬ Bechatona ꝗ teñ Ailſi[9] &c. This peculiar tenure of the lands at Bicton continued in a succession of great families during the long space of seven hundred years, and, according to Lysons, was only abolished so late as 1787.   Hence arose the names Portitor, De Porta, De la Porte, and Janitor, which these keepers of the jail bore at different periods.   The last time I was in Normandy, making researches, I came upon an original charter of John Janitor at the archives at St. Lo, dating about the end of King John, by the names of the subscribers, or the beginning of Henry III.   The seal still remained, though much defaced.   It was circular, and bore the words—" Sigill Johannis Janitoris," but only the last word is plain.   The device consists of a hand and arm upholding a key, or two large keys back to back, before some object—perhaps a tower, or the gate of the jail.*   Some very strange and, at the same time, very false impressions respecting the place of this jail have long existed among our old and respectable writers.   There is a tradition still lingering in the neighbourhood that at a remote period the jail of the county of Devon was situated first at Harpford (about ten miles east of Exeter), then at Bicton (the same distance south-east from the metropolis of the county), and finally at the city of Exeter itself. Both the Isaacks, in their Histories of Exeter, at page 110 in each History, have been misled by this popular but thoughtless belief.   Westcote, page 239, says it was Henry I. who placed the jail at Bicton ; whereas, what Henry I. did was to confirm to John Janitor the keeping of the gate of Exeter Castle and of the jail ; that Joan, daughter and heir of the last of the Janitor blood, carried the manor of Bicton, with its mode of tenure, to Siccavilla, Sacheville, or Sackville, who removed the jail to Exeter.   Lysons, *Mag. Brit.* vi. 47, writes :—" The county jail, which was formerly at Bicton, under the superintendence of the lord of this manor, was for greater security removed to Exeter in 1518.   It was not till 1787 that the Lord of Bicton was exonerated from the custody of the county jail."   At page 256 he alludes to the tradition respecting Harpford.   He says :—" The ancient manor house [at Harpford, of which place he is now speaking], called Court Place, now a farm house, is the property of the Rev. Sydenham Peppin.   There is a tradition, evidently groundless, that it was in ancient times the county gaol, before it was removed to Bicton."   I know this farm house well.   It lies between Harpford Church and the river Otter.   In or about the year 1860 it was accidentally burnt down ; but it has been rebuilt, and of course every feature is now modern. The Rev. Edmund Butcher, at the commencement of the

* See also *Journal Brit. Arch. Assoc.* for Sept., 1862, p. 257, for seal of Roger Janitor.

present century, brought out the first Sidmouth Guide, under the title of *The Beauties of Sidmouth Displayed;* and, speaking of the adjoining parish of Harpford, he says:— "The jail was removed from thence to Bicton by the family of the Rolles, and thence to Exeter, where it now remains." All this is an absurd jumble. These are our Historians! They seem to have thought that because the lord of Bicton held that manor for the service of keeping the county jail, that the jail was necessarily at Bicton; whereas, in reality, it was never there at all. How it could ever have been placed at Harpford is still more unaccountable, and still more absurd. They seem all to have been content with a baseless tradition, and to have copied confidingly from one another. It is necessary, however, to hark back sometimes, and recur to the fountain head. The following is one of those fountain heads, and by referring to it we shall get correct information. I took it from the Hundred Rolls, temp. Edw. I., m. 9, dorsum, at that time preserved in the Chapter House at Westminster; and it is expressly stated that the jail was at Exeter.

Ᵽ Iť Ᵽra de Buketon debeȝ teneri de · r · in Ᵽiauntia p̃ Ᵽvic c°tod̄ Gaolam Exoñ. t nūc in manu dnῑ r · rõe c°todῑe filii Ᵽ hr Regin Le arbelestr · qui ȝ inf* etatem. cui⁹ c°todiā ht Thoɱ de pyn . a ῑpe q° fuit Escaetor · bienñ elaps̄ · sȝ nefciūt q° Warent.

The next I took from the Testa de Neville, compiled in the reigns of Henry III. and Edward I., Vol. I., page 837. It is equally explicit respecting the nature of this ancient tenure, as also the place of the jail. It runs thus:—

ω Joñes Janitor tenet Bukinῑ cum ptin de dno Regē p̃ feriantiam cuftodiendi Januam Caftʳ Exoñ Ᵽ gaiolam prifonū de dono · H.R. pᶦmᶦ· antecefforibȝ fuis p̃ idem ferviciū.

The above ought to be enough to clear up every obscurity. The descent of the manor of Bicton from the conquest downwards may be briefly stated thus:—Ailsius the Saxon had it before the Domesday survey. Afterwards the Janitors had it for several generations; then the family of Balistarius, or Le Arbalister, had it for at least five descents, until the heiress Joan (though it is not quite clear which family she was heiress of) carried it to Siccavilla, whose heiress carried it to Copple-stou, who sold it to Robert Denis, whose heiress Anne carried it to Sir Henry Rolle of Stevenstone, from whom it descended to the late Lord Rolle. Since his lordship's death it has been held by trustees during Lady Rolle's life, for their relative the Hon. Mark [Trefusis] Rolle.　　　　P. O. HUTCHINSON.

ON THE EARLY HISTORY OF DAWLISH.

BY JAMES BRIDGE DAVIDSON, M.A.

(Read at Dawlih, July, 1881.)

THE history of Dawlish may be said to begin in the year
1044, when King Eádweard the Confessor was on the throne;
when the government of the southern counties, from Kent to
Cornwall, was in the hands of Earl Godwine; whilst the
Bishop of Devonshire still had his chair at Crediton; and
shortly after the sees of Devon and Cornwall had become
united in the person of the existing Bishop, Lyfing. In this
year seven manses of land at Dawlish were granted by the
king to his "worthy (idoneo) chaplain," Leofric.

Of Leofric's origin, all that is known is contained in two
short phrases, one of Florence of Worcester (writing before
1118), who says* that he was "Regis cancellarius" and
"Britonicus;" the other of William of Malmsbury, who
(writing in about 1125) states† that he was "apud Lothar-
ingos altus et doctus." To this man then, of Saxon name, of
British race, and of German education, who had come to be
King's Chancellor‡ (not Chancellor of England, as Prince§
has it) and Royal Chaplain,‖ was granted this extensive and

---

* FLOR. WIG., sub anno 1046; M. H. B., 602 B.
† *De Gestis Pontificum*, ii. 94; Rolls edition, p. 201.
‡ This, Mr. Freeman thinks, is the first mention in English history of the
office of Chancellor; *Norm. Conq.* ii. 84.
§ *Worthies*, ed. of 1810, p. 561.
‖ John Hoker, of Exeter, probably mistaking the meaning of "altus," and
taking it to mean "a man of high birth," or "nobleman" (an error into
which Mr. N. E. S. A. Hamilton, the Rolls editor, has also inadvertently
fallen, p. 536), improves upon Malmsbury's statement, and says that Leofric
was "a man descended from the blood and line of Brutus, brought up in
Loreine." This statement was imported by Godwin into his *Lives of the
Bishops*, ed. of 1615, p. 395; and when that work was Latinized appeared as
follows: "Vir nobili prosapiâ, in Burgundiâ natus" (ed. of 1743, p. 400),
"Burgundia" being simply a rendering for "Lorraine." As Lotharingia,
when Leofric was born, which must have been somewhere about A.D. 1000,

fertile tract of territory at the place, which "by the inhabitants of that region is called DOFLISC."* Up to this date Dawlish had been "ancient demesne of the Crown;" that is, had been part of the private possessions of the Kings of Wessex, probably since the first occupation of the country.

Of Dawlish, this grant of 1044 contains the first known mention; but the Dawlish of 1044 included, as will be presently seen, the modern parish of East Teignmouth; and respecting Teignmouth, Camden has something to say in his *Magna Britannia*. In the edition of 1610,† the passage runs thus: "Then meet you with Teignemouth, a little village at the mouth of the river Teigne, whereof it hath also the name; where the Danes that were sent before to discover the situation of Britaine, and to sound the landing places, being first set ashore about the yeere of Salvation, 800, and having slaine the governor of the place, tooke it as an ominous good token of future victorie; which indeede afterward they followed with extreme cruelty thorow the whole Iland." A story in Risdon ‡ is to the same effect. Both these statements are manifestly erroneous in point of locality. The first landing of the Danes in England took place near Weymouth in the year 787, and the governor who was slain was the king's reeve at Dorchester, Dorset.§ That a "governor" should have existed at Teignmouth in 800 is an historic impossibility.

The valley of the Teign was no doubt invaded by the Danes in A.D. 1001. This appears from the *Winchester Chronicle*,‖ of which the following is a translation: "And

was a district reaching from Basle to Ghent, and from Dijon to beyond Cologne, it may well be that part of its upper or southern portion was at sundry periods afterwards covered by portions of the shifting area of the duchy, kingdom, and province of Burgundy. Prince, without any authority whatever, boldly claims Leofric as a native of Devon. Dr. Oliver, *Lives of the Bishops*, p. 6, follows the Latinized version of Godwin's narrative.

* As this is the first extant form of the name, its spelling deserves attention as a guide to the meaning. There can be no reasonable doubt that the signification is "Devil Water." The writer, however, no longer (*Trans. Dev. Assoc.* x., 1878, 252 n.), supposes the word to be Saxon. For this it must needs be an adjective, but adjectives were never used as proper names. With greater probability the name is a compound of two Cornish words, "deawl," diabolus, and "isc," aqua. Of like origin are the names Dewlish, with its associated forms, in Dorset, and Dowlish (Wake) in Somerset. The theory is confirmed by the fact that in this parish there are a rivulet and hamlet called Dawlish Water. Whether or not this hamlet was the original nucleus of the settlement, it is highly probable that some impurity, natural or artificial, in this little brook gave a reproachful name to the whole stream and valley.

† p. 208.
‡ p. 143.
§ *A. S. Chronicle*, sub anno 787 ; "Æthelweard," M. H. B., p. 509 C.
‖ Sub anno MI.

then" (*i.e.* after the fight with the men of Hampshire at
Æthelinga-dene [Alton], where the king's high reeve, Æthelweard,* was slain) "they" (the Danish host) "went westward
till they came to the Defenas" (men of Devon), "and there
came to meet them Pallig, with the ships that he could
gather. . . . And they burned Tegntun, and also many other
good hams" (homesteads) "which we cannot name; and
peace was afterwards made there with them." It has been
often assumed that this Tegntun was Teignmouth.† Professor
Earle‡ was the first to point out that it was Kingsteignton.
There is no positive statement that Teignmouth was burnt in
1001, or indeed that there was anything at Teignmouth to be
burnt. But it is highly probable that a fishery had been
established there, and if so, there can be no doubt that the
property of the inhabitants perished in the general destruction. It is perhaps not too much to assume that the
fortress-church of East Teignmouth was built as a result of
this harrying.

The charter of 1044 has been printed by Dr. Oliver,§ but
without the Saxon boundaries; and as these have never
hitherto, it is believed, appeared in print, the document is
here produced in its entirety.‖

✠ Regis cunctorum regum regimine reguntur omnia supera,
ima, profundaque; cuius quoque immensa beniuolentia subinde
quem sibi obtemperantem perspexerit, et præsentibus locup-
letat habunde opibus, et post istius miseræ uite decursum
facit eum pennis angelicis transcendere ad regna supernorum
gaudiorum. Qui etiam solus uoluntate æterni Patris disponit
sceptra iuraque regnorum; est nempe dux ducum, rexque
omnium proculdubio regum. Cuius rei autem gratia a nobis
inchoatus sic hic donationis libellus consequenter manista-
bitur ¶ in præcedente paginula. Igitur ego EADVVARDVS
opitulante potentissimo Deo, possidens totius monarchiam

---

* Mr. Freeman, *N. C.* i. 308, suggests that this was probably the Sheriff
of Hampshire; but from a charter printed by Kemble, *C. D.*, DCXCVIII.
(iii. 304), it appears that he was Sheriff of Devon and Cornwall.

† Thus Polwhele (i. 198) writes: "In 970 the Danes committed horrid
devastations at West Teignmouth." This statement is not borne out by the
English chronicles, which record, however, that in 981 Petrockstow, in
Cornwall, was ravaged; and great harm done everywhere by the sea-coast,
both in Wales and Devonshire.

‡ *Sax. Chron.* p. 334.

§ *Lives*, p. 8.

‖ In this copy the first letters of proper names, where in small letters in
the original, have been printed in capitals. All contractions have been
extended, except "m̄," which has been printed for "minister" at the foot;
and all stops have been supplied.

¶ *i.e.* "manifestabitur."

Angelicæ * necne et Brittanniæ telluris, haud modice concedendo, concessus sum cuidam meo idoneo capellano, LEOFRICO onomate nuncupato, quoddam rus in uilla quæ ab incolis regionis illius uocitatur DOFLISC, scilicet, vii. mansos illimet ad arandum, eo tenore quo omnibus diebus uitæ suæ, absque aliqua machina, sub illius honorofice regatur dominio atque potestate, postque finem dierum illius habeat potestatem cuicumque placuerit tribuendi aut erogandi. Præcepimus autem ut antefatum rus sit liberum ab omni fiscali tributo uel uectigali, cum omnibus ad se rite pertinentibus tam in maximis quam in modicis rebus, campis, pascuis, pratis, siluisque : exceptis istis tribus, expeditione, pontis arcisque constructione. His itaque a nobis prout debuimus ceuque placuit reuerentiæ nostræ et uoluntati stabilitis, adhuc quod minime est obliuioni tradendum, uolumus ut hic præsens codicillus nostræ licentiæ scriptus, dampnet, conculcet, atque anathematizet cunctos emulorum, si qui contra eundem reperti fuerint, libellos. Si quis autem, quod futurum minime autumo, præsumptione audaci instinctuque diabolico contra nostrum decretum hanc donationis karterulam adnihilare uel pro nibilo ducere temptauerit, in primis, quod grauius est, iram Dei omnipotentis genetricisque eius uidelicet almæ et intactæ Mariæ incurrat, dehinc meam omniumque satellitum meorum, noscatque se obnoxium atque reum omnibus horis atque momentis solorum, fiatque pars illius cum Datham et Abyron cumque tortuoso Beelzebub, Principe Muscarum, in baratro inferiori, et quod indigne seu procaciter reperit non eum dicet, sed cum dedecore multimodo expulsus sit a nobis, nisi prius hic digna penitudine studuerit, ultro, non coactus, emendare. Anno incarnationis dominicæ m̅. xliiii., indictione xii., epactaque xviii., et concurrente vii., scilicet bissextili anno, karaxata est hæc kartula, gubernante piisimo Anglorum cateruam rege feliciter EADVVARDO.

Ðys sindo tha landgemæro. Ærest on Tenge muðan, upp and lang thæs fleotes on crampan steort; and swa eft ongean be tham sealternon on tha stræte on west healfe Michaheles ciricean; and swa norð andlang thære stræt on tha greatan dic; thanon norð eft ongerihte on thone blindan will; on tham wille norð on gerihte on thone dunnan stán; thanon eft norð rihte on tha ealdan dic; and swa and lang thære dic norð on gerihte ofer wætersceota cumb; thanon up and lang thære ealdan ræwe on tha stapulas; fram tham stapulon on gerihte and lang hricges on sand holcan; of sand holcan andlang strete on blacan penn; thanon andlang stræte on

* Sic, pro "Angliæ."

bradan mores heafdon; and thanon on gerihte and lang
stræte oð eorð birig; and swa norð and land stræte on stan
beorh; and swa niðer and lang stræte on Doflisc ford; and
thanon norð of tham forda and lang thære port stræte on risc
slædes heafdon; swa niðer and lang streames on Cocc ford;
and swa and lang thæs fleotes ut on Exan; niðer eft and lang
Exan thær sciterlacu ut scit; and swa up and lang sciter
lace on thæs fleotes heafod, thanon siððan suð on tha ealdan
dic; and swa on gerihte to tham readan stane; of tham
stane suð ut on tha sæ; swa west be sæ eft on Tenge muðan.

Ego EADVVARDVS rex totius Anglice gentis huius donationis
libertatem hilari animo fieri concessi.

Ego Eadsinus Christi æcclesiæ archi-presul corroboraui.

Ego Ælfricus Eboracensis æcclesiæ archi-episcopus consolidaui.

Ego Lifingus Crydianensis æcclesiæ pontifex rogatus a rege
calomo (sic) scripsi.

Ego Æluuinus episcopus assensum præbui.

Ego Brihtuuoldus episcopus confirmaui.

Ego Dodico episcopus consignaui.

Ego Ealdredus episcopus corroboraui.

Ego Ælfuuinus abba nouæ æcclesiæ.

Ego Ægeluuardus abba Glestoniensis æcclesiæ.

Ego Æthelstanus abba.

Ego Uulfuueardus abba.

Ego Goduuinus abba.

Ego Goduuinus dux stabiliui.

Ego Leofricus dux.

Ego Suuegen dux.

Ego Sigeuuardus dux.

Ego Haroldus nobilis.

Ego Tosti nobilis.

Ego Leofuuinus nobilis.

Ego Odda nobilis.

Ego Ordgarus nobilis.

Ego Ælfgarus nobilis.

Ego Ordulfus nobilis.

Ego Dodda nobilis.

Ego Brihtricus nobilis.

Ego Osgodus m̃.

Ego Ælfstanus m̃.

Ego Ecglafus m̃.

Ego Æthelmærus m̃.

Ego Karl m̃.

Ego Atsorus m̃.

Ego Godricus m̃.
Ego Ælfuuinus m̃.
Ego Ulfcytel m̃.
Ego Osmarus m̃.
Ego Ecgulfus m̃.
Ego Goduinus m̃.
Ego Ælfricus m̃.
Ego Æthelwerdus m̃.
Ego Wulfwerdus m̃.
Ego Æthelricus m̃.
Ego Liuingeus m̃.
Ego Wulfgarus m̃.
Ego Brihtwinus m̃.
Ego Uulfsige m̃.
Ego Thurkyl m̃.
Ego Toui m̃.
Ego Æthelwinus m̃.
Ego Thurstanus m̃.
Ego Ælfgeat m̃.
Ego Manni m̃.

The following is a translation:

"All things—above, below, and in the deep—are governed by the sway of the King of all kings,* whose unmeasured favour, as soon as it has recognized the man who obeys Him, both enriches him abundantly with present wealth, and, after the course of this miserable life is ended, causes him to ascend on the wings of angels to the kingdoms of heavenly bliss; who also alone, by the will of the eternal Father, regulates the sceptres and the laws of kings; for He is in truth the Lord of lords, and without doubt the King of all kings. For what purpose, therefore, this charter of donation has been commenced by us will appear consequentially from the foregoing paragraph. Wherefore I, Eadward, by the aid of Almighty God, possessor of the monarchy of the land of all England, and moreover of Britain, have granted to a certain worthy chaplain of mine, named LEOFRIC, a certain tract of land in the vill, which by the inhabitants of that region is called DOFLISC; that is to say, seven manses at that place, by the tenure that the same shall be governed in all honour, under his dominion and power, all the days of his life, without any machination, and that he shall have power of appointing or nominating the same, after the end of his days, to whomso-

* Namely, Christ, whose name is indicated by the monogram at the beginning of the deed.

ever he may think fit. Moreover, we decree that the aforesaid land be free from every fiscal tribute or tax, together with all things rightly pertaining thereto, whether in great or in minor things—fields, pastures, meadows, and woods—except these three things—military service, and the building of bridges and castles. Having thus established these things as we have felt bound, or as it has been pleasing to our dignity and pleasure to do, in order moreover that they may not be consigned to oblivion, we will that this present written testimony of our license may condemn, tread under foot, and anathematize all the charters of rivals, if any such shall be found in opposition to this grant. And if any one, which I desire may never happen, shall attempt, with audacious presumption and by diabolical instigation, contrary to our decree, to annihilate or bring to nought this charter of grant, first of all, which is most serious, may he incur the wrath of Almighty God, and of his Mother, the pure and intact Virgin Mary; then may he incur my wrath, and that of all my officers; may he feel himself to be hostile and guilty during all hours and moments of his life, and may his lot be with Dathan and Abiram, and with the crafty Beelzebub, the Lord of Flies, in the lower gulf; and may that which he unjustly or insolently acquires not acknowledge him, but may he be with abundant disgrace expelled from our presence, unless by adequate repentance he shall, voluntarily and not under compulsion, labour to undo the evil.

"This charter was executed in the year of the Incarnation of the Lord, MXLIV, the twelfth indiction, the eighteenth year of the epact, being bissextile, whilst the most pious King Eadward was happily governing the nation of the English.

"These are the land boundaries. First at Teign mouth; up along the estuary to crampansteort (anchor point); and so back again by the salterns along the street on the west side of St. Michael's church; and so north along the street to the great dike; thence north back right on to the blind well; from the well north straight on to the Dun stone; thence back north right along the old dike; and so along the dike north right on over Watershed comb; thence up along the old row to the staples; from the staples right on along the ridge to Sand holcan (the sand beds); from Sand holcan along the street to Black penn; thence along the street to Broadmoor's head; and thence right on along the street to the earth barrow; and so north along the street to the stone barrow; and so down along the street to Dawlish ford; and thence north from the ford along the market street to Rushslade's head; so down

along stream to Cocc ford ; and so along the estuary out on
Exe ; down back along Exe to Sciterlake's out-fall ; and so
up along Sciterlake to the estuary's head ; thenceforward
south on the old dike ; and so right on to the red stone ; from
the stone south out to the sea ; so west by the sea, back to
Teign mouth."

This grant, it will be observed, is of the most absolute
kind ; both expressly and in terms it is without limit. No
reference is made in it to any intended elevation of Leofric
to a bishopric, nor is any obligation laid upon him to dispose
of the land otherwise than he may think proper in any event
whatsoever.

The boundaries are easy to trace, and will be found to
comprise a space corresponding almost exactly with the
present parishes of Dawlish and East Teignmouth combined.
The line begins at the mouth of the Teign, and follows the
coast of the harbour to " crampan-steort." This word, not to
be found in any of the dictionaries, is taken to mean the
little promontory or spit of land thrown up by the silt of the
small river Tame, which discharges itself into the harbour.
Here, it is presumed, boats and vessels formerly anchored ;
and here, for the old mooring place, a jetty is now substituted.
The Tame still, for the greater part of its course, divides East
and West Teignmouth, though its stream is for the most part
covered by streets and buildings. The boundary of Dawlish
in 1044 followed this rivulet back by the salterns.* The

---

* Professor Skeat, of Cambridge, informs the writer that this early use of
the word " saltern " in a piece of Old English writing is of considerable
philological value. An " ern," or " ærn," was literally a shed, or roofed
structure, not originally designed for the dwelling of man. When we say
" cow-house," " barley-house," our ancestors said " cow-ærn," bere-ærn," or
" barn." So " win-ærn," a wine cellar ; " holm-ærn," an ocean house, or
ship. A saltern, then " salina," was a shed for the manufacture of salt. To
this industry, besides the salt water, a stream of fresh water was necessary.
As was the case until comparatively recent times in the Bay of Cancale, a
saltern was a cabin with four clay walls, thatched, and having two openings
in the roof to let out the smoke. There was a single door. The process was
as follows : A heap was collected of sand, which had been thoroughly soaked
in sea water by the action of the tide. This was placed on a floor of clay, and
beaten flat with shovels ; then placed in a common wooden trough, where
fresh water was allowed to trickle upon it. The water, impregnated with salt,
was drawn off as brine, and stored in casks or tubs, where it was tested by a
rude instrument in the form of a float weighted with lead. The more fully
the water was saturated with salt, the higher the float swam. From the casks
the brine was drawn off by buckets, and poured into leaden vats, having fires
under them, and turned into salt by evaporation. The dry salt was stored
in the saltern itself, or in separate sheds or cellars. The Combe cellars, in
Combe-in-Teign-head parish, on the south of the Teign estuary, were either
salt cellars or clay cellars. Sometimes the vats began to overflow when the
fire below was too brisk. Then the overflow was guided, and the edges of the

mention of these salterns shows that the sea formerly flowed and ebbed up and down this little stream. After the salterns the boundary left the bank of the Tame, and crossed over to the west of St. Michael's Church, much in the course of the present main street of East Teignmouth. On its way it may have passed a cross, which formerly stood in the middle of the town.* Thus a strip of land between the church and the river Tame, now in East Teignmouth parish, was not in the ancient Dawlish. This strip, in which the homestead of Brimley stands, was probably, in 1044, an outlying part of Kenton parish.†

The mention of St. Michael's Church is especially interesting. Not only is a reference in Saxon boundaries to a church very rare, but proof of the existence of this venerable structure as a Saxon edifice twenty-two years before the Conquest will be welcome to all antiquaries.‡

vats were shored up, by means of a flat stone. This dirty black stone was called the "mistress" or "lady" of the saltern, and every one who entered was supposed to salute the mistress. Generally, adds the French writer, the appearance of people who had visited a saltern testified to their politeness. There was also used an iron stamp, at the end of a rod, to crush down the blisters that rose upon the bottom of the vats when they were beginning to melt. Sometimes the saltmakers, male and female, slept in the saltern. "To smoke like a saltern" was a proverb; and the workpeople were so blackened and begrimed with the smoke that they and their habitation resembled an abode of African negroes. (From *Avranchin*, by Le Héricher, 1845, vol. i. p. 342.) This industry, both in France and England, was severely taxed. In England a large quantity of salt was made by solar evaporation only; but evaporation from leaden vats heated by wood fires was also practised, as appears abundantly from Domesday. At Bremesgraue (Bromsgrove), in Worcestershire, the loads of wood and leaden vats are enumerated; fol. 172 (2). See Sir H. Ellis's Introduction, *Salt Works*. The important point is, that here we have undoubted evidence of the use at Teignmouth of "salterns," *salt-houses* (not mere ponds or pans), twenty-two years before the Conquest.

* This cross was discovered not long since, and has come into the possession of G. W. Ormerod, Esq., by whom it has been presented to the Teignmouth Infirmary.

† Polwhele, iii. 146; and see Dr. Lake's valuable paper, entitled "Sketch of the History of Teignmouth," published in the *Transactions* of the Association for 1874 (vi. 381).

‡ Leland's account is as follows: "There be two towns at this point of the haven by name of Teignemouth, one hard joining to the other. The southern of them is Teignmouth Regis, where is a market and a church of St. Michael, and a piece of an embattled wall again the shore; and this is taken for the elder town." (*Itin.* vol. iii. fol. 31.)

Of old East Teignmouth church, one of the best descriptions is that given by Polwhele (i. 233) from a correspondent, whom, from Dr. Lake's paper, we know to have been the late Mr. R. Jordan, of Teignmouth. "This church," says Mr. Jordan, "is dedicated to St. Michael . . . and it is thought the oldest in the Dean of Exeter's jurisdiction. The first structure was small, and was built, according to the account of the ancient inhabitants, for the conveniency of the fishermen going to prayers before they went about their fishery; and as an emblem thereof, several golden herrings were hung up in the church; since which a large addition has been made to it on the north

From the east side of the church the boundary proceeds north along the street to the great dike; in other words, half-

part, much larger than the first building. In this church there is nothing remarkable, except the screen which parts the chancel from the body of the church, which is about seven feet high; in the upper part of which there is a

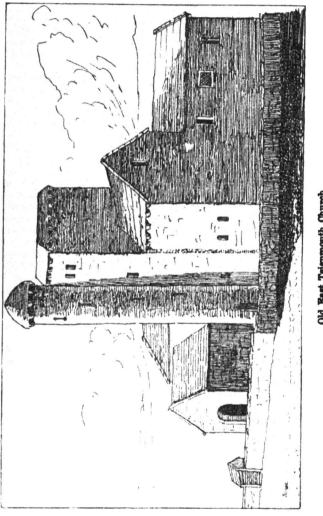

Old East Teignmouth Church.

cornice, in the large hollow of which there is a rude hieroglyphical carving of several grotesque figures. . . . The construction of the roof of the original part of the church is worth the observation of the curious. Formerly this church, as appears by old deeds now in the church, had a large quantity of land belonging to it, and which maintained it in repairs, and part thereof was appropriated to provide candles to burn in the church, with several other

H 2

way up the hill, to the point where the road branches into two, the "great dike," or main road, continuing on the right. The boundary takes the road on the left, and follows it past a place formerly called "blind well," and then turns northwards to the "Dun" or "down" stone. This stone no longer exists, but the meeting of roads where it once stood sufficiently indicates its locality, at the spot where the open ground of

Romish ceremonies, as reading masses for the requiem of the souls of the deceased, &c. &c., but is now irrecoverably lost by neglect or otherwise; indeed, at this time it is not known where it lay. There are now a few houses and several closes of land belonging to the church vested in twelve trustees, chosen as those of West Teignmouth."

An excellent engraving of old East Teignmouth church was published in the *Gentleman's Magazine* for September, 1793 (vol. lxiii. part ii. p. 785), with a letter by J. S. (the Rev. J. Swete), of Oxton House. From this drawing (of which we print a *fac-simile* copy) it appears that the ancient part of the church consisted of two square blocks of building, placed side by side, west and east, the north and south walls being continuous. The western block was a tower, and its walls were twice as high as those of the eastern block, which was the chancel. The tower had a parapet, slightly overhanging, and sloping for a short distance inwards, as if intended as a stone foundation for a pyramidal wooden roof. The parapet had ornamental supports in the shape of corbels, about five on each side, consisting of heads of men or animals. The windows of the tower shown in the drawing are four only— one on the ground floor, another on a level with the top of the chancel wall, the other two near the top. All are small square-headed openings, without chamfers or relief of any kind. At the south-west angle of the tower was a a cylindrical staircase, with a conical cap, resembling an Irish round tower, having corbels round the parapet. These corbels were slightly higher than the parapet of the tower. From the drawing they appear to be of the same character as the other corbels, but bolder. At the foot of the staircase was an entrance doorway, fronting south-east, and there were openings for light at intervals, drawn like arrow-slits. The chancel roof was a saddle-back, resting on a set-off in the east wall of the tower, and terminating in a gable. Only three windows are represented, two being small round-headed lights on a level with the ground-floor window of the tower, and the other in the gable, on a level with the middle window of the tower. Mr. Swete, in the article referred to, supposes that this structure was built for military purposes. It stood within an enclosure, which had a wall to protect it from the sea.

Mr. Polwhele says, "I consider the Church of East Teignmouth (or rather its towers) as the oldest in the county. The style of its architecture, or that of its towers, may be referred to the Saxons. . . . Take away the church from these towers, and they would favour more of a military than a religious structure; and probably they might have been appropriated to the purpose of defence, and that part of the edifice which is the church (though very ancient) might have been added." (i. 233.)

Dr. Oliver, in his *Ecclesiastical Antiquities* (ii. 140), also gives a lithographic view of this old church, copied from a print published by Edward Croydon, at Teignmouth, in 1822. Dr. Oliver adds that this very ancient church being in a most dilapidated state, an Act of Parliament for enlarging and repairing it, received the royal assent on July 12th, 1815. On May 18th, 1821, the parishioners resolved to rebuild it; and on November 5th, 1822, the foundation of a larger edifice, in the Saxon style, from the designs of Andrew Patey, Esq., architect, was laid by the Rev. Charles Phillott. This church was consecrated by Dr. William Carey, Bishop of Exeter, on October 21st, 1823.

In the year 1875 the church was again rebuilt.

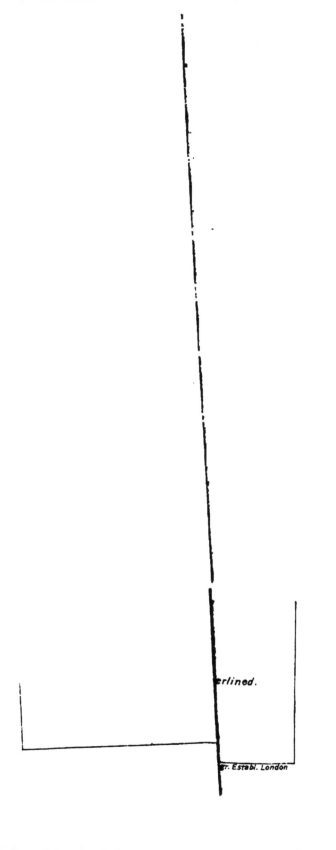

erlined.

Tr. Establ. London

Holcombe Down formerly began. Thence the boundary proceeds, again north, to the "old dike." This old dike exists to this day. Upon it is constructed the modern road to Little Haldon, and it has on its western or left side the deep ditch from which it was constructed. The next station, still on this same road, is "Water-shoot Coomb," a name now seemingly lost, but probably designating the very steep-sided valley of Lidwell, which lies to the right. Thence along the old row to "the staples." This spot, "the staples," was probably the boundary of the open land of Little Haldon. Thence the boundary ran along the ridge to the "sand holcan," the veins or beds of sand; thence along the street to the "black penn," or "top;" thence along the street to Broadmoor's head; thence straight on along the street to the "earth barrow." The sand-beds, the black top, and Broadmoor's head, can perhaps no longer be identified; but it is with the utmost interest that we find mention in these boundaries of the small circular camp on Little Haldon. From the earthwork the boundary proceeds to the "stone-barrow." This station can only be supplied conjecturally. From the stone-barrow it goes down, along the street, to Dawlish ford, precisely following the modern parish boundary. Thence it proceeds along the "port" or market street to Rush slade's head. This seems rather a summary description of a line reaching from Dawlish ford, past the four cross roads, through the hamlet of Gulliford, as far as the middle of the west valley, or rather "slade."* From this point the boundary proceeds to Cock ford, now Cofford; thence along the estuary out on the Exe; thence down and back along the Exe to the outfall of Sciter lake, now Shutterton or Shutton; thence to the head of the estuary; thence to the "old dike," on which the present Teignmouth and Dawlish road was constructed; thence to the "red stone;" thence south to the sea, and from the sea back again to the mouth of the Teign.

From the map which accompanies this paper these stations will be shown more distinctly than is possible by verbal description.

The charter is purported to be signed† by Eadsine (Eadsig), Archbishop of Canterbury; Ælfric, Archbishop of York; Lifing, Bishop of Crediton; Ælwine (Ælfwine), Bishop of Winchester; Brihtwold, Bishop of Ramsbury, and Dodico

---

* This is a good specimen of a "slade," namely a shallow basin of land with an outfall, without a spring, and so without a stream of water except from rainfall.

† It may be added that the indiction, epact, and concurrent, are all correct.

(Dudeca), Bishop of Wells; also by Ælfwine, Abbot of New-minster; Ægelward, Abbot of Glastonbury; Æthelstan, Abbot of Ramsey; Wlfweard, abbot,* and Godwine, Abbot of Winchcombe.

It will be seen that there is no exception to the generality of this grant. It purports to convey seven manses, and the area is shown by the line of boundary to coincide with the modern parishes of Dawlish and East Teignmouth (4980 acres together), all but the Brimley valley.

The next noteworthy event is the death of Lyfing, which took place on the 23rd of March, 1046, perhaps at Tavistock, where he was buried. Leofric, the chaplain and chancellor of King Eádweard, and lord of Dawlish, now became, at Credi-ton, bishop of the united sees of Devon and Cornwall. This union, commenced in the person of Lyfing in 1026, has at length in our day been again severed, with the happiest auspices, after a duration of 850 years.†

Next came, in 1050, the transfer of the united sees from Crediton to Exeter, accompanied by the often described cere-mony of the installation of Leofric in his new chair by the personal assistance of King Eádweard and Queen Eadgyth. The church in which the bishopstool was thus newly set up was the church of the monastery of St. Mary and St. Peter at Exeter.

There is good documentary evidence to show that this monastery of St. Mary and St. Peter was founded by Ædelstan. It was in 926, probably, that King Ædelstan, having defeated the Cornu-Welsh, having expelled the British from Exeter, having taken the government of Devon-shire into his own hands, and committed that of Cornwall to Howel, as his viceroy, began to build the walls of the city, and also began to construct the church of this monastery, sending abroad for relics for its enrichment; and it was probably at the great gemót, held at Exeter, on the Wednes-day after Easter, the 16th of April, 928, that Ædelstan's laws were promulgated, and this church consecrated. Tra-dition states that the site occupied that of the east part of the present Lady Chapel.‡ It must have been in this build-ing, restored under Eádgár in 965, and almost entirely rebuilt under Cnut in 1019, that Leofric was installed. That Leofric

---

* This abbot's name appears in several contemporary charters, but his see
s not mentioned.
† The Order in Council, constituting the bishopric of Truro, is dated the 15th of December, 1876.
‡ GODWIN, Ed. of 1615, p. 390 ; Archdeacon FREEMAN, *Arch. Hist.*, p. 12.

himself ever built a cathedral church is, considering the state of his revenues, extremely unlikely. In all probability what Bishop Warelwast found, when he set to work in 1112, was no other than this old re-edified Saxon church. An idea of its outward appearance may, as Archdeacon Freeman suggests,* be derived from a seal of the Bishop and Chapter, figured by Dr. Oliver,† of which a copy appears in the margin of the page.

King Ædelstan is said to have endowed the church of St. Mary and St. Peter with six and twenty cotlifs, or manors, and with one third of the relics which he had collected. Of these manors the names of four appear from the testimony of charters, or copies of charters, still extant; namely, Topsham, Monkerton in Pinhoe, Stoke Canon, and Culmstock. Those of two others—Sidbury and Branscombe —are furnished by the Hundred Roll.‡ Two others are mentioned by Godwin § (following Hoker)—Morkshut (*i.e.* Morchard) and Treasurer's Beare, now Traysbere, in Honiton Clist. Polwhele furnishes another; namely, Ide.‖ The rest can be gathered only conjecturally from the list of Leofric's acquisitions, from Domesday, and from the remote traditions of the see.

Of this vast rent-roll, however, such had been the spoliation and loss, that Leofric found, when he took to the minster, no more land in possession than two hides at Ide, with no more live stock thereon than seven head of cattle. To remedy this enormous deficiency, and to recover these lost properties, became one of the most constant occupations of the bishop's life and his first temporal care.¶

Leofric, on his arrival at Exeter, is said to have found three

* p. 68.
† *Lives of the Bishops*, p. 168, Seals, No. 14.
‡ pp. 66a, 66b.
§ Ed. of 1615, p. 391.
‖ He says: "I have a copy of King Athelstane's grant of Ide to the church of Exeter. It is written on a parchment 14 inches by 9. Dated 937." (i. 221.) And then he refers to an appendix, which was amongst the things that were not to be. What has become of this parchment copy?
¶ An entry in Leofric's missal (fo. 3a) describes him as a man temperate in life and manners, a learned preacher to the people, a teacher of doctrine to the clergy, a builder of churches, and a strenuous administrator of the duties of his office. *Domesday* states expressly that at the death of King Eádweard, 5th January, 1066, Leofric, as bishop, was the holder of eleven manors in Cornwall, of which the principal were St. Germans, Tregel, Pawton-in-St.-Breock, Lawhitton, and St. Winnow.

monastic establishments, all within what afterwards became St. Peter's Close. The first, according to Godwin (following Hoker), was a house of nuns, where the dean's house and (according to Risdon, p. 108) the Calendar Hay, or vicars' close, then stood (1615). The second was a monastery for monks, supposed to have been founded by King Æðelred, third son of King Æðelwulf, and immediate predecessor of Ælfred the Great, in about 868. The third was the Monastery of St. Mary and St. Peter, of which we have been speaking, "for monks of the order of St. Benet" (says Godwin), founded by Æðelstan. The narrative goes on to state that, in terror of the ravages of the Danes, the monks fled, and the house remained destitute, until King Eadgar, taking pity on its forlorn condition, re-established it in about 968.* Then, in all probability, it was that the Benedictine rule was adopted, under the influence of the king and Archbishop Dunstan. A second period of affliction passed over the house, on that darkest day in the history of Exeter, when the city was betrayed by the French traitor, Hugh, reeve of Queen Emma-Ælfgifu, to the Danish tyrant, Swegen, in 1003. The buildings were demolished and the ancient charters burnt. Moreover, the king's reeves (regis praepositi), including no doubt this same Hugh, had "imposed the yoke of servitude on the manors of the Church of St. Mary and All Saints, in Exeter" (imponebant iugum seruitutis praediis sanctae Mariae, etc.), a difficult expression, which perhaps means that they had reduced to a condition of serfdom many tenants who before were free. From these disasters the monastery was restored by the piety of Cnut, to whose zeal a charter of restoration to Abbot Æðelwold in 1019,† and a re-grant of Stoke Canon in 1031,‡ bear testimony.§ The latter is purported to be made to a thegn named Hunuwine, but was really for the benefit of the episcopal church.

For the nature of Leofric's reforms we have the excellent authority of William of Malmsbury. He says that Leofric expelled the nuns (not mentioning any monks) and established canons, who were made subject to the Lotharingian rule, enjoining that they should eat at a common table and sleep in a common dormitory. The historian adds that the rule was transmitted to their successors, but owing to the

---

* See *N. M.* ii. 525.
† K. *C. D.*, DCCXXIX. ; iv. 3.
‡ Not printed.
§ Risdon says (p. 81) that a representation of Cnut, wearing a triple crown, was, not long before 1620, to be seen in a window of Stoke Canon Church.

luxury of the age had (in 1125) become relaxed; and the clerks then had a steward, appointed by the bishop, who provided them their food daily and their clothing each year.* Godwin (following Hoker) adds that the expelled monks (not saying what became of the nuns) were sent to Westminster, and that the buildings of the nunnery and of Ædelred's monastery were pulled down† and added to Leofric's own church. In the later Latin edition of Godwin, it is further stated that of the Lotharingian rule not a shadow or vestige at that date (1725) remained, and that there were then twenty-four resident canons, each of whom had a separate house, large enough to entertain a party of guests in good style if other means were forthcoming.

On the 5th of January, 1066, occurred the death of Leofric's patron, King Eádweard; and in the same memorable year came the battle of Hastings, with its momentous results. To the first Bishop of Exeter, however, neither the territorial nor the legal conquest of England seems to have brought any change. It was no part of the policy of William to disturb the possessions of the Church, and Leofric obtained the support of the Conqueror just as he had enjoyed the favour of the Confessor.

Two years afterwards, in 1068, the West of England was subdued by the Normans, Exeter was besieged and taken, and Rougemont Castle was built.

In the following year the defences of the new fortress were put to their first proof. A band of insurgents, espousing the cause of the sons of the unfortunate Harold, assailed the walls; but were easily beaten off by the Norman garrison, aided probably by the citizens of Exeter themselves.

In this same year, 1069, King William made another grant to the Church of St. Peter at Exeter. This deed is also printed by Dr. Oliver,‡ but also without boundaries. It cannot, however, be said that they have never appeared in print; for Dr. Hickes, in his letter to Sir Bartholomew Shower, prints the whole document.§ This is now reproduced.

✠ MVNDO ACCRESCENTIA MALA MINANTVR ETIAM MVNDI APPROPINQVARE EXCIDIA ET BEATIVS EST HOMINEM mortalem illuc mentis passibus tendere ubi post finem huius uitæ beatis datur perenniter uiuere. Hoc enim uiuere beatissimum oportet regem Christianum omni mentis conamine sibi alacriter emere, quia miserabile est regem hoc sæculo coronari, et

---

* *De Pont.* p. 201.
‡ *Lives*, p. 10.
† Ed. of 1615, p. 391.
§ *Diss. Epist.* 77, 8.

in futuro æternis poenis mancipari. Haec uero uigili mente
iutuens, his quoque ne succumbam precauens, EGO WIL-
HELMVS uictoriosus Anglorum basileus concessi fidelem meum
LEOFRICVM episcopum septem mansos terræ in priuatis locis,
hoc est apud BEMTVN et ESTTVN et CEOMMANYG, ac HOLA-
CVMB æcclesiæ sancti PETRI apostoli in Exonia ubi eius
episcopalis sedes est, donare, et canonicorum euisdem æcclesiæ
uictum ampliare, hereditario iure, tam in magnis quam in
modicis rebus ad se rite pertinentibus, uidelicet, agris, siluis,
pratis, pascuis, cultis et incultis exitibus et reditibus, eo
tenore ac concessu ut prefata terra ab omni censu sit libera,
excepta expeditione, pontis ac urbis constructione et restau-
ratione. Si quis autem, quod absit, diabolo instigante, meum
regalem concessum presumat euertere et beneficia predictæ
æcclesiæ et canonicis data detrahere, uel in aliquo minuere,
nisi conuersus reddendo et dupliciter restituendo sanctæ Dei
æcclesiæ satisfaciat, in resurrectione beatorum diuina uoce
damnatus fiat socius omnium demoniorum.

Anno dominicæ incarnationis MILLESIMO LXVIIII., consen-
tiente WILHELMO rege data est hæc terra æcclesiæ sancti
PETRI apostoli in Exonia ciuitate a uenerabili presule
LEOFRICO sub testimonio eorum qui subscripti sunt.

Ðis synd tha landgemæro thæs landes the Eadwig cyning
ageaf tham halgan were æt Bemtune, and tham hyrede, and
siððan Leofric bisceop, be Willhelmes cynges unnan, let*
gebocyan into sancte Petres mynstre on Exancestre. Ærest
thær ceoman lace ut scytt; and lang ceoman lace thæt hit
cymeð on Temese; anlang Temese westward; swa West-
sexena gemære is and Myrcena; thæt hit cymeð up to tham
gemyðan; thonne went hit on ða norðeran ea; thæt hit
cymeð to anre lace; betwix berhtulfingyge and hrisyge;
thæt on ða norð ea; thæt anlang thære ea; thæt hit cymeð
eft to ceomanlace; and thæt land æt cyngbrycge norð and
lang broces thæt hit cymð thær holanbroc ut scytt; and lang
broces up to tham wege be norðan cynstanes treowe; and
lang weges to fulan broces heafdon; andlang broces on tha
stanbricge; of thære stanbricge andlang weges on burg dyc;
andlang dyc on thone broc; andlang broces eft on cyng-
bricge; á onecnisse into sancte Petres mynstre on Exancestre,
and ealle tha teoðunga thæs cyninges.

---

* *Sic*, though from a slight inaccuracy in the writing of the "l," one is
inclined to think that the scribe was copying from a MS. which rightly read
"het," and that he was at first disposed to copy correctly; but not understanding the word, substituted the inferior reading "let." Afterwards he
writes "let" without hesitation.

✠ This synd tha landgemæro thære anre hyde and thære oðerhealfan gyrde æt Holacumbe the læg into Doflisc, the Leofric bisceop let gebocyan for his sawle into sancte Petres mynstre on Exancestre. Ærest on crampansteort; of crampansteorte on floraheafdo; and of floraheafdo up on thone weg be westa ðære cyrcan up to tha ferngara; of tham ferngara to tham dunnastane; of ðam dunnastane up to thære dyc; and swa east andlang thære dyc to than wætere; of tham wætere norð on thæs crohtes heafod; and swa norð on tha smala paðe; swa on dun to thære thwirsc díc; and swa to Dofolisces landscore adun to arietes stane; and swa andlang strandes to crampansteorte.

✠ Ego WILHELMVS Dei gratia rex Anglorum hanc donationem perpetuæ memoriæ mandaui.

✠ MATHILDA regina adiuui.

✠ Ego STIGANDVS archiepiscopus Christi æcclesiæe Confirmaui.

✠ Ego ODO episcopus consolidaui.

✠ Ego HERIMANNVS episcopus corroboraui.

✠ Ego LEOFRICVS episcopus concessi and subscripsi.

✠ Ego GOSFREDVS episcopus consensi.

✠ Ego GYSO episcopus assensi.

✠ Ego WILHELMVS episcopus confortaui.

✠ Ego BALDVVINVS abbas dignum duxi.

✠ Ego RODBERTVS comes.   ✠ Ego WILHELMVS uicecomes.

✠ Ego Wilhelmus comes.   ✠ Ego Rodbertus uicecomes.

✠ Ego Brient comes.   ✠ Ego Rocgerius uicecomes.

✠ Ego Eduuinus comes.   ✠ Leofnodus minister.

✠ Ego Morkerinus comes.   ✠ Ego Ricardus minister. .

✠ Ego Raulfus comes.   ✠ Ego Folco minister.

✠ Ego Arfastus cancellarius. ✠ Ego Hugo minister.

✠ Ego Angelricus presbiter. ✠ Ego Raulfus minister.

The following is a translation :

"The increase of evil in the world warns us that the end of the world is approaching; and it is better that man who is mortal should by the footsteps of his mind strive to attain to that region where after the close of this life it is given to the blessed to live everlastingly. To this most blessed life it behoves a Christian king with all the energy of his mind diligently to attain; for it is a miserable thing that a king should be crowned in this world, and himself suffer eternal punishment in the future. Viewing these things, then, with watchful mind, taking precaution that I may not be overwhelmed by these evils, I, WILLIAM, the victorious king of the English, have agreed to grant to my faithful bishop, LEOFRIC, seven manses of land in private localities,* that is, BEMTUN, and ESTTUN, and CEOMMANYG, and HOLACUMB, to the Church of St. Peter the Apostle, in Exeter, where his episcopal see is, and to increase the maintenance of the canons of the same church, by hereditary right, as in great, so in minor things thereto rightly appertaining, to wit, woods, meadows, pastures, cultivated lands and wastes, outgoings and rents, by the tenure and grant that the land aforesaid shall be free from every tax, except military expedition, and the building and repair of bridge and castle.   But if any one, which may Heaven forbid, shall presume, at the instiga- tion of the devil, to overthrow my royal grant, and to detract from or in any way diminish the benefits granted to the aforesaid church and canons, unless, being converted, he shall, by restoration and double restitution, satisfy the holy church of God, may he, in the resurrection of the just, be condemned by the divine voice to become the companion of all demons.

"In the year of our Lord's incarnation 1069, with the con- sent of King William, this land was granted to the church of St. Peter the apostle, in the city of Exeter, by the venerable bishop Leofric, by the testimony of those whose names are subscribed.

"These are the land boundaries of the land which King Eadwig gave to the holy men at Bemtune, and to the convent; and (which) since then bishop Leofric, by command of King William, has caused to be conveyed by charter to Saint Peter's minster, at Exeter."

(Then follow the boundaries of the Bampton lands.)

✠ "These are the land boundaries of the one hide, and of the yard and a half at Holcombe, adjoining Dawlish, which bishop Leofric caused to be conveyed by charter, for his soul, to Saint Peter's minster at Exeter.

"First at crampan steort (anchor-point); from crampan steort to the floraheafdo (floor-heads); and from floraheafdo up along the way by the west of the church up to the ferngara (fern-gores); from the ferngara to the Dun stone; from the Dun stone up to the dike; and so east along the dike to the water; from the water north to the head of the croht (croft); and so north to the small path; so upon the down to the thwart dike; and so to the land boundary of Dawlish down to Ariet's stone; and so along the strand to crampan steort."

This grant, it will be observed, differs materially from the former, in that it is not simply a donation to Leofric person-

* Manors of ancient demesne.

ally; it is a grant to him as bishop, for the benefit of the episcopal church of St. Peter, and also for the maintenance of the canons; and further it is a re-grant by the bishop to the church of St. Peter, this re-conveyance being the thing which was witnessed by the persons whose names are subscribed. Then when the Saxon portion is examined (this being evidently framed by a different hand than the author of the Latin part), the Oxfordshire lands are represented as re-conveyed by *the king's command*, whereas the Holcombe lands are re-conveyed voluntarily. It seems as if the document was intended to be held by the chapter of Exeter as an evidence of title as against both king and bishop.

The boundaries in this instance are not very easily followed. Beginning at the "crampan-steort" or promontory in the harbour, the line proceeds to the "floor-heads," a name which the writer is unable to explain. The corresponding station in the Dawlish boundary is "the salterns." Thence the line proceeds to the west of the church, as before; then mounts the hill about half-way, and, as before, proceeds to the "ferngores," which here take the place of the "blind well," and thence, as before, to the Dun stone and to the dike. From the dike the line proceeds to "the water." Here, it is presumed, the line breaks off from the former boundary, which went "north right on over Watershed comb," and now descends into the valley. From the water the line proceeds north to the head of the "croht," a word which Professor Skeat thinks may possibly be an early form of "croft," thence north to the small path, then along the down to the thwart dike, and so to the boundaries of Dawlish, down to Ariet's stone.

No express mention is made of an important object, Gorway Cross, which was standing until comparatively recent times. Gorway, formerly Godaway, Cross marked the boundary of Dawlish, so far as it was separate from Holcombe, and hence the boundary must have passed this spot. On the meaning of "Ariet's stone," the writer is unable to throw light. This boundary, which cannot be traced with the same certainty as the former, is marked with a yellow line on the accompanying map. Roughly speaking it corresponds with East Teignmouth parish, which was doubtless made up out of it, with certain additions and subtractions. Its area would be about 600 acres.

Amongst the signatories to the deed are King William and Matilda his queen; Stigand, Archbishop of Canterbury; Odo, Bishop of Bayeux; Hermann, of Sherborne; Leofric of Exeter (the donee and donor); Geoffrey of Coutances;

Gyso of Wales; and William of London. The Abbot Baldwin, who signs, was probably the Abbot of St. Edmund's Bury. Amongst the rest, Rodbertus *comes* is Robert Duke of Normandy; Wilhelmus *uicecomes*, William Rufus; and Wilhelmus *comes* and Brient *comes* represent William Fitz-Osborn, governor of Winchester, and Brian of Brittany, who in this year, 1069, relieved the garrison of Exeter, thus holding the new castle of Rougemont in the interest of the king, as above mentioned.* Next come Edwin *comes*, and Morcar *comes*, the two handsome sons of Algar, and grandsons of Leofwine, younger son of Earl Godwin, and of Leofwine's wife, the famed Lady Godiva, foundress of Coventry Abbey. In the year 1066 Edwin and Morcar had rebelled against William; finding the issue of the contest doubtful, had by submission been admitted, "to all appearance," says Orderic, to the king's favour.† Amongst the rest appears a "chancellor," "Arfastus cancellarius." This was the Herfast, who in 1070 was made bishop of Elmham, and in 1075 transferred his see to Thetford, dying at an advanced age in 1084.

So far as the Oxfordshire lands at Bampton, Aston, and Chimney are concerned—Aston and Chimney being hamlets in the parish of Bampton—this grant is stated to be a confirmation of a former donation by King Eadwig. But as to the Holcombe land there is no reference to any former grant. Why it was that King Eádweard's grant of 1044 was not referred to in this deed does not appear, nor why a new grant of Holcombe to Leofric should have become necessary. Possibly Holcombe, like Topsham, had been appropriated by Earl Harold, and unlike Topsham, which was never recovered, was by this act of King William, restored.

On the 10th of February, 1073,‡ Bishop Leofric died, and

---

* ORD. VIT. iv. 5.

† "Gratiam regis petierunt, et specie tenus obtinuerunt," iii. 4.

‡ Or 1072, according to the reckoning of the commencement of the year. If the year is taken as beginning on the 1st of January, it was in 1073; if on the 25th of March, it was 1072. As to this date there is some contrariety of statement. The entry in Leofric's own missal (Bodl. MSS. 579, fo. 3 b) is to the effect that he died in 1071, which is clearly wrong; but it also states that the death was on the 10th of February, in the twenty-sixth year of his episcopacy, which is probably right. Now Lyfing died on the 23rd of March, 1046; hence the 10th of February in the twenty-sixth year of Leofric's episcopacy must have been in 1073. With this agrees the epitaph set up by John Hoker in the Cathedral in the year 1569, the last two lines of which, according to Prince (*Worthies*, ed. of 1810, p. 563), were as follows:

"Quatuor adde decem lustra, et tres insuper annos
Mille, Leofricum mors tremebunda petit."

The statement in the Exon. Eccl. Chronicon, Laud MSS. Bodl. No. 627, is to the same effect.

was succeeded by Osbern, the Norman. As to his place of burial there has been some doubt. Archdeacon Freeman * points out the discrepancy. In Leofric's missal the statement is, "Sepultus est in criptam ejusdem æcclesiae;" *i.e.* in the crypt of his own church. Hoker, on the other hand, as cited in Godwin,† says he "was buried in the cemetery or churchyard of his own church, under a simple and a broken marble stone, which place, by the sithence enlarging of this church, is now within the south tower of the same." The matter is cleared up by an entry in the Codex Exoniensis.‡ In that marvellous old book it is recorded that a certain serf was manumitted from the land at Bishop's Teignton by Bishop William Warelwast, "on the day on which the remains of Bishop Leofric and Bishop Osbern were removed from the old monastery into the new." In other words, Hoker must have been mistaken, and Leofric was never buried in the cemetery. He and Osbern were buried in the crypt of the Saxon church; and when William of Warelwast had completed his church, including its two noble towers, the bodies of the bishops were moved into the southern tower, Leofric's being placed against the eastern wall, and Osbern's against the southern. There, to his honour, "that painful antiquary," as Prince calls him,§ John Hoker, in 1569, raised to the memory of Leofric a monument, at the charges, as he himself says, of the Dean and Chapter; but as Prince says, chiefly of Bishop William Alley.

Of the famous bequest of Leofric to the minster of St. Peter, the seat of his bishopric, the original is entered on the first leaf of his copy of the gospels, now in the Bodleian.‖ Another original, hardly second in value, is the copy which is entered on the first page of the Codex Exoniensis. Of the opening sentences of this bequest we here, for the sake of completing our narrative, give a translation, though the passage has been often before printed.¶

"Here is declared, upon this Christ's book what bishop Leofric hath given to Saint Peter's minster at Exeter, where his bishop's stool is. That is, that he has, by God's support, and by his own pleading, and by his own treasure, recovered that which before was alienated—that is, first the land at

---

* *Arch. Hist.* pp. 2, 3.
† Ed. of 1615, p. 396.
‡ Fol. 5 b ; HICKES, *Diss. Epist.* p. 16 ; THORPE, *Dipl.* p. 646.
§ Page 563.
‖ Now *Auct.* D. ii. 16 ; see Wanley, p. 80.
¶ See DUGDALE, *N. M.* ii. 526 ; KEMBLE, *C. D.* DCCCCXL. (iv. 274) ; PEDLER (with translation), pp. 136, 138 ; THORPE (with translation), p. 428.

Culmstock, and the land at Branscombe, and at Salcombe, and the land at St. Mary church, and the land at Staverton, and at Sparkwell,* and the land at Morchard, and Sidwell Huish, and the land at Brixton (and the land at Topsham, although Harold unlawfully took it away †), and the land at Stoke,‡ and the land at Sidbury, and the land at Newton,§ and at Norton,‖ and the land at Clist,¶ that Wid had. Then, this is the addition, in lands of his own, with which he has endowed the minster, for the souls of his lords, and for his own, for the sustenance of God's servants, who have to intercede for their souls—that is, first the land at Bampton, and at Aston, and at Chimney; and the land at Dawlish, and at Holcombe, and at Southwood.** And when he took to the minster, he found no more land (of) that (which) had been given thereto, than two hides of land at Ide, and there were thereon of cattle no more than seven oxen."

The bishop, it will be observed, makes a distinction between the lands which had anciently been the property of St. Peter's, and lands of his own with which he himself was endowing the minster. This distinction agrees with what we know of Æðelstan's grants, and with the above extracted deeds of King Eádweard and King William. The land at Dawlish was a free gift to Leofric, and is disposed of by him as his own. So is the land at Holcombe, and the land at Southwood. It would almost seem as if Southwood came to him by virtue of King William's above-stated grant of Holcombe. The boundaries rather negative this, but the point is doubtful. ††

* A separate manor in Staverton parish.
† The words in brackets are, in both originals, an insertion over the line of the main writing. This looks as if both the entries were by the same hand, possibly that of Leofric himself. The expression forcibly speaks the mind of the bishop, lamenting the spoliation which his church has suffered. At first the writer seems to have forgotten all about Topsham ; but after both entries had been made, he remembers that Topsham also, the gift of Æðelstan, had been recovered, but lost again, by the unlawful act of Harold. See Mr. Freeman's remarks, *N. C.* ii. 562 (App. E.) and iv. 166. The supposition that Topsham was needed for the defence of the coast will not commend itself to any one acquainted with the locality. Exmouth would have been more to the purpose. The weirs and salmon pools of Topsham, and possibly also its haven dues, were doubtless irresistible temptations.
‡ Stoke Canon.   § Newton St. Cyres.
‖ Query, a manor in the parish of Newton St. Cyres.
¶ Afterwards Treasurer's Beare, now Traysbere, in Honiton Clist.
** Southwood, in Dawlish, is here spoken of as a separate manor.
†† Two ancient chapels existed until lately in Dawlish, one on the east side of the parish, at Cockton, now Cofton, the other in the upper part of the Southwood valley, at Lidwell. Both are described by Polwhele (iii. 153), and by Dr. Oliver (*Eccl. Antiqq.* ii. 142). Further particulars respecting each are highly to be desired.

In 1086 came the Domesday Survey, when it is found that out of the manors which Leofric had recovered —ten, namely, Newton St. Cyres, Culmstock, Branscombe, Salcombe, the church and a small portion of the land of Marychurch, Staverton, Brixton, Stoke Canon, Sidbury, and Ide—and out of the manors which had been granted to him personally, one—namely, Dawlish—was still in the hands of his successor. To one of these properties, namely, Newton St. Cyres, Bishop Osbern had to establish his claim by legal process. One would have supposed that Leofric's devise would have been sufficient, but Osbern seems to have preferred to rest his title on proof that Newton was a manor appurtenant to Crediton. At any rate he succeeded, on production of his charters.* Out of the rest four, namely, Dawlish, Ide, Staverton,† and the church of Marychurch, were now (1086) set apart "de victu canonicorum," for the maintenance of Leofric's and Osbern's canons. Of the remainder, five, namely, Sparkwell, Morchard, St. Sidwell's, Norton, and Treasurer's Beare had been temporarily alienated. Sparkwell in Staverton had become the property of Baldwin the sheriff. This was owned in 1066 by Brihtric; had probably passed to Queen Matilda, and probably by her been bestowed upon the see at Leofric's request; but after his death his successor, it seems, was unable to hold it. Morchard Bishop had gone to Queen Matilda, or rather to her estate, she having died some three years before, on the 3rd November, 1083. This also was part of the lands of Brihtric. St. Sidwell's was probably in lay hands. Norton had, strangely enough, become the property of the Abbot of Buckfast. Beare in Clist Honiton, was no longer in the hands of the bishop. All these five, however, returned like lost sheep to the fold, and remained the property of the Dean and Chapter for centuries. Not so Topsham, of which only the church continued to belong to

---

* The charters showed that the Bishop of Exeter's church was seized of Newton before the reign of King Eádweard. As to this the *Exon* entry, p. 107, is clear: "De hac mansione (Niuuentona) ostendit Osbertus episcopus cartas suas quæ testantur ecclesiam suam esse inde saisitam antequam regnaret rex Eduuardus." The Exchequer Domesday introduces confusion by substituting "ecclesiam Sancti Petri," for "ecclesiam suam." The church of the bishop to which Newton belonged before King Eadweard's reign was not St. Peter's at Exeter, but the Church of the Holy Cross, at Crediton; and Newton went over, along with the manor of Crediton, to St. Peter's, in 1050.

† Risdon, p. 257, confuses the name of this manor, called in the *Exon.* p. 110, Stouretona, and in the *Exch.* fo. 101 (4) Sovretone, with Sourton parish, in Lifton hundred. A sorry sustenance would the canons have gleaned from the heaths and moorlands of Sourton! This hungry place belonged in 1066 to a king's thane named Aluric, under the name of Siredone. (*Exch. D.* fo. 118-3.)

the chapter. Of the lands which had been conveyed to Leofric personally, Dawlish, with Southwood, remained annexed to the see, and Holcombe—that is to say, East Teignmouth—after an interval, followed. In the mean time a portion of it had been appropriated by the powerful baron Ralph de Pomerei, to whom it yielded six shillings and five pence, as the produce of four salinæ,* the amount of land held with the salt-works being inconsiderable. In these salinæ we recognize, almost without doubt, the salterns, which are shown to have existed on the bank of the Tame brook at East Teignmouth in the year 1044; and Ralph de Pomerei's Holcombe it probably was which was afterwards known as the manor of Teignmouth Courtenay.†

* *Exon. D.* p. 315 ; *Exch. D.* fo. 114 (1).
† See Polwhele, iii. 146.

MISCELLANEOUS DEVONSHIRE GLEANINGS.

PART II.

BY W. PENGELLY, F.R.S., ETC.

(Read at Dawlish, July, 1881.)

Prefatory:—It will be found that some of the *Gleanings* which make up this Paper are said to have been "copied from the Note Book of Mr. O. Blewitt." The following facts are offered in explanation:—In the winter of 1880–1, Mr. Octavian Blewitt, author of the *Panorama of Torquay*, was so good as to lend me his MS. Note Book, with permission to copy and utilize anything I found in it; and I have taken the earliest opportunity of availing myself of the privilege. Some of the members of the Association will be pleased to be referred to an interesting Biographical Sketch of Mr. Blewitt in the *Biograph* for February, 1881 (v. 170–185).

I. " BONESHAVE."

Every one acquainted with the Glossaries of the Dialects of the south-western counties of England, is aware that the word *Boneshave* (= *Sciatica*) occurs in the famous *Exmoor Scolding* as well as in its companion, the *Exmoor Courtship;* in Mr. Rock's *Jim and Nell*, written in the dialect of North Devon; in Mr. Palmer's Glossary to *A Dialogue in the Devonshire Dialect,* (but, so far as I have been able to find, not in the Dialogue itself); and in *A Glossary of Provincial Words and Phrases in use in Somersetshire*, by Mr. W. P. Williams and Mr. W. A. Jones. It is equally well known that, though there are several other valuable Glossaries in the counties just specified the word does not occur in any of them. In short, *Boneshave* appears to be now restricted to

I 2

Exmoor and the immediately adjacent parts of Devon and Somerset shires.

Nevertheless, that this, instead of being one of the autochthones of Exmoor, is probably a survival there of a word once used in other districts, I have been led to believe from the following fact :—The Rev. Thomas P. Wadley, of Naunton Beauchamp, Worcestershire, writing to *Berrow's Worcester Journal* for August 30th, 1879, said " I send you a few extracts from a " [MS.] " book of Receipts written, it would seem, at various times from the reign of Henry VII. until the end of that of his successor, or a little further on."

Amongst the Receipts is the following :—

" ffor the boneshawe—

"Take the hyldyr beryse, & a boles or a oxes galle & ij p'tys of hony & seth he' to gedre & scome it clene, & set it down & put it in a glas & anoynt ye y'wt a yens ye fire."

It will be observed that, as written in the Receipt, the word is *Boneshawe* not *Boneshave* ; but, as the letters *u* and *v*, as well as *u* and *w*, are constantly exchanged for each other throughout the Receipts, the two words may, no doubt, be accepted as variations of one and the same.

The following noteworthy instance of the substitution of *w* for *v* occurs in the *Faerie Queene* (B. II. C. xii. St. 4, Gilfillan's ed. 1859), to meet the emergencies of rhyme :—

" For, whiles they fly that Gulf's devouring jaws,
They on the rock are rent, and sunk in helpless wawes."

Mr. Wadley writes me that the Receipts " would appear to have been written for the most part by members of the medical profession, in more than one part of the country." Direct mention is made of " Worcestre," Gloucester, Chepstow, and "lyttyl tynterne;" thus connecting, apparently, some of the writers, at least, with the country near which the Severn and the Wye enter the Sea. Norwich is also spoken of, but there is no allusion to Devon or Somersetshire; nor are there any dialectical finger-posts pointing distinctly to either of these counties.

Further, the Receipt for the *Boneshave* is strictly *medical ;* it is not a *charm*, though charms are found, and by no means sparingly, amongst the Receipts. The prescribed ingredients are " hyldyr beryse," a " a boles or a oxes galle," and " hony ;" and the compound is to be applied externally. It is well known, however, that the Exmoor treatment for *Boneshave* is the following *charm* :—" The patient must lie on his back on the bank of a river or brook of water, with a straight staff by his side, between him and the water; and must have the following words repeated over him :—

> ' Bone-shave right ;
> Bone-shave straight ;
> As the water runs by the *stave,*
> Good for bone-shave.'   (See *Exmoor Scolding.*)

In short, I have little or no doubt that the word was formerly used far away from Exmoor, and do not despair of detecting it, sooner or later, in Glossaries of ultra-southwestern dialects.

II. BROCKEDON, William.

Mr. Octavian Blewitt's *Panorama of Torquay*, 2nd edition, 1832, p. 271, contains a Biographical Sketch of the late Mr. W. Brockedon, who, as is well known, was a native of Totnes. From the character of the sketch, as well as from a foot-note, I concluded that it had been submitted to the artist—then in his 45th year,—that it had met his approval, and that its publication had been sanctioned by him.

To leave no room for doubt on the point I wrote Mr. Blewitt, who, in his reply, dated " Nov. 9, 1880," after remarking " Brockedon was one of my dearest friends," says " My Biography in the *Panorama* was drawn up, as you have correctly inferred, from information given to me by himself ; but as you may like to have his own words, I enclose a copy of extracts from two letters which he wrote me in 1832 in reference to his work as a watchmaker.

"The second extract is interesting as showing how proud he was of the share he had in making the Church clock—a fact which I have often heard him mention, and in the presence of many friends, from whom he had no desire to conceal the fact that he had been a working watchmaker.

"He was a fine noble-minded fellow, above all the pride which would have made a mystery of his early life."

The following are the extracts mentioned by Mr. Blewitt :—

Extract, (1) from a Letter from Mr. Brockedon, dated "Aug. 29, 1832," addressed to " Octavian Blewitt Esq." :—

. " ' My Father was a man of singularly fine and powerful understanding. His natural talents I have never seen surpassed, and whatever turn my own character may have taken, if the world thinks highly of it, it grew under his instruction and advice, and the impressions they made upon me before I was 15, for prior to this age I had the severe misfortune to lose him (in Sept 1802).

"'He had instructed me in his business, and the taste then acquired for mechanical pursuits has never left me. During his long illness, nearly 12 months, young as I was, I conducted his business. After his death, in accordance with an arrangement made by him whilst he was living, I spent 6 months in London in the house of a watch manufacturer to perfect myself in what I expected would have been my pursuit in life. On my return from London I continued to carry on my business for my mother for 5 years.'"

Extract (2) from a letter dated 'Nov. 17, 1832,' from Mr. Brockedon to Mr. O. Blewitt.

"'In the mention of my early pursuits in life which still so much influence me, Mechanics, you will smile, perhaps, at my calling to mind and mentioning what I recollect with such pleasure,—*the hand I had* in making the present Parish Clock in the church at Totnes.

"'An order was given to my Father to make a new Church Clock a short time before the Accident by lightning which, in Feb. 1799, struck the Tower, threw down the S. E. Pinnacle, and did so much damage to the Church as to require nearly 3 years to repair. This accident prevented the clock being put up until the Summer of 1802, during my father's last illness; . . . .

"'I was set to do some of the work, though only about 13 years of age, particularly cutting the *fly pinion* out of the solid steel.'"

It will be found that the substance of the first of the foregoing extracts has been faithfully incorporated in Mr. Blewitt's biographical sketch in the *Panorama of Torquay*, mentioned above.

The following extract from a letter from the late Governor A. H. Holdsworth to Mr. Blewitt, dated "Brookhill" [Kingswear, Dartmouth] "Feb. 20, 1837" will not be considered out of place here :—

"I am daily expecting Brockedon, he has come down to bury his mother, who has been carried off by the Influenza. He has been very ill himself & I hope he will benefit by the air of this place."

III. COLTON, Rev. Caleb C.

(Copied from the Note Book of Mr. O. Blewitt.)

" Mr. Dickinson of Knightshayes, Tiverton, who afterwards took the name of Walrond, on succeeding to the Estate of Bradfield near Collumpton, ... told me that Caleb Colton, the author of ' Lacon,' was considered the best shot in the county.

" When Colton lived at Tiverton, he had apartments in a house which overlooked the Exe. One day, a friend of Mr. Dickinson called on him, and found him sitting in the window, with pistols lying on the table, and a row of empty bottles by his side. He asked him what he was doing. ' Practising with the pistol,' replied Colton ; and, taking up a bottle, he threw it out of the window, and seizing a pistol smashed the bottle to pieces before it reached the river.

" On another occasion, Mr. Dickinson said, Sir John Trevelyan, of Nettlecombe Court, Somerset, had a dispute with a neighbouring farmer, who finding it impossible to bring Sir John to terms, wrote off to Colton, and promised him a good day's sport if he liked to come over from Tiverton. Colton was only too glad to accept the invitation, and on his arrival the Farmer took him out to some of his land adjacent to Sir John Trevelyan's preserves, and contrived to frighten the birds so as to make them fly over his fields. Colton, of course, had rare sport ; and when the Gamekeeper, alarmed by the incessant firing, came out to see what it meant, he was so amazed at the destruction going on, that he ran into the house and told his master that the Farmer had got a man in his fields who brought down everything that flew across them, and that not a bird would be left at Nettlecombe at the end of the day. Sir John Trevelyan immediately went out and looked over the hedge, when he exclaimed, as he saw bird after bird fall under the gun of the stranger, ' If that is not Caleb Colton it is the devil. Go round to Mr. —— and say that if he will stop the firing I will agree to his terms.'

" The ' Mysterious Disappearance of the Rev. Caleb Colton' was almost a standing heading of paragraphs in Devonshire Papers for many years after this occurrence. He died in Paris by his own hand. O. B."

IV. COOKWORTHY, William and the DIVINING ROD.

The late Mr. William Cookworthy, a native of Kingsbridge, but popularly connected with Plymouth on account of his

long residence there, takes a well-won place amongst Devonshire Celebrities, mainly, perhaps, on account of his discovery
of the existence, in England, of the China Clay and China
Stone ; and of his connexion with the Plymouth China
Factory.

Mr. Cookworthy was, it is well known, a firm believer in
the Divining rod, and left a treatise on its uses. (See *Trans.
Devon. Assoc.* viii. 481, 1876.) Though it is not necessary to
add anything to the evidence already before the world on this
belief of Mr. Cookworthy, it appears to be desirable to give a
place in the *Transactions* of this Association to the following
anecdotes, which I have recently met with—one in a somewhat scarce volume, and one in manuscript.

*Topographical and Historical Sketches of the Boroughs of
East and West Looe in the County of Cornwall.* By Thomas
Bond (1823), contains the following paragraph :—

"Though no metallic Ore of any kind has been discovered
near Looe, yet if confidence may be given to the Virgula
Divina, a load of some kind of metal passes under the houses
near the Conduit in East Looe. This I was informed of by
the late Miss Elizabeth Debell, of East Looe, who stated that
her cousin Wm. Cookworthy (the late celebrated Chemist of
Plymouth), made several trials with the rod outside her Quay
door, at the back of her house near the Conduit, and who
was persuaded from his trials that such was the fact. Mr.
Cookworthy always put great confidence in the divining-rod."
p. 141.

(*Copied from the Note Book of Mr. O. Blewitt.*)

"My great uncle, Bartholomew Dunsterville, was serving
his time as a Pupil of Dr. Mudge." [John Mudge, M.D.
1720–1793], "when Dr. Johnson arrived at Plymouth, on a
visit to the Doctor.

"Old Mr. Cookworthy, who professed to have discovered
a Divining Rod by which he could detect the existence of
metal underground, begged Dr. Mudge to allow him to show
the powers of his Rod in the presence of Dr. Johnson, if the
latter could be induced to witness the operation.

"Dr. Johnson was so much amused with the idea that he
suggested that they might take advantage of the opportunity
to play Mr. Cookworthy a trick by burying an iron 'crock' in
the garden, and seeing if he could find it by his Divining Rod.
Dr. Mudge agreed ; and, on the evening before the appointed
day, an iron vessel was buried, and the ground above made

smooth. When Mr. Cookworthy arrived next day, he walked about the garden testing it in different parts with his Rod, until he came to the place where the iron vessel had been buried; when he at once stuck the Rod into the ground, and exclaimed that there was metal underneath. The Gardener was ordered to dig away, when the iron crock made its appearance, to the great amusement of Dr. Johnson, while Mr. Cookworthy was very angry with Dr. Mudge at allowing such a trick to be practised on him, declaring at the same time that the result, though intended to throw ridicule on him, had really proved the efficacy of his Divining Rod. O. B."

We learn from Boswell (ed. 1851, vol. i., ch. 11, p. 245) that Dr. Johnson and Sir Joshua Reynolds visited Devonshire during the summer of 1762, and were the guests of Dr. Mudge during their stay at Plymouth. Johnson was then about 53 years of age, Reynolds 39, and Mudge 42, whilst Cookworthy was 57.

Boswell makes no mention of Cookworthy or the rod ; but he had not at that time made the acquaintance of Dr. Johnson, and he states that he was obliged to Sir Joshua for the information concerning the excursion. Perhaps neither of the travellers was tempted to mention the clumsy trick.

V.   LETHBRIDGE, John, Inventor of a DIVING APPARATUS.

In their sketch of Mr. John Lethbridge, of Newton Abbot, who invented early in the 18th century a very successful Diving apparatus, it is stated by the Lysonses that "The apparatus, about twenty years ago, was at Governor Holdsworth's, at Dartmouth, but it was then in a decaying state." (*Devonshire*, p. 569)

The authors just quoted state in a foot-note (p. 570) that their sketch of the clever and successful machinist was "from the information of Capt. Thomas Lethbridge, of the navy, a grandson of Mr. John Lethbridge." The Lysonses' *Devonshire* was published in 1822, so that, assuming that Capt. Thomas Lethbridge furnished the information not long before that date, the apparatus would appear to have been in the keeping of Governor Holdsworth about the end of the 18th century, that is fully 40 years after the death of the inventor, which occurred in December, 1759.

It seems somewhat strange that Capt. Lethbridge's curiosity had not been sufficiently ardent to enable him to speak with certainty respecting the actual fate, at the time he wrote, of a machine which made his grandfather famous, and had been very beneficial in its effect on the history of his own family. He seems, however, to have had no doubt that *about twenty years ago it was at Governor Holdsworth's*, and was in a decaying state ; and it must be admitted that his statement on the matter *ought* to be trustworthy.

It was accordingly copied by Mr. O. Blewitt, in the second edition of his *Panorama of Torquay*, published in 1832 (p. 261), and, in substance, by Mr. J. S. Amery in 1880, in his interesting paper on *John Lethbridge and his Diving-Machine.* (*Trans. Devon. Assoc.* xii. 495.)

The letter from the late Governor A. H. Holdsworth to Mr. O. Blewitt, whence a passage respecting Mr. Brockedon was quoted above (p. 134), contains the following paragraph :— " Of the history of Leathbridge " [*sic*] " or his diving bell I know nothing, and am, therefore, led to believe that you have mixed me up with some other person when you ask ' whether I still possess the machine.' I should like to get at anything connected with that affair."

At first sight we appear to have here a *Slip connected with Devonshire*—" The apparatus," says Captain Thomas Lethbridge, " was at Governor Holdsworth's at Dartmouth." Governor Holdsworth, writing at Dartmouth, in February, 1837, replied, " Of the history of Leathbridge or his diving bell I know nothing."

The solution of the problem lies probably in the suggestion made by Governor A. H. Holdsworth, in his letter just quoted. " I am led," he says, " to believe that you have mixed me up with some other person." The "some other person" was probably his own father, as the following statements appear to show.

Dr. Newman, in his Paper *On the Antiquity of Dartmouth,* (*Trans. Devon. Assoc.* iii. 130), says, " In 1725 the office of Governor " [of Dartmouth Castle] " was given to Fort-Major Arthur Holdsworth, and it continued in that family till 1860. When the late Governor died it became extinct. The last Governor held the office just fifty years, though since 1832 no pay has been attached to the office." (*op. cit.* p. 134.)

The last Governor—Arthur Howe Holdsworth—died at Torquay in 1860, and, accepting Dr. Newman's statement that he " held the office just fifty years," he must have succeeded his father in 1810—about twelve, not " twenty years " before the publication of the Lysonses' *Devonshire.* The Governor Holdsworth they mentioned as being in possession of the machine, was, from the facts before us, not Mr. Blewitt's correspondent, but his father. According to the *Gentleman's Magazine* (vol. 77, Pt. 2, p. 1053, 1807.) A. M. Holdsworth, Esq., was appointed Governor of Dartmouth Castle, *vice* Arthur Holdsworth, deceased.

It can scarcely be supposed that had the last Governor Holdsworth ever seen the machine, or understood its character, he would have called it a " *Diving Bell* "—a name to which it seems to have been by no means entitled. Moreover, he is known to have taken so much interest in machinery that one is prepared to find him writing, as he did to Mr. Blewitt in the passage quoted above, "I should like to get at anything connected with that affair." Such was his enthusiasm on kindred topics, that, in the letter now under notice, he writes to Mr. Blewitt, "I wish I could give you any information about Newcomen, as I have long taken a great interest about him. . . . . . I confess to you that it is with real regret that I have often heard such things said of Watt, who after all was but an *improver;* and the *Inventor* of that instrument now so common thro' the world totally forgotten. I have expressed that feeling in public in every way that has come within my means; but it is of little use, for ignorance gives to *Watt* the credit, and few take the pains to search beyond the surface of anything."

It cannot be supposed that a man of such tastes and feelings as the writer of these paragraphs could have utterly forgotten that he was at one time the possessor of a diving apparatus with which its inventor, born in a neighbouring part of the same county as himself, "had recovered from the bottom of the sea, in different parts of the globe, almost £100,000 for the English and Dutch merchants which had been lost by shipwreck." (See *Trans. Devon. Assoc.* xii. 495).

VI. TEIGNMOUTH visited by the DANES, A.D. 787 ?

Mr. S. H. Slade, of Torquay, has favoured me with the loan of an oblong pamphlet, 6.5 × 4.25 inches, and consisting of 6 unnumbered pages only, the first of which is occupied by a quaint map of Devonshire, whilst the remaining five are devoted to ten numbered paragraphs. It bears neither date nor author's name, is headed " Devonshire Chapter ix," and the bottom of the last page has the word " Cornwall" so placed as to show that it was to be the first word on an immediately succeeding page. In short, there can be no doubt that it is the Devonshire Section of a work descriptive of England, or perhaps of Britain. It contains internal evidence of having been written before 1676, and is said by experts to be the work of John Speed (1542-1629). See P.S., p. 149.

The following statement occurs in it :—

"The *Danes* at *Teigne-mouth* first entred for the invasion of this Land, about the year of Christ 787, unto whom *Britrick* King of the *West Saxons* sent the *Steward* of his house to know their intents, whom resistantly they slew: yet were they forced back to their Ships by the Inhabitants, though long they stayed not, but eagerly pursued their begun enterprises." (par. 4.)

The *Anglo-Saxon Chronicle* (Bohn's ed., 1859, p. 341) has the following statements :—

"A. 784. This year . . . Bertric obtained the kingdom of the West-Saxons, and he reigned sixteen years, and his body lies at Wareham."

"A. 787. This year king Bertric took to wife Eadburga, King Offa's daughter; and in his days first came three ships of Northmen, out of Hæretha-land [Denmark]. And then the reve* rode to the place and would have driven them to the king's town, because he knew not who they were: and they there slew him. These were the first ships of Danish-men which sought the land of the English nation."

There can be no doubt that the "Britrick" of the one passage is identical with the "Bertric" of the other. Teignmouth in Devonshire and Tynemouth in Northumberland are often confounded; and this is not surprising, at least in the present day, since each of the names is popularly pronounced *Tin-mouth*. Speed clearly understood the place mentioned to be the Devonshire town. It may be of interest, therefore, to see what mention is made of the incident by other writers.

Ethelwerd, whose *Chronicle* is usually assigned to the 10th century, says, "Whilst the pious king Bertric was reigning over the western parts of the English, and the innocent people spread through their plains were enjoying themselves in tranquility and yoking their oxen to the plough, suddenly there arrived on the coast a fleet of Danes, not large, but of three ships only: this was their first arrival. When this became known, the king's officer, who was already stopping in the town of Dorchester, leaped on his horse and galloped forwards with a few men to the port, thinking that they

---

* "Since called sheriff; *i.e.* the *reve*, or steward, of the shire.—INGRAM."

were merchants rather than enemies, and, commanding them in an authoritative tone, ordered them to be made to go to the royal city; but he was slain on the spot by them and all who were with him.   The name of the officer was Beaduherd." (*Ethelwerd's Chronicle.* Ed. by Dr. Giles. Bohn, 1866, p. 19.)

According to William of Malmesbury, whose *Chronicle* was probably written between 1095 and 1143, "After Cynewolf, king of the West Saxons, "for sixteen years, reigned Bertric: more studious of peace than of war, skilful in conciliating friendship, affable with foreigners, and giving great allowance to his subjects, in those matters which at least could not impair the strength of his government . . . he had already begun to indulge in indolent security, when a piratical tribe of the Danes, accustomed to live by plunder, clandestinely arriving in three ships, disturbed the tranquility of the kingdom.   This band came over expressly to ascertain the fruitfulness of the soil, and the courage of the inhabitants, as was afterwards discovered by the arrival of the multitude which overran almost the whole of Britain.   Landing then, unexpectedly, when the kingdom was in a state of profound peace, they seized upon a royal village, which was nearest them, and killed the superintendent, who had advanced with succours; but losing their booty through fear of the people, who hastened to attack them, they retired to their ships." (*William of Malmesbury's Chronicle of the Kings of England.* Ed. by Dr. Giles.   Bohn, 1866, p. 40.)

We learn from Florence of Worcester, who died in 1118, that in A D. 787, " Brihtric, king of Wessex, married Eadburga, King Offa's daughter; in his time, Danish pirates came to England with three ships.   The king's reeve hearing of their arrival, hastened to meet them with a few followers, and being in entire ignorance who they were, or whence they came, tried to drive them, unwilling as they were, to the royal vill, but they presently slew him.   These were the first Danes who landed in England." (*Chronicle of Florence of Worcester.* Ed. by T. Forester.   Bohn, 1854, p. 46)

Henry of Huntingdon, whose *Chronicle* was written in instalments from 1135 to 1154, states that in A.D. 787, " In the fourth year of his reign, Bertric took to wife Eadburga, daughter of Offa, King of Mercia, by which alliance the king's power was strengthened and his arrogance increased. In those days the Danes landed in Britain, from three ships, to plunder the country. The king's officer descrying them, set upon them incautiously, making no doubt that he should carry them captives to the king's castle; for he was ignorant who the people were who had landed, or for what purpose they had come. But he was instantly slain in the throng. He was the first Englishman killed by the Danes, but after him many myriads were slaughtered by them, and these were the first ships the Danes brought here." (*Chronicle of Henry of Huntingdon.* Ed. by T. Forester. Bohn, 1853, p. 138)

Roger de Hoveden (A.D. 1189–1201) makes the following statements respecting this first Danish landing in England:— " In the fourth year of his reign, Brithric took to wife Eadburga, the daughter of Offa, king of Mercia. Strengthened on the throne by this alliance, he gave way to pride. In these days, the Danes came to Britain, with three ships, for the sake of plunder; the king's reeve in that province, seeing this, went to meet them without taking due precautions, in order that, having captured them, he might carry them to the king's town; for he was ignorant who they were, or for what purpose they had come; but, being immediately surrounded by them he was slain. He was the first person of the English nation slain by the Danes . . . . these too were the first ships of the Danes that arrived here." (*Annals of Roger de Hoveden.* Ed. by Henry T. Riley. Bohn, 1853, i. 28.)

Roger of Wendover, who died 6th May, 1237, gives the following version of the incident :—" In the year of our Lord 790, Brithric, king of the West Saxons . . . . married the daughter of Offa, king of the Mercians, who was at that time in the height of his power; strengthened by whose alliance, he drove into France Egbert, the only one remaining of the royal race. . . . . On his expulsion the king lived in security, when a piratical band of Danes arrived in three vessels and disturbed the peace of that province. It is to be suspected that they came to spy out the fertility of the country; and this is made clearer than light by the subsequent arrival of a multitude of Danes, who filled the whole of Britain. But at this time they landed stealthily, and, attacking a royal vill in the neighbourhood, slew the king's bailiff, who gave them battle. He was the first of the English nation that was slain, but afterwards many thousands of them fell. At last a multitude of people attacked the Danes, and drove them, with the loss of their spoil, to their ships." (*Roger of Wendover's Flowers of History.* Ed. by Dr. Giles. Bohn, 1849, i. 157.)

Coming down to later times, we find that Camden, in his *Britannia*, the first edition of which appeared in 1586, described Teignmouth, in South Devon, as "a little village at the mouth of the river *Teign*, whence its name; at which the Danes, who were sent before to discover the situation and approach to Britain, first landed about A.D. 800, and, having killed the commanding officer of the place, took it for an omen of future victory, which they afterwards pursued with the most horrid cruelty over the whole island." (*Britannia.* By William Camden. Richard Gough's Translation, 2d ed., in 4 vols., 1806, i. 35.)

N.B.—The passage here cited is not from Gough's "Additions."

Risdon (1560–1640), in his *Survey of Devon*, tells the story thus:—"West Teignmouth, is an haven . . . remarkable for the Danes first arrival for the invasion of this kingdom, a nation accustomed to piracy upon the coast of France and Normandy. Here, in the year 970" [*sic*], "they landed out of their ships to discover the country for a greater force to follow; whereof the king's lieutenant, more hasty than advised, demanded their name, and cause of coming and arrival, and attempted to seize on them by force, to have presented them to the king, was himself slain. After which they so prosecuted their begun attempt in this island, with inhuman and unheard of cruelty; even unto the Norman conquest; that the very clift here red, seems yet to memorize the bloodshed and calamities of their times according to these verses :—

> In memory whereof, the clift exceeding red,
> Doth seem thereat again full fresh to bleed."

(The *Chorographical Description or Survey of the County of Devon.* By Tristram Risdon. 1811, p. 143.)

Rapin, whose *History of England* appeared first in 1724, alludes incidentally to the question now under consideration, in the following few sentences :—

"Whilst Egbert was enjoying the fruits of his victories, the Danes, who had before made two descents on England, arrived at Charmouth with thirty-five vessels."

In a foot-note on the previous "two descents," the author says "the first was in 789, at Portland." (*History of England. By M. Rapin de Thoyras. Translated, with additional Notes, by N. Tindal*, M.A., 4th ed., 1757, i. 290.)

Hume writing, in 1761, of the Danes, says, "Their first appearance in this island was in the year 787, when Brithric reigned in Wessex. A small body of them landed in that kingdom, with a view of learning the state of the country; and when the magistrate of the place questioned them concerning their enterprise, and summoned them to appear before the king, and account for their intentions, they killed him, and, flying to their ships, escaped into their own country." (*History of England*, vol. i. chap. i.)

Mr. Sharon Turner having (1807) described the murder of Cynewulf, king of Wessex (A.D. 784), says, "This melancholy catastrophe produced the dignity of Brihtric. He was of the race of Cerdic, and married Eadburga, the daughter of Offa. The year of his accession was distinguished as that in which the Danes first landed on the English shore. The gerefa of the place went out to see the strangers, who had arrived with three vessels, and was instantly killed. Their incursion was repeated on other parts of the island." (*History of the Anglo-Saxons*, 2d ed., 1807, i. 174.)

According to the Lysonses (1822), "Both Camden and Risdon say that the Danes first landed in England at West Teignmouth, in 787; but it appears to have been mistaken for Tynemouth, in Northumberland, which is certainly the Tinemutha of the Saxon Chronicle." (*Magna Britannia.* By Rev. Daniel Lysons, A.M., F.R.S., F.A.L.S., and Samuel Lysons, F.R.S., F.A.S. Vol. vi. *Devonshire*, p. 489.)
See also a passage on the question, p. v. of the same authors.

It will be seen that, with the exception of Risdon only, all the writers quoted above concur in placing the event under notice in the reign of Bertric—known also as Brihtric, or Brithric—King of Wessex, which extended from 784 to 800 A.D. Risdon's statement of "970 A.D." as the date, may probably be a clerical or typographical error in which the 9 and 7 have been transposed, so that for "970" we should, perhaps, read "790."
It is noteworthy, perhaps, that the Lysonses fall into the

error of saying that both Camden and Risdon say the date was 787; instead of which they give different dates, and neither of them gives 787. Camden's statement is "about A.D. 800," whilst Risdon says "970," but probably means "790."

There is not a corresponding approach to unanimity of opinion amongst the various writers respecting the exact *spot* at which the landing took place, as the following brief recapitulation of the foregoing quotations show:—

1. With the exception of the Lysonses, of whom more subsequently, all the writers, either explicitly or by implication, place the landing within the dominions of Bertric—the Wessex of the eighth century.

2. With the exception of Ethelwerd, no writer before the latter part of the 16th century gives any clue or opinion as to the exact spot at which the landing took place.

3. Ethelwerd, who, with the exception of the compiler of the *Anglo-Saxon Chronicle*, seems to have been the first to mention the event, and wrote within 200 years of its occurrence, states by implication that it occurred not far from Dorchester.

4. Some of the writers towards the close of the 16th century—but no one before that date—name Teignmouth as the place of landing.

5. Camden, Risdon, and Speed concur in the opinion that the Teignmouth spoken of was the town of that name on the coast of South Devon, whilst the Lysonses contend that it was Tynemouth in Northumberland.

6. M. Rapin de Thoyras states that the landing took place at Portland.

In attempting to adjudicate on the rival claims of Tynemouth, Teignmouth, and Portland—assuming that one of them was the exact spot—there seems no need for hesitation in dismissing Tynemouth. It is probably true that, as the Lysonses state, "Tynemouth in Northumberland is certainly the Tinemutha of the Saxon Chronicle;" but to this it is enough to reply that neither the Saxon nor any other Chronicle says that the landing took place at Tinemutha. Indeed, with the exception of Ethelwerd's Chronicle, not one of them ventures to give any name.

We have seen, moreover, that it was in Wessex, and therefore not in Northumbria, but certainly on the south coast, somewhere in Hampshire or west of that county.

It is to be feared that the Wessex test is scarcely less fatal to Teignmouth in Devonshire, inasmuch as there seems to be no reason to believe that the Wessex of the eighth century— Bertric's Wessex—included a foot of coast west of the river Axe.

We learn from *Ethelwerd's Chronicle*, written, it will be remembered, much sooner after the event than any other of the Chronicles, except the Anglo-Saxon only, and with fuller detail of the circumstances, that the place of landing was a port such as merchants might be expected to visit; that it was within a comparatively easy gallop of Dorchester; that Dorchester was, apparently, a royal city; and that the king's officer wished to take the visitors thither.

It must not be forgotten, however, that there are two Dorchesters, one in Dorset, the other in Oxfordshire. The Dorsetshire town was certainly in the Wessex of the eighth century, but whether its namesake was also included in that kingdom is anything but certain. The county of Oxford is always regarded as having formed a part of the kingdom of Mercia.

Be this as it may, the fact that the Oxford Dorchester is at least 60 miles from the coast, whilst that in Dorsetshire is barely 6, is, no doubt, conclusive in favour of the Dorset town, inasmuch as a ride of 6 miles, but not of 60, harmonizes well with Ethelwerd's statement, that "the king's officer, who was already stopping in the town of Dorchester, leaped on his horse and galloped forwards with a few men to the port."

It will not be out of place to remark here that the Dorsetshire town was called "Villa Regalis," whilst that in Oxfordshire was called "Villa Episcopalis," it having been given to Bishop Birinus, there to settle his see. (*Bede's Eccles. Hist.* Ed. by Dr. Giles, 3d ed. Bohn, 1859, p. 119.)

That part of the coast to which Dorchester is nearest, is about a mile east of Weymouth, and therefore in the neighbourhood of Portland, where Rapin says the landing was made.

With the evidence at present to hand, it seems certain that the first landing of the Danes was not at Tynemouth in Northumberland, improbable that it was at Teignmouth in South Devon, but in all probability it occurred at some spot on the western shore of Weymouth Bay.

VII. WOLCOT, Dr. John = "Peter Pindar."

(Copied from the Note Book of Mr. O. Blewitt, where it is said to have been "Written by Walter Prideaux, of Kingsbridge.")

"Doctor John Wolcot, commonly called Peter Pindar, was born in Dodbrooke, in the county of Devon, it is believed in the year 1739, but the Register of the Parish of Dodbrooke having been in the custody of Mr. Gillard, the Churchwarden, when his house at Well was burnt, the register was unfortunately destroyed, by which means the exact period of his birth cannot be found. His father was a surgeon and apothecary of considerable eminence in his day, and gave his son a good classical education under a Mr. John Morris, an exceedingly clever man, who kept a large boarding and grammar school in the town of Kingsbridge, which adjoins the village of Dodbrooke, where the Doctor was born. The house in which that event took place, on the death of his father, became his property, and was sold by him 30 years since to the Rev. Nath¹ Wells, who resided in it till his death . . . .

"When he had finished his education, the Doctor was placed as an apprentice with his uncle, who was a surgeon of great respectability and large practice at Fowey, in Cornwall, with whom he served out his time, and" [then] "attended the hospitals to complete himself in his profession. Amongst his uncle's patients was the Trelawny family" [residing, no doubt, at Trelawny, in the parish of Pelynt, about 6 miles E.N.E. from Fowey], "with whom the Doctor was very intimate, and of whose abilities they had a high opinion.

"Not long after the completion of his studies, and when he was not fixed as to the place in which he should settle in business, Sir Wᵐ Trelawny was appointed Govʳ of Jamaica. Wolcot, on hearing it, applied to him to be taken out as his Surgeon, when Sir William expressed great regret at having before engaged to take out another young man in that capacity, but told him if he could get a diploma, of which Sir William had little doubt, he would most willingly take him out as his Physician.

"Upon this Wolcot immediately applied to Doctors Huxham of Plymouth and another Physician there, from whom he obtained the necessary certificate of his capability, and immediately procured a diploma as an M.D. On being asked by an intimate friend and old schoolfellow of his (in the presence of the writer of this), who was acquainted with

Huxham, how he had contrived to prevail on old Dr. Huxham to sign the certificate, ' Oh,' says Wolcot, ' I found Huxham fond of flummery, I gave it to him liberally, he swallowed it greedily, and signed the certificate readily.'

" On obtaining his diploma he accompanied the Govr to Jamaica, but being a very young man, and several old men, who had settled there, running away with all the practice, he found his success did not answer his expectat^{ns}, and expressed thoughts of returning to England, when the Gov. said to him one day, ' Doctor, I wish you was a Parson, as I should then most likely soon have it in my power to provide for you handsomely.' Wolcot asked him if he was serious, and upon his saying he really was, replied, ' Then I will go to England, get ordained directly, and return to Jamaica ;' and he did accordingly come to England, applied to the Bishop of London, and after being examined, the Bishop ordained him to preach the gospel in foreign parts ; upon which he returned to Jamaica in full hopes and expectation of the promised living, but here again he was disappointed, as almost immed^y after his return the Governor died, before he had an opportunity of presenting him with the promised preferment.

" On the death of the Governor the Doctor returned to England, and settled at Truro, where he would have had a large practice, but unfortunately for his prospects, Truro was a Borough Town, and the members were returned through the influence of Lord Falmouth, whose interest being opposed by Sir Fra^s Basset, Wolcot took the part of Lord Falmouth, and giving way to his poetic vein, he held up the opposite party, who were the most numerous and proved successful in overthrowing his lordship's interest in the Borough, in a most caustic satire, which the writer of this has seen in manuscript, and been almost convulsed with laughter at reading it.

" The consequence of this talent for rhyming at Falmouth " [sic ? Truro] " was the loss of his practice, two of the most prominent characters attacked by him, being medical men in large practice as Surgeons and Apothecaries, did everything in their power to destroy it. Finding his business gone, he then removed to London, and soon after published his *Ode to the Reviewers*, as a prelude to his *Lyric Odes* addressed to the painters, which were his first publications, and finding after a little time that his satires took with the public, he afterwards gave himself up entirely to writing and publishing his poetic pieces, which speak for themselves ; and although some of them are coarse, and perhaps not to be defended as to their propriety, still the genuineness and originality of their wit are undeniable.

"The Doctor never afterwards left London, except now and then to visit his uncle at Dartmouth, and his sisters at Fowey; but those visits were of short duration, London being the only place in which he could find and enjoy the society he delighted in, and have his relish for music, to which he was much devoted, sufficiently gratified.

"He lived to a very advanced age, and died at Somers-town; and at his own earnest desire was buried at St. Paul's, Covent Garden, close to the remains of Butler, the author of Hudibras."

P.S.—Since this Paper was in type, I have obtained a copy of the work of which the "pamphlet," mentioned and quoted on pp. 139-140 above, is a Section. It is entitled "England Wales Scotland and Ireland Described and Abridged With yᵉ Historic Relation of things worthy memory from a farr Larger Voulume Done by John Speed Anno Cum privilegio 1627."

THE GEOLOGY OF DAWLISH.

BY W. A. E. USSHER, F.G.S.

(WITH THE PERMISSION OF THE DIRECTOR-GENERAL OF THE GEOLOGICAL SURVEY.)

(Read at Dawlish, July, 1881.)

IN a previous paper "On the Mouth of the River Exe," read at Paignton, 1878, a brief allusion was made to the Triassic rocks of the Dawlish district, but no detailed description of the geology of this most interesting neighbourhood, as exemplified in the fine railway cliff coast sections, was attempted beyond the Post Tertiary phenomena. I now propose to supply this deficiency, devoting some preliminary remarks to the gravels.

Gravels.—Upon Langstone Point the relics of an old river deposit are observable. The gravel is finely exposed in the railway cutting for nearly 50 chains from the Point toward Dawlish. It has been mentioned by De la Beche and Godwin-Austin, and figured by Mr. Parfitt. The composition of the deposit where best exposed was given in my paper above referred to. The coarser detritus, consisting of subangular and well-worn fragments derived from Cretaceous and Triassic rocks, is invariably overlain by red sand, generally with an intervening bed of ancient alluvial loam. The sand overlapping the gravel and loam, and resting directly upon soft Triassic sandstones, renders the termination of the gravel patch toward Dawlish exceedingly indefinite. The cliffs range from 80 to 120 feet in height. At a gully in the upper part of the cliff, near the termination of the gravel, the surface is at 125 feet above the sea. Near Langstone Point the gravel occupies an eroded hollow in the Trias between two faults, giving it the appearance of a faulted displacement. At about 38 chains, and at 20 chains from

Dawlish Station, gravels cap the cliff, which is about 80 feet in height.

The low cliff, extending for 12 chains from the Hotel opposite the Railway Station, is composed of rounded and subangular stones of grit, &c., flint and chert, often of large size and, seemingly, unstratified. The exposure behind the Hotel is from 15 to 20 feet in height. Similar gravel occurs on the S. margin of the Dawlish-water alluvium, resting on Triassic sandstones.

Apart from its thickness and extent, the gravel patch near Langstone Point is of interest, owing to the preservation of the old alluvial loam upon it. The regenerated Triassic sand upon the alluvial deposits may be a Head of materials washed from higher ground by rains, &c. Although the configuration of the ground in the immediate vicinity of the gravel does not lend itself readily to this idea, yet it is difficult, on the one hand, to account for the absence of signs of fluviatile deposition in it, which would be likely to produce a discolouration of the material; and on the other, to believe that the friable alluvial deposits on the gravel would have escaped denudation in an exposed site without some such covering as the shedding of atmospheric *débris* would be likely to have afforded.

On the hill between Dawlish and Cliff Cottage a patch of gravel occurs at a height of about 160 feet above the sea. It is exposed by the road to Teignmouth, and consists of subangular and well-worn fragments derived from the Triassic breccia, with flint and chert, resting unevenly upon the Triassic rocks.

By the stream gully E. of Country House, old river gravel, consisting of flint, chert, grit, and igneous fragments in brown loam, caps the cliff, which is about 140 feet high. At the end of the road to the beach from Lower Holcombe, near the mouth of the Clerk Rock Tunnel, a trace of old river gravel occurs, at 60 to 70 feet above the sea.

The positions of the higher gravel patches, in sites totally distinct from the present lines of drainage, and at such height above the sea, indicate a date of deposition sufficiently remote to have permitted the obliteration of their connection with the present stream valleys, and to have enabled the sea to cut back the ancient coast line (breached by their embouchures) to the present line of cliffs.

There is no means of correlating such gravels with the raised beaches, as the soft secondary rocks between Portland Bill and Hope's Nose have been cut back too far to allow of the preservation of any portion of the coast line of the raised beach period. It is not improbable that the higher gravel patches may be of older date than the raised beaches, whilst the Dawlish gravel may have been, roughly speaking, contemporaneous. The Dawlish gravel indicates the selection of the present line of drainage, and during the raised beach period the streams appear to have flowed in the valleys now tenanted by them.

The gravels on Langstone Point cliffs seem to mark the site of an old line of drainage subsequently deserted for sites marked by the present valleys to N. and S. of it.

Similarly, the higher gravels on S. of Dawlish may represent a deserted line of drainage in part roughly coincident with that taken by the principal tributary of the Dawlish-water.

The present alluvial flat bordering the Dawlish-water represents the erosion of the old bed, of which the bordering gravels formed a part, during an elevation, possibly that which carried up the old beaches ; and likewise denotes the decreasing volume and force of the stream.

The presence of large boulders of igneous and other rocks in the beds or gravels of the Dawlish-water or its tributaries, no matter how far up stream (as at Ashcombe, *vide* paper by Mr. Pycroft) they may be found, are plainly referable to the disintegration of the Triassic breccia in which the stream courses are situated. The common occurrence of boulders of large size in the breccia near Haldon, and its rubbly and friable character, afford especial facilities for the manufacture of boulder stream gravels.

Upper Greensand Area.—The conspicuous landmarks of Great and Little Haldon are the remnants of an old plain of Cretaceous rocks, which may have abutted on the flanks of Dartmoor on the west, and was continuous with the Blackdown Range on the east. Standing upon either summit and gazing over the fertile vales and grassy knolls of the Triassic area at one's feet to the horizon line of the Blackdowns, some idea of the extensive denudation from which the country has suffered in Post Cretaceous times cannot fail to be suggested. The broad valley excavated by the Exe and its tributaries lies mapped out at the observer's feet, and beyond, the elevated range of Woodbury Common, forming the feature of the Lower Keuper Pebble Beds, separates the drainage of the Exe from that of the Otter.

The Haldons are capped by that remarkable accumulation of loam and clay, with broken unworn flint and chert stones, which cover the summit levels of the Blackdowns. But besides this, waterworn materials are here and there scattered over Haldon; schorlaceous fragments, which may have been transported from the Dartmoor area at a time when the Cretaceous tableland abutted against its flanks, and well-worn flints, probably due to the reassortment of the clay with flints in the stream courses of that long bygone time. These waterworn materials appear to have been attributed by Mr. Godwin-Austen to marine action. There can be little doubt that the Cretaceous high-lands of Devon are portions of a great plain of marine denudation, whether the uplifted bed of the Cretaceous sea, or the result of a depression of Cretaceous strata in tertiary times, I do not pretend to say; if the latter, the waterworn materials in question may be the relics of Tertiary deposits.

The presence of such quantities of flint as occur on Haldon affords an excellent proof of the westerly overlap of the Cretaceous subdivisions. If they are the relics of chalk with flints, disintegrated by atmospheric and other causes, *in situ*, which appears almost certain, we have a hiatus between them and the greensands on which they rest, of the lithological equivalents of the chalk without flints and the upper beds of the Upper Greensand, although the chloritic marl may be in part represented by the coarser grained beds forming the uppermost part of the Haldon greensand.

By this extension of chalk *débris* the presence of flints in the old and more modern gravels is amply accounted for.

Lower Trias.—In the railway cutting between Langstone Point and Dawlish no less than 30 faults are visible. The amount of downthrow can in most cases be estimated, as seams of breccia are of frequent occurrence in the most part of the sandstone cliffs, and beds of sandstone occur in the parts of the cliff in which breccia prevails.

Langstone Point is composed of red-brown sand rock, closely studded with subangular fragments of grit, jaspideous rock, quartz, &c., and analagous to the breccia in Exmouth Shrubbery. A nearly vertical fault line, having a direction N. 20° W. and S. 20° E., throws similar breccia, but with bands and beds of sand rock, against the breccia of Langstone Point.

For 13 chains from Langstone Point the cliff is composed of breccia with intercalated seams and beds of sandstone, disturbed by 5 faults, at 1, 4, 5, 2 chains apart, respectively. The downthrow of the first of these faults cannot be estimated;

it is probably small. The respective amounts of throw of the other faults are 6 inches, 1 foot, 5 feet to S.E., and 4 feet to S.E.

At from 13 to 21 chains from the Point the intercalation of sandstone with breccia becomes more evenly balanced, the former finally prevailing. In this distance of 8 chains, no less than 8 faults are observable, with north-easterly downthrows of from 2 to 6 feet, with the exception of 2 small faults with 8-inch shifts in an opposite direction.

At 21 chains from the Point the cliff is composed of red sand rock, with irregular beds of breccia.

At from 28 to 54 chains from the Point, red sand rock forms the cliff, breccia being very occasionally represented by impersistent seams.

At 25 chains from the Point, a crack intersects the cliff; it may be a reversed fault, in which case its downthrow would be on S.E. side and about 5 feet; but there is nothing to negative the idea that its hade may be normal and its downthrow very considerable. Below the gorge, near the top of the cliff, at about 43 chains from the Point, the sandstones contain corrugated slabs of black ironstone [pan], and are intersected by a crack, which may mark a fault of considerable amount.

At 5 chains from the last-mentioned spot, near the termination of the old river gravel patch on the cliff, a crack or fault traverses the sandstones. In this, as in the two preceding cases, owing to the homogeneous character of the sand rock, and the impersistent indications of its bedding planes, no clue as to the effect of the faults (if such) is afforded. It seems very probable that one of the cracks, at least, may be a fault of importance, tending to repeat the sandstone beds for a considerable distance; but it might reasonably be asked, if such were the case, would not the dislocation have a marked visible effect on the relations of the sandstones and breccias in inland localities? To this objection the very unstable lithological character of the Lower Triassic rocks is a sufficient answer; for, with the exception of the Langstone Point fault, which acts as a general lithological boundary line for 2 miles from the coast, no faults can be traced with certainty in inland localities, where the upper beds of the Lower Trias are alone affected.

At 50 chains from the Point, 2 tiny faults of 6 inches counteract one another. From this spot to a bridge over the railway, 4 chains further on, the sandstones contain a bed of breccia and a seam of loam, displaced by 2 faults apparently from 2 to 5 feet in downthrow. At the bridge the section is wholly composed of rock sand.

At from 3 to 10 chains from the bridge, the presence of marked beds of breccia and seams of pan render the smallest faults distinguishable. Eleven small faults are visible in a distance of 6 chains, but the majority are subsidiary cracks, so that they may be embraced in 5 or 6 distinct faults with downthrows of from 1 to 3 feet. Near this, at from 24 to 36 chains from Dawlish Station, the railway cutting is concealed by grass and scrub. The beds concealed appear to be sandstones, with beds of breccia and seams of pan.

At from 12 to 15 chains from Dawlish Station, the cliff is chiefly composed of breccia, with intercalated beds of sandstone. In this part of the cliff 2 faults occur with north-easterly throws; one of them may be of some importance, as sandstone is thrown down by it, but the other has a downthrow of 2½ feet only. Indications of another fault are visible at about 16 chains from Dawlish Station, of the same indefinite character as in the case of the three cracks, distant respectively 25, 44, and 48 chains from Langstone Point.

On crossing the alluvium of Dawlish Water, cliffs composed of red sand rock are visible behind the houses and for some distance southward; they are intersected by a fault in one spot.

A nearly N. and S. fault cuts across the tunnel-mouth on the S. of Dawlish beach, the seaward face of the cliff-promontory, in which the tunnel has been excavated, being thrown down by it. An interesting section is afforded in the cliff at the gentlemen's bathing-place; a small projection from the promontory has been thrust up between converging faults, and forms a cliff more than 100 feet in height, composed of breccia with a conical capping of sandstone; sandstones upon breccia being let down against it on the N., and massive bedded red sandstones, let down on the S., are exposed in the fine railway-cutting cliff, the south entrance to the tunnel being in a receding cliff face along the hade of the fault. This fault has a downthrow of 100 feet or more. A thick bed of sandstone, about half-way up the cliff on the downthrown side, exhibits false bedding on a large scale. The next tunnel is driven through a promontory of breccia, which dips under the sandstones. From this point to Clerk Rock continuous examination of the cliffs is almost impossible, owing to the numerous tunnels and the high sea wall, which precludes observation of the cliffs from the beach.

A fault at the S. entrance to the second tunnel from

Dawlish throws the breccia against an irregularly intercalated series of sandstones and breccia (somewhat similar to that near Langstone Point), much cut up by faults between the tunnels. Twelve faults are visible, but owing to the variability of the beds affected, their downthrows can seldom be ascertained with any degree of certainty. In a distance of a quarter of a mile, proceeding from N. to S., we have breccia with a thick mass of sandstone, faulted against sandstone (or sand rock), with a thick bed of breccia displaced by a fault, which appears to have a downthrow of about 20 feet. The next fault brings on breccia upon a thick stratum of sandstone resting upon breccia with intercalated beds of sandstone, faulted against sandstone upon sandstone partly brecciated upon breccia with beds of sandstone upon breccia; here we have a gradual downward passage into breccia. By the next faults a mass of breccia is thrust up, breccia upon sandstone being thrown down against it. What appears to be the base of the last-mentioned sandstone, resting on breccia, is next brought up by fault, being cut off against sandstone with a thick bed of breccia, faulted against an intercalated series of breccia, upon sandstone, upon breccia, upon sandstone, upon sandstone with beds of breccia. The next fault brings on sandstones upon sandstones with beds of breccia upon breccia; a succession slightly disturbed by a fault and cut off against the most southerly patch of recognisable sandstone in this part of the Lower Trias, which rests upon breccia containing no further distinguishable masses of sandstone. The breccia affords, N.E. to N.N.E., dips, of from 7° to 10°. It is affected by 3 or more faults near the entrance to the tunnel on N. of Clerk Rock.

From the sections between Clerk Rock and the gentlemen's bathing-place, one would be inclined to regard the transition from sandstone to breccia as gradual and irregular, presenting some such downward succession as the following:—Sandstone, breccia, sandstone, breccia, sandstone, sandstone with beds of breccia, or breccia with beds of sandstone, breccia. But the distinction between the beds of sandstone and breccia might at any time be lost through irregularity of intercalation.

It now becomes very difficult to assign their true place to the sandstones faulted down at the gentlemen's bathing cove; they are either represented by the intercalated series just described, which would then be a modified continuation of them repeated by fault; or the sandstones rest upon a mass of breccia, separating them from a downward succession of intercalated sandstones and breccias, before the breccia finally prevails. It seems probable that the sandstones and breccias with intercalated sandstone beds, may be faulted representatives of the lower part of the beds between Dawlish and Langstone Point. In the Langstone and Dawlish section, were we to judge by lithological analogy, the parts of the cliff composed wholly of sandstone would appear to be the uppermost, and the intercalated sandstones and breccias a downward passage into breccia, regarding the breccia of which Langstone Point is composed as the lowest. But this does not appear to be the case; for on tracing the rocks by lithological characters, we find that the Langstone Point breccia terminates, forming a kind of outlier on sandstones, at Kenton, which appearance could not be entirely accounted for by faults. The faulted patches of Lower Trias by the Exe at Lympstone are associated with breccia, and there is every reason to think that they form the upper beds of the Lower Trias, which is almost entirely composed of sandstone between Honiton's Clist and Topsham. Impersistent bands of breccia occur in the upper part of the Lower Trias near St. George's Clist and Bishop's Clist; so that there may be a considerable amount of breccia in the upper part of the sandstones between Powderham and Exmouth, and no hard and fast stratigraphical boundaries can be inferred from the occurrence of breccia in mass in the sandstone area.

In South Devon the deposition of breceia (during the later stages of the Lower Trias) may have been irregularly protracted at various periods leading to its inosculation with the sandstones, such appearances being mainly due to variable sources of derivation and the facilities afforded for the spread of coarser materials outward from the then existing coasts.

In endeavouring to arrive at an estimate of the thickness represented by the coast section between Dawlish and Langstone Point, a distance of a mile and a quarter, 25 of the faults mentioned may be ignored as too insignificant to affect the results. It is quite possible that the effect of one or more of the remaining faults may be such as to reduplicate the beds, in which case the distance would have to be reduced to one-half, or 50 chains; but, as we have seen, there is no means of distinguishing the displacements produced.

If the whole distance, $1\frac{1}{4}$ mile, be taken, an average dip of 8° would give a thickness of more than 900 feet, ignoring faults. If, however, we take half the distance, to allow for possible reduplication by fault, a dip of 8° would give a thickness of about 460 feet, and a dip of 10° a thickness of more than 600 feet. The former (460 feet) estimate appears to me to be the least open to objection, because the low dips furnished by the sandstones of the Honiton's Clist district do not seem to argue any great thickness for the upper part of the Lower Trias, where sand prevails.

The breccia thrown against Middle Trias marls by fault, at the end of the Shrubbery at Exmouth, as well as that which forms Langstone Point, may belong to the uppermost beds of the Lower Trias, and pass into pure sandstones northward.

THE TRIAS AT DAWLISH.

BY G. WAREING ORMEROD, M.A., F.G.S.

(Read at Dawlish, July, 1881.)

THE continuous line of Trias that forms the cliffs bordering a considerable part of the southerly sea coast of Devon has been described by various authors (see Appendix), so that a memoir relating to it would for the most part repeat a well-known tale. Within the last few years, however, " Pseudo-morphous Crystals" of salt were discovered near Sidmouth by myself; bones of a " Labyrinthodon " near Sidmouth by Mr. Johnston Lavis; bones of the "Hyperodapedon" at the mouth of the Otter by Mr. Whittaker; and that " Murchisonite " was the characteristic of certain beds near Dawlish by myself.

The " Keuper " crops out from under the chalk near Branscombe Mouth and extends to Exmouth, where the " Bunter " appears, and extends thence to near Babbacombe Bay; the portion of this district that lies between the Ex and the Teign will be the subject of this memoir.

At the western end of the Beacon at Exmouth a bed, consisting mostly of small angular and subangular fragments of hard brown rock, Lydian stone, and porphyry crops out from below soft red and grey sandy beds; this conglomerate so closely resembles one at Cockwood, on the right bank of the Ex, and also the conglomerate overlying a red sandy rock where the road from Cofton to Kenton crosses that from Staplake to Mowlish, that there can scarcely be a doubt that the Beacon beds are a portion of those just mentioned, and that they form the upper part of the Bunter.

Between Cofton Chapel and Cofton Cross a soft red rock crops out from under this conglomerate, and may be traced from Staplake brook, on the north-west, to the cliffs west of Langstone Point. Near Mowlish, and in a cutting by the roadside, about half a mile to the south-west of Cofton Chapel, detached crystals of Murchisonite occur in this sandstone. The existence of Murchisonite at Dawlish has been known for many years; it has also been found at Heavitree near Exeter, and at Arrau. It is an opalescent felspar, possessing a third cleavage, in addition to the two at right angles to each other, of Orthoclase; and it is upon this third cleavage plane that the opalescent play of light is observable. This mineral, as found at Dawlish, according to the analysis of Mr. R. Phillips as given in Greg and Letsome's *Mineralogy*, consists of silica 68·6, alumina 16·6, potash 14·8. A fault running in a northerly direction passes to the west of Langstone Point, but I have not been able to decide the exact position in the Bunter beds of the rock at that point. Soft sandy beds, in which Murchisonite has not been detected, form the cliffs between Langstone Point and the steps at the Dawlish Coastguard Station, where they are succeeded by a soft sandy conglomerate, containing small angular and subangular fragments of rocks and Murchisonite, which can be traced along the line of strike by Gatehouse, Gulliford, and Newhouse, for a distance of about two miles and a half, to the entrance to the grounds of the parsonage at Mamhead and the cross roads at Whistlade, where the lower part of the bed may be seen; Dawlish Water may, as a general line, be considered its western boundary. Below this bed a soft sandy rock with Murchisonite occurs, as shown in the cliffs to the south of Dawlish. Up to this place Murchisonite is found mostly in small detached crystals, in soft rock; but the underlying rocks are of a more compact nature than those that have been described. These rocks, being those between the Second Tunnel and Smuggler's Lane, consist of a conglomerate composed of angular and subangular fragments of hard shale, black siliceous rock, quartz, carbonate of lime, porphyry, granite, limestone with and without organic remains, and Murchisonite both in the porphyritic and granitic pebbles, and in detached crystals. Between Smuggler's Lane to within a short distance of the Teignmouth Railway Tunnel, the cliffs consist of an alternation of soft marly and pebbly beds, with in some places grey bands; in the conglomerate of the low cliff to the south of the tunnel mouth, Murchisonite may be found occasionally, and large rounded blocks of various descriptions of rock, some three feet in length, occur. The level part of Teignmouth is built for the most part on gravel from the sea, but the Trias may be traced on the rising ground at the back, and in the low cliffs by Bitton and the northerly end of Shaldon Bridge. At the Ness, on the south side of the Teign, and from thence to Maidencombe, the upper beds are of a conglomerate very similar to that at Shaldon Bridge; below these there are beds of soft red rock, and these lie upon a coarse conglomerate containing large rounded fragments of limestone and granitoid rocks. Near Petit Tor the nearly continuous cliff exposure of the Trias ceases, giving place to the Devonian beds of Mary Church and Babbacombe. A bed of recomposed Trias, containing fragments of flint and other rocks, overlies the Trias, at the station at Dawlish and the cliffs between that place and Langstone Point; it also occurs near Beavis Bridge, Spratford, Rixtail, and Ideford, to the west of the Exe, and between Otterton and Ladram Bay to the east of that river.

The inland exposure of the Trias between the Exe and the Teign is bounded by Carbonaceous beds; these, for the greater part of the distance between Exeter and the Belvidere on Great Haldon, contain beds of porphyry, and near Bishopsteignton beds of greenstone; a considerable area of the Trias is capped by the Greensand on Great and Little Haldon.

APPENDIX.

LIST OF THE CHIEF MEMOIRS AND OTHER. PUBLICATIONS RELATING TO THE TRIAS OF SOUTH DEVON.

From the Publications of the Geological Society.

AUSTEN (R. A. C. Godwin). "On the part of Devonshire between the Exe and Berry Head, and the coast and Dartmoor." Vol. ii. *Pro.* p. 414.

——————————— "On the Geology of the south-east of Devonshire." Vol. vi. *Trans.* 2nd series, p. 433; vol. ii. *Pro.* p. 584.

BUCKLAND (Rev. Prof.) "On the occurrence of Keuper Sandstone in the Upper Region of the New Red Sandstone formation or Poikilitic System in England and Wales." Vol. ii. *Pro.* p. 453.

——————————— "On the excavation of Valleys by Diluvial Action, as illustrated by a succession of Valleys which intersect the south coast of Dorset and Devon." Vol. i. *Trans.* 2nd series, p. 95.

DAVIDSON (T.) "Notes on the Brachiopoda hitherto obtained from the 'Pebble Bed' of Budleigh Salterton, near Exmouth, in Devonshire." Vol. xxvi. *Q. J.* p. 70.

DE LA BECHE (Sir H. T.) "Remarks on the Geology of the south coast of England from Bridport Harbour, Dorset, to Babbacombe Bay, Devon." Vol. i. *Trans.* 2nd series, p. 40.

——————————— "On the Geology of Tor and Babbacombe Bays, Devon." Vol. iii. *Trans.* 2nd series, p. 31; vol. i. *Pro.* p. 31.

DE LA BECHE (Sir H. T.) "Note on Trappean Rocks associated with the New Red Sandstone of Devonshire." Vol. ii. *Pro.* p. 196.

EDGELL (A. W.) "Notes on some Lamellibranchs of the Budleigh Salterton Pebbles." Vol. xxx. *Q. J.* p. 45.

HOLL (H. B.) "On the older Rocks of South Devon and East Cornwall." Vol. xxii. *Q. J.* p. 400.

JOHNSTON-LAVIS (H. J.) "On the Triassic Strata which are exposed in the cliff sections near Sidmouth; and a note on the occurrence of an Ossiferous Zone containing Bones of a Labyrinthodon." Vol. xxxii. *Q. J.* p. 274.

MURCHISON (Sir R. J.) and SEDGWICK (Prof.) "On the Physical Structure of Devonshire, and on the Subdivisions and Geological relations of its old Stratified Deposits." Vol. v. *Trans.* 2nd series, p. 633; vol. i. *Pro.* p. 556.

ORMEROD (G. W.) "On the 'Waterstone Beds' of the Keuper, and on Pseudomorphous Crystals of Chloride of Sodium in Somersetshire and Devon." Vol. xxiv. *Q. J.* p. 546; vol. xxv. *Q. J.* p. 50.

———————— "On the Murchisonite Beds of the Estuary of the Exe, and an attempt to classify the beds of the Trias thereby." Vol. xxxi. *Q. J.* p. 346.

USSHER (W. A. E.) "On the Triassic Rocks of Somerset and Devon." Vol. xxxii. *Q. J.* p. 367.

———————— "On the Chronological Value of the Triassic Strata of the South Western Counties." Vol. xxxiv. *Q. J.* p. 459.

WHITAKER (W.) "On the succession of Beds in the 'New Red' on the south coast of Devon, and on the locality of a new specimen of Hyperodapedon." Vol. xxv. *Q. J.* p. 152.

Reports of the Plymouth Institution.

PENGELLY (W.) "The Red Sandstones and Conglomerates of Devonshire." Part I. 1861–2, p. 13.

———————— "The Red Sandstones, Conglomerates and Marls of Devonshire." Part II. 1862–3, p. 13.

———————— "The Red Sandstones, Conglomerates and Marls of Devonshire." Part III. 1864–5, p. 13.

Report of Devon Association, 1863.

PENGELLY (W.) "On the Chronological Value of the New Red Sandstone System of Devonshire." p. 31.

CONYBEARE (W. D.) and PHILLIPS (W.) "Outlines of the Geology of England and Wales, 1822." pp. 293–295.

DE LA BECHE (H. T.) "Report on the Geology of Cornwall, Devon, and West Somerset, 1839." pp. 204–208.

NOTES ON THE SUBMARINE GEOLOGY OF THE ENGLISH CHANNEL OFF THE COAST OF SOUTH DEVON.

PART II.

BY ARTHUR R. HUNT, M.A., F.G.S.

(Read at Dawlish, July, 1881.)

SINCE the last meeting of this Association, I have been again indebted to Mr. Walter M. Baynes and the intelligent crew of his trawler, the *Pelican*, for additional specimens of stones from the English Channel. Though not numerous, being only four in number, without reckoning a set of flints, two of them are of considerable interest, and will, I think, justify my resuming my notes on the submarine geology of the English Channel without waiting for further material.

15 and 16. On the 27th September, 1880, I accompanied Mr. W. M. Baynes to Brixham, to see two stones, numbers 15 and 16, that had been taken—No. 15 on the 22nd of that month, No. 16 on the 24th, and both in the same locality; viz., about 16 miles south of the Start. Thinking it better to preserve these stones entire, instead of keeping only hand specimens, I agreed with the crew to land them at Torquay; this was done the same morning, and they were conveyed to my own residence, Southwood. The largest (No. 15) is fairly symmetrical in shape, its greatest dimensions being about 2 feet 8 inches × 1 foot 8 inches × 1 foot 6 inches; whilst in form it approaches an oblique rhomboidal prism. As will be seen in Mr. Tawney's description in the appendix, it is a gabbro, a purplish and green mottled rock with opaque white spots. An interesting feature in this stone is a small patch of a sedimentary slaty rock attached to one of its sides, and described by Mr. Tawney, who saw a piece of it, as "killas." So that this comparatively

L 2

small block, brought up in a fishing-net from the bottom of the sea, is an instance of what is not always easy to get even on land ; viz., a good specimen in small compass of a junction between a stratified and a non-stratified rock.   The smaller stone (No. 16) is of irregular shape, and its greatest dimensions 2 feet 6 inches × 1 foot 10 inches × 1 foot 2 inches.   Its chief component seems to be actinolite.   It was taken in the same locality as the stone previously described, viz., 16 miles south of the Start.

17. On the 30th September, 1880, the *Pelican's* crew took another stone (No. 17), whose weight they estimated at 7 or 8 cwt., and whose form they described as being " more three-cornered " than the gabbro first described.   This stone (No. 17) Mr. Tawney pronounces to be " a diabase of ordinary type."   It was trawled some 17 or 18 miles S.W. by W. of the Start.

18. In the same locality, on the 28th September, some flints were trawled.   Three were sent to me ; the largest (No. 19), weighing 1 lb. 9½ oz., now exhibited, shows no sign of the rolling action of water, and the condition of the other two is similar.

The stones I have now described add little to the knowledge we already possessed.   The three blocks were all detached, and therefore of uncertain origin, and the flints are similar to Nos. 14 and 14A, taken in the same neighbourhood, and described last year.

19. We now come to a specimen (No. 19) trawled on the 12th October, 1880, 20 miles south-west of the Eddystone, and which is of great interest as affording good evidence of the rock that forms the bed of the Channel in that locality. Shortly after it was taken, Mr. Baynes informed me that his crew had recently brought up in their trawl a small piece of granite, which they had given to him just as they found it ; that is to say, they had not broken it off a larger stone, as they usually do when saving hand specimens for me.   This piece of news was not only not satisfactory to me, but quite the reverse, as I felt sure that such a small stone was either a piece of ballast, or that at any rate nobody would believe to the contrary.   Through my lack of interest this stone remained on board Mr. Baynes's yacht for about a fortnight, and it was not till the 1st of November that I possessed myself of it.

My first glance at it convinced me that it was no ballast, and that, whatever the crew of the *Pelican* might say to the contrary, they had broken it off a larger mass.   This was very disquieting, as, unless the inconsistency could be explained, my faith in the reliability of the statements of the fishermen must necessarily be greatly shaken. On asking Mr. Baynes for further particulars, he reminded me of a fact that had escaped my memory; viz., that when the stone was taken, the *Pelican* had been fast some hours in what the crew supposed to be a wreck, and that on heaving up the trawl, the stone was found in it just as it was when sent on shore. On hearing this, the conclusion seemed inevitable that the trawl of the *Pelican* had been fast in a rock, not in a wreck, that the small stone with its one clean fracture had been torn off the parent rock by the foot-rope of the trawl, and that thus the fishermen had broken it off a larger mass without knowing it. From the state of the fragment, and the circumstances of its capture as described to me, the evidence of granite *in situ* at the bottom of the Channel seemed unanswerable; but everything depended on the accuracy of the statement that the stone had not been broken on board the *Pelican*. In order to get this information direct from the crew, at my request the master and first hand signed a certificate as to the facts. It is as follows :—

"This is to certify that the piece of granite stone taken in the trawl of the *Pelican*, about 20 miles S.W. of the Eddystone, on Tuesday, October 12th, 1880 (after the trawl had been fast for some hours in what we supposed to be a wreck), was not broken on board, but handed to Mr. W. M. Baynes just as we found it.

"GEORGE HAYDEN.*

"Witness—W. M. Baynes,   J. DYER.
      "Owner of the *Pelican*."

This certificate will probably be accepted as conclusive evidence that the fragment of granite in question was torn off a larger mass at the sea bottom; but it may possibly be objected that there is nothing to show that the larger mass was *in situ*, and that it was not a detached block too large for the trawler to move. An examination of the fragment will throw some light on this point. The dimensions are about $10\frac{1}{2} \times 4\frac{1}{2} \times 2\frac{1}{2}$ inches, and it has all the appearance of having formed part of a flat ledge of rock. It shows no signs of having been either rolled by waves, or scoured by sands, pebbles, or other agency, and in this it differs from all the detached blocks that I have seen, all of which have

---

* Master of the *Pelican*.

their angles rounded in a greater or less degree. Further, it is thin and slab-like, and in this respect differs from the trawled blocks, which have been, as a rule, so massive that it has been a matter of difficulty to knock off hand specimens. Accustomed as I am to get my own dredge fast in the sedimentary rocks of Torbay, and either to part the rope or bring away a piece of the rock in the net, the evidence of this fragment in the trawl, with its one clean fracture, is conclusive both as to the nature of the rock when it was taken, and as to the manner in which it was taken. But with those unaccustomed to this sort of geologising, a scrap of broken stone brought up in a net will, in all probability, not carry the same weight.

This stone is of especial interest for several reasons. It appears to have been taken *in situ*, and therein differs from all the detached blocks, which, for all we know to the contrary, may have been carried by the trawlers from one spot to another from time to time before being finally brought away; for it is well known the blocks frequently break through the nets when brought to the surface, and after the vessel has drifted many miles during the process of heaving the trawl.

When we examine the composition of this stone, we find that we at last have a rock from the Channel that is not totally different from all previously obtained from the same source of supply ; for although by no means identical, it is not unlike the block (No. 2) that forms the doorstep of the Brixham Orphanage, and described last year.

No. 19, under consideration, is a true granite. The slice, as Mr. Tawney tells us, shows neither hornblende nor schorl, but the components are black and white micas, a little triclinic felspar in addition to the orthoclase, quartz with fluid enclosures containing bubbles, and apatite. Now, on reference to Mr. Tawney's analysis of No. 2, published last year, it will be seen that the composition of the two rocks is almost identical, the only difference being that whilst certain " microlite needles, and hair-like delicate crystals of undetermined nature," are stated to be present in No. 2, no mention is made of them in No. 19. The similarity of these rocks is interesting, as No. 2 is one of the pair which, as stated last year, cannot be referred to any British rock above water. It would seem now that if not of British extraction, we can, at any rate, assign it a place under the waters of the English Channel.

In a paper read to the Association last year, Mr. R. N. Worth described several varieties of the rock on which the new Eddystone Lighthouse has been built, and stated that the area, though small, had "afforded examples, in every stage of gradation, from what we may regard as the typical gneiss of the 'house-rock' to pieces which in hand specimens cannot be distinguished from the common red granitic veins of Dartmoor." . . . Mr. Worth has been kind enough to supply me with characteristic specimens of the above-mentioned varieties from the new Lighthouse rock. One is a good example of gneiss; a second is a piece of that part of the rock that has been for a long time considered granitoid, if not granite; and Mr. Worth informs me that "no part of of the reef has produced more decidedly granitic rock" than this specimen; two others are portions of the rock compared to the "red granitic veins of Dartmoor." All these specimens were sent to Mr. Tawney for examination. He pronounced the red rocks as similar to the veins in the Malvern gneiss, and being veins, scarcely worth slicing for the microscope. However, one of the pieces was so treated, and proved to be "a clastic rock," consisting "nearly entirely of quartz and felspar." The two gneisses, when put to the test of the microscope, turned out to be almost identical, both containing the same minerals, though differing a little in their arrangement. Thus it appears that the theory so long held, that the Eddystone reef is more or less granitoid, except in so far as gneiss itself is considered granitoid, is not borne out by the four specimens kindly presented to me by Mr. Worth. Passing on from the subject of the Eddystone reef, Mr. Worth, in the paper referred to (*Devon. Assoc. Trans.*, vol. xii. p. 362), proceeded to make the startling announcement that the Shovel Rock, inside Plymouth Breakwater, on which a fort had been built 12 years previously, was also gneiss, and as such, conclusive proof "that the Eddystone reef is no isolated phenomenon." . . . . Mr. Worth was kind enough to send me a piece of this rock also, with permission to make any use of it. Of this permission I have gratefully availed myself to the fullest extent. The rock has been submitted to Mr. Tawney, and, as will be seen by his microscopic analysis appended, it is not only gneiss, but "a typical gneiss; in appearance and structure very like that from the Eddystone rock (No. 1)."

In a paper such as the present, whose primary object is to record notes of observed facts, it is well to defer drawing deductions for as long a time as possible, lest the deductions

of one year be demolished by the discoveries of the next.
But it may, perhaps, be permissible briefly to indicate the
direction in which our recently acquired knowledge seems
to point.   We find a large tract of sea-bottom off the south
coast of Devon where large blocks of stone abound; and to
such an extent that the fishermen are greatly inconvenienced
by them.   In proof of this assertion, I need only mention
what Hayden, the master of the *Pelican*, told me last September; viz., that on Monday, the 20th of that month, some
40 smacks shot their trawls together, and that only about five,
of which the *Pelican* was one, escaped being brought up by
stones or "pick-ups."   But though she escaped that day, we
have seen that she was not so lucky during the rest of the
week, as she trawled a stone on the Wednesday and another
on the Friday.   But if the number of these detached blocks
is remarkable, their character is equally so.   Of all the
Channel stones received hitherto, only one is a simple sedimentary rock; viz., the fragment of sandstone (10) presumed
to have been broken off the parent rock by the trawl.   All
the others, thirteen in number, are eruptive, granitic, or metamorphic, with perhaps one exception, viz., the conglomeratic
grit (5); and even that one Mr. Tawney cannot pronounce free
from alteration.   To these thirteen we may add the gneisses of
the Eddystone and Shovel reefs, making in all fifteen specimens of Channel rocks, none of which are, strictly speaking,
sedimentary.   As already stated, many varieties are represented.   Out of the present total of fifteen, we have at least
thirteen different rocks, which the meagre evidence available
suffices to prove to be of several different ages.   The collection may be roughly grouped into granites, gneisses, syenitic
rocks, both igneous and metamorphic, serpentine, diorite,
diabase, gabbros, and conglomeratic grit.

The granites appear to agree in one thing; viz., to disclaim any connection with the family of the same name on
shore.   On this point, and more especially with reference to
the typical granite (No. 19), Mr. Tawney speaks without
hesitation.   Closely connected in mineral composition with
these typical granites (Nos. 2 and 19), and presumably of
the same age, we have the Eddystone and Shovel gneisses
and the fine-grained rock No. 3.   The same minerals occur
in all; viz., orthoclase, plagioclase, biotite, muscovite, and
quartz, but no hornblende and no schorl.   Moreover, in all
these rocks, excepting the Shovel gneiss, the quartz contains
fluid enclosures.   Now it so happens that the Eddystone
rock is as nearly as possible S.W. (magnetic) of Plymouth,

and as the granite No. 19, which we believe to be *in situ*, was trawled 20 miles S.W. of the Eddystone, we find these three rocks, the Shovel, the Eddystone, and the granite, so like in mineral composition, almost in line with each other. Now, if we are right so far, I think we shall be able to show that, given the contemporaneity of these gneisses and granites, they are all much older than the granites of Dartmoor, from which mineralogically they differ so much. The facts are as follows:—About 31 miles S.W. of Plymouth we have typical granite, composed of mica, quartz, and felspar; 20 miles to the N.E. of this rock we find the same minerals in the metamorphic rock of the Eddystone reef, "a well characterised gneiss; 11 miles further to the N.E. we find the same minerals reappearing in Plymouth Sound in the Shovel Rock, "a typical gneiss . . . . very like that from the Eddystone." But though we find these indications of intense metamorphic action extending from 30 miles seaward right up to the Devonian rocks of Plymouth Sound, we find these Devonian rocks, though undoubtedly much contorted, quite unaltered, and exhibiting no trace of the immediate neighbourhood of such a large area of granites and gneisses. The fair inference seems to be that the Devonian rocks of Plymouth were not in existence when these gneisses were formed, or, in other words, that the Shovel and Eddystone gneisses and their corresponding granites are of preDevonian age. Nor are these gneisses and granites quite alone in their evidence of the antiquity of certain of the Channel formations; for the conglomeratic grit No. 5 has been thought by more than one geologist to be of great antiquity; and Dr. Hicks, writing on the pre-Cambrian rocks of the British Isles, speaks of the specimens I exhibited to the Geological Section of the British Association at Swansea in the following terms:—"I have seen some of the specimens . . . . and believe that among them are types only known in pre-Cambrian rocks in this country." (*Proceedings of Geological Association*, vol. vii. No. 1.)

If these typical granites and gneisses are of the age suggested, they can clearly have no claim to having had anything to do with the metamorphosis of the more modern Devonian slates of the Start and Bolt district, and it is equally clear they can have nothing to do with the Dartmoor granites, which have long been known to be of Post-Carboniferous age. But these typical granites and gneisses apart, there remain many other rocks from the Channel to whose age we have no clue. Such are the hornblendic granite (4), the syenitic rocks, igneous (7), and metamorphic (?) (9), the gabbros (8, 15), the diabase (19), and the diorite (?) (17; sufficient indications of igneous action of unknown date off the south coast of Devon to enable us to dispense with the typical granites and gneisses, supposing these can be proved to be of greater antiquity than the period of metamorphosis of the mica-schist of the Bolt and Prawle.

. In my papers on the Submarine Geology of the Channel I have endeavoured, by giving full details of persons, times, and places, to enable any other worker in the same field to verify and, if requisite, to correct my statements. One such statement recorded, on the authority of others, in my first paper, from further information, I have reason to believe incorrect in two particulars, and I take this opportunity to correct it.

In pp. 316 and 317 of vol. xi. of the *Trans. Devon. Assoc.* the reader is informed that a certain block of granite, now the foundation-stone of St. Peter's Mission Chapel, at Brixham, was trawled by a fisherman named George Eden, that a builder had declared it to be artificially cut, and that he could see the marks of the chisel upon it. When on board the *Pelican*, on the 27th of September, 1880, to see the two stones, Nos. 15 and 16, her new master, George Hayden, in the course of conversation, volunteered the information that some people fancied that the large stone in St. Peter's Chapel, *which was brought on shore by his father*, was worked—an idea which he, George Hayden, ridiculed. Much surprised, I asked him whether his name was not Eden, for I had been told that that particular stone had been trawled by a George Eden. He assured me to the contrary, and I then saw clearly that the mistake in the name must have arisen through a confusion caused by the ordinary Devonshire pronunciation. To test this point, I enquired of a relative living in a Devonshire village how she would spell the name of a Devonshire man who announced himself as Hayden. Without any hesitation she replied, "Eden." But, on the other hand, should a man's name really be either Hayden or Heyden, there is no room for variation in pronunciation, except as to the aspirate, which would vary in different speakers. This discrepancy of the name is thus explained, and I am very glad to have the opinion of the son of the supposed George Eden that the block in St. Peter's Chapel was not artificially worked when first found; a supposition, however, which no one who has studied the detached blocks from the Channel could entertain for a moment.

NOTES OF MICROSCOPIC EXAMINATION OF FOUR SPECIMENS OF ROCKS TRAWLED IN THE CHANNEL, THREE SPECIMENS OF THE EDDYSTONE ROCK (NEW LIGHTHOUSE), AND ONE SPECIMEN OF THE SHOVEL ROCK.

BY E. B. TAWNEY, M.A., F.G.S.

Trawled Rocks.

15. Trawled about 16 miles S. of Start Point, 22nd September, 1880. Gabbro, a purplish and green mottled rock, with opaque white spots. Some "killas" is said to have been adherent to the block, so that its not very characteristic appearance may be due to the junction with the sedimentary rock.

The diallage scarcely retains its own physical properties; much of it has become altered to an aggregate of diverging fibrous, colourless or pale greenish crystals, which may probably belong to the actinolite group. The plagioclase is in places opaque from decomposition, and is everywhere much penetrated by the pale green actinolite microlites.

This gabbro is no longer in its original condition, the diallage being seen changing to actinolite.

16. Trawled about 16 miles S. of Start Point, September 24, 1880. A sap-green coloured rock, in which the large actinolite crystals chiefly catch the eye; it is coarsely crystalline. The microscope shows the long actinolite crystals, green in colour, and at the borders often connected with diverging bundles and needles of pale green crystals, also actinolite, which penetrate the felspars.

The plagioclase still preserves its twinning for the most part, but much of it is attacked by decomposition, and it is everywhere permeated by long actinolite fibres and particles. Apatite is present. Secondary quartz has been deposited in little veins and interstices. The rock, if a diorite, is evidently much altered.

17. Trawled September 30, 1880, 17 to 18 miles S.W. by W. of the Start. A dark green rock of medium grain, with minute specks of pyrites. A diabase of ordinary type. The plagioclase is much decomposed, the twinning being often lost. Quartz has been secondarily deposited. The augite has also been partly attacked by decomposition, and chloritic matter has resulted thereby. A little apatite is present. Magnetite or black oxide is much more abundant than the pyrites.

19. Broken off by the trawl, about 20 miles S.W. of Eddystone, 12th October, 1880. Granite of coarse grain. The slice shows neither hornblende nor schorl, but both white and black micas are present; so that the rock comes under granite proper, of which it is a good example. A little triclinic felspar is present in addition to the orthoclase. The quartz contains large fluid enclosures with bubbles, and in some smaller ones moving bubbles were noticed. Apatite is abundant in rather large crystals.

Eddystone Rock (New Lighthouse).

E. 1. The hand specimen is a grey rock, a well characterised gneiss, with distinct foliation; small garnets of salmon colour, visible to the naked eye.

The microscope shows that it contains two micas; the brown one strongly dichroic; the second has sometimes a delicate straw tint, sometimes colourless. This mica shows much brighter colours, but is noticeable chiefly for in some cases containing long needle prisms, crossing at an angle of 60°, reminding us of the phlogopite, from Grand Burgess, Canada. Other minerals present are garnet of pinkish colour, titanite, and another mineral which does not often show good crystal outlines, but which we are inclined to refer to zircon. Of felspars, both orthoclase and triclinic are present, their condition fresh; both contain flakes of mica. The quartz is clear, contains scattered fluid enclosures, in which, however, no motion was detected.

E. 2. The second specimen has the same grey colour, but is less distinctly foliated, the quartz being rather more in lumps; garnets present in less quantity.

The microscope shows that all the minerals of the former slide are present, and it is the same rock with a little different arrangement merely of components. There are the two felspars, both full of mica at times: the quartz over a part of the slide is very full of capillary crystals; garnet, titanite, and the mineral referred provisionally to zircon are present.

E. 3. The third specimen is quite a different rock in appearance; a mixture of colourless quartz, red felspathic portions with chloritic veins and patches between the other materials.

The microscope shows that it consists almost entirely of quartz and felspar, with in parts what we might call a pseudofelsitic arrangement of these factors; it is traversed in numerous directions by strings and veins of brownish ferric matter. There are also vermiform collections of clinochlore (Helminth?) The quartz is very dirty-looking, from the abundance of minute enclosures. It is evidently a clastic rock, but its alteration has resulted in a structure of great confusion.

Shovel Rock.

S. 1. Gneiss from the Shovel Rock, at the foundation of Iron-cased Fort, within the Plymouth Breakwater. This is a well-foliated rock, a typical gneiss; in appearance and structure very like that from the Eddystone Rock (No. 1). The felspar is mostly triclinic; it encloses frequently a great number of oval and bar-shaped minute pale green crystals, which are probably mica. Both white and brown mica are present, the former being more abundant. Quartz layers, alternating with mica and felspar bands, are of the usual type. Pink garnet occurs, and may be seen in the rock with a hand lens. Titanite is chiefly mixed up in the mica layers. A well characterised gneiss.

THE PRINCE OF ORANGE IN EXETER, 1688.

BY T. W. WINDEATT.

(Read at Dawlish, July, 1881.)

In the paper I read at the meeting of this Association at Totnes, on "The Landing of the Prince of Orange," founded mainly on Whittle's *Diary*, I followed the Prince on his march to Newton, postponing an account of his subsequent proceedings in Devon to a future occasion.

While I cannot profess to have gathered very much additional information, the account in Whittle's *Diary* is so complete, graphic, and interesting, and the book itself so scarce, that extracts from it would alone form ample material for another paper.

It will be remembered that the Prince, having landed at Broxholme (Brixham), on Monday, November 5th (old style), arrived at Ford House, Newton Abbot, on Wednesday, 7th, Dr. Burnet and Lord Mordaunt, with a troop of horse, having gone on in advance to Exeter, to prepare for the Prince's advent there. They arrived at the West Gate of the city on the morning of Thursday, 8th. This gate had been closed by order of the Mayor and Aldermen, who were for the King; but, as I find stated in an account * of the Prince's actions, published in 1690, "without barricading or fastening, so that being soon opened, an advance party entered, and was joyfully received by the inhabitants, a great many of them having before their coming listed themselves for the service of the Prince." This enlistment had been made by Captain Hicks, the son of Mr. John Hicks, deceased, a Nonconformist divine, for which he had been committed to prison by the Mayor. The concourse of people, however, about the Guildhall was so great that he could not be removed there-

* *An Historical Account of the Memorable Actions of the Most Glorious Monarch, William III., King of England, &c.* London, 1690.

from, so had to be kept there in the custody of two constables. Lord Mordaunt on entering the city went first to the Guildhall and set the captain at liberty, and finding on enquiry that he had been well treated by the Mayor, gave the attendants a guinea.

The Bishop (Lamplough) and the Dean had both fled, and the Bishop's palace and the deanery being both viewed, the deanery was thought to be the more convenient place for the accommodation of the Prince, and was therefore prepared for his reception. The Mayor, Sir Thomas Jefford, had recently been knighted by King James, and had been continued in office for a second year by the mandate of the King, the charter having been purposely surrendered. * It is evident, from the fact of the mandate dispensing with his taking any oath for the execution of his office, that he was a Papist. Burnet and Mordaunt pressed him to meet the Prince at the gate, but he excused himself, and said that he was under the obligation of an oath to his lawful sovereign, James II., and hoped the Prince would lay no commands upon him prejudicial to his conscience. The army proceeded to march from Newton to Exeter, crossing the Teign at or near Newton, and passing over Haldon. Whittle thus refers to the march of the army from Newton to Exeter, and some of its incidents :

" The Army moved toward Exeter, some Regiments being at one Town, and some in another : And as they were marching over the Heath, or Common, between Newton Abbot and Exeter, about five miles off the City, sundry companies of young Men met them, with each a Club in his Hand ; and as they approached near they gave sundry Shouts and Huzza's, saying, God bless the Prince of Orange, and grant him victory over all his Enemies ; We are his true Servants, and come to fight for him as long as we are able : So we all bid them welcome. Here the Army passed by a Popish Lady's House, which was cruel to all her Protestant Tenants ; she forced some to turn Papists or Apostates : But had the French King's Army passed thus by a Protestant House, it should soon have been fired, the People put to the Sword, or burnt : But we have not so learn'd Christ, nor been thus taught by his Minsters in our Land ; for no Man molested this House, nor did any visit it unless a Captain and some Gentlemen, which would have bought themselves Horses there, having lost their own at Sea, and so constrained to walk on foot till they could supply themselves with more.

" It must needs be acknowledged by all People that his Highness took special care in marching of the Army, that no Disorders should

---

* OLIVER'S *History of Exeter.*

be committed; and never better Order could be kept in any Army than in this, as all sorts of Men confess: Nay, they told us at Exeter, that when we were there, the City was more quiet in the Night, and freer from debauched and disorderly Persons than 'twas before. The poor Souldiers began now to grow lame, and so marched slip-shod, which was irksome."

The "Heath or Common," referred to by Whittle, is undoubtedly Haldon, and the Popish lady's house was probably Ugbrooke.

The remarks of Whittle as to the good order kept by the army are borne out by other authorities, and this fact is one which must always reflect credit on the expedition.

The Prince, who had remained at Ford House two nights, arrived at Exeter, somewhat in advance of the main army, on Friday, November 9th, and made his entry into the city through the West Gate. The following is Whittle's account of it:

"After the Prince of Orange had tarried two or three Nights at Sir Will. Courtney's, he, with a brave Train of Nobles, Knights, and Gentlemen to attend him, rode unto Exeter; they long'd much for his coming. It was a very wet and rainy Day when he came into Exeter with his Army. The manner of his coming into this City, being so glorious, was long since published, so that I shall not speak much about it: The Guards rode, some before and some behind him, with their Swords drawn, their Colours flying, Kettle-Drums beating, and trumpets sounding joyfully, their Officers courteously bowing unto the People; all sorts and conditions of Men thronging on each side the Streets making great "Acclamations and Huzza's as the Prince passed by. The Windows of every House were extremely crowded and beautified; the bells ringing. The Foot souldiers did not appear well, because they were sorely weather-beaten, and much dabled in marching in the Dirt and Rain, and look'd very pale and thin after such a hard days march which made some people conjecture that they were dull sluggish Men.

"As the Prince of Orange was riding thus towards the Deanary through the City, attended with Mareschal Schomberg, Count Solms, Count Nassau, Heer Zulustein, Heer Bentein, the Earl of Shrewsbury, the Earl of Macclesfield, Lord Viscount Mordant, Lord Wiltshire, Earl of Argile, Colonel Sidney, Sir Rowland Guyn, and divers other Lords, Knights and Gentlemen; Such was the Resolution and Desire of an old woman to see the Prince that she throng'd in amongst the Horse Guards, and tho she was divers times in Jeopardy of her Life, yet for all, says she, I will see him though it cost me my Life: so coming at length to him, she touched his Hand and said, I pray God bless you, Sir, and so was thrust away by the Guards : but as she was going from him, she put her Hand to her Heart and spake out aloud, Now my very Soul within me is the better for seeing him ; at which speech and humour of this Woman his Highness himself seem'd to smile."

In the British Museum there is a broadside, apparently published at the time, entitled, "A True and Exact Relation of the Prince of Orange His publick entrance into Exeter," which gives a detailed account of the Prince's cavalcade, and the order in which it entered the city. This account, with the exception of a few words at the commencement and at the close, is almost word for word the same as that given in the pamphlet entitled, "An account of the Expedition of His Highness the Prince of Orange for England," referred to in my previous paper, and quoted by Mr. Pengelly in his "Miscellaneous Devonshire Gleanings," read at the Torrington meeting, though he omits this very interesting portion of it. It must have been one of these papers to which Whittle refers, and on account of the previous publication of which he refrains from going more into detail, with reference to the manner of the Prince's entry.

I venture therefore to set out the paper in the British Museum in full, as follows :

"A TRUE AND EXACT RELATION OF THE PRINCE OF ORANGE,

HIS PUBLICK ENTRANCE INTO EXETER.

" Since the foundation of Monarchy, Imperial Orations or the triumphs of the *Cæsars*, in the Manner, Grandeur and magnificence of their most sumptuous cavalcades, there was never any that exceeded this of the most Illustrious Hero the Prince of Orange his Entrance into Exeter, which was in manner and form following :

" 1. The Right honourable the Earl of Macclesfield with 200 horse, the most part of which were *English* Gentlemen, Richly mounted on Flanders Steeds, manag'd and us'd to war in Headpieces, Back and Brest, Bright Armour. *

" 2. 200 Blacks brought from the plantations of the *Netherlands* in *America*, Imbroyder'd Caps lined with white Fur and plumes of white Feathers to attend the Horse.

" 3. 200 *Finlanders* or *Laplanders* in Bear Skins taken from the Wild Beasts they had slain, the common Habbit of that cold Climat, with black Armour and Broad Flaming Swords.

* In a MS. Treatise on Armour, written about 1792 by Thomas Barrett, a Manchester antiquary, it is stated that "armour was last worn in England on the March of the Prince of Orange to Exeter."

" 4. 50 Gentlemen, and as many Pages to attend and support the Princes Banner, bearing this inscription GOD and the PROTES-TANT RELIGION.

" 5. 50 Led Horses all Managed and brought up to the Wars, with 2 Grooms to each Horse.

" 6. After these Rid the Prince on a Milk White Palfrey. Armed Cap a Pee. A Plume of White Feathers on his head. All in Bright Armour, and 42 Footmen Running by him.

" 7. After his Highness followed likewise on Horseback 200 Gentlemen and Pages.

" 8. 300 Switzers with Fuzies.

" 9. 500 Voluntiers each 2 led Horses.

" 10. His Captain and Guard 600 Armed Cap a Pee. The rest of the Army in the rere, his Highness with some Principal officers entered the Town, where they were not only Received but entertained with Loud *Huzzas* Ringing of Bells, Bonfires, and such acclamations of joy as the conveinence of the place, and their abilities cou'd afford.

" FINIS."

It is stated in Blewitt's *Panorama of Torquay*, published in 1832, that the flag placed in the bow of the first barge in the procession at the opening of the Exeter Canal was the identical banner under which William landed at Brixham, it having become the property of a member of the Watson family; who was engaged in his retinue.

Whittle's Diary continues as follows :

" After the Prince was come unto the Deanary, and had refresh'd himself, with all his Lords and Gentlemen, then was he pleased to go and render his hearty Thanks to Almighty God in the Cathedral Church for his safe Arrival and the whole fleet. The People thronged the Streets to see him as he went, and crowded the Quire where he was to come very much. Now there were sundry Men with Hol-bards who cleared the way, besides Sentinels ; so being conducted to the Bishop's Seat, he sat down with about six of his Life-Guard men on his Right hand, and many more before him and about him in the Quire. As he came all along the Body of the Church the Organs played very sweetly, though 'twas not the right Organist himself, he being gone aside on purpose, as I was informed there. And being sat the quire began, and sung Te Deum for the save Arrival of the Prince of Orange and his Army in England (as also for his whole Fleet) : After the Collects were ended, the Reverend Dr. Burnet began to read the Declaration of his Highness : William Henry, by the Grace of God, Prince of Orange, &c. Of the Reasons inducing him to appear in Arms in the Kingdom of England, for preserving of the Protestant Religion, and for the restoring the Laws and Liberties of England, Scotland, and Ireland, &c. At the very beginning of which Declaration the Ministers of the Church there present rushed immediately out of their seats, and bustled through all the Crowd going out of the Church; the people remained, and were very attentive to the Doctor's reading, and the Declaration being ended, he said, God save the Prince of Orange, unto which the major part of the Multitude answered, Amen. So his Highness return'd to the Deanary, the People echoing forth Huzza's as he went along. Another Evening at Service, one of the Ministers reading that Prayer for the pretended Prince of Wales, a certain Noble-Man or two being present, stood up at the same and put on their Hats, kneeling down to all the other Collects; and this they did to demonstrate their abhorrence of it. The Right Reverend Bishop of this place and Diocess as soon as he learn'd (for certain) that the Prince of Orange was landed with an Army at Tor-Bay, in Devonshire, took his Coach and came up to give the late King James Information thereof, for which he gave him the Bishoprick of York. The Reverend * Dean likewise took his Coach and went about six or seven Miles in the Country, where he remain'd some days, but returned unto his own House or Deanary before the Prince came away; for we tarried at Exeter many days to refresh the Army after it had been so long on shipboard, and to recover the Horses to their former strength, as also for the Gentlemen of the Country thereabout to come and joyn his Highness there. The Train of Artillery Magazine and the whole Baggage of the Army was brought hither by Water; there were one and twenty good Brass Pieces for the Field, divers of which were too heavy for those Roads, and more than sixteen Horses could draw. Arms for sundry thousand Men were now given out here, which we brought with us out of Holland. The first Sunday after the Prince was come unto Exeter, being Novemb. 11, the Reverend Dr. Burnet preached before him at the Cathedral Church in the Morning, the Quire and Body thereof being extreamly throng'd with People which came to see his Highness, some placing themselves in Seats by eight in the Morning. When his Highness came he was for to sit in the Bishop's Seat in the Body of the Church as he had done in the Quire before: Sundry Sentinels stood just behind him, two just before him, and many more in the Church-Isle; the Doctor's Text was Psalm 107. 43. Whoso is wise and will observe those things, even they shall understand the loving Kindness of the Lord. The Doctor very accurately shewed the loving Kindness of the Lord unto the Prince of Orange, and his Fleet; how he caused the Winds to turn at Tor-Bay where the whole fleet was to tack about to come into the Bay; and then shew'd the upright Design of the Prince to promote the Glory of God, and good of his Church in England, Scotland, and Ireland; having ended his Sermon, he read the Prayer for the Expedition, and so concluded with the Blessing, &c. Some time was passed here before the

* The Honourable Richard Annesley.

Gentlemen of the West joyned his Highness, but when once they did begin to come in, then they came daily: The Mayor and Aldermen of the City came to visit the Prince, and were busie in their Consultations among themselves. The late King James we heard now was advanc'd as far towards us as Salisbury, with a very brave Army, of about thirty five thousand Men, and a prodigious great Train of Artillery, which made the poor Country People tremble. Moreover we heard, that he was fully resolved to encamp his Army about Sarum, in the Plain, where he intended to fight us. Some of our men, being of the Van-guard were advanc'd as far as Wincaunton to provide Carriage, at which place there was a small Skirmish or Action between 26 of our Souldiers, and about 150 of the late King's Party; which you shall have a particular account of by and by. We soon received information of the Skirmish at Exeter: Order was now given to get Waggons to carry the Magazine and Baggage of the whole Army, together with all sorts of Utensils fit and convenient for War, and Horses to draw the Artillery, and for the Country People round to bring in their Horses to be sold at Exeter, that so the loss of our Horses might be made up here: According to which Order the Country People came daily in with their Horses to sell, and the Officers gave great Prices for them, because they must have them there or nowhere. The Souldiers were ordered to keep themselves and their Arms in good order, and to get everything here which they wanted. Much Money was laid out in this City for all sorts of Commodities which the Officers or Souldiers lacked. Here at first the People were scrupulous about the Dutch Money, and many Country People refused it, but were forc'd to take it, because all the Army had little else, but Guineas and Dutch Money. The People of the City began now to be more and more inclin'd towards our Army, and all fear almost of the other Army was banish'd out of their thoughts, so that they would discourse more freely now than at the first. The Drums beat for Volunteers, and every Regiment of English or Scotch which wanted any Men, was now compleated: The Regiment of Sir John Guyes, and Sir Robert Peyton fill'd up very fast; for Men came into the City daily from all Parts to list themselves, insomuch that many Captains pick'd and chose their Souldiers. Very great crowding was here at the Deanary, (it being the Prince of Orange's Court) by all sorts of People: Many coming 20 Miles on purpose to see him, and all the People of the adjacent Places were waiting there daily; insomuch that the Sentinels could hardly keep them out. The Guard was before the entrance into the Deanary, and sundry Sentinels two at each door. Now his Highness received Information, that the late King James was gone back from Sarum towards London, (with his whole Army) by reason of the false Report of some Tumult in the City, made by the Apprentices, which News did not in the least discompose us. The weather being somewhat favourable, the Prince of Orange, with all his Lords and Gentlemen attending him, was pleased to ride and view the City, and Castle; and this Day the Deanary was embroider'd with the Officers in their Gold and Silver-Lace Coats. The Country People brought all sorts of Provisions in abundance because it yielded them Money, and went off well.

"We heard here that our Friends were up in the North of England, as the Lord Delamore, Earl of Devonshire, Earl of Stamford, Earl of Danby, Sir Scroop How, Sir William Russel with divers others: By this time the Gentlemen of Somersetshire and Dorsetshire were coming in to join his Highness; and on Thursday, November 15, they waited on him at Exeter, upon which he was pleased to speak to them as follows:

"'Tho we know not all your Persons, yet we have a Catalouge of your Names, and remember the Character of your Worth and Interest in your Country. You see we are come according to your Invitation and our Promise. Our Duty to God obliges us to protect the Protestant Religion; and our Love to Mankind, your Liberties and Properties. We expected you that dwelt so near the place of our Landing, would have join'd us sooner, not that it is now too late, nor that we want your Military Assistance so much as your Countenance and Presence, to justify our declar'd Pretensions, in order to accomplish our good and gracious Design. Tho we have brought both a good Fleet, and a good Army, to render these Kingdoms happy, by rescuing all Protestants from Popery, Slavery, and Arbitrary Power; by restoring them to their Rights and Properties established by Law, and by promoting of Peace and Trade, which is the Soul of Government, and the very Life-Blood of a Nation; yet we rely more on the Goodness of God, and the justice of our Cause, than on any Humane Force and Power whatever. Yet since God is pleased we shall make use of Humane means, and not expect Miracles for our Preservation and Happiness; let us not neglect making use of this gracious Opportunity, but with Prudence and Courage put in Execution our so honourable Purposes. Therefore, Gentlemen, Friends, and Fellow Protestants, we bid you and all your Followers most heartily Welcome to our Court and Camp. Let the whole World now judg, if our Pretensions are not Just, Generous, Sincere, and above Price since we might have even a Bridg of Gold to Return back; but it is our Principle and Resolution, rather to dye in a Good Cause, than live in a Bad one, well knowing that Vertue and True Honour is its own Reward, and the Happiness of Mankind Our Great and Only Design.'"

It was after this interview with the Prince that, at the suggestion of Seymour, the country gentlemen of Devon formed themselves into an association, and publicly and formally pledged themselves to the Prince's cause by signing a declaration drawn up by Burnet.

The following is a copy of the declaration from one in my own possession, purporting to have been "printed at Exon in 1688:"

"The General

ASSOCIATION,

Of the Gentlemen of *Devon*, to his Highnefs

THE

Prince of Orange.

WE Whofe Names are hereunto Subfcribed who have now joyned with the Prince of *Orange*, for the Defence of the *Proteftant Religion*, and for maintaining the Antient Government, Laws and Liberties of *England*, *Scotland*, and *Ireland*, do ingage in Almighty God, to his Highnefs the Prince of *Orange;* and to one another, to ftick firm to this Caufe, and to one another, in the Defence of it; and never to depart from it, until our Religion, Laws, and Liberties are so far fecured to us, in our Free Parliament; that we shall be no more in danger of falling under *Popery* and *Slavery:* And as we are Ingaged in this common *caufe*, under the Protection of the Prince of *Orange;* by which means his Perfon may be expofed to Dangers, and Defperate, and Curfed Attempts of Papifts and other Bloody Men; we do therefore Solemnly Ingage both to God and one another; that if any fuch Attempts are made upon him, we will purfue not only thofe who make them, but all their Adherents, and all that we find in Arms against us, with the utmost Severity of a juft Revenge to their Ruin and Destruction; and that Execution of fuch attempts, which God of his Mercy forbid, shall not prevent us from Profecuting this *Caufe*, which we now undertake, but that it shall ingage us to carry it on, with all the Vigor that fo Barbarous a Practice fhall deferve."

Whittle continues:

"The late King James coming up towards London, the Regiment of Dragoons belonging to Lord Cornbury came away from him to join the Prince of Orange, and the Lord Cornbury with many other Lords, Knights, and Gentlemen, came unto Exeter, and attended on his Highness, which made all the Army to rejoice. The Prince rode about five miles out of Exeter, to view some new Regiment of Horse which were just come into His Service.   He gave the Officers and Souldiers a courteous Reception, and made a Speech unto them, upon which the whole Regiment shouted and Huzzad for Joy."

In the Seventh Report of the Historical Manuscripts Commission, there is published a letter from Exon referring to the Prince's visit to the troops, and containing a list of some of those who had joined the Prince. Among them we recognize names of men whose descendants still hold a leading position in the county. It is noticeable that in this list occurs the name of Mr. Roope, whom I stated in my first paper to have been by his own account the first to join the Prince. The fact that the name of the Dean also occurs there confirms Whittle's statement of his having returned to the deanery.

The following is a copy of this letter :

"1688 Nov. 21st.

"To Mr. Richard Musgrave, at the Chancery Office in Chancery Lane.

"Saturday last the Prince went 8 miles to view the Lord Cornbury's and the other Troops which came to him, and ordered them their pay, which is in arrear, and a month's advance. This morning his Highness marched towards Salisbury; the baggage and artillery marched yesterday. Our town hath been full of gentlemen from many counties; Dorset and Somerset came in very briskly. Most of ours have offered their service to his Highness. They are provided with all things that can be useful in such an expedition in abundance, especially with the sinews of war. Coll. Lutterell hath a regiment, which is to be here with some others; Mr. Sp. Seamor another, and is one of the Council. Since you desire a list, take it in part as underneath : the Prince being gone there's little more at this time. E. of Abbington, E. of Montrose, Capt. Burrington, Major Northcote, Mr. Edm Cary, Mr. ffulford, Mr. Lee, Sir William Drake, ffr. Drake, Capt. Cholwick, Dean of Exeter, Mr. Beavis, Coll. Port, Mr. Elwill, Capt. Martyn, Capt. D. Rolle, Mr. Northleigh, Sir Wm. Portman, Coll. Lutter[ell] and his brother, Major Palmer, Mr. Speak. Seamor, Mr. Th. Seamor, Capt. Rodd, Mr. Hattou Compton, Capt. Brewer, Mr. Row, Mr. Wharton, Mr. Russell, Coll. Bampfield, Coll. Tho. Wyndham, and his son, Capt. Est, Sir J. Fowell, Coll. Rolle, Mr. Champernown, Coll. Cooke, Sir Tho. Lear, Mr. Stawell, Mr. Mallett, Capt. Tydecomb, Capt. Braddon, Sir Rob. Pye's son, Sir Rob. Peyton, Mr. Geo. Courteny, Sir ffr. Northcote, Mr. Roope, Coll. Godfry, Capt. Osbourn, Capt. Hooper, Capt. Colman, Sir P. Prideaux, Sir B. Wray, Sir H. Carew, *cum multis aliis.*"

(Endorsed by Tempest. A letter from Exon containing a list of several in the Prince of Orange's army.)

Accompanying the Prince there were doubtless also many

English Protestants who had fled from England owing to the persecutions, and returned again in his fleet. Among these was one Robert Hodge or Hodges, a physician, who with his brother Elaxander, had sought a refuge in Protestant Holland. Robert Hodge had studied in Holland, and been employed as a physician about the Court, and is said to have come over in the same ship with the Prince. He doubtless must have felt a peculiar interest in the old city and its neighbourhood; for from the Church of St. Thomas his brother had been ejected in 1662. A lady resident at Ashburton, descended from another brother, has large portraits of three of the family, two of them being those of Elaxander and Robert. In the latter portrait is a sea view in the background, with ships and land in the distance, with a town on the sea-shore, which resembles Torbay, and a church with a square tower. The lady has some pieces of old Dutch china, supposed to have been brought over at this time by Robert Hodge.

There are several other letters set out in the same report of the Commission, more or less interesting, and confirmatory of the facts stated by Whittle. To set them all out would occupy too much space, I therefore quote the following only, which is too interesting to be passed over: .

"1688, Nov. 17th. Letter from Exon. The Prince hath appointed Commissioners for the managing the revenue which are my Lord Wiltshire, Mr. Herbert, and Mr. Roe. Yesterday they collected the monthly duty of excise for this city and say they will have the whole revenue. They have been with me about ours and said they would have all the money that was received here, but I being a Deputy, and Mr. Parsons wanting, Mrs. Parsons hath persuaded Mr. Roe, (who is her kinsman) to suspend the matter till Mr. Parsons comes home, she having sent for him. The Prince is gone this morning to Ottery with a great number of English and foreign noblemen and gentlemen to view some of my Lord Cornbury's dragoons, and some horse of my Lord of Oxfords, who are come to his assistance, and returns at night. Several gentlemen of the county come in every day to him; but our magistrates are suspended during the Prince's stay here, they not complying with him. The army is so great that I am told Sir William Waller's regiment, that was almost full of new raised men is disbanded. Some time next week the Prince marches from hence, but will leave two or three regiments here."

The next portion of Whittle's *Diary* is interesting, on account of its referring to a personal incident.

"I preached at St. Carion's Church in Exeter, November 18. My Text being in Isa. viii., 12, 13, 14. Neither fear ye their fear, nor be afraid. Sanctify the Lord of Hosts himself, and let him be your fear, and let him be your dread, and he shall be for a Sanctuary. Now the Church Wardens of this Parish, altho there was no Minister to preach, were unwilling to give the keys (because they were no true friends of our good cause) insomuch that I was forc'd to threaten them for their great rudeness. The Clerk of the Parish going along with me the Day before for the Key, one of the Church Wardens very rudely broke his Head in Sundry places, for which intolerable Action I immediately had him brought before the Honourable Colonel Cutts for this bold Fact, who upon a due submission and acknowledgment of his faults, dismissed him with a sharp reprehension. For Modesty-sake I conceal his name, hoping that he's reformed with the Times."

Whittle, after referring to the news that King James had returned to Sarum, with a view of giving battle, continues:

"The Army being now well refresh'd, and one Man as good as two when we were at Torbay, Order was given for the Army to march in three Lines: The first Line march'd out of the City as far as St. Mary Ottrie, and were quarter'd in and near that Place: The next day the second Line march'd forth of Exeter to the same place, and the first Line advanc'd to Axminster: The third Day the last line march'd, as before, to St. Mary Ottrie, the first Line advancing some to Beminster, and some to Crookhorn, the second to Axminster and the adjacent towns; and the Regiments march'd some one road and some another; as the first Line advanced, so the whole Army moved, which was according to the Motion of our great Master: For when he remained any where, then did the whole Army abide in the same Quarters. The City of Exeter was now freed of all its Souldiers, only the Regiment of Sir John Guyes (which was new raised) was order'd to keep the City, and he made Governour thereof. Now many Oxen being brought into this town to draw the Artillery, and many Horses being come to carry the Ammunition, and all things necessary for War appertaining to our whole Army; we then were soon on the March; A Captain with some other Officers and about a hundred Men, came along with it to guard it. Here at Exeter was a certain Person kept in custody some Days, for speaking very threatening Words against his Higness the Prince of Orange; but within a while was released. Another was apprehended for a Spy because he said he had a Commission from the late K. James to go into any Man's House, to search for Goods: This Man was also accused for stealing about ten pound from the People of the House where he lodged, but no money could be found about him, whereupon he also was dismissed in few Days. I suppose our Army was now in

Circumference between 20 and 30 Miles.   The Prince with all his Lords, Knights, and Gentlemen attending him rode from Exeter unto St. Mary Ottrie; the Weather was very Rainy, and the Roads bad for Marching; however we had time enough, for our Stages were not far distant one from the other: The Places where we Quarter'd were scarce able to receive us, insomuch that every House was crowded."

The remainder of the *Diary*, though very interesting, refers to what transpired after the Prince and his army had passed beyond this county.

THE SHIPPING AND COMMERCE OF DARTMOUTH IN THE REIGN OF RICHARD II.

BY PAUL Q. KARKEEK.

(Read at Dawlish, July, 1881.)

AMONG the many valuables in that vast collection of treasures, the Record Office, is a series of Rolls extending from Edward I. to James I., which give the returns of the officers appointed to collect the customs at the various ports. By the kind assistance of Mr. Walford Selby, and Mr. J. H. Greenstreet, I have become possessed of accurate copies of such rolls as relate to Dartmouth during the early part of the reign of Richard II. The reprinting of these intact would be a rather bulky contribution to the pages of the Devonshire Association, and I shall therefore content myself with extracts only.

These Rolls are among the so-called "Ancient Miscellanea" of the Queen's Remembrancer's side of the Exchequer. Generally the information contained is the class and name of the vessel, the name of the master, the date of the sailing, and the description of such portions of the cargo as were liable to duty.

There was a great variety of ships in use at this period, and some of the species are not now easy to recognise. In these lists the following are to be found, "Navis," "Cog," "Barge," "Craiera," "Trygo," "Batell," "Carvela," "Balingera," and "Scapho." Even when these terms are employed, the name of the ship sometimes implies a contradiction of the recorder's accuracy, or knowledge of nautical matters. For instance, in $\frac{34}{17}$ is the following: in the column where the species of vessel is given is the word "Balingera," and in that for the name, is "Seint Mary Cogge." Now it is very evident that the owner believed his vessel to be a Cog or Cogge, but the government officer describes her as a Balinger; thus confounding two distinct varieties of vessels.

The Cog, or Cogge, was the first-class vessel of the 14th century, and was sometimes as much as 200 tons burden;

nearly round in shape, having very broad bow and stern, somewhat resembling a cockle-shell, from which the word cog is supposed to be derived. The Barge was a small edition of the Cog. The Navis, or Nef, was a small coaster. The Craiera, or Crayer, was a small trading vessel of between 30 and 60 tons burden. The Trygo, or Trier, is supposed to have been a miniature of the Genoese Carack, which was a large vessel but little known in these waters until later in the 15th century. The word Trier is said to be a corruption of Trireme. The Batell resembled a large boat more than a ship. The build of the Carvela at this period is somewhat uncertain, but it was probably the original and predecessor of the Caravella, such as Columbus sailed in on his celebrated voyage of discovery. The Balinger was about the same size as a barge, it had a rounded bow, a high built stern, and bulging sides. All that is known of the Scaffa or Scapha is that it was very long in proportion to its breadth.

The names given to the ships do not show that variety which might be expected. In one list of thirteen entries there are no less than three "Christophers," two of which were Crayers and one a Barge. In the same list were also three "Marys," and all apparently of the same class. Among the names are "Trinitie," "Robynet," "Jovet," "Clere," "Welfare," "Johan," "Alianore," "Michiel," "Seinte Marie," "Katerine," "Bartholomew," "Mary Ffitzwaryn," "Mary sauns "Pere," "Nicholas," "Mary Bower," "Alisot," "George," "Margerete," "Leonard," "Elizabeth," "Elinor," "Lydenard," "Peter," "Chenawe," and "Magdeleine."

In the paper on the "Early History of Dartmouth," contributed by me to the *Transactions of the Devonshire Association*, 1880, allusion was made to the description by Chaucer of the Dartmouth Shipman—

> "His barge y-cleped was the Maudelayne."

Among the names of the vessels in these lists are two Magdeleines. Both are described as Navis, or Nef, and there is every reason to believe that the Nef was a small coasting vessel. The original "Maudelayne" was a barge; one calculated to go such expeditions as Chaucer's Shipman is described as making. Too much importance must not be ascribed to the description of vessels in these government returns, as has already been pointed out in the case of "St. Mary Cogge," which is described as a Balinger. If therefore, there had been only one "Magdeleine," or "Maudelayne," we might have jumped to the conclusion that this was a mistake in the description only. It is of course possible that this "Magdeleiné," which is entered in the second and ninth years of Richard II., may have been one and the same ship, and that between the two dates she may have changed owners.

If this is to be taken as a solution of the difficulty, then either George Coventre or Peter Risshenden—the names of the masters in the two entries—may have been the Dartmouth Shipman who rode a pilgrimage to Canterbury with the thirty-one companions, whose portraits are shewn in that famous gallery of speaking likenesses—the Prologue to the *Canterbury Tales.*

- The entries in respect to the cargoes simply relate to those portions only which were liable to duty. This is evident from the fact that some vessels are recorded as paying on such small quantities as four and six pieces of cloth, which by themselves would be but small shipments. The King had the right to levy a tax on wool, but his officers argued that the King ought to have the same from cloth made in the kingdom and exported, as from wool exported, according to the total amount of cloth made from a sack of wool. This was eventually fixed by Parliament at sixpence per pound on the value of the cloth exported. (Stat. 2, 5 Rich. II. c. 3.) Some of the entries relating to the payment of this tax appears as follows. No. $\frac{345}{11}$ A⁰ 8. (Rich. II.)

Carvela, "le Mary Ffitzwaryn," Walter Cok, sailed 24 Nov.
     pro 15 pann' alb' strict' 17s. 6d.
Carvela, "le Mary sauns pere," John Harrye, sailed 24 Nov.
     pro 18 pann' alb' strict' 18s. 8d.
     pro 5 ,, ,, ,, 9s. 4d.
Navis, "le Trinite," Walter Culvercock, sailed 13 Jan.
     pro 10 pann lat sine color 11s. 8d.
Navis, "le Mary," Roger Abraham, sailed 3 Jan.
     pro 15 pann' strict 17s. 6d.

The word pann', or pannus, cloth, is sometimes qualified by adjectives, and on some rolls these are quite omitted. The various sorts of pannus, or cloth, mentioned in these rolls are—

pro 4 pann' alb' strict'	. .	white, stretched.
pro 4 pann' russett .	. .	dingy brown.
pro 1 pann' de kersey	. .	
pro 3 pann' strict' color sine	.	stretched, but not dyed.
pro 12 pann' lat'	. .	latus = broad.
pro 6 pann' sine g^{d}no	. .	
pro panno' de blankett	. .	
pro pann' de Galeys .	.	Welsh flannel

Most rulers have from time to time endeavoured to fill their exchequers by taxing that necessary of life, common salt; Richard II. was no exception to this rule.

pro 15 charges Sal .   .   . val. £5

A Charge of Salt was some mode of measurement, query Load.

. Fish seems to have contributed to the revenue, for instance,

pro j last allec' alb .   .   . val. 30s.

One last (twelve barrel, or 20,000, Halliwell) of White Herrings.

pro ij ᴍ de Brodefysshe   .   . value £20

What these two thousand Brode or Broadfish were, is not easy to say, perhaps Ray; they certainly were not Hakes, as the following entry in the same list testifies—

pro vijc. Hakes   .   .   . value 46s. 8d.

These entries of 2000 Brodefysshe and 700 Hakes testify to what was probably an important industry having died out. The fish must have been salted, smoked, sun-dried, or otherwise preserved; and certainly there is but little done in the way of fish-curing in Dartmouth now. In the days when the fasts of the Church were rigidly observed, there was a large demand for cured fish; indeed most of the pilchards caught and cured on the Cornish coast to day are exported to and consumed by the Roman Catholic nations on the shores of the Mediterranean, and the market was much more extensive prior to the Reformation.

Other articles of food, beside fish, were taxed.

Pro figes & Raisons .   .   . val 33s. 4d.
pro fabis (broad beans)   .   . val 13s. 4d.
pro 1 dol' fab'   .   .   . val 13s. 4d.

This seems to imply that the beans were either packed in barrels (dol' = dolium, a tim, or barrel) or had been measured. If we consider that the real value of 13/4 at this period was probably eight to ten times as much, then we must conclude that beans were very dear in those days.

Wine, of course, was liable to duty then as now, and a special subsidy was raised on its importation, and entered on the rolls as distinct from the ordinary customs levied.

Here is one ship's cargo in wine.

Pro 15 dol' vini .   .   .   (subsidy)   45s.
   „ 15   „   „   ·   „   45s.
   „   6   „   „   ·   „   18s.

Pro 3 dol & 1 pip vini .   (subsidy) 10s. 6d.
,, 18 doliis vini.   .   ,,   54s.
,, 12 dol' & 1 pip vini .   .   ,,   37s. 6d.

Three shillings a tun on all wines, irrespective of quality, good, bad, or indifferent; a very simple method, but somewhat unfair.

In 1390, Dartmouth was the port from which all the tin raised in the country was shipped, but this absurd arrangement had expired prior to the period to which these records relate. It still was convenient for some mining districts, doubtless those on Dartmoor, to send their produce to Dartmouth for shipment. In $\frac{11}{10}$ An. 2–3 Rich. II. are the following entries:

pro 1 c stanni in gridell .   .   .   value 20s.
,, 3 c ,,   ,,   .   ,,   £3
,, 2 c .   40s.
,, 4 c ,   £4
,, 1 m ,   £10
,, 5 c ,,   ,,   .   .   .   ,,   £5

In $\frac{11}{12}$ the record of tin exported is made somewhat differently.

pro 10 pecis stanni .   .   . pecis = peciis or pieces.

I can find no clue to the word *gridell*; doubtless it means the shapes or blocks into which the tin was run after it had been smelted; in the second quotation from $\frac{11}{12}$ they are simply described as pieces.

There is only one mention of lead; viz., $\frac{11}{10}$.

pro 8 c Plumbi: val £8. Eight hundredweight of lead.

In the same roll is the following—

pro 1 c de pewtr' vessell' val 20s. Pewter vessels.

In $\frac{11}{11}$ is the following allusion to iron—

pro ferro   .   .   val £16
,,   ,, £8
,,   ,, £8
,,   ,, 106s. 8d.
,,   ,, 53s. 4d.
,,   .   .   ,, £4

The only entries of interest remaining to be noted are—

pro 8 duoden' pell' vitulanor'   .   . val 26s. 8d.

8 duodenis pellium vitulanorum = 8 doz. calves skins.

pro 2 tables de Alabast' val 40s. Alabaster.

DEVONIANA.

PART I.

BY J. T. WHITE.

(Read at Dawlish, July, 1881.)

UNDER this title I venture to offer the following notes for the *Transactions* of the Devonshire Association for the Advancement of Literature, Science, and Art. In the first I have endeavoured to show that a tradition current at Paignton, relating to Miles Coverdale, Bishop of Exeter, is unsupported by reliable testimony. The second relates to the domestic economy of Torwood Grange, a manor house that existed in Torquay several years ago, but about which very little is known beyond the fact that it was the residence of the Ridgeways, one of whom, the first Earl of Londonderry, was born in it.

I. DID MILES COVERDALE TRANSLATE THE SCRIPTURES AT PAIGNTON ?

It would be rank heresy to answer this question in the negative in the presence of some of the inhabitants of Paignton, where it is firmly believed that not only did Miles Coverdale, Bishop of Exeter, live at the Episcopal Palace, the remains of which still exist in that town, but that in it he undertook the translation of the Scriptures. It is useless to explain to such people that the story is erroneous, for they say, "It has been handed down by tradition, and therefore must be true." Those who have read the chronicles of the Reformation are aware that the so-called "tradition" has no warrant whatever, and it might be passed over unnoticed were it confined only to village gossip. But unfortunately it is gravely stated in the London papers from time to time, and, as a consequence,

many visitors to Torquay make a pilgrimage to the spot
where the good bishop is supposed to have done such excellent work. Only last year, one of the London high-class
weeklies, in a leaderette, referring to the visit of the Prince
of Wales during the Torbay Regatta, said:—"The Prince
slept on board his yacht, which was anchored within sight
and almost beneath the shadow of the Palace tower where
Miles Coverdale translated the Scriptures."   Under these
circumstances it may, perhaps, be allowable to set forth, however briefly, a few facts showing the entire absence of ground-
work for such a tradition.

Miles Coverdale was born (1487) in Yorkshire. His con-
version to the reformed faith took place about 1530. Owing
to his attachment to the principles of the Reformation, he was
compelled to take refuge in Germany, where, it is said, he
assisted Tindal in his translation of the Bible; but this has
been questioned. Tindal suffered martyrdom, but Coverdale
followed up the object in pursuit of which his colleague had
surrendered his life, and in 1534 the translation was not only
completed, but was dedicated to Henry VIII. When Edward
VI. ascended the throne, Miles Coverdale returned to England,
and having been appointed chaplain to his patron, Lord
Russell, he accompanied that nobleman in his expedition
(1549) to the West for the suppression of the rebels in
Devon. This service did not last many weeks. We know
from the public records the route Lord Russell's force took,
and at no time did it approach this part of the county. For
his piety and zeal, Miles Coverdale was raised to the see of
Exeter in 1550, when he was at least 63 years of age. The
bishop had been in office less than three years when Mary
came to the throne. Coverdale was imprisoned; his life was
threatened; indeed, it was only by the intercession of the
King of Denmark that, after two years' confinement, he was
permitted to go into exile. He retired to Geneva, where he
was soon busy at work in aiding other English refugees in
producing the Geneva Bible, which made its appearance in
1560.

It is a question whether Miles Coverdale ever visited
Paignton. He occupied the see less than three years; the
times were troublous; there were few facilities for travelling;
it therefore appears unlikely that the bishop, at the age of
63, visited this portion of his diocese; for at that time the
only means of travelling was by horse or mule.

Again, the probability is that the Bishop's Palace did not
at that time belong to the Bishops of Exeter, because we

know that Bishop Coverdale's predecessor, Bishop Voisey, kept such great state that he wasted the revenues of the diocese. "Out of twenty-five lordships and manors, enjoyed and left by his predecessors, of great yearly income, he left but three, and these leased out; of fourteen houses, well furnished, and the demesnes well stocked with cattle, deer, &c., he left to his successor only one, and that plundered of its furniture and charged with several annuities." This solitary house is understood to be the Palace at Exeter. In the *Antiquarian Itinerary*, vol. v. [ed. 1817], there is a notice of the Bishop's .Palace at Paignton, in which this passage occurs :—" Tradition, as well as history, is silent as far as respects the last bishop who lived here."

In the above an endeavour has been made, very shortly, to prove—

1. That Coverdale's translation of the Bible (a great portion of which was Tindal's work) was completed *before* he was made Bishop of Exeter, during his first exile, and therefore could not have been accomplished at Paignton.

2. That his later translations were made *after* his deposition, and during his second exile.

3. The extreme improbability of his ever having visited Paignton.

It may be remembered that the Rev. Treasurer Hawker read an excellent paper on Miles Coverdale at the Paignton Meeting of this Association, in 1878, but very little was said with regard to the bishop's connection with Paignton. Perhaps some member of the Devonshire Association who has the privilege of access to the archives of Exeter Cathedral may be able to throw further light on the subject.

II. Torwood Grange.

About forty years ago there stood a large building, known as Torwood Grange, on an eminence in the Babbacombe Road, Torquay. It was at one time the residence of the Ridgeways, the lords of the manor of Tormohun. One of these, Thomas Ridgeway, was knighted in 1600, was created a baronet in 1612, a baron in 1616, and Earl of Londonderry in 1622. The Grange, together with the rest of the property, passed into the hands of the Earl of Donegal, on his marriage with Lucy, the heiress of the last of the Londonderrys; and after his death the building was used as a farmhouse. There is very little known of the house, or of the home-life of the Ridgeways while they were there; but possibly the following fragment, narrating certain domestic economies during the last days that the Ridgeways held the property, will interest many of the members of this Association. The original is a quaint old document, covering both sides of four sheets of letter paper (sixteen pages) closely written. It was brought to light in a curious manner. Several years ago a solicitor had occasion to clear out a box which contained old deeds, letters, and other papers, some of which related to Torwood Grange. The deeds were preserved, but the "old letters" and papers were thrown aside as worthless. Amongst these presumedly worthless papers was the document referred to. Mr. S. Johnson, of Torquay, seeing that it possessed a local interest, asked that he might preserve it, and it is now in his possession.*

"An Account of John Blatch for disbursements since he made up his last account with my Lord London Derry. 1712.

for a Shoulder of Mutton	0	1	2
for a Leg of Mutton	0	1	2
for Bacon	0	0	8
for mending A Warming pan	0	0	11
for Seven hogsheads of Cyder drankt att Torwood during my L^{ds} stay there	7	0	0
for a Man and two horse's when my L^d went away	0	6	0
for a Letter from my L^d	0	0	10
for Letters to my L^d after he was gone	0	1	4
for the Land Tax for the mills	0	05	1½
for A Letter from Mr Holwell	0	0	6
for A Letter from my L^d	0	0	10
for Charges when Mr Holwell was att Torwood	0	2	6
for Sendeing my Son to Plymouth	0	10	0
p^d Mary Blatch by my L^d order	2	0	0
p^d the Window Tax	0	7	6
p^d Margaret & Betty Blatch by my L^d order	0	15	0
A Letter from my L^d	0	0	10
for Nailes for the Windmill	0	07	6
p^d Dearing for 2 Dayes worke on foxes house	0	03	0
for drawing a tree to the Windmill	0	02	6
A Letter from Mr. Manscome	0	00	6
Charges when Mr. King was at Torwood	0	07	6
A Letter from my L^d	0	00	10
Renewing the Bounds	0	10	0
pay^d Mr. Cowell for making the Windmill Sailes	0	05	0

* Since the above was written, Mr. Johnson has presented the original document to the Torquay Natural History Society.

	£	s	d
p^d for glazing the Windows of the Windmill	1	02	2
A Letter from my L^d	0	01	2
October—Mr. Holwell was at Torwood Charges	0	05	6
October—my Son went to Plymouth	0	12	0
A quarter of a: 100: of Reed by order for Job: Dining	0	05	0
Halfe A Quarter for Ann ffoxes house	0	02	6
Michlemas Court Charges	0	16	6
Lime and Nailes for the Windmill	0	02	0
Nailes & Worke on Ann ffoxes house	0	02	0
Swifts for the Barnes Doore	0	00	10
halfe a: 100: of Nailes	0	00	8
p^d Mr. Baker for his help to carry the beds to Sarcross	0	03	0
for my horses and Labor about the Beds	0	18	0
three: 100: of Lafts	0	03	3
for fore hogsheads of Lime	0	16	0
for A Hooke for the Barnes Doore	0	00	6
for mending the Key of my Ld Chamber doore	0	00	6
A Letter from my L^d	0	00	10
p^d for fetching of Stones for the Garden wall	0	02	6
p^d for Nailes and mending the Gate	0	00	6
A Letter from Mr Holwell	0	00	10
p^d for Lafts & Nailes	0	01	8
p^d Ann ffox for keepeing the oar	0	05	0
payed to the Land tax for the Yeare: 1712 due the 25 of March 1713	10	18	0
payed to the Window Tax: 1712	01	10	0
the Church & poore Rates: 1712	07	03	4
for Blatch Sallary for gott is put under	02	00	0

For the Year 1713.

	£	s	d
Charges at the Court	0	17	6
p^d to Margaret ffox for keeping the ore	0	05	0
for carrying timber to the Windmill	0	01	6
for Six: 100: of Lafts & Nailes	0	10	0
for making A Doore to Coles Sellar	0	03	0
A Letter from my L^d	0	00	10
for Carrying twenty pounds to Darth^mo	0	02	0
for Rideing twise to Bogams	0	04	0
p^d for Nailes & Spooks	1	09	9
p^d for fetching the Spooks & Nailes from Exon	0	05	0
p^d for 6: Hogsheads & A halfe of Lime	0	18	6
A Letter from Mr Holwell	0	00	6
for Renewing the Bounds	0	10	0
A Letter from my L^d	0	00	10
p^d to Tho: Jeffryes for the Barnes floore	0	13	0
Sending A Letter to my L^d	0	00	2

	£	s	d
Charges att Michlemas Coart	0	18	6
for halfe 100: of board nailes	0	00	8
for Mr Clarke & his horse	0	14	6
for three: 1000: Laft Nailes	0	03	9
for three: 1000: Laft Nailes	0	03	9
for A: 100: Board Nailes	0	01	4
for two bushells of hair & fetching	0	01	7
for halfe: 100: board Nailes	0	00	8
for : 1000 Lafte nailes	0	01	3
A Letter from my Lord	0	00	10
for two Locks & Keys	0	01	6
for halfe : 100 : Board Nailes	0	00	8
for 2000 : & A Quarter of Laft Nailes	0	03	0
for Mr Kings Clarke	0	01	0
A Letter from my L^d	0	00	10
for drawing of Timber for the house	3	10	0
for one hogshead & halfe of Lime	0	04	6
p^d for pantils & fetching	0	14	6
p^d Bouchers for Slats	1	08	0
for ploughing for my L^d trees	0	02	8
p^d for making the pigs house doores	0	09	0
for Sending A Letter to my L^d	0	00	2
March 2th for glazeing the Windows	0	06	0
for making the lafts	1	10	0
p^d Tho. Jeffryes for Selling the Timber	0	15	0
for carrying my Ld Survey books to Exon	0	03	0
A Letter from my L^d	0	0	10
p^d Tho: Jeffryes for building the house	13	0	0
p^d the mason in parte	01	04	0
Rec^d three Letters from my Ladye	00	02	6
for Four hogsheads of Cyder	05	00	0
p^d for 22000 of Slatts	08	05	0
for fetching Sand & water for the house	0	03	6
for one to Cleare the Rubble	0	02	6
p^d Walter Dearing for Heyling the Bruehouse	03	02	6
for one : 1000 : stones	00	08	0
payed to the Land Tax for the Year 1713 due the 25 : of March 1714	05	09	0
payed to the Window Tax 1713	01	10	0
the Church and poor Rates : 1713	05	17	5
my Sallary	02	00	0

For the Year 1714

	£	s	d
p^d Tho. Jeffryes for Laying the Barns floore	1	04	0
p^d him more for takeing up the Seats for my L^d burying	0	04	8
October the 28 p^d Walt Dearing for Healing	7	04	6
p^d margaret ffox for keeping the ore	0	05	0

	£	s	d
April the 29ᵗʰ Charges for the Court . . .	1	01	6
two letters from my Ladye	0	01	8
for Renewing the Bounds	0	10	0
pᵈ the Glazer in parte	0	08	0
A Letter from my Ladye	0	00	10
pᵈ Hydon the mason	2	00	0
Charges att the Court October the : 25 : .	0	19	6
pᵈ Mʳ King October 25 . . .	15	00	0
pᵈ for Lafts & Nailes & Lock & Key . .	0	06	0
pᵈ for : 6 : hogsheads of Lime . .	0	18	0
for fetching Water & Sand . . .	0	03	0
for : 1000 : & Quarter of board nailes ⅓ 100 hatch nailes	0	02	0
for : 3000 : of Lafts nailes . . .	0	03	9
pᵈ Philip Stooke for Iron Work . .	0	06	4
A Letter from Mʳ Holwell . . .	0	00	6
pᵈ the Glazer in part . . .	1	12	11
pᵈ Tho: Jeffryes for Staning A Ladder . .	0	02	6
payed to the Land Tax for the Yeare 1714 due the 25 of March 1715 . . .	5	09	0
payed the Window Tax 1714 . . .	1	10	0
the Church & poor Rates : 1714 . . .	9	11	2
my Sallary	2	00	0

For the Year 1715 :

	£	s	d
pᵈ Taylor the Glazier in part . .	0	12	0
Charges at Michlemas Coart . . .	0	17	6
for the Survey att Torwood for Vitreys Estate .	0	15	6
pᵈ the Poor Rate for yᵉ mills . .	0	12	8
for two men to mend the mill hedge . .	0	02	0
A Letter from my Ladye . . .	0	00	10
for carrying Jeffry Bickforde Leas to Mr. Holwells .	0	02	6
for carrying Timber to Torkey . .	0	01	6
for carrying the Recits to be sent to London . .	0	02	6
A Letter from Mʳ Holwell . . .	0	00	6
for A hogshead of Lime . . .	0	02	6
for halfe 1000 of Laft Nailes . . .	0	00	8
for one Hogshead & halfe of Lime . .	0	03	9
for two hogshead of Cyder to London . .	2	00	0
A Letter from my Ladye . . .	0	00	10
for : 2000 : Laft nailes . . .	0	02	8
ffeb. mʳ Holwell was at Torwood Charges .	0	12	0
for drawing of Stones to the Water Mill .	0	10	0
for a Line for the Jack . . .	0	01	8
for 7 Lobsters att the Court . . .	0	03	8
pᵈ for Glazing the Windows . . .	2	03	3½
pᵈ for hookes and swifts for the pigs loose door .	0	01	0
A Letter from my Ladye . . .	0	00	10

payed to the Land Tax for the year 1718 due the 25
of March 1716 . . . 5 9 0
payed to the Window Tax 1715 . . 1 10 0
the Church and poore Rates 1718 . . . 8 16 10
my Sallary 2 00 0

For the Yeare 1716

p^d for carryage of the box from London to Exon . 0 05 0
for fetching the box from Exon . . . 0 03 0
p^d Willm Baker the miller for 2 days worke . . 0 02 0
for A man & horse to carry freth . . . 0 01 0
for A man one day 0 01 0
To the mason for one day Ripping stones for the Stable 0 01 6
for two Load of Straw to make Cob for the stable to the
mill 0 02 0
for A man & A horse to Cary Earth to ye Stable . 0 03 0
p^d for two Letters brought to Tor Abby for m^r Holwell 0 00 8
April 27th Court Charges . . . 0 18 6
p^d margaret ffox . . 0 05 0
two pounds of Wooll for the mill . . . 0 00 6
p^d for : 1000 : of Slatts . . . 0 08 0
p^d in part for Holles Estate . . . 0 00 7½
Drawing of Timber to the mill stable . . . 0 03 0
one : 100 : of Lafts . . . 0 01 1
one : 1000 : of Laft Nailes . . . 0 01 3
p^d for 4 hogshead & A halfe of Lime . . 0 11 3
fetching water to temper the Lime . . . 0 01 6
A Letter from Mr Holwell . . . 0 00 6
Mr Holwell at Torwood Charges . . 0 03 6
when my Son carryed the money to Mr Holwells . 0 02 0
for two : 100 : of Lafts . . . 0 02 2
one : 1000 : Laft Nailes . . . 0 01 3
for A new Ladder 0 06 0
for Crying the mill at Totness & Nuton . . 0 01 0
for two hogsheads of Lime . . . 0 05 0
A Letter from m^r Holwell . . . 0 00 6
Renewing the bounds . . . 0 10 0
Drawing of timber for the mills . . 0 07 6
October Court Charges . . . 0 19 6
Nouember : p^d for planke and Board sawing . . 0 19 0
Wooll for the mill . . . 0 01 0
to Baker the Glazier . . . 0 00 6
October : p^d for makeing A house of office . . 1 07 3
for painting it 0 07 4
for nailes for it 0 02 3¼
one : 1000 : of Laft Nailes . . . 0 01 3
for 4 Spookes . . . 0 00 8
for Board Nailes & Hatch Nailes . . 0 00 6

malt & Hops for the Survey . . . 0 06 0

p^d to George Jonson for the thatchin Spears & Rope
Yarn 01 02 6

for one : 100 & A Quarter of Reed . . . 01 02 6

p^d June the twelft to Tho : Jeffres for things done when
my Lord was hear by his order . . . 01 00 5

June 10th p^d John Hydon for makeing the steps to the
forgate 0 08 0

p^d to Tho : Cowell for Lime to the Water Mill . . 0 05 0

A parte of Willm Curtese's Tax . . . 0 00 9

p^d to Tho : Jeffryes for Worke on Coles celler . . 0 02 3

for Nailes 0 00 4

for nailes for the house of office . . . 0 01 9

to the Carpenter one day on the pound doore . . 0 01 6

To Sr Bradwardine Jackson by his Bill given to me is 16 06 7

p^d to Amy Baker for drinke at the Court . . 0 11 6

for mending A Lock & Key . . . 0 00 6

for Ironworke for the Gates . . . 0 03 0

for Cleansing the Jack . . . 0 02 0

for Ironworke for the Gate . . . 0 00 8

for mending three Locks & Keys . . . 0 01 0

for mending A pair of Jemmes . . . 0 00 6

for makeing two Scrapers . . . 0 02 6

for makeing A new Lock & Key . . . 0 01 4

for makeing A new Key . . . 0 00 6

for makeing the Ireworke of the pound doore . . 0 03 0

bought : 21 ; Apple trees in 1715 . . . 01 10 0

bought : 10 ; more in 1716 . . . 0 15 0

p^d the workemen on the Key . . . 10 00 0

p^d Sr Bradwardine Jackson . . . 01 10 0

p^d to the Land Tax for the year : 1716 due the 25 : of
March : 1717 . . . . 10 18 0

payed to the Window Tax : 1716 . . . 01 10 0

the Church and poore Rates : 1716 . . . 12 04 3

my Sallary as Bayliffe 02 00 0

*An Account of the Charges at my Ld London Derry's funerall not
mentioned in the Accounts : 1713.*

for Beer att the Church house . . . 1 4 5

for makeing three Graues . . . 1 4 0

for three Women to Carry Eearth . . . 0 1 6

for Lime Sand & Labor . . . 0 2 6

to Tho : Jeffryes . . . 0 1 6

for Beer att Sandy Gate . . . 0 3 6

for Beer att Joan Cowells . . . 0 8 0

for meat & Drinke & Wine att Tor towne for the
Beares & Gentlemen . . . 4 0 0

for A murning Suit for my Selfe by order . . 3 15 0

An Account of John Blatches Disboursements by my Lady London Derryes order when my Lord Dunnigall was at Torwood in August 1716.

	£	s	d
for three y^{ds} of Cloath to mend & Couer the beds	0	1	6
for : 12 : y^{ds} of poledany to Couer : 2 : beds	0	7	1
for two White Chamber p—ts	0	1	6
for y^{ds} of Canvas for the beds	0	2	8
To A Taylor for two Days Work and thread	0	2	8
for two White porrengers	0	0	6
for two muggs	0	0	6
for Wood for the fire	0	5	6
for three Geese	0	3	9
for Butter	0	13	6
for milk & Cream at times	0	5	6
for one pound of Loaf Sugar	0	1	0
for : 5 p^d of powdered Sugar	0	2	8
for spice	0	1	2
for : 11 : Chicken at 5^d p piece	0	4	7
for : 6 : Ditto att 3½ p. piece	0	1	9
for Tinning A Sauce pan	0	0	8
for A brush for the Chambers	0	1	3
for A mopp	0	0	8
for Onions	0	0	11
for fish at times	0	1	2
for two bed Cords	0	4	3
for A dozen Lobsters	0	5	0
for Capers	0	0	10½
for Bread & fflower	0	10	6
for Beer	1	4	6
for A man fetching Wine from Topsham	0	2	6
for one fetching Wine from Darth^{mo}	0	1	6
for two men Cleansing the Court	0	2	0
for a man & two horses to fetch Sande	0	2	0
for 2 women for. Cleaning the house	0	10	0
for Beefe & mutton	1	10	0
for A man & horse to fetch Wine from Totness	0	1	0
for Soape & Washing the Linning	0	3	6
for Candles	0	5	6
for Eggs	0	0	8
for : 2 : Dozen of Wine from Totness	2	0	0
for : 2 : bottles of Clarett from Ditto	0	4	0
for two Dozen of Wine from Topsham	1	13	0
for one Dozen of Wine from Darth^{mo}	0	14	0
for A Woman makein beds & Washing	0	1	6
for Glasses	0	4	4
for meat for ten horses : 5 : dayes	1	5	0
for Beer at Joan Cowells	0	17	6
June the 29 : 1717 p^d the Land Tax	2	0	10½

NOTES ON SOME DEVONSHIRE PLANT NAMES.

BY REV. HILDERIC FRIEND.

(Read at Dawlish, July, 1881.)

In my wanderings up and down the country I have been struck with the want of definiteness in the application of local names to our commonest plants and flowers. At the same time, many names are preserved in the most distant parts of the country, which help to throw light on each other, though they are applied to different plants in different localities. My meaning will be made plain as we proceed. The present collection of names makes no pretension to being complete. The notes have been made up during country rambles taken within the past few weeks, but it was thought that some good might result from placing them before the Association, since other collectors, with more leisure, more scientific knowledge of botany, more familiarity with the local dialect, and with a better knowledge of the names used in other parts of the country, could be thereby stimulated to take up the work. I have not yet seen the *Glossary of Plant Names* by Mr. Britten, but have no doubt it would prove very helpful to collectors. One of the incidental advantages of a study like this is the aid it gives to the study of philology, especially the philology of the English tongue and of our local dialects.* An illustration of this will be afforded under such words as Eglet, Maiden's Ruin, and Slones.

1. *Arb-rabbit.*

This word is a corruption of " Herb-Robert " (*Geranium Robertianum*). I was passing through some fields near

* See " *English Plant Names from the Tenth to the Fifteenth Century.* By John Earle, M.A. Oxford: At the Clarendon Press. MDCCCLXXX." This is a valuable little work, with an Introduction of more than 100 pages, teeming with information. There is also an Index for the Latin names, another for English and Saxon, and a third for French, by means of which the value of the book as a work of reference is greatly enhanced.

Newton Abbot one day with a friend, plucking flowers, and discussing them, when a woman who was passing by volunteered the following information: "Us calls that *Arb-rabbit*. The oal people gathers it, an' lays'en up for winter, to make arb tea." The flowers are called by various names, as *e.g.* "Bird's-eye," or "Little Robins;" and by the peasants in Sussex "Little Bachelor Button." Herb-Robert is also known as "Stinking Crane's-bill" (the name, as in many other cases, being given to the flower on account of the shape of the seed-pods), the whole plant emitting a very unpleasant smell on being bruised. I extract the following note from *Fragments of Two Essays on Philology*, by Rev. J. C. Hare, M.A.:

"*Herb-Robert, Robertskraut* or *Ruprechts-kraut*, a sort of wild geranium, flowers in April, the 29th of which was consecrated to St. Robert. Adelung deduces the German name from a certain disease, which used to be called *Sanct Ruprechts-plage*, and against which this plant was held to be a powerful remedy. But how then did the disease get this name? Far more probably was it so called because St. Robert cured it by means of his herb."

I may here add a note on the curious provincialism contained in this word. In Sussex we have a word "robert" or "robbut," a corruption of "rabbit." Thus, whilst in Devonshire "robert" becomes "rabbit," in Sussex the change is just the other way, and "rabbit" becomes "robert." The Sussex form, however, is really more near the old form (compare Dutch *robbe, robbeken*) of the word for rabbit.

2. *Aver; see Iver.*

3. *Archangel.*

In some parts of Devonshire the Dead-nettle (*Lamium album*, "White Dead-nettle;" or, as it is often called, "Blind-nettle" and "Dumb-nettle") is called Archangel. The name properly belongs to the Yellow Weasel-snout (*Galeobdolon luteum*). Bentham places this among the Lamiums, however, so that it is quite possible that the name Archangel may be found to be given to each of the Lamiums (red, white, and yellow) of Bentham. In some parts of England the Archangel (*Lamium*) is eaten as a pot herb; so in Sweden.

4. *Bird's-eye.*

This is a very vague term, being applied to several flowers, the names of which are not otherwise known. Thus the various kinds of wild geranium are called "Bird's-eye." There is also a pretty little blue flower (see "*Cat's-eye*") which is so called. The garden flower commonly known as London Pride, Prince's Feather, or Garden-gates (which see), is sometimes called Bird's-eye in South Devon, and possibly • elsewhere. The Campion (see "Robin" below) is frequently so called. In Sussex the wild geranium (see "Arb-rabbit"), and the *Lychnis diurna* (or *L. dioica* ; Linnæus), are generally called Bachelor Buttons. (See Bull's-eye" below.)*

5. *Bluebell.*

Here we have another very ill-defined term, the name being applied variously to the wild Hyacinth and the Campanula.

6. *Boy's Love.*

This* is one of the names by which Southernwood (*Artemisia abrotanum*) is known. In Sussex it is called Lad's Love. Other names are "Old Man" and "Maiden's Ruin," which see.

7. *Bugloss.*

As this word occurs in some botanical works, it may be said not to be, strictly speaking, a Devonshire name; but it is introduced here on account of the fact that whilst you will often hear the word used by the common people of Devon, it is unknown in many parts of the country. There are two flowers which bear this name; viz., (1) *Echium vulgare*, "Common Viper's Bugloss;" and (2) *Lycopsis arvensis*, "small Bugloss." In Devonshire the Forget-me-not is called Bugloss.

8. *Bull's-eye.*

This name (like "Piskies" below) is limited to some parts of the county. It is applied by some to the Campion or *Lychnis diurna*. (See under "Robin-flower.")

9. *Buttercup.*

A common name for the Marsh Marigold (*Caltha palustris*), which it resembles. (See under "Cowslip.") The name "Gold Cup" often takes the place of Buttercup for the Meadow Ranunculus. (See "Drunkard" below.)

10. *Butter and Eggs.*

An expressive name for the Narcissus (*N. biflorus*), the petals of which are white and the nectary yellow. In Sussex

* In Somersetshire the name "Bird's-eye" is applied to quite another flower ; viz., the Pansy, Heart's-ease, or Violet. Thus a large yellow Pansy will be pointed out by the expression, "Look at thik yellow Bird's-eye !"

"Butter-and-eggs" is the name for *Cypripedium*. (See "Lady's Boots" below.) The Narcissus is also called "Hen-and-chickens."

11. *Cat-mint.*

The *Nepeta* or ground-ivy. This plant (known as *Nepeta glechoma* or *Glechoma hederacea*) is called "Lion's Mouth" by the Sussex peasantry. Compare "Weasel-snout" and other names for *Labiatæ*, compounded of words with *mouth.* The Snapdragon (*Antirrhinum majus* and *A. Orontium*) are in some places called "Rabbit's Mouth." (See "Rabbit's Flower" below.)

12. *Cat's-eye.*

The common Speedwell (*Veronica*) sometimes receives this name. The flower is a bright blue, and though it is often called Bird's-eye (which see), the term Cat's-eye is much more appropriate.

13. *Cat's-tail.*

A common name for the Reed-mace (*Typha latifolia*); but to a native of Sussex the word "Cat's-tail" would suggest quite a different thing, that name being applied to the male blossom of the Hazel or Willow, and to a cultivated flower common in cottage gardens.

14. *Cheese.*

In Devonshire, as in Sussex, the Mallow (*Malva sylvestris*) is known by this name, on account of its peculiar cheese-like fruit. In both these counties the White-thorn is also called "Bread-and-cheese tree," the leaves, and especially the early buds, being eaten by the children. (See "Cuckoo-flower.")

15. *Chibble.*

Small green onions are called Chibbles. This is a most interesting word, on account of its renowned family connections. In the diminutive form we find it represented by the following words: German *Zwiebel,* Spanish *cebolla,* Italian *cipolla,* and with double diminutive suffix *cipalletta.* On the other hand, we find the simple form in Anglo-Saxon *ciepe, cipe ;* Latin *cœpa,* &c. With this are connected the words *chives, cives,* &c. In Mrs. Whitcombe's *Bygone Days in Devon and Cornwall* we read (p. 47), "The fairies had even their musicians; hautboys were syves (*i.e.* chives) :

"Excepting one, which pufte the player's face,
And was a *chibole,* serving for the base."

16. *Chickens.*

See "Garden-gates," and compare "Hen-and-chickens." Also see "Bird's-eye" above. The London Pride is sometimes so called.

17. *Cowslip.*

The Meadow Ranunculus (*Ranunculus acris*), commonly known as Buttercup or Gold-cup (Somerset, "Go'-cup"), is called Cowslip in some parts of Devon, where the Cowslip proper (*Primula veris*) is seldom seen. The same name is also applied to the Foxglove.

18. *Cress.*

This word is used with others in cases which are unknown in some parts of the country. Thus "Swine's-cress" and "Wart-cress" are the common names of the *Senebiera;* "Water-cress" for *Nasturtium* (shortened to *Stertion*) *officinale;* "Mustard-cress" for *Sinapis nigra;* and "Garden-cress," or "Pepper-cress" (or "Pepper-wort") for *Lepidium campestre.* The *Thlaspi arvense* is called "Penny-cress," and the Cardamine "Bitter-cress," &c. &c. The word (as in some other places) is often pronounced *crease.*

19. *Cuckoo-flower.*

To deal fully with the subject of "Cuckoo-flowers" would be to write quite a treatise. I may refer to the *Folklore Record*, ii. 78, *seq.* for a valuable collection of notes, but this work will only be in the hands of members of the Folklore Society, and is not quite exhaustive. The Cuckoo's Garland (says Mr. Hardy) consists of several ingredients. The true Cuckoo-flower is *Cardamine pratensis*, known as "Bitter-cress" and "Lady's Smock;" and on the Borders as Pinks or Wild Rocket. Gerard, in his *Herball* (p. 261), says: "These flower for the most part in April, when the cuckowe doth begin to sing her pleasant notes without stammering." (See "Milkmaid" below.) Miss Baker thinks that the "Cuckoo-flower of Clare is the red-flowered Campion (*Lychnis diurna*, see "Robin"); a name which is given it in some parts of Devon. According to Halliwell's *Archaic Dictionary* the Hare-bell is called "Cuckoo." But there is some confusion respecting what flower is really meant by the Hare-bell. (See below.) By some the *Campanula rotundifolia* (or Bell-flower, sometimes called "Blue-bell") is so called; whilst others call the *Agraphis nutans* (or Wild Hyacinth) Hare-

bell, others Blue-bell.*   Now it is true that the latter
(*Agraphis nutans*) is called "Cuckoo-flower" in Devon,
although this is probably on account of the similarity this
flower bears to the Orchis, which is specially known in this
county as the Cuckoo-flower. (See under "Ramsey.") But it
is not in Devonshire alone that the *Orchis mascula* is thus
known, as Mr. Hardy (*loc. cit.* p. 79) has shown.   In Bucks
and Essex any spring-flowering plant which has no other
name is called "Cuckoo," and in Devonshire the term is not
much more definite.   In Sussex the White-thorn is called
"Cuckoo's bread-and-cheese tree." (See "Cheese" above.)
There is an old proverb—

> "When the cuckoo comes to the bare thorn,
> Sell your cow and buy your corn."

In reference to the *Orchis mascula*, we find that instead of
being called "Cuckoos," they in some places, as in Sussex,
bear the name of "Long-purples," which reminds us of Shakespeare's words—

> "And *long-purples*,
> That liberal shepherds give a grosser name."

20. *Damzel*.

The small black plum which grows wild in hedgerows,
called *Scads* in some parts of England. Damzel is probably
connected with "Damson," the change of *n* to *l* being quite
common, and may be taken as a diminutive form, meaning
"the little damson" (from Damascus, Damascene).

21. *Dog-violet*.

Not peculiarly local. The wild violet is so called in many
parts of the country, although not universally known by that
name, any more than the wild or hedge rose is known everywhere as Dog-rose. But the name Dog-violet is intelligible in
the face of the Latin *Viola canina*. I draw attention to the
word in order to show that the word "dog," as a synonym of
"wild" in plant names, is not peculiar to ourselves. We
have the following names (among others) in illustration—

> Dog-violet and Wild-violet,
> Dog-rose and Wild-rose,
> Dog-wood and Wild-cornel,
> Dogs-mercury and Wild-mercury,

which latter is termed *Mercuriale sauvage*, or *chou de chien*,
by the French, and by the Greeks κυνο-κράμβη.

---

* Also known as *Hyacinthus nonscriptus*, the Sussex "Blue-bottle."

21A. *Drunkard.*

As already stated, the Marsh Marigold is often called
" Buttercup." But another name for it is " Drunkard." When
I was told this by a young person in South Devon, I asked
why it had received such a name. " *They say* that if you
gather them you will get drunk, and so they are called
Drunkards," was the prompt reply. The true explanation
lies in their fondness for water.

22. *Eglet.*

The fruit of the White-thorn. A long list might be formed
of the names used in various places. We have the following:
" Gazels " (French *Groseiller,* a currant tree), " Gogs," " Hog-
gazels," " Alves " (or " Halves " from) " Agarves," " Hogarves,"
" Hads-and-halves," " Hazles," &c.

23. *Floptop.*

The Foxglove *(Digitalis purpurea)*; also called " Flox,"
" Rabbit's Flower," " Flapdock," " Cowflop," and " Cowslip."

24. *Flox.*

The foxglove. (See " Floptop " and " Rabbit's Flower.")

25. *French Pink.*

The *Armeria Maritima,* Thrift, Sea-pink, or Sea-gilliflower,
which grows in the cliffs by the sea-shore, and forms a very
pretty border for gardens. The flowers are sometimes white,
more generally red (pink). In Somerset known as "Cushions."

26. *Garden-gates.*

" What do you call that flower ?" I enquired of a woman at
Bovey Tracey one day as I pointed to a clump of Saxifrage,
the flower elsewhere known as London Pride, Prince's Feather,
and Pink. " We call it *Garden-gates,*" was her reply. Other
names for the flower in Devon are " Bird's-eye," and " Chickens "
(which see), and also " Kiss-me-quick."

27. *Harebell.*

The white Hyacinth *(Orchis mascula,* or *Orchis masculata)*
is sometimes called Harebell in this county. But, as before
remarked (see " Cuckoo-flower "), there is considerable confusion on the subject; and this not merely among the vulgar.

Thus, in his *Handbook of the Torquay Flora*, Mr. Stewart gives us, under Campanulaceæ—

"CAMPANULA ; BELL-FLOWER.

Campanula rotundifolia (round-leaved Bell-flower, or *Harebell*)." Turning to *Folklore Record*, ii. 79, we read: "In Devonshire, according to Mr. Halliwell (*Archaic Dictionary*), the Harebell (*Agraphis nutans*) is called Cuckoo." Now it is true, as shown above, that *Agraphis nutans* is called Cuckoo, but not Harebell; and turning again to *Handbook of Torquay Flora*, we find *Agraphis nutans* described as the wild Hyacinth or Blue-bell. What we wish to notice is, that the Orchis is sometimes called Harebell in Devonshire. The Hyacinth (or *hyercind*, as it is vulgarly pronounced in Devon) is called Blue-bottle in some places.

28. *Hazle.*

See "Eglet," above.

29. *Hen-and-chickens.*

The name by which a hybrid kind of Daisy is known. It is also applied to other flowers, one of which is the Narcissus.

30. *Horse-daisy.*

The Ox-eye or *Chrysanthemum leucanthemum.* Probably Horse-daisy is as common a name in other parts as is Ox-eye; but it is strange that people should suppose it is so called because the horse is fond of it, seeing cattle will not eat it while green. Sir Thomas Brown long since remarked, in his *Vulgar Errors:* "And so are they deceived in the name of *Horse-radish, Horse-mint, Bull-rush,* and many more; conceiving therein some prenominal consideration, whereas that expression is but a Grecism, by the prefix of ἵππος or βοῦς ; that is, *Horse* and *Bull,* intending no more than *great.* According whereto the *great* Dock is called *Hippolapathum,*" &c. In Somerset the Ox-eye is called "Thunder-daisy."

31. *Iver.*

This word is variously pronounced as *Aver, Iver,* &c. The farmers in this neighbourhood speak of "Clover and Iver," with which they sow their fields. The "Iver" forms what would in some parts of England be called "Seed-hay;" the word being a corruption of "Eaver," Rye-grass, or *Lolium perenne.* In Somersetshire, if the farmers require Rye or Ray-grass, they ask for "Devon evver."

32. Jack-by-the-hedge.

In Devonshire the Garlic-mustard (*Alliaria officinalis*) is thus known, another name being "Sauce-alone." But in some parts of England (as in Sussex for instance) "Jack-in-the-hedge" is the name given to *Lychnis diurna* (or *L. dioica*, Linnæus), the Campion or Red Robin. (See "Robin" below.)

33. Lady's Boots.

It has been often remarked that what was formerly consecrated to Venus, was often transferred in the middle ages to the Virgin Mary. Among the Scandinavians Freya used to occupy the place now taken up by the Virgin. (See Hare's *Essays*, vol. i. p. 21. Farrer, *Primitive Manners and Customs*, p. 313.) "*Our Ladies Slipper*, so called from the shape of the flower, is the *Calceolus Mariæ*, or Cypripedium; in Germany the same plant is *Venusschuh*, sometimes *Marienschuh*, *Marienpantoffel*." Hence the form "Lady's Boots" stands for "Our Lady's Boots;" and it is interesting to find this word preserved in Devon, now that it has in some other places given way to such forms as "Shoes and Stockings," "Pattens and Clogs," "Butter and Eggs." There seems to be some confusion between the *Cypripedium* and *Lotus corniculatus*. The flowers of the latter are very like those of *Hippocrepis comosa*, or the Horse-shoe Vetch, which grows very freely and prettily in our hedgerows. (See "Lady's Smock" below.)

34. Lady's Smock.

Contracted from "Our Lady's Smock;" referring, as in the last case, to the Virgin Mary. But it is strange that in Devonshire the Lady's Smock is called "Milkmaid" (which see); many of the common people never using the name Lady's Smock at all.

35. Lammint.

A corruption of "lamb-mint," or mint for lamb. Does this indicate that in Devonshire lamb is a commoner article of diet than in some parts? The word *mint* is differently used in Devon to what it is in some other places. What is here called peppermint is called *spare* (for *spear*) *mint* elsewhere; whilst the word *lamb-mint* is unknown in many places.

36. Maiden's Ruin.

Southernwood (*Artemisia abrotanum*); also called "Old Man," and "Boy's Love." The form here used should be observed. One will often hear the words "Boy's Love and Maiden's Ruin" joined as one name. In Devonshire a "maid," or "maiden," means a "girl;" but you will never hear such a phrase as "They have three boys and two maidens" in some counties.

Archbishop Trench has said, "Words not a few were once applied to both sexes alike, which are now restricted to the female; it is so even with girl, which once meant a young person of either sex. Compare the word *virgin*, and the fact that in Sussex the word *maid* is still sometimes used for a child of either sex who is too young to work."

37. *May.*

The Lilac is called May in this part, though the word May is elsewhere applied to the White-thorn. Some people apply the name to both Lilac and White-thorn.

38. *Milkmaid; Milkymaid.*

This name is given to the Lady's Smock (*Cardamine pratensis*), also called Bitter-cress and Cuckoo-flower (which see). In some places the *Lotus corniculatus*, or Bird's-foot trefoil, is so called; and the flowers of the *Convolvulus sepium* (or "Old Man's Night-cap)," also bear the name of Milkmaids in some parts.

39. *Old Man.*

Southernwood: see "Boy's Love" and "Maiden's Ruin."

40. *Pink.*

The following flowers among others bear this name. (1) The Garden Pink (*Dianthus*); (2) Thrift (*Armeria*, see "French Pink"); (3) London Pride (see "Garden-gates"). Any flower with a pink or red blossom, whose name is not easily remembered, is frequently spoken of under this name.

41. *Piskies.*

The flowers (*Stellaria holostea*, Stitchwort), which are usually called Snappers, or Snapjacks, are known as Piskies in some parts of Devon.

41A. *Prince's Feather.*

The name given to Pampas Grass, though London Pride is called Prince's Feather in some places. Also applied to Love-lies-bleeding.

42. *Rabbit's Flower.*

The Foxglove (*Digitalis purpurea*), also called Flop-top and Flox (which see). The Snapdragon is likewise so called.

43. *Ramsey.*

One form of Ramsons or Ramsins; another form into which it is corrupted being "Ransom." The Broad-leaved Wild Garlic (*Allium ursinum*), which emits a very strong smell when in blossom. A curious illustration of the way in which plant names get confused is afforded by this word. In Sussex the children gather the Orchis and call it Rams' Horns, which is, I believe, only another corruption of Ramsons. See Anglo-Saxon *Hramse*. In Aubrey's *Gentilisme and Judaisme*, 1686, we read :

"The Vulgar in the West of England doe call the month of March, Lide. (They have) a proverbiall ryhthme—

"'Eate Leekes in Lide, and *Ramsins* in May,
And all the yeare after Physitians may play.'"

This reminds us of another Devonshire proverb—

"Eat an apple as you go to bed,
Physicians then may beg their bread."

43A. *Robin-flower.*

The different kinds of Campion (*Lychnis*) are known as Red Robin, Ragged Robin, and White Robin (including the Bladder Campion). In some places the Red Robin (*Lychnis diurna* or *dioica*) is called "Jack-in-the-Hedge," the White Robin being "Grandmother's Night-cap." Some Devonshire folk call Herb-Robert by the name Robin-flower, just as in Sussex it, in common with the Campion, is called Bachelor Button. The Red Campion is also called Bull's-eye in some parts of Devon. In Somerset it is "Robin Hood."

44. *Shaking-grass.*

Quaking-grass (*Briza media*); known in the North as "Doddering Dick," and in the South as "Doddle-grass," or "Toddling-grass," because it is constantly in motion.

44A. *Shepherd's Needle.*

Venus' Comb (*Scandix pectens*) is often so known; but in some places this flower is called "Hedgehog."

45. *Slones.*

The fruit of the Black-thorn—a small sour plum. The Anglo-Saxon word was *slá*. We now form the plural Sloes; but the Devonshire form is very interesting, as it preserves the Anglo-Saxon plural ending. The plural of *slá* (*slág* or *sláh*) was *slán, slágan,* so that *Slones* is a double-plural. Does the name *Slagthorn* (sloe-thorn) still survive in the sense of Black-thorn? In Sussex the Sloe is called "Winterpick."

46. *Snapjack.*

The Stitchwort (*stellaria*); also called Snappers—because when the seed-pod is ripe it will snap on being pressed—and Piskies.

47. *Strawberry.*

The Cinquefoil (*Potentilla reptans* and other varieties), with bright yellow flowers; which with the leaves have much the appearance of wild strawberries, though they are easily distinguishable. It is not in Devon alone that this name is given to Cinquefoil.

48. *Sweet Alice.*

Belongs to the Cruciferæ or Brassicacæ. A small white flower, which blossoms in April, and is largely used in garden borders. It is also called Snow-in-Summer, and Snow-on-the-Mountain; and in some parts Milk-and-Water, from the colour of the blossom. On account of its use as a border plant, it is frequently known only by the name "Seedling" or "Bordering."

49. *Traveller's Joy.*

This is the name here given to the Clematis, but in various parts of the country the plant affords joy in another way; for the lads cut up the young wood and smoke it. Hence a common name is Boys' Bacca, Tombacca, and Smoking-cane. In Sussex, on account of its climbing tendency, it is called *Bethwine.*

50. *Water Lily.*

The Iris (*fœtidissima,* stinking, in common with the *pseudacorus,* Yellow Water Iris, or Corn Flag) is so called. In an old book we read:

> "His cloake was of the velvett flowres, and lynde
> With *flowre-de-lices* of the choicest kinde."

Some write flower-de-luce, others *fleur-de-lis.* It is also called Flag-flower, Dragon-flower, and Dagger-flower.

51. *Wind-flower.*

The Anemone (vulgar *nemony* and *enemy*) is sometimes called "Wind-flower, because it is so delicate that it almost succumbs to a gust of wind." Such was the information once given me in Devonshire. Is it possible that this was a lingering tradition to account for the etymology? The Anemones are said to have received their name from an old opinion that they never blossomed except when the wind blew; they do in fact flower in the rough March winds, and will thrive in exposed and elevated situations.

NOTE.—The list of Plant Names is continually swelling, and the writer earnestly solicits the hearty co-operation of Members, that a more perfect list may be presented to the Society next year. Will those who have [leisure kindly send the smallest items of information to me as early as possible, that time may be afforded for arranging and re-writing?

THE POTTER'S ART IN DEVONSHIRE.

BY J. PHILLIPS.

(Read at Dawlish, July, 1881.)

AT the Ashburton meeting of this Association I called attention, in a paper on " The Ashburton Urn," to the evidence which the pottery found in the parish church afforded of skilled potters having worked in Devonshire during the Roman occupation.

There is in the possession of the Messrs. Watts, of Newton, a very unique piece of Anglo-Roman pottery, with a " twist" handle, which demonstrates the great plasticity of the clay of which it was made ; for it is improbable that the artificial method of amalgamating the clay with gum was applied during that period, and the local clays, or some of them, have sufficient plasticity to admit of this twist.

Numerous specimens of pottery exhumed in Devonshire, being of well-known types, are certified by antiquaries as coming from the chief site where that type of pottery has been found. Thus, much is classed as Durobrivian most illegitimately; good pottery having been made in Devonshire at the same period as at Castor. And while the best specimens of the so-called Samian, were no doubt imported, and are probably Gallo-Romaine, numerous specimens, which may easily be distinguished, and which were made on the wheel, are unquestionably of Devonshire manufacture, and clay.

The next evidences — chronologically — of uncommon pottery which we find in the county are in the form of tiles used in church floors ; and, so far as can be traced, the chief seat of this manufacture was in the Bideford district. An unpleasant feature of many of these tiles is the unevenness of the surface. The pattern on them is sometimes in considerable *relief*, as notably the *fleur-de-lis* on the tiles of Down St. Mary Church ; while some in the collection of Mr. Harry

Hems—fourteenth century—are as good encaustic as those which are now made.

Coming to later times, it is interesting to find the date of 1609 on the top of the chimney of the Bideford Pottery; and in this North Devon district, specimens of pottery are often turning up, much of it good, in its quaint simplicity of form and decoration. Only in North Devon do we find that, until quite recent times, the usual mode of obtaining artificial light was by burning oil in pottery lamps quite similar to those in modern use in Algeria. Many persons living, remember no other light being used in the country cottages, and have a keen remembrance of the "smitch" which they emitted. "Bideford ovens" have been known all through the West of England and South Wales from time immemorial.

A simple method of sgraffito decoration appears to have been practised in this county from very early times, and specimens of this abound in North Devon,* and of a more advanced type at Bovey Tracey, where also domestic pottery (ordinary earthenware) has been made for over 150 years. Originally, only local clays and local fuel—lignite—were used.

A few years since, a new direction was given to the sgraffito pottery of North Devon by Mr. Fishley, of Fremington,† whose acquaintance I then made, and subsequently, on his application, had the pleasure of accompanying him through some of the best collections of pottery in London, which were likely to be useful to him, including Dr. Schlieman's, many pieces of which he sketched, and very cleverly reproduced.

The late Mr. Brannam, of Barnstaple, exhibited some of his pottery in this style in the Great Exhibition of 1851, where it was classed as *stoneware*—obviously in error—and now his son is producing some most excellent work in this true Devon style of pottery decoration.

Mr. Webber, of Honiton, has also, in this same style, produced highly-decorated and quaint pottery.

With some examples of the Barnstaple pottery before him, Professor Church, in his recent lectures at the Society of Arts, thus speaks of this style of pottery:

"The productions of this old Barnstaple pot-work stand quite alone in the material, decoration, and manner of their execution. They are decorated with washes of white clay,

---

* Mr. Rock, of Boutport Street, Barum, has a jug with this decoration, bearing date 1733.

† Fremington appears to be the source of the clay for all the North Devon Potteries.

with incised patterns and coloured glazes of flowing and pulsating lines. This 'Barum ware' reminds one at once of the rare Italian sgraffito ware, and of some of the quaintest English work of the 17th century."

Turning into an altogether different direction, we have the highly-finished and completely artistic work of the Torquay Art Potteries, on which neither time nor expense is spared.

The great revival which has of late taken place in the potter's art in Devonshire, is so fresh in everyone's mind that it is needless here to say much.

The two potteries at Torquay have performed a work far beyond the mere fabricating of things of beauty in red earth. They have created, and, by the facilities which they afford, have fostered, a keen appreciation of ceramic art.

In 1868 there were some good pieces of terra-cotta work, and of amateur pottery painting, in the Art Exhibition held that year in the townhall at Bovey Tracey. But amateur work in that direction did not fairly take root and become general in the county (and specially in South Devon) till some years after, when it became first extensively practised in Torquay and neighbourhood, and then both in Plymouth and Exeter.

Since the Bovey Exhibition of 1868, four other potteries have sprung into existence in the same district, and now are in full and extensive work.

Elsewhere in the county, extensive pottery work has been, and is being, largely practised.

In 1835 fire-bricks were first made in the West of England at the Morley Clay Works, and subsequently stoneware socket pipes. Some years later, the manufacture of stoneware pipes was commenced at Annery, near Bideford, the clay being had from Peter's Marland, where, now that a light railway has been constructed, very extensive pottery works exist, producing glazed bricks and tiles of excellent quality.

By this recital it will be seen that the natural advantages which Devonshire possesses over every other county, by her geological formations in respect of clays, are more highly appreciated, and turned to much more practical account, than is generally supposed, or than Devonshire people themselves have allowed.

Opportunities have been presented in the county, during this year, for those who are interested in any way in the potter's art to study some of the most rare and beautiful specimens which exist; and the very considerable show of amateurs' work seen at the recent exhibitions in Exeter,

Newton, and Plymouth, speaks for the widespread interest in this art, and the widespread practice of pottery decoration in Devonshire.

If any apology were needed—which I am sure is not the case—for bringing this art work before the notice of the Association, it would be found in the large number of persons who are interested in and now practising it in Devon.

The exhibition held during Easter week of this year at Newton has given an impetus to amateur ceramic art work in the county, and much is looked for as resulting from it, and from the work of the Art School at Newton. The Princess Louise (Marchioness of Lorne), in granting her patronage to the Newton Exhibition, was pleased to express her interest in it, and the hope that it might be instrumental in giving an impetus to ceramic art work in Devonshire.

There are in the county numerous and most valuable collections of art pottery in the possession of private persons, containing rare examples of the most perfect work of the potter's art; also numerous choice pieces of simple decoration from the South of France and elsewhere. A very great service indeed may be rendered to Devonshire art by the loan of such, for specified periods, to responsible bodies, such as art school committees, for the purposes of study by the students of the schools.

If in the past Devonshire, groping in the dark, and oblivious to what was doing elsewhere, has yet produced meritorious work, and in fact developed a special school of pottery decoration, what may not be anticipated for the future, with all the aids and opportunities now at command, not for a moment overlooking the fostering care which associations of this nature are designed to afford?

Looking through the catalogues of the painted pottery exhibitions in London, the eye meets on every page familiar Devonshire names; and last year, one of the best pieces of design and decorated vases so exhibited was by a Devonshire lady, and both in design, adaptation, and execution, was in all ways excellent. Painting on the biscuit is a more advanced stage of pottery decoration than on the enamel, and we find it largely practised in this county.

It surely will be a most legitimate work, for this Association to take full cognizance of the special development of the potter's art which claims Devonshire for its home, and which is becoming so worthily represented by the North Devon potters, and is taken up in a higher degree by the Art potteries of Torquay.

ART IN DEVONSHIRE.

PART I.

BY GEORGE PYCROFT.

(Read at Dawlish, July, 1881.)

INQUIRY leads men to doubt. To hold fast our belief in any historical fact we should ask no questions about it. If there is a well-grounded faith, say our fellow-countymen, it is, first, that Devonshire has produced more artists than any other county in England; secondly, that the inspiration proceeds from the ever-changing atmospheric effects, and the inexhaustible variety of the Devonshire climate and scenery. It is so pleasant a faith that I approached the inquiry into the subject with something like dread, lest the belief should prove to be the product of the warping effect of a patriotic bias.

I find that it is true that more artists can claim Devonshire for their birthplace than any other county, but that it is not true that this fact is due to the inspiriting effects of the climate and scenery. There are thirty-three Devonshire artists who have died and left a name behind them. This seems a very small number for so large a county, and for a period ranging from Henry VIII. to Queen Victoria; but we must remember that there was hardly any art in England before the days of the great Sir Joshua.

In carefully analyzing Redgrave's *English School of Painting*, I find that there have been 1,127 painters whose names have been preserved. Of these he has been able to trace the birthplaces of only 438, leaving 689 unaccounted for. These 438 have been distributed among the English counties in the following manner:

Middlesex	.	166	Cornwall	. .	7
Devon	.	33	Kent	. .	5
York	.	22	Hertford	. .	4
Somerset	.	22	Cheshire	. .	4
Lancashire	.	17	Lincoln	. .	2
Norfolk	.	27	Surrey	. .	7
Cumberland	.	9	Derby	. .	8
Northumberland	.	11	Dorset	. .	3
Stafford	.	9	Suffolk	. .	5
Essex	.	7	Leicester	. .	2
Shropshire	.	7	Wilts	. .	5
Westmoreland	.	5	Berks	. .	3
Sussex	.	6	Nottingham	. .	4
Hants	.	5	Cambridge	. .	2
Durham	.	5	Worcester	. .	6
Northampton	.	1	Gloucester	. .	1
Hereford	.	5	Isle of Wight	.	1

Thus, leaving London-bearing Middlesex out of the question, we find that our county really heads the list as an art-producing land.

Of all English provincial cities, Plymouth and its neighbourhood stands first, as the parent of six painters of the highest order, whose works have been held worthy of a place in our National Gallery; viz., Sir Joshua Reynolds, Prout, Eastlake, Haydon, Northcote, and Solomon Hart, and also of Rogers and Johns, the landscape painters.

In the first class of painters may be ranked fifteen out of our thirty-three artists; viz., Brockedon, Cosway, John Cross, Eastlake, James Gandy, Gendall, Haydon, Hart, Hilliard, Northcote, Prout, Reynolds, Lee, Traies, and Johns; a goodly band, of whom any country might be proud.

Our historical painters are nine in number—Brockedon, John Cross, Eastlake, Haydon, Hart, Jenkins, King, and Northcote.

The portrait painters number fifteen, and among them, first in order of time, and in merit second to none, stands Nicholas Hilliard, the portrait and miniature painter of Queen Elizabeth's reign; second, James Gandy, of Exeter; third, Hudson, who, if he did not paint as well as his pupil, Sir Joshua, painted more portraits than almost any man, and was the first fashionable painter of high life in England; fourth, Sir Joshua Reynolds, than whom, if our county had produced no other, she might have sat down in her self-complacency for ever, for he not only produced works of the highest art, but by his eloquent lectures, teaching, and example, was the cause of art in others; fifth, the eccentric and vain Cosway, of Tiverton, with his unrivalled miniatures; sixth, Downman, with his delicately-handled portraits of our grandmothers in their prime; seventh, Northcote, R.A.; eighth, Leaky, with his miniatures in oil; and then came Thomas Mogford, cut off too early in life for his fame, and William Mineard Bennett, R. A. Clack, R. Crosse, J. King, and W. Score.

Among our thirty-three artists it is remarkable that only seven practised landscape, and among these but five can be said to have drawn their inspiration from Devonshire scenery; viz: John Gendall, Thomas Mogford, Fred. R. Lee, Traies, and Johns. It is also worthy of note that all these practised their art within the last fifty years, and that previous to this time the seasons might change, the clouds and haze might give their beautiful atmospheric effects, the granite lichen-covered boulders might break the glistening moor streams into cascades; it was all lost upon the Devonshire men, who slept like the inhabitants of the Lotos islands, unmoved by the surrounding loveliness, never dreaming of fixing it on canvas. This is the more remarkable, because at the same period, in flat unpicturesque Holland, and in that English Holland, Norfolk, landscape painters abounded.

We have changed all this now. The classical school of landscape is dead, I trust, for ever. We have no longer compositions for real transcripts from nature; we have no more Roman temples in the middle distance and nymphs and philosophers in the foreground. Our artists no longer work in garrets, like Wilson, but in daylight face to face with nature. They are to be met with by the moor streams, and among the granite boulders, catching the tints as they fly, and giving to their work an air of reality, and a degree of daylight, that is not to be found among the works of men of old time. On our Devonshire painters' canvasses the sunlight now dances upon the broken stream; the moss, lichen, and ivy grow on the rock, and you can tell what rock it is; the anatomy of trees is correctly given; the season of the year is depicted with its delicate greens, or its golden russets; the very time of day is seen at a glance, and instead of fancy shepherds or bald-headed sages in the foregrounds, we find sleek cattle knee-deep in ferns and wild flowers, seeking the water or the shade. Moreover, our eyes are charmed with that endless variety of hue which always exists in nature, but which is seldom, if ever, found in the work of the old masters, because our artists endeavour to hold the mirror up to nature, and not that gloomy substitute, the Claude Lorraine. So work Widgery of Exeter, the two Dingles, father and son, of Plymouth, Pike of the same town, Philip Mitchell, Morrish, of Chagford, Mary Isabella Grant, of Hillersden, Cullompton, and some others. We may therefore reasonably hope that we shall ere long possess a school of landscape painters of our own, owing their inspiration to that loveliness of the earth, the air, and the water, with which Devonshire is endowed before all the counties of our land.

There is one branch of art not yet referred to, which is represented in our county by one man—I mean mezzotint engraving. It is one of those branches of the art that has flourished most in England during the last hundred years, and our island can boast of many excellent professors, notably Lupton and C. Turner, in pure mezzotint, and C. Landseer, and our county man, Samuel Cousins, in a mixed style. There is no man of whom his native city is more proud than of Samuel Cousins, who has added a lustre to the county of Devon by his unrivalled works. He stands without cavil the greatest engraver in his style and in his age.

The information contained in the following biographies I have gathered from Walpole's *Anecdotes of Painters*, Bryant's *Dictionary of Painters*, Ottley's *Dictionary of Painters*, Redgrave's *English School of Painters*, obituaries from the *Art Union* and the *Times*, and from notes of my own, which I have made during many years:

ASHWORTH, EDWARD, architect, born at Colleton, near Chumleigh, Devon, in 1814. His father, the son of a barrister, followed agricultural pursuits; but from failing health left that part of the country in 1822. Turning his attention to architecture, Edward Ashworth was first articled to Mr. Cornish, of Exeter, and afterwards became a pupil of Mr. Charles Fowler, of 1, Gordon Square, London. After passing some time in other London offices, he went, in 1842, to New Zealand, then in a languishing state. From thence he proceeded to Hong Kong, where he was employed in carrying out works in that rising place in 1844 and 1845.

Returning to England in 1846, he wrote for the Architectural Publication Society an essay on Chinese Architecture, also from time to time, between 1847 and 1877, papers on Church Architecture, which were read before the Exeter Diocesan Architectural Society. He rebuilt the churches of Dulverton, Tiverton, Bideford, Lympstone, Romansleigh, and East Anstey. He built the new church at Withecombe, Exmouth, Topsham, and St. Mary Major, Exeter, and partially restored the churches of Seaton, Axminster, Shute, Wooton Courtney, Selworthy, Cheriton Fitzpaine, Somerset.

BENNETT, WILLIAM MINEARD, a miniature painter, was born in Exeter, studied art under Sir Thomas Lawrence, and attained reputation in London as a miniature and portrait painter. He exhibited at the Academy in 1812, sending oil portraits and miniatures, in 1813, 1815, 1816, and again in 1834 and 1835. He then settled in Paris, where he was decorated by Louis XVIII. He attained also proficiency in music, and cultivated a taste for literature. In 1844 he returned to Exeter, and pursued art only as an amusement. He died in his native city October 17th, 1858, aged 80.

BROCKEDON, WILLIAM, subject and history painter, born at Totnes, October 13th, 1787. His biography has already appeared in our *Transactions* from the pen of Mr. Windeatt, vol. ix. p. 243, and was read at Kingsbridge in July, 1877. We merely therefore give a list of his works. He exhibited in 1812 two portraits, and the next year one of Miss Booth, the actress, which gained him notice. In 1814 he again exhibited, and sent in a plaster model of Adam and Eve, in competition for the Academy medal. In 1815 he visited France for the purpose of study, and on his return painted the large picture of the "Acquittal of Susannah," now in the Exeter Castle. In 1818 he again competed in sculpture for the Academy medal, and painted "The Resurrection of the Widow's Son," now at the parish church, St. Saviours, Dartmouth. In the ancient Guildhall of Dartmouth is a large picture by him from a scene taken from Ossian's poems, another in Dartington parish church of a scene in the life of St. Peter, and a Crucifixion in the parish church of Cornworthy. From the number of very large canvases he presented to churches and public institutions, it is perhaps fair to conclude that, like B. R. Haydon, he lived to find that such works are not marketable. In 1822, after spending a winter in Rome, he settled in London, and painted more saleable pictures of popular subjects and of smaller size, "Pifferari," "Psyche borne by Zephyrs," "L'Allegro," "Galileo visited by Milton in Prison," "Burial of Sir John Moore," "Raphael and the Fornarina." Between 1828–30 he published *Illustrations of the Passes of the Alps; Journals of Excursions on the Alps;* wrote the literary part of Finden's *Illustrations of the Life of Byron* in 1833–4; the *Road Book from London to Naples* in 1835; *Italy, Classical and Picturesque,* 1842–3; *Egypt and Nubia,* from drawings by David Roberts, R.A., 1846–9. He died, August 29th, 1854, in his 67th year, and was buried in the cemetery of St. George-the-Martyr, Bloomsbury.

CLACK, RICHARD AUGUSTUS, portrait painter, the son of a Devonshire clergyman. He studied at the Royal Academy, and exhibited from 1830 to 1845. He practised portrait painting in Exeter for many years, and died in 1881.

COLLIER, THE RIGHT HON. SIR ROBERT, amateur landscape painter, was born in 1817. He is the son of John Collier, Esq., of Grimstone, M.P. for Plymouth from 1832 to 1841. He was educated at Trinity College, Cambridge (B.A. 1841), was called to the bar at the Inner Temple in 1843, and was made Q.C. in 1854. He was sometime Recorder of Penzance; was Judge-Advocate for the Fleet, and Counsel to the Admiralty, from 1859 to 1863; appointed Solicitor-General in 1863, and as Attorney-General served from 1868 to 1871. He was appointed a Justice of Common Pleas in November, 1871, and a few days subsequently a Judge of the Judicial Committee of Privy Council. He represented Plymouth in Parliament from 1852 to 1871; was created K.B. in 1863, P.C. in 1871. Sir Robert is a devoted lover of art, and has practised it with so much success that it is fair to say of him, that had he followed painting as a profession he would probably have attained as great eminence in it as he has in the law. He was President of the Devonshire Association in 1879 at the Ilfracombe meeting, and delivered an address on art, than which no better essay on the subject has appeared since the publication of the *Modern Painters*. An excellent and representative specimen of his work—in his case, holiday work—may be seen in the Alpine landscape presented by him to the Plymouth Athenæum.

CONDY, NICHOLAS MATTHEWS, marine painter, born at Plymouth. Exhibited at the Royal Academy in 1842–44. Some views on the Thames by him were published. He died at Plymouth, May 20th, 1851, aged 52 years. He was an artist of great merit.

COSWAY, RICHARD, R.A., portrait and miniature painter, was born at Tiverton, where his family had been long settled, and where his father was master of the public school. To any one at all familiar with the history of art in the reign of George III., the career of Cosway is well known. He was so prominent a figure, from his amusing vanity, self-conceit, and eccentricity that he kept himself much before the public. He was a little man in person, and gave himself the greatest airs. His portrait may be seen in Zoffany's portraits of the Royal Academicians. He married at St. George's, Hanover Square, in 1781, Maria Hadfield, a handsome, clever woman, and an artist, and set up house on the verge of Carlton Gardens, and afterwards in Stratford Place. Here they lived sumptuously; the Prince was their visitor, and they made themselves the mark for satirists and caricaturists. He believed in Swedenborgianism, in animal magnetism, professed to be able to raise the dead, and declared that the Virgin Mary had sat to him several times for the half-length portrait of the Virgin which he had just finished. He felt himself greater than he was, and he left a request that his remains should be carried to Antwerp, and deposited near the bones of Rubens; the vaults of Marylebone Church had, however, to serve his turn.

With all his foppery and eccentricity, which amused him and injured no man, he had great talent. He was an admirable draughtsman. Two large oil paintings by him are to be seen at Powderham Castle, and one at Haldon House. He is chiefly esteemed as a miniature painter, an art in which he had no rival. His works are eagerly sought for at the present day, and command large prices. The lovely Mrs. Fitzherbert, and the beauties of the court, sat to him, and he sailed along in the full tide of courtly favour. Ivory was the medium on which he generally worked; but he sometimes drew whole lengths in blacklead pencil, and painted the faces in miniature, somewhat after the manner of Downman.

In 1755 he gained the premium for drawing at the Society of Arts; in 1766 became a member of the Incorporated Society of Artists; in 1769 was admitted as student of the Academy; in 1770 as associate, and 1771 as full member of that body. He died July 4th, 1821. In him, and in Hilliard, Devonshire may boast of two of the best miniature painters our island has produced.

COUSINS, SAMUEL, the greatest mezzotint engraver of the English school, born at Exeter, May 9th, 1801. He showed a talent for drawing at a very early age, and at the age of eleven he gained in competition the silver palette given by the Society of Arts for a copy in pencil of Heath's engraving of the "Good Shepherd," after Murillo, and in the following year received the silver medal of the same society for a drawing in black and white.

Mr. Cousins was taken notice of by that generous patron of struggling or youthful talent the late Sir Thomas Dyke Acland, Bart., and was sent to London, and articled to S. W. Reynolds, the best mezzotint engraver of the day. With him he served his apprenticeship, and remained as his assistant for three years after, and during this time Mr. Cousins's name appears upon many plates in conjunction with that of Reynolds. He started in business on his own account late in 1828.

Sir Thomas Dyke Acland gave him his first commission, to engrave the picture by Sir Thomas Lawrence, of Lady Acland and her sons, and this plate is the first upon which Mr. Cousins's name appears alone. Sir Thomas Lawrence was so pleased with his work that he wished to engage him to engrave in future for him alone; but this he would not agree to. Mr. Cousins tells me as an anecdote, at which he can now afford to smile, that when a boy under fourteen years of age, he drew many portraits in pencil from nature, for which his charge was five shillings each. I here exhibit a series of photographs taken from these early portraits, sent to me by Mr. Cousins. On examining the face of the old man in the wig, who was a builder employed by the Earl Ashburnham, I doubt not you will agree with me that no artist of any age, or at any age, could have modelled a face better.

Subjoined is a chronological list of his works:

ENGRAVED

1826.	Lady Acland and her sons	Sir T. Lawrence, P.R.A.
	Master Lambton	ditto
	Prince Metternich	ditto
	Doctor Brown	... ...
1827.	La Surprise	Dubuffe.
	Sir Stamford Raffles	Sir F. Chantrey, R.A.
	Vice-Admiral Lord Collingwood	F. Howard.
	Miss Croker	Sir T. Lawrence, P.R.A.
	Sir M. Shaw Stewart, Bart.	Sir H. Raeburn.
	Earl Grey	Sir T. Lawrence, P.R.A.
	Pope Pius the Seventh	ditto
1828.	Duke of Wellington	Sir T. Lawrence, P.R.A.
	Rt. Hon. J. Wilson Croker	ditto.
	Davies Gilbert, P.R.S.	H. Howard, R.A.
	Rev. Mr. Cogan	T. Phillips, R.A.
	Sir Joseph Banks (statue)	Sir F. Chantry, R.A.
	Michael Faraday	W. H. Pickersgill, M.A.
	Mr. John Bell	Thos. Stewardson.
	Sir James Moncrieff	ditto
	Bishop Heber	T. Phillips, R.A.
	Lord Jeffrey	... ...
1830.	Sir Thomas Munro	Sir M. Shee, P.R.A.
	Mrs. Woolff	Sir T. Lawrence, P.R.A.
	Lady Grey and Children	ditto
	Sir Thomas Lawrence, P.R.A.	ditto
	Lady Dover	ditto
	Miss Macdonald	ditto
1831.	Lady Gower and child	ditto
	Lady Peel	ditto
	The Earl of Aberdeen	Sir T. Lawrence, P.R.A.
	Robert Burns	Alex. Nasmyth.
	Dr. Croft	Mrs. Carpenter.
1832.	Dr. Buckland	T. Phillips, R.A.
	Dr. Sedgwick	ditto
	Miss Peel	Sir T. Lawrence, P.R.A.
	Lady Grosvenor	ditto
	Thomas Campbell	ditto
	Mr. Vaughan	ditto
	Mr. Grenfell	Sir M. Shee, P.R.A.
	Miss Juliana Homfray	Sam. Lane.
1833.	The Rev. James Tate	... ...
	William Wilberforce, M.P.	G. Richmond, R.A.
	Rt. Hon. George Canning (marble statue)	Sir F. Chantrey, R.A.
	Christ in the Garden	Correggio.
1834.	Dr. Sumner	Sir M. Shee, P.R.A.

ENGRAVED

1834.	Lord Canterbury	W. Pickersgill, R.A.
	Mrs. Lister	G. S. Newton, R.A.
	Duchess of Rutland	G. Sanders.
	Mr. Bridge	John Jackson, R.A.
	William Pitt (statue)	Sir F. Chantrey, R.A.
1835.	Dr. Jones	T. Phillips, R.A.
	Beatrice Cenci	Guido.
	Nature	Sir T. Lawrence, P.R.A.
	Master Hope	ditto
	Dr. Gilbert	T. Phillips, R.A.
	The Rev. Edward Bather.	W. Etty, R.A.
	The Orphan	H. Leversedge.
	The Visionary	ditto
	Pet Rabbits	Miss Corbaux.
	Lady Ravensworth and Daughter	... ...
	Rev. Wm. Stanley Goddard, D.D.	... ...
	John Milford, Esq.	W. Owen, R.A.
	Mr. Biddle	Thos. Sully.
1836.	The Maid of Saragossa	Sir D. Wilkie, R.A.
	Lady Rolle	Mrs. Robertson.
	Lady Lyndhurst	Sir T. Lawrence, P.R.A.
	Earl of Durham	ditto
	"The Letter"	Raoux.
	Mr. Hallam (bust)	Sir F. Chantrey, R.A.
	Mr. Mclean, M.P.	John Bridges.
	Interior of the old House of Commons	... ...
1837.	Bolton Abbey in the Olden Time	Sir E. Landseer, R.A.
	Lady Blessington	Sir T. Lawrence, P.R.A.
	The Abercorn Family	Sir E. Landseer, R.A.
	Sir Wm. Knighton	Sir T. Lawrence, P.R.A.
	Sir J. T. Coleridge	Mrs. Carpenter.
	Mr. Justice Patteson	ditto
	J. Andrew Knight	S. Cole.
1838.	Queen Victoria	Alfred Chalon, R.A.
	Return from Hawking	Sir E. Landseer, R.A.
	Mr. Joseph Neeld, M.P.	Sir M. Shee, P.R.A.
	Mr. Earl (bust)	... ...
	Dr. Copplestone	... ...
1839.	Lady Clive	Sir T. Lawrence, P.R.A.
	Sir John Malcolm (statue)	Sir F. Chantrey, R.A.
	Dr. Sumner	Mrs. Carpenter.
1840.	Duke of Wellington	J. Lucas.
	Lady Eveline Gower and Marquis of Stafford	Sir E. Landseer, R.A.
	Queen Victoria receiving the Sacrament at her Coronation (commenced this year)	C. R. Leslie, R.A.

ENGRAVED

1841.	Dr. Selwyn	G. Richmond, R.A.
	Earl Brownlow	Sir M. Shee, P.R.A.
1842.	Queen Victoria receiving the Sacrament at her Coronation (finished)	C. R. Leslie, R.A.
1843.	Lady Durham	Sir T. Lawrence, P.R.A.
	Sir Charles Forbes (statue)	Sir F. Chantrey, R.A.
1844.	The Queen and two Children	Sir E. Landseer, R.A.
	Early Dawn	Christal.
	Head of Napoleon I.	Mansion.
	Dr. Blackall	R. R. Reinagle, R.A.
1845.	Mr. Keble	G. Richmond, R.A.
	Mr. Robert Bateson	... ...
1846.	Christ Weeping over Jerusalem	Sir C. Eastlake, P.R.A.
	Beauty's Bath	Sir E. Landseer, R.A.
1847.	Duke of Wellington	Sir T. Lawrence, P.R.A.
	Mrs. Braddyl	Sir J. Reynolds, P.R.A.
	The Prince of Wales as a Sailor Boy	F. Winterhalter.
1848.	Group of Royal Family (commenced this year)	ditto
	Rev. Mr. Marker	J. P. Knight, R.A.
1849.	Shakespeare	Unknown.
	Mrs. Elizabeth Fry	G. Richmond, R.A.
1850.	Dr. Pindar	Sir Wm. Boxall, R.A.
	Mr. Hodgson	Partridge.
1851.	Rt. Hon. Sir Robert Peel, Bart.	Sir T. Lawrence, P.R.A.
	Viscount Palmerston	Jno. Partridge.
	Mr. Adams	T. Mogford.
	"The first of May"	F. Winterhalter.
1852.	Bishop of Moray and Ross	G. Richmond, R.A.
	Peter Barlow	Sir Wm. Boxall, R.A.
	Dugald Stewart	Sir David Wilkie, R.A.
1853.	Mr. Ledsham	E. U. Edis.
	The Infant Samuel	J. Sant, R.A.
	Samuel Taylor Coleridge	Alston.
1854.	The Emperor of the French	F. Winterhalter.
	The Order of Release	J. E. Millais, R.A.
	The Infant Timothy	J. Sant, R.A.
1855.	"Comedy"	ditto
	"Tragedy"	ditto
	Rev. Mr. Griffiths	G. F. Watts, R.A.
1856.	Empress of the French	F. Winterhalter.
	Princess Royal of England	ditto
1857.	A Midsummer Night's Dream	Sir E. Landseer, R.A.
1858.	Rosa Bonheur	Dubuffe.
	Sir Bartle Frere	W. Phillips.
	Saved	Sir E. Landseer, R.A.

ENGRAVED

1859.	Mrs. Naylor	.	Sir F. Grant, P.R.A.
	The Mitherless Bairn	. .	T. Faed, R.A.
	Mr. Frederick Huth	.	Sir Wm. Boxall, R.A.
1860.	Duke of Northumberland	.	Sir F. Grant, P.R.A.
	Sir Henry Rawlinson	.	W. Phillips.
	Dr. Beasley	. -	H. T. Wells.
	Abel Smith	.	F. R. Say.
	Lord Winmarleigh	.	G. Richmond, A.R.A.
1861.	Marie Antoinette	.	E. M. Ward, R.A.
	Lord Clyde	.	Sir F. Grant, P.R.A.
	The Maid and Magpie	.	Sir E. Landseer, R.A.
1863.	H.R.H. the Princess of Wales	.	... ...
	From Dawn to Sunset	.	T. Faed, R.A.
	The Rev. J. C. Woodhouse	.	Wyndham Phillips.
1864.	"Whittington"	.	J. Sant, R.A.
	W. Gibbs, Esq.	.	Sir W. Boxall, R.A.
	Duchess of Northumberland	.	Weigall.
1865.	Piper and Pair of Nutcrackers	.	Sir E. Landseer, R.A.
	Lady Mary Hamilton	.	F. Winterhalter.
	"My First Minuet"	.	J. E. Millais, R.A.
1867.	"The Connoisseurs"	.	Sir E. Landseer, R.A.
	Earl Spencer, K.G.	.	H. T. Wells, R.A.
1868.	Mater Dolorosa	.	F. Goodall, R.A.
	Sir Thos. Watson	.	G. Richmond, R.A.
	Mater Purissima	.	F. Goodall, R.A.
	J. Pemberton Heywood, Esq.	.	G. Richmond, R.A.
1870.	"The Queen"	.	Lowes Dickenson.
1873.	The Strawberry Girl	.	Sir J. Reynolds, P.R.A.
	"Yes or No"	.	J. E. Millais, R.A.
1874.	The Age of Innocence	.	Sir J. Reynolds, P.R.A.
	New-laid Eggs	.	J. E. Millais, R.A.
	Penelope Boothby	.	Sir J. Reynolds, P.R.A.
	Simplicity	.	ditto
1875.	Miss Bowles	.	ditto
	Picture of Health	.	J. E. Millais, R.A.
	Lady Caroline Montague as "Winter"	.	Sir J. Reynolds, P.R.A.
1876.	Lady Ann Fitzpatrick as "Sylvia"		ditto
	"No"	.	J. E. Millais, R.A.
	Moretta, a Venetian Girl	.	F. Leighton, P.R.A.
	The Countess Spencer	.	Sir J. Reynolds, P.R.A.
	The Hon. Ann Bingham	.	ditto
1877.	Lavinia Countess Spencer	.	Sir J. Reynolds, P.R.A.
	Playmates	.	H. Merle
	Lady Spencer and her Son, Lord Althorp		Sir J. Reynolds, P.R.A.
	The Dauphin, son of Louis XVI.		Greuze.
	Miss Rich	. .	W. Hogarth.

ENGRAVED

| 1877. | Duchess of Rutland | . | . | Sir J. Reynolds, P.R.A. |
| | "Yes" | . | . | J. E. Millais, R.A. |

Since
1877.

Duchess of Devonshire .	.	Sir J. Reynolds, P.R.A.
The Princes in the Tower	.	J. E. Millais, R.A.
The Princess Sophia of Gloucester		Sir J. Reynolds, P.R.A.
"Muscipula"	.	.	ditto
Mrs. Brown		.	Edwin Long, R.A.
"Imprisoned"		.	Briton Rivière, R.A.
Cardinal Newman		.	Lady Coleridge.
Ninette		.	Greuze.
Benedicta		.	Frank Dicksee, A.R.A.
Head of Italian Girl	.	.	Sir F. Leighton, P.R.A.
Cherry Ripe	.	.	J. E. Millais, R.A.

Mr. Cousins is still working on, more to the advantage of the public than of himself. His eye has not grown dim, nor his hand unsteady. His heart is kind and generous as ever, and many persons who have no personal claim on him can show precious gifts from him of his handicraft, kindly and thoughtfully presented, solely because he has observed that they love and appreciate them.

He was elected by the Royal Academy an associate engraver in 1835, and was transferred to the new class of associate engravers in 1854, and was the first to receive (1855) the honours of the newly-created rank of academician engraver.

CRANCH, JOHN, was born at Kingsbridge, Devon, October 12th, 1757. Self-taught as a boy, he made progress in drawing, then went to London, where he was befriended by Sir Joshua Reynolds. He never gained excellence. His best picture was a "Death of Chatterton." He excelled in what are called Poker pictures. He died at Bath in February, 1821. He published two works, one on *The Economy of Testaments*, and the other, *Inducements to Promote the Fine Arts of Great Britain*.

CROSS, JOHN, historical painter, a native of Tiverton, born in 1819. His father, who was superintendent of the lace factory at that place, removed to St. Quentin, to become foreman of the English factory established there. Here young John Cross worked at the factory in the machinery department; but as he showed a strong disposition for art, he was admitted into the School of Design, founded by Delatour. Here he worked so well that at the end of the last year but one he was presented with a medal. From this place he removed to Paris, and entered the studio of M. Picot, a painter of the classical school, and acquitted himself so well that he was appointed treasurer and director of the studio, and won several medals. At the time of the completion of his studies at M. Picot's, the British Government offered prizes for the best cartoons portraying subjects from English history or poetry, the competing cartoon to be exhibited in Westminster Hall. To this Cross sent a cartoon, the subject of which was "The Assassination of Thomas à Becket;" but owing to certain conditions not having been complied with, he did not obtain a prize. The picture, however, was very highly approved, and had been much admired when previously exhibited at the hall at Fervaques. A second competition, two years later, opened by the same authority, took place at Westminster Hall, and to this Cross sent a picture, representing "Richard Cœur de Lion, at the Siege of Chaluz, pardoning the archer who had wounded him." This painting obtained the first premium of £300, and it was thought so highly of that it was purchased by the Government at £1,000, and placed in the hall of the Fine Arts Commissioners in the Palace of Westminster. He had now gained early in life the summit of his reputation. Everything looked well with him, and for a time he was sought after and looked upon as the rising historical painter of the day. The Fine Arts Commissioners engraved the picture at their own expense, and he received a commission to repeat it in reduced size for Mr. Heathcot, of Tiverton, together with an order for a new picture, "Lucy Preston, imploring the pardon of her father from Queen Mary II." His health unfortunately began to fail, and to this circumstance must be attributed the fact that he did nothing after to sustain his reputation. He painted pictures certainly which showed great talent, but nothing which took with the public as his early ones did. He received commissions to paint two pictures, "Edward the Confessor naming Harold his successor," and "William of Normandy swearing Harold on the reliques." These have been well spoken of. He next took to teaching drawing and portrait painting for a livelihood. His paintings became weak and feeble, and in 1860 two pictures which he sent to the Academy were actually rejected. His last works of any note were a picture from his prize cartoon, "The Assassination of à Becket," and "The Coronation of William the Conqueror," which was exhibited at the Royal Academy in 1858. Both remained unsold at the time of the artist's death, which took place on the 26th February, 1861. The paintings he left were exhibited at the Society of Arts, and a subscription was raised to a small amount for his family. His friends purchased his "Murder of à Becket," and placed it in Canterbury Cathedral; and his Devonshire friends purchased "The Burial of the two Princes in the Tower," and presented it to the Albert Memorial Museum at Exeter.

CROSSE, RICHARD, miniature painter, born in Devonshire. He received a premium at the Society of Arts in 1758. In 1763 he was a member of the Free Society of Artists. He exhibited miniature and water-colour portraits at the Royal Academy. In 1790 he was appointed enamel painter to the King. He died at Knowle, near Cullompton, in 1810, aged 65 years.

DAVEY, ROBERT, portrait painter, born at Cullompton, Devon. He commenced as a portrait painter, and studied at Rome. On his return he settled in London, but met with little success. He taught drawing at Woolwich and other schools. He died September 28th, 1793.

DOWNMAN, JOHN, A.R.A., portrait and subject painter, born in Devonshire, was a student of the Royal Academy in 1769, and an associate in 1795. He studied under Benjamin West, P.R.A. His portraits, almost of a miniature size, may be found not unfrequently in the country houses of Devon. They are in pencil, generally in profile, and slightly coloured. Two or three good specimens are at Sir John Duntze's house, Exeleigh, Starcross, and an excellent example of full-length portraiture at the mansion of Mr. Henn Gennys, Plymouth. He exhibited at the Academy a kitcat portrait of "A Lady at Work" in 1770, and in the following year a painting of "The Death of Lucretia." In 1777 he practised portrait painting at Cambridge, visited Plymouth in 1806, and in 1807–8 set up at Exeter. He then returned to London, and after some years residence, during which time he continued to exhibit, he removed to Chester, and died at Wrexham, in Denbighshire, on Christmas-eve, 1824. One of his best works was "Rosalind," which he painted for the Shakespeare Gallery. He worked chiefly in water-colour, and his pictures, though low in tone, were gracefully designed and delicately painted.

EASTLAKE, SIR CHARLES LOCKE, was born at Plymouth on the 17th of November, 1793. He was the youngest son of Mr. George Eastlake, solicitor to the Admiralty, and Judge Advocate General. He began his education at the Borough School, but was soon moved to the Charter-house. Here, stimulated by the example of Haydon, who in 1807 exhibited his first picture, "Riposo," he begged his father to allow him to follow painting as a profession. He was then 15 years old.

He became a student of the Royal Academy in 1809. Mr. Jeremiah Harman, a connoisseur, gave him the commission for his first picture, "The Raising of Jairus's Daughter;" and after he had painted several others, generously sent him to Paris. Here he studied till compelled to leave on the return of Napoleon from Elba.

Young Eastlake now returned to his native town, and painted some portraits. It so happened that the *Bellerophon* put into Plymouth with Napoleon on board. Eastlake was fortunate enough to get a sight of him, and painted the well-known picture of "Napoleon at the Gangway of the Bellerophon." This picture gained him much reputation, and the sale of it assisted him in his tour to Italy and Greece. Returning home, after a brief visit to Plymouth, he visited the Netherlands, Germany, and then repaired to Rome, where he remained twelve years, and where he must have acquired that knowledge of Italian art for which in after life he was so esteemed.

In 1823 he exhibited at the Academy his first contribution, consisting of three views of Rome.

In 1825 he sent from Rome "A Girl of Albano leading a Blind Woman to Mass."

In 1827 he exhibited "The Spartan Isadas rushing undraped from the Bath to meet the Enemy," and was elected Associate.

In 1828, "Pilgrims in Sight of Rome."

In 1829, "Byron's Dream."

In 1830, "Una delivering the Red Cross Knight," and was elected a full member of the Academy.

Eastlake now returned to England, and in 1831 exhibited two Italian subjects, with "Haidée, a Greek Girl."

In 1833 his famous "Greek Fugitives."

In 1834, "The Escape of Francesco da Carrara" and the "Martyr."

In 1839 his picture, "Christ Blessing Little Children."

In 1841, "Christ Weeping over Jerusalem."

These comprise his best works, and the greater number of them have been engraved.

In the same year his knowledge of art and his attainments in letters, combined with great aptitude for business, caused him to be selected for the honourable post of Secretary to the Commission, presided over by Prince Albert, for the decoration of the new Palace of Westminster.

In 1842 he was appointed the Librarian of the Royal Academy; in 1843 Keeper of the National Gallery; and in 1850 was elected President of the Royal Academy, and received the honour of knighthood.

In 1855 he received the appointment of Director to the National Gallery. It was his duty now to travel year by year on the Continent in quest of pictures for that institution, and it is universally acknowledged that from his taste and knowledge of the Italian school he added greatly to our national collection. He had now little leisure for the practice of his art, and having exhibited a replica of the "Escape of Francesco da Carrara," which is now in the National Gallery, he did not again exhibit.

He wrote *Materials for a History of Painting*, 1847; *The Schools of Painting in Italy, translated from Kugler*, 1851; *Kugler's Handbook of Painting*, 1855; and some treatises and addresses of his own.

The University of Oxford conferred on him the degree of D.C.L., and he was decorated with the Cross of the Legion of Honour. Sir Charles married, in 1849, Miss Rigby, authoress of the *Baltic Letters* and other works.

He died at Pisa, of a malady from which he had long suffered, on December 23rd, 1865.

FOWLER, CHARLES, architect, born at Collumpton, May, 1792, served his apprenticeship with a builder and surveyor at Exeter. His first work was the Court of Bankruptcy, in Basinghall Street. He competed successfully for the design of London Bridge, and gained the first premium, although the design was not carried out. He built Covent Garden Market, Hungerford Market, Exeter Lower Market, restored and built additions to Powderham Castle, built churches at Charmouth, Buckley, and Honiton, and the Devon County Lunatic Asylum. He died at Great Marlow, September 26th, 1867, in his 67th year.

GANDY, JAMES, portrait painter, born in Exeter in 1619. He is said to have been a good painter, and his name has been handed down by tradition as one of our best Devonshire artists. The greater part of his works remain in Ireland, whither he went with the Duke of Ormond; his portraits are rare in this country. He received instruction from Vandyke; and as Sir Joshua Reynolds owned to the impression made upon him by this painter, it is fair to conclude that he deserved his fame. He is sometimes credited, to his disadvantage, with works performed by his son William, an artist inferior to himself. The portrait of Sir Edward Seaward, Kt., at the Exeter Workhouse, and that of John Patch, sen., at the Exeter Hospital, are by his son. He died in Ireland in 1689.

GENDALL, JOHN, landscape painter, born in Devonshire in 1790. In early life, having shown a talent for drawing, the gentleman in whose house he was living as a lad sent him to London, with a letter of recommendation to Sir John Soane. Having shown him some drawings, Sir John was much pleased, and gave him his first commission—a drawing of one of the windows of Westminster Abbey. He next introduced him to the house of Ackerman, the well-known print-seller and publisher in the Strand. Here, while improving himself in art, he made himself useful in many ways to his employer. At one time he had the management of the *matériel* in the house; at another he was employed in carrying out and perfecting the new art of lithography, which had just then made its appearance. He was sent on a sketching tour through Normandy, to illustrate the river scenery of that country, and the water-colour drawings he then made gained him great credit when exhibited very many years after. Indeed one of them was shown by a friend, at a meeting of the Society of Arts, as a genuine " Turner," and it passed as such till the critics were undeceived. He also illustrated views of country seats, with Westall and T. H. Shepherd. After leaving Mr. Ackerman's house, Mr. Gendall resided in Exeter, joining business with Mr. Cole; and in the picturesque timber-built house in the Cathedral Close, formerly known as Moll's Coffee-house, a true artist's home, he continued to reside till his death, in March, 1865. Mr. Gendall possessed a great knowledge of pictures, and his opinion on works of the old masters was much prized. In early life he worked in water-colour, contenting himself with a sketch rather than a finished picture, but the success he gained in oils made his admirers regret that he did not commence that branch of the art earlier. His oil-paintings are chiefly of Devonshire scenery, of the Avon and Teign more particularly. He delighted in the calm and quiet repose of nature, the still, dark pool, and the moss-covered boulder; the rippling streamlet, and the dewy weeds growing by its banks. He never attempted the high tone of colour. He exhibited at the Royal Academy from 1846 to 1863. He was much honoured in Exeter, not only as an artist of whom the citizens were proud, but because in everything where taste was required he was at hand to lend his aid, not only to objects of public interest, but also to such private individuals as might seek his help. There were few men employed in carrying out works of decorative art who have not had his refined taste to assist them ; and most of the young artists of the neighbourhood sought, and never sought in vain, his friendly guidance.

Gendall worked to the last. Even while suffering from the illness which brought him to the grave, he struggled on till his strength failed him, and he could do no more. A lady sent him a commission to illustrate a little work of her own. Gendall looked at it, took his small bit of pencil, which he always carried in his waistcoat pocket, and thought a few minutes ; then lifting it up in the air, he opened his hand and let it fall. "It is all over," said he, and he never used pencil more. To stamp for ever the name of John Gendall as a true artist, it is only necessary to say that his paintings were highly esteemed by that greatest of all landscape painters, living or dead, J. W. M. Turner. He died March 1st, 1865, aged 75.

HART, ALEXANDER SOLOMON, R.A., historical painter, born at Plymouth in 1806, the son of Samuel Hart, who, while serving his apprenticeship to a goldsmith, studied art, and painted under Northcote in 1785. Solomon Hart entered the Royal Academy as a student in 1823, and exhibited his first work, a miniature of his father, in 1826. He practised miniature painting for a livelihood, but showed his first painting, "Instructions," at the British Institution in 1828, and "The Elevation of the Law," which noble picture was purchased by Mr. Vernon, was engraved in the *Art Union* and is now in the National Gallery. Subsequently he painted "Isaac of York in the Donjon of Front-de-Bœuf," 1830 ; "English Nobles privately receiving the Catholic Communion early in the 16th century," 1831 ; "Giacopo Guerini refusing to enter into the compact with Boemondo Theopolo to put to death the Doge Gradenigo," 1832 ; "Wolsey and Buckingham," 1834 ; "Richard and Saladin," 1835, which last two pictures secured him the honour of election as associate. He afterwards painted "Milton visiting Galileo in Prison," 1847; the "Three Inventors of Printing," 1852; and many interiors of cathedrals and ecclesiastical buildings. Of still later works, "Manasseh ben Israel pleading with Oliver Cromwell for the admission of the Jews," was the most successful. Great pains were taken with this work, which was designed by the artist as an offering to the memory of the great Protector, by whose wise statesmanship the ancestors of the painter had been permitted to settle in England. The head of the Lord Protector was copied from a photograph of the portrait in Sidney Sussex College, Cambridge. The picture was hung in the Academy, and purchased by the late Sir Francis Goldsmid. Mr. Hart also painted landscapes and portraits, and contributed to the *Athenæum*, the *Jewish Chronicle*, and other periodicals. He served repeatedly on the Hanging Committee of the Royal Academy. In 1857 he succeeded Mr. Leslie as Professor of Painting in the Royal Academy, and in 1865 was appointed by the Queen Librarian of that body, in which capacity he took part in the Librarians' Conference in London in 1877. He died in London in June, 1881, aged 75 years.[*]

HAYDON, B. R., historical painter, born at Plymouth, January 26th, 1786, and died June 26th, 1846. His biography has already appeared in our *Transactions*, vol. vi., p. 73, from the graphic pen of the Rev. Treasurer Hawker, M.A., I will therefore merely give a list of his best paintings.

His first picture was "Joseph and Mary." He exhibited in 1809, "Dentatus;" 1810, "Lady Macbeth;" also painted "Judgment of Solomon;" 1820, exhibited "Christ entering Jerusalem," at the Egyptian Hall, Piccadilly; 1823, "Raising of Lazarus;" 1826, "Venus appearing to Anchises." He also painted at various times "Alexandra Taming Bucephalus," "Euclus," "Mock Election," and "Chairing the Member," "Waiting for the *Times*," "The Reform Banquet," "The Retreat of the Ten Thousand," "Napoleon at St. Helena," "Pharaoh dismissing Moses," "Wellington at Waterloo," "Banishment of Aristides," "Nero playing on the Lyre," "Curtius plunging into the Gulf," "Alexander the Great encountering a Lion."

HAYMAN, FRANCIS, historical painter, born in Exeter in 1708. He was pupil of Robert Brown, a portrait painter, went to London while young, and was employed by Fleetwood, the manager of Drury Lane, as scene painter. He also decorated the alcoves of Vauxhall. The booksellers employed him as an illustrator, and his

* Solomon Hart failed very much in his later pictures, and was the subject of much ridicule and facile criticism; but the members of the Academy, says a critic in the *Magazine of Art*, were never blinded to the utility and worth of a painter whose scholarship, intellectual capacity, and theoretical knowledge were as fine, as his later pictures were unworthy of his earlier powers. He was a lecturer on art of uncommon ability.

designs may be found in Hanmer's editions of Shakespeare, Milton, Pope, and Cervantes. He was considered the first historical painter of his day, the best in England before the arrival of Cipriani. He was the first librarian of the Royal Academy, a member of the St. Martin's Lane Academy, and President of the Incorporated Society of Artists. He was of a very convivial turn, a member of the Beef-steak and Old Slaughter, and several other clubs. A jolly fellow, in fact—a friend of Hogarth, and fast men about town. He presented his picture, "The Finding of Moses," to the Foundling Hospital; and there is a portrait of himself in the National Portrait Gallery. He died February 2nd, 1776, in Dean Street, Soho, London.

HILLIARD, NICHOLAS, portrait and miniature painter, and one of the first-class, who, though born in Exeter in 1547, and practising his art during the reign of Elizabeth and James I., is still regarded as inferior to few who have succeeded him. His father was high sheriff of Exeter in 1560.

He was apprenticed to a goldsmith, and afterwards studied miniature painting, taking for his example the work of Hans Holbein, and the best models he could follow. He was appointed goldsmith, carver, and portrait painter to Queen Elizabeth, and painted her portrait several times; and the same office was continued to him by the patent of James I., who also gave him during twelve years the exclusive privilege "to mint, make, engrave, and imprint any pictures of our image or our royal family."

He painted several pictures of Queen Elizabeth, a portrait of Mary Queen of Scots at the age of 18, and many of the nobility and celebrities of the age. In the collection of the Duke of Buccleuch are miniatures by him of Edward, seventeenth Earl of Oxford, a portrait of himself, of his wife Alicia Brandon, of Robert, Earl of Southampton, four of Lady Arabella Stuart, famous for her beauty and misfortunes, seven of Queen Elizabeth, also of George Clifford, third Earl of Cumberland, his father Richard Hilliard, Sir Philip Sidney, Edward Seymour, Duke of Somerset, and many others. Mr. W. H. Pole Carew has a portrait of Sir Gawen Carew, Kt.; Sir John Salusbury Trelawny, one of Queen Elizabeth; the Earl of Portsmouth has two by his hand— Sir Henry Wallop, Kt., and Sir Oliver Wallop, Kt.; and the Marquis of Salisbury has a portrait of Mary Queen of Scots.

He engraved the Great Seal of England in 1587. He painted a view of the Spanish Armada, and a curious jewel containing the portraits of Henry VII., Henry VIII., Edward VI., and Queen Mary. On the top was an enamelled representation of the battle of Bosworth, and on the reverse the red and white roses.

Peacham *On Limning* says: "Comparing ancient and modern painters brings the comparison to our own time and country; nor must I be ungratefully unmindful of my own countrymen, who have been, and are still able to equal the best if occasion served, as old Hilliard, Mr. Isaac Oliver, inferior to none in Christendom for the countenance in small," &c. Richard Heydock, of New College, Oxon, in his translation of *Domazzo on Painting*, published in 1598, speaks of the "rare perfection we now see by the most ingenious, painful, and skilful master, Nicholas Hilliard." Of him Dr. Donne said, in his poem of *The Storm* —

> " An hand or eye
> By Hilliard drawn is worth a historye
> By a worse painter made."

His works are still held in high esteem, and a collection of them was exhibited at the Exhibition of Old Masters at Burlington House, in 1879. He died January 6th, 1619, and was buried at St. Martin-in-the-Fields.

HOSKING, WILLIAM, architect, born at Buckfastleigh in 1808. In early life was taken to New South Wales, where he learned the elements of his business at the hands of a builder. Later in life he became Professor of Architecture at King's College. He wrote many treatises on the principles and practice of his profession, and the articles on architecture, building, and masonry, in the *Encyclopædia Britannica.* He died in London, August 2nd, 1861, and was buried in Highgate Cemetery.

HUDSON, THOMAS, portrait painter, born in Devonshire in 1701. He studied under Jonathan Richardson, a leading portrait painter of the day, and married his daughter. He became a member of the Incorporated Society of Artists, and for many years was the fashionable portrait painter of the day. He is said to have merely painted the faces of his sitters, and to have left the figure and drapery to an assistant. It is impossible to class him among the great painters. There certainly was considerable grace in some of his figures. A portrait of a lady in Powderham Castle is as dignified and as graceful as ever was drawn; but taken as a whole his pictures are weak, and not worthy of the fame he enjoyed during his day of fashion. They are so numerous as to be seen in the mansions of most country families. His paintings are not valued at the present day, and Hudson is chiefly spoken of as the master of the great Sir Joshua Reynolds. He died at Twickenham, January 26th, 1779.

Excellent specimens of his work are to be found at Powderham Castle. In the board-room of the Exeter Hospital are portraits of John Tuckfield, Ralph Allen (whom Fielding copied for Squire Allworthy), and William Lee Dicker, and in the Exeter Guildhall are portraits of Sir Charles Pratt and George II.

JACKSON, WILLIAM, amateur, born in Exeter in 1730. He was a friend of Gainsborough, and painted some clever landscapes. He died July 12th, 1803.

JENKINS, THOMAS, historical painter, born in Devonshire, a pupil of Hudson's. He went to Rome, and studied historical subjects. He traded in antiquities, and amassed a large fortune, becoming the chief English banker at Rome. Through his means many works of antique sculpture were acquired by his countrymen. He died at Yarmouth in 1798.

JOHNS, AMBROSE BOWDEN, born in Plymouth in 1766. This excellent artist practised as a landscape painter. He was originally a bookseller, carrying on his trade in his native town, but his intelligence and agreeable manners procured him the friendship of the first gentlemen of Plymouth, among whom several took great interest in the young bookseller's progress in art. Johns employed all his leisure in sketching, and in process of time he gave up business, built a cottage close to Plymouth, and started in life as a landscape painter. There he was constantly encouraged by the society of his art friends, among whom were Northcote, brother of the portrait painter, Haydon, Bidlake, Rogers, R. King, Ball, Sir Chas. Eastlake, early in his career, and Prout, Opie, Mitchell, and Cook, somewhat later.

The great Turner sketched by his side, and spent a few days at the cottage. Indeed Turner and Johns frequently worked together, and our artist must have caught some of his fellow-student's style, for in after years one of his pictures was engraved by Turner's favourite engraver, John Cousen, and published with Turner's name to it in one of the old "Annuals." Johns was very angry when informed of the occurrence (a great mistake on his part, for a higher compliment could not have been paid him), and he wrote to the publisher, who behaved in a very handsome manner. This, however, gave rise to a coolness between the two painters ; not an actual rupture, but a cessation of intercourse. This engraving was taken from a picture in the possession of S. C. Hall, and after passing out of his hands was being offered for sale at Christie's as a genuine Turner, when a gentleman present stepped up to the auctioneer and named Johns as the artist. Mr. Christie immediately mentioned the fact to the audience, but added, " Whether it be by Turner or not I know not ; one thing I do know, that I have not had a sweeter thing pass through my hands for a long time." This picture was sold by Mr. Palmer to Dr. Yonge, at whose house it hangs, almost spoiled (I am told) by cleaners or daubers. At another time a large canvas was publicly exhibited in Plymouth as a Turner, which his family at once recognized as the work of their father. After his death a gentleman of York purchased a picture as a Turner at Christie's for £600, which the Johns' family proved to be the work of their father, by producing the original sketch.

Some of his pictures are at Saltram ; many are in the hands of the widow of Dr. Yonge, at Plymouth, and of Mr. Fisher, of Taunton. One of his finest works is in the gallery of Lord

Darnley of Cobham, and this picture was singled out for high praise by the art critic Waagen.

Unfortunately, from his great carelessness as to medium, and from his having used asphalte too freely, many of his pictures have blackened sadly.

Johns had no regular art education. He exhibited at the Academy, "Evening—Pirates landing their Cargo and a Female Captive," and views in the neighbourhood of Plymouth. He died at Plymouth, December 10th, 1858.

KING, JOHN, history and portrait painter, born at Dartmouth in 1788. He studied at the Academy, and first exhibited in 1817. He painted historical subjects for several years, but obtained scant encouragement. Latterly he tried portrait painting. He continued to exhibit till 1845, and died at his native town on the 12th July, 1847.

LEAKY, JAMES, portrait and miniature painter, born in Exeter, 1773. He established himself in Exeter, and judging from the number of his pictures still to be found in Devonshire houses, must have had considerable practice. His miniatures were in oil, well coloured, and finished with great care. He was much esteemed as an artist. He resided in London in 1821–22, and exhibited at the Academy, "The Marvellous Tale," "The Fortune Teller," and two Devonshire landscapes. In 1838 he sent from Exeter three portraits and two landscapes to the Academy. He died in Exeter, February 16th, 1865, aged 92 years. There are two of his portraits in Exeleigh House, Starcross.

LEE, FREDERICK RICHARD, R.A., landscape painter, born at Barnstaple in 1799. He was in his day one of the leading landscape painters of the English school, with such eminent men as Linnel, Creswick, Francis Danby, and Sidney Cooper. His career is especially interesting as showing the advance of a genuine nature-taught painter, for he began as an amateur, continued his study when he was serving as a young officer in the 56th Regiment, and leaving the army on account of weak health, entered as a student at the Academy in 1818. He soon attracted notice by his pictures contributed to the British Institution, and the directors awarded £50 as a mark of his merit. Born at Barnstaple, he was from his boyhood to old age a lover of the sea, and he painted almost as many sea pictures as landscapes. His pictures were for many years taken from the rich pastoral and river scenery of Devon, in several of which the cattle were painted by his friend, Sidney Cooper, who survives him; and in one, "The Cover Side," painted in 1839, just after he was made a full Academician, the dogs, figure, and game were painted by Sir Edwin Landseer. This, with three other works, is in the National Gallery, the bequest of Mr. Vernon and Mr. Jacob Bell. During the next decade of his work he was a constant contributor of Devonshire landscapes, in which he distinguished himself as a painter of trees in the rich, full foliage of summer and autumn, bending over some shady shallow of the river, where the cows come to enjoy the cool stream, or some " silver pool," where the trout lie watching for the fly, or hiding the old mill, with its wheel and tumbling stream rushing among the rocks. One of his largest and best works was "A Summer Morning," with cattle by Sidney Cooper, exhibited in 1848, which was recently sold at Christie's for £798. His passion for yachting led him to paint sea subjects, and in these he was even more happy than in his favourite Devonshire valleys. In 1859 he astonished his old admirers with a most spirited sea piece, "The Coast of Cornwall near the Land's End," with a dismasted ship tossed on a wild sea under a stormy sky being rescued by a steamer ; and "The Bay of Biscay, March 11th, 1857," his own little yacht struggling bravely with the huge dark waves—a scene of danger which he contrasted by a charming little picture of his "Cottage by the Brook," in the same exhibition. Again, in 1861, he had not only two remarkable views of Gibraltar, but a fine sea piece of the Plymouth Breakwater, which was compared favourably with Stanfield's "Homeward Bound," in the same exhibition. In the following year his large picture of "The Pont du Gard," the ancient Roman aqueduct near Nismes, another fine view of Gibraltar, and two or three of his pastorals, showed what a true artist he was in the versatility and vigorous exercise of his pencil. In 1864 he paid a visit to Garibaldi in his island home at Caprera, and painted many sketches, from which he did the picture of the General's house looking across the Straits of Bonifacio towards Corsica, exhibited next year along with one of his yacht, *King-fisher*, in a gale off the coast of Malaga. He was now, however, naturally losing his power with advancing years, and though he contributed a few more pictures to the exhibition, and had no less than six pictures in the first exhibition at Burlington House, in 1869, he retired as honorary Academician in 1871, and died at Vlees Farm, Cape Colony, aged 81 years.

THE FAUNA OF DEVON.

ORDER HYMENOPTERA.

FAMILY ICHNEUMONIDÆ.   SECTION PUPIVORA.

BY EDWARD PARFITT.

(Read at Dawlish, July, 1881.)

IN my contribution to the Fauna of Devon, last year, I enumerated the various species belonging to the first section of the order Hymenoptera; namely, the Aculeata. This year I have done my best, by the aid of friends and my own collections, to continue the order in the division Ichneumonidæ. We saw in the first section that the habits both of the parasites and of their hosts, and their modes of life, were very peculiar, and also that the extraordinary order, arrangement, and the degrees of intelligence displayed by the industrious ants, surpass anything known amongst insect life.

The present section of the great order Hymenoptera, so far as is known, is entirely parasitic; that is, the larvæ of the Ichneumons subsist either on the caterpillars of butterflies or moths, or on the pupæ of the order Lepidoptera, and are termed, from their habits, pupivora, and I may add larvivora, or pupæ and larvæ eaters, both of which are strictly true. They may also be denominated anatomists and vivisectionists, both of which are likewise true. The application is particularly true as regards the latter, for they are the most persistent vivisectionists known; their own lives, in fact, depend upon their skill as operators in this apparently disgusting and cruel work of torturing, and ultimately destroying, the lives of those caterpillars which they may fix upon as their hosts or victims. This, seen from a vivisectionist's point of view, is a merciless and cruel act; that the beautiful caterpillars of the most gorgeous of the insect world should be tortured and tormented and eaten up piecemeal by these silent workers of their destruction. They might be termed the "teeth and claws" of nature.

The insects of this section cannot, so far as is known, be traced further back in time than the Upper Miocene formation, and in this they are found associated with the gnats and flies of most of the families now living, as also with ants and bees and a few Lepidoptera. Considering that these insects are mostly parasitic on the larvæ of Lepidoptera, they were probably not introduced much before them. At the same time, they are not entirely confined to the butterflies and moths, as one new species, or one unknown to science, will be found described in this list; it was bred from the pupa case of the small whirligig-beetle, *Gyrinus natator*, found by the Rev. J. Hellins. I have named it, from its habit, *Hemitelcs gyrini*. I have bred species from the larvæ of the beetle which infests our houses and furniture, the different species of Anobium; also from the larvæ and pupæ of Dipterous insects, and from the nests of spiders, on whose nests of eggs the larvæ of the parasites feed; so that it will be seen that their habits range over most of the great orders of the insect world. In some cases the parasite, so far as is known, is attached to one species of insect; and as there is never a rule without an exception, we have others which seem to attack butterflies and moths indiscriminately. To understand the habits of these various species it is necessary to collect the larvæ of such Lepidoptera or other orders and feed them and keep them separate and watch the result. My friend Mr. Bignell, of Stonehouse, and the late Mr. D'Orville and myself have been very successful in rearing some new and interesting species, which will be found enumerated further on, with their hosts.

The development of these parasites from the larvæ or pupæ, as the case may be, was a great source of speculation amongst the earlier philosophers, who conceived it possible that one animal had occasionally the power of being absolutely transformed into another; and Swammerdam records as a thing very wonderful that 545 flies of the same species were produced from four chrysalides of a butterfly; so that the life of the four seemed to have transmigrated into that of the 545 others. And we may still say with Swammerdam that it is wonderful that a creature should go on living, with so many lesser creatures living and fattening on its flesh, without directly taking its life. This fact alone is very significant, and shows that the life, whatever that may be, is not equally distributed throughout the animal, but that it is confined to certain nervous systems in the structure of the animal, termed "vital organs." Hence these parasites can, and do, feed upon the adipose or fatty flesh, if I may so call it, of the victim, without taking its life.

Dean Swift may well exclaim, in the following lines (although his verses do not run so smoothly as the modern version of them), that—

> * " The vermin only teaze and pinch
> Their foes superior by the inch ;
> So nat'ralists observe, a flea
> Hath smaller fleas that on him prey,
> And these have smaller still to bite 'em,
> And so proceed *ad infinitum.*"

This is literally true, as these parasitic Ichneumons have parasites which live in them and destroy them ; the lesser ones are called hyper-parasites, the Pteromali, and others too numerous to mention here.

·In the larva state the Ichneumons subsist entirely on the fluids and adipose matter of other insects, and are either attached singly to the external surface of the bodies of their victims, or are located internally between the tissues : they drink up the life-blood prepared for another without entirely destroying the means of its production.

The larvæ, writes Mr. George Newport,† undergo the same mode of growth, the casting of the skin, and gradual development, as a common Lepidopterous larva ; the chief difference between the larvæ of the parasites and other larvæ is in their earlier stage, when their digestive apparatus is merely a simple sac, or bag, rounded and closed at its larger extremity, with an imperforated intestine proceeding from it without an outlet.

Very little undigested substance remains after the assimilation of the nourishment imbibed, and consequently no excretory outlet to the organ is required. This is a beautiful adaptation to the creature's mode of life, that the assimilation of the one should be so exactly adapted to the wants of another, so equally balanced, that nothing remains over and above. No change in the economy or in the development of the internal organisation of the creature takes place, so far as is known, until the individual is replete with nourishment,

---

* *Swift's Works,* v. vii., p. 268.
† *Linnæan Society's Transactions,* vol. xxi. p. 61, *partim.*

or, in other words, full fed and ready to undergo its change into a pupa.

"When this period of its existence has arrived, it is first necessary that the unassimilated portion of food, together with the worn-out materials of the body, should be removed, and this necessitates the change from a closed receptacle to a canal."

It would appear from this that the old or worn-out materials of the internal organs, the epithelial cells, &c., of the bag-like stomach, could not be digested, and therefore accumulated, and consequently necessitated a cloacal arrangement.

Professor Owen says, speaking of the habits of the larvæ, that "they avoid penetrating the alimentary canal, but evidently destroy many of the minute branches of the tracheæ which ramify in the adipose tissue; such wounded tracheæ probably permit the escape of sufficient air for the respiration of the parasitic larvæ; for though the caterpillars so infested survive and go into the pupa state, they are uneasy and evidently diseased; the loss of the adipose store of nutriment prevents the completion of the metamorphosis; they perish, and instead of a butterfly, a swarm of small Ichneumons emerge from the cocoon."[*]

The marvellous instinct or knowledge displayed by the parent Ichneumons in searching out the victims for their oviposition is something to be seen, but not understood. We cannot, with all our knowledge of the habits and peculiarities of insects, divine how it is that certain species of Ichneumons should know, out of the numerous larvæ of butterflies and moths, to say nothing of the wood-boring beetles, &c., the special ones for the purpose of depositing their eggs, and, of course, at the same time seeking their destruction. The caterpillars, at the early stage at which they are generally sought, are so much alike in a great many instances that they are with difficulty distinguished by the student; and yet these keen-sighted (if it be sight) Ichneumons are able to distinguish them. Do they, I wonder, reason to themselves, when passing by those that are nearly like the ones they are looking for, and say, "Am I right?" This selection passes our comprehension. We call it instinct; but this does not help us to a knowledge of what it really is. This power of discrimination is quite as great, if not greater, in the lower forms of life than it is even in man himself. Take the oviposition of a moth or a butterfly: the greater number of moths are nocturnal in their hours of flight, and

* *Invertebrates*, p. 432, 2nd edit.

yet they are able to distinguish one plant from another, and select the one proper for the food of their progeny, so that when these leave the egg they shall not have to search for food.

We may apply this same reasoning to the minute Ichneumons, which are parasitic on the eggs of certain butterflies and moths. The eggs of insects, of course, are extremely small, but even they are subject to the attacks of minute creatures, which deposit an egg in each egg of the insect on which the young larva is to feed: it does not eat or injure the shell of the moth's egg until it is full fed and ready to undergo its transformation, and in most they even make the egg-shell a kind of protecting covering, for they undergo their pupation inside, and only emerge when they are ready to fly away to perform the same round as did their parent.

To pursue this instinctive peculiarity of the Ichneumonidæ further, there are certain kinds attached to some species of Aphis, the *bête noire* of the gardener, and especially the rose cultivator. It may be observed, by those who will take the trouble to investigate this subject, that generally amongst a number of Aphides, say feeding on a rose tree, there are many with bodies much swollen, which have changed from a green colour to nearly white. These Aphides have been (so-called) stung by the Ichneumons; that is, an egg has been deposited in each of their bodies, and has hatched; the young larva has devoured the contents of the Aphis, and has utilised its body as a protection for its own thin pupa skin. By collecting these white-looking Aphides, and keeping them under a glass, the Ichneumons may be seen to emerge. These, when once ascertained, should be encouraged as benefactors to man.

The same may be said of those species of Ichneumons that attack the larvæ of several species of Dipterous insects, so destructive to the growing crops of wheat and barley. The larva of the fly, when feeding inside the growing plant, and in the early stage, is not discoverable by man until it has eaten away some of the centre of the corn plant, when its presence may be discovered by the young blades growing pale and yellow; but prior to this a little Ichneumon, called *Cephus pygmæus*, has had his eyes on this so-called diseased plant, and has deposited, by some means not exactly understood, an egg in this devouring larva. But the mystery is, how did this Ichneumon know that there was a larva in this growing wheat plant, and how did she know whereabouts to perforate the plant so as to deposit her egg in the larva feeding inside unseen by human eye? The egg could not have been dropped in at the top, for the closely-sheathing leaves of the plant would preclude this; she must, therefore, have perforated the stem with her ovipositor, but we are left entirely in the dark as to her knowledge of ascertaining its whereabouts. The probability is that some, if not all, these internal feeding insects may give off a scent, which although imperceptible to us, is perceptible to the Ichneumons; for, whenever they are on the search for victims in which to deposit their eggs, they are constantly vibrating their antennæ, waving them to and fro, as if beating the air. Nearly all these insects are provided with very long antennæ, but the sense of smell in insects is still an open question. Various experiments have been tried to prove or negative this sense, but it is still doubtful how insects obtain the knowledge which they possess; they certainly know how to apply it.

Some of the Ichneumons have a very peculiar, an indescribable kind of scent or smell when handled, the larger ones more especially. Many insects have a disagreeable smell; the plant bugs, for instance, the Oil Beetle, &c. The Devil's Coach-horse Beetle, *Staphylinus olens*, however, has a very agreeable smell to us, which may be very objectionable to insects or animals which might attack it. The scent given off by the Ichneumons may probably serve as a means of defence to repel the attacks of other parasites to which these insects are liable.

One of the most remarkable things in the history of these insects is recorded by Messrs. Kirby and Spence, under the head of "Affection of Insects for their Young." These accurate observers remark, on the selection the parent Ichneumon makes when searching for a proper caterpillar in which to deposit her eggs:—" Perhaps, however, she discovers by a sense, the existence of which we perceive, though we have no conception of its nature, that she has been forestalled by some precursor of her own tribe that has already buried an egg in the caterpillar she is examining. In this case she leaves it, aware that it would not suffice for the support of two, and proceeds in search of some other yet unoccupied." This, it must be admitted, is very wonderful, and how she obtains the knowledge is entirely beyond human ken.

Much more might be said upon this interesting and at the same time difficult subject, did time and space permit. The vast field of study of insect life is one that ought to attract more attention than it does. The present section is one, perhaps, of the least known of any in this country, and it has, perhaps, fewer workers in it than in almost any other. In 1872 the Rev. T. A. Marshall catalogued all the species, so far as was then known, in the United Kingdom, and they only amounted to 1,654. Since then many have been discovered; but still the list does not represent half the number that ought to, and, I believe, does exist in this country. Of this number I have enumerated 342 species, and I have many yet undetermined.

In conclusion, I have much pleasure in tendering my best thanks to E. Fitch, Esq., of Maldon, Essex; and J. B. Bridgman, Esq., Norwich; for their kind assistance in determining some difficult species; and also to Mr. Bignell, of Stonehouse, for the good work he has done in breeding so many interesting insects of this group.

CATALOGUE.

WITH NOTES AND OBSERVATIONS.

BIBLIOGRAPHY.

Gravenhorst, Ichneumonologia Europea. 1829.
Nees ab Esenbeck, Hymenopterorum Ichneumonibus Affinium Monographiæ.
    1834.
Haliday, in Annals of Natural History. 1839.
Newport, G., in Linnæan Society's Transactions. 1845.
Stephens, Illustrations of British Entomology. 1835.
Curtis, J., Farm Insects. 1860.
Devignes, Catalogue British Ichneumonidæ. 1856.
Marshall, Catalogue British Hymenoptera. 1872.
Donovan, British Insects.
Curtis, J., British Insects.
Marshall, Rev. T. A., in Entomologist's Annual. 1874.
Westwood, Introduction to the Modern Classification of Insects. 1840.
Messrs. E. Fitch and J. B. Bridgman, in Litt. 1881.
Owen, Prof., Lectures on the Invertebrate Animals. 1855.
Goss, H., Fossil Entomology, Ent. Mont. Mag. 1879–80.

Order, HYMENOPTERA.
Family, ICHNEUMONIDÆ, *Leach.*
Section, PUPIVORA, *Latreille.*
GENUS, **ICHNEUMON**, *Linnæus.*

(Scutellum and abdomen black.)

BILINEATUS, *Gml.*

> *Grav.*, Ich. Europ., i. p. 127; *Steph.*, Ill., v. vii. p. 138,

This has been bred by Mr. Bignell, from *Bryophila glan-difera*, and also from the Gooseberry Moth, *Abraxas grossulariata.*

LINEATOR, *Fab.*

> *Grav.*, Ich. Europ., i. p. 120; *Steph.*, Ill., v. vii. p. 190.

Captured on Prawle Point, in August. Variety of female, with abdomen entirely castaneous red.

COMITATOR, *Linn.*

> *Grav.*, Ich. Europ. i. p. 108; *Steph.*, Ill. v. vii. p. 127.

Taken on heads of umbelliferous flowers, frequently near woods, &c.

NIGRITARIUS, *Grav.*

Ich. Europ., i. p. 113 ; *Steph.*, v. vii. p. 128–132.

Beaten from hedges in June, and bred by Mr. Bignell from *Abraxas grossulariata.*

CORUSCATOR, *Linn.*

Grav., Ich. Europ., i. p. 133 ; *Steph.*, Ill., v. vii. p. 133.

Taken on flowers near woods in June.

MACULIFRONS, *Steph.*

Ill., v. vii. p. 133.

Very rare ; taken near Exeter in April. This varies a little from the type, in having the base of the antennæ black.

(Scutellum pale or with pale spots, abdomen black.)

OCHROPUS, *Gml.*

Grav., Ich. Europ., i. p. 182 ; *Steph.*, Ill., v. vii. p. 143.

This appears to be very scarce ; I have seen only one female. Stephens says the larvæ feed on that of *Abraxas grossulariata.*

FABRICATOR, *Fab.*

Grav., Ich. Europ., i. p. 185 ; *Steph.*, Ill., v. vii. pp. 137, 143, 196.

The females of this species are so extremely variable in size and colouration that they have been named by naturalists as so many different species. It is one of our handsomest insects, and is generally distributed.

OSCILLATOR, *Holmg.*

Grav., Ich. Europ., i. p. 233. (*I. Pallipes.*)

Taken by Mr. Bignell near Plymouth.

MULTIANNULATUS, *Grav.*

Ich. Europ., i. p. 223 ; *Steph.*, Ill., v. vii. p. 151.

Frequent, by the sides of roads, on flowers of the large umbelliferæ, in June and July.

FUSCIPES, *Gmel.*

Grav., Ich. Europ., i. p. 224 ; *Steph.*, Ill., v. vii. p. 151.

Not very common ; taken by Mr. D'Orville and myself.

FUSCIPES, *var.* SUBGUTTATUS, *Grav.*

Ich. Europ., v. p. 449 ; *Steph.*, v. vii. p. 187.

This was taken by Mr. D'Orville at Alphington, and I have bred it from pupæ dug up at the roots of trees.

LANGUIDUS, *Wesm.*

Grav., Ich. Europ., i. pp. 200-213.

This is very closely related to the one above, so much so that they require very nice discrimination. I have taken it on umbelliferous flowers in July.

TRILINEATUS, *Gmel.*

Grav., Ich. Europ., i. p. 173; *Steph.*, Ill., v. vii. p. 142.

Bred by Mr. Bignell from *Abraxas grossulariata.*

(Scutellum white or dotted with white, abdomen black, the ultimate segments spotted with white.)

SATURATORIUS, *Linn.*

Grav., Ich. Europ., i. p. 237; *Steph.*, Ill., v. vii. p. 154.

By no means a common species, but widely distributed.

ANATOR, *Fab.*

Grav., Ich. Europ., i. p. 250; *Steph.*, Ill., v. vii. p. 156.

Not common, but generally distributed.

COMPATORIUS, *Müll.*

Grav., Ich. Europ., i. p. 256; *Steph.*, Ill., v. vii. p. 158.

Common and generally distributed,

CINGULIPES, *Steph.*

Ill., v. vii. p. 157.

A fine but scarce insect; captured on flowers of umbelliferæ.

LEUCOMELAS, *Grav.*

Ich. Europ., i. p. 255; *Steph.*, Ill., v. vii. p. 156.

Stephens says captured in Devonshire in June.

SUBMARGINATUS, *Grav.*

Ich. Europ., i. p. 244; *Steph.*, Ill., v. vii. p. 155.

Taken by Mr. Bignell near Plymouth.

GRACILENTUS, *Wesm.*

Nov. Mem. Ac. Brux, 1844, p. 47.

Taken by Mr. Bignell in the Plymouth district.

(Scutellum pale or spotted with white, abdomen of three colours, black, red, and white or yellow and white.)

CONFUSORIUS, *Grav.*

Ich. Europ., i. p. 276; *Steph.*, Ill., v. vii. p. 160.

So far as my observation goes, this does not seem an abundant species.

RUDIBUNDUS, *Grav.*

> Ich. Europ., i. p. 229.

Taken at Laira by Mr. Bignell.

SUSPICIOSUS, *Wesm.*

> *Grav.*, Ich. Europ., i. p. 281 (?); *Steph.*, Ill., v. vii. p. 161 (?)

This conspicuous insect is not uncommon on flowers of umbelliferæ. It is, however, rather uncertain whether this is the true *Suspiciosus* of Wesmael. I have a specimen named by Mr. Marshall, but he added a note of interrogation to it.

(Scutellum pale, abdomen black, the middle belted or spotted with yellow or white, apical segments black.)

VAGINATORIUS, *Linn.*

> *Grav.*, Ich. Europ., i. p. 357; *Steph.*, Ill., v. vii. p. 174.

An abundant species, and very variable in its markings; found generally on flowers of the umbelliferæ, on the borders of woods, in July.

XANTHORIUS, *Forst.*

> *Grav.*, Ich. Europ., i. p. 361; *Steph.*, Ill., v. vii. p. 173.

Taken by Mr. D'Orville and myself; generally and sparsely distributed in July.

(Scutellum pale, abdomen either with pale marks or the segments yellow, with the apical one black.)

SUGILLATORIUS, *Linn.*

> *Grav.*, Ich. Europ., i. p. 440; *Steph.*, Ill., v. vii. p. 185.

Of this I have seen but one specimen only.

LUCTATORIUS, *Linn.*

> *Grav.*, Ich. Europ., i. p. 411; *Steph.*, Ill., v. vii. p. 182.

A common species, parasitic on *Triphæna pronuba* and other noctuidæ; a very variable insect as regards both size and colouring.

INQUINATUS, *Wesm.*

> Ich. Europ., i. p. 418; I. luctatorious, var. i.; I. crassorious, of Desvigne's Catalogue.

This fine insect would seem to be very rare; one only has fallen to my net.

LEUCOSTIGMUS, *Grav.*

 Ich. Europ., i. p. 446.

Captured by Mr. Bignell in the Plymouth district.

JUGATUS, *Grav.*

 Ich. Europ., i. p. 452.

Bred by Mr. Bignell from *Tephrosia extersaria.*

(*Scutellum pale, abdomen either entirely red or red and black.*)

LANIUS, *Grav.*

 Ich. Europ., i. p. 499; *Steph.*, Ill., v. vii. p. 192.

This little species was taken by Mr. D'Orville, probably at Alphington.

FUSCOCASTANEUS, *Grav.*

 Ich. Europ., i. p. 486.

Of this I have only seen one; it was presented to me by the late Mr. Style, who purchased the Raddon Collection. I presume, therefore, that this was taken in North Devon.

VACILLATORIUS, *Grav.*

 Ich. Europ., i. p. 500; *Steph.*, Ill., v. vii. p. 192.

Bred by Mr. Bignell from larvæ of *Depressaria Heracleana,* August 12, 1878.

(*Scutellum black, abdomen either entirely red or red and black.*)

CULPATOR, *Schr.*

 Grav., Ich. Europ., i. p. 548; *Steph.*, Ill., v. vii. p. 194.

A scarce species with us, so far as my experience goes.

CASTANEIVENTRIS, *Grav.*

 Ich. Europ., i. p. 556; *Steph.*, Ill., v. vii. p.

I bred this from pupæ dug up at the roots of trees, but am not sure what they were.

LATRATOR, *Fab.*

 Grav., Ich. Europ., i. p. 572; *Steph.*, Ill., v. viii. pp. 200, 206.

I bred this from pupæ of *Orthosia stabilis* in March, 1857.

RUFATOR, *Steph.*

 Ill., v. vii. p. 201.

Captured by Mr. W. G. Woollcombe, near Hatherleigh, North Devon.

GASTERATOR, *Stephens.*
Ill., v. vii. p. 199.

This species was named for Mr. D'Orville by Mr. Marshall, but he had some doubt as to the correctness. So far as the description given by Stephens goes, it agrees very closely. I have three specimens of it. Mr. D'Orville bred this from *Depressaria Heracleana.*

GENUS, **EXOPHANES,** *Wesmael.*

OCCUPATOR, *Grav.*
Ich. Europ., i. p. 425.

Taken by Mr. Bignell in the Plymouth district.

GENUS, **AMBLYTELES,** *Wesmael.*

(*Scutellum and abdomen black.*)

CASTIGATOR, *Fab.*
Grav., Ich. Europ., i. p. 124 ; *Steph.,* Ill., v. vii. p. 131.

Captured by Mr. Bignell near Plymouth.

(*Scutellum pale or spotted with white, abdomen black.*)

SUBSERICANS, *Grav.*
Ich. Europ., i. p. 161 ; *Steph.,* Ill., v. vii. p. 139.

Captured at Ide on August 3rd, 1880.

FOSSORIUS, *Grav.*
Ich. Europ., i. p. 164 ; *Steph.,* Ill., v. vii. pp. 139, 140.

Not common, so far as my experience goes ; taken in July.

FUNEREUS, *Fourc.*
Grav., Ich. Europ., i. p. 206 ; *Steph.,* Ill., v. vii. p. 148.

This was captured by Mr. D'Orville, probably in his garden at Alphington ; taken also by Mr. Bignell near Plymouth.

PROTEUS, *Christo.*
Grav., Ich. Europ., i. p. 217; *Steph.,* Ill., v. vii. p. 150.

This fine insect has been bred both by Mr. D'Orville and Mr. Bignell from the Elephant Hawk Moth, *Deilephila elpenor.*

(*Scutellum pale or spotted with pale colour, abdomen of three colours.*)

VADATORIUS, *Rossi.*
Grav., Ich. Europ., p. 304 ; *Steph.,* Ill., v. vii. p. 166.

Captured on flowers of the umbelliferæ, on the borders of woods, in July.

GRAVENHORSTII, *Wesm.*
> *Grav.*, Ich. Europ., i. pp. 266, 321.

This pretty insect is widely distributed, but not common.

(*Scutellum pale, abdomen black, the middle belted or spotted with yellow or white, the apex black.*)

PALLIATORIUS, *Grav.*
> Ich. Europ., i. p. 385 ; *Steph.* Ill., v. vii. p. 177.

This is one of the most abundant of the whole group, found on the large heads of umbelliferæ.

INFRACTORIUS, *Panz.*
> *Grav.*, Ich. Europ., i. p. 368 ; *Steph.*, Ill., v. vii. p. 172.

A widely distributed species, found on flowers by wood sides in July.

ORATORIUS, *Fab.*
> *Grav.*, Ich. Europ., i. pp. 394-397 ; *Steph.*, Ill., v. vii. p. 179.

Not common ; found near woods and thick hedges in July. Bred by Mr. Bignell from *Aplecta nebulosa.*

ARMATORIUS, *Forst.*
> *Grav.*, Ich. Europ., i. p. 370 ; *Steph.*, Ill., v. vii. p. 175.

A common and widely distributed species ; the males are frequently to be met with on flowers by wood sides in June and July. This is parasitic on many kinds of butter-flies and moths. See *Entomologist*, vol. xiv. p. 110.

(*Scutellum pale, abdomen either with pale marks or the segments generally yellow, with the apical always black.*)

NOTATORIUS, *Fab.*
> *Grav.*, Ich. Europ., i. p. 429 ; *Steph.*, Ill., v. vii. p. 184.

I have only seen one specimen, a female, of this very hand-some insect ; this I took near Lydford, in August, 1868.

Genus, TROGUS, *Panzer.*

LUTORIUS, *Fab.*
> *Grav.*, Ich. Europ., i. p. 374 ; *Steph.*, Ill., v. vii. p. 270.

This has been bred by Mr. Bignell from pupæ of *Sphinx Ligustri*, the Privet Hawk Moth.

ALBOGUTTATUS, *Grav.*
> Ich. Europ., ii. p. 373 ; *Steph.*, Ill., v. vii. p. 269.

I have not seen a Devonshire specimen, but Stephens records it as taken in the country. Mr. Bignell has bred this from *Orgyia pudibunda.*

PLATYURI, *Wesmael.*
GENUS, **EURYLABUS,** *Wesmael.*

DIRUS, *Wesm.*

Grav., Ich. Europ., i. p. 137 (*I tristes*).

Taken by Mr. Bignell in the Plymouth district.

GENUS, **PLATYLABUS,** *Wesmael.*

ORBITALIS, *Grav.*

Ich. Europ., i. p. 490; *Steph.,* Ill., v. vii. p. 191.

This appears to be rare with us. Mr. D'Orville captured one, and I have taken another. Var., with the face black, the inner orbits of the eyes alone pale yellow. Bred from a larva that was feeding on leaves of citron, in a greenhouse at Coaver, Exeter, March, 1852.

PNEUSTICI, *Wesmael.*
GENUS, **HERPESTOMUS,** *Wesmael.*

BRUNNICORNIS, *Wesm.*

Ich. Europ., i. p. 145; *Steph.,* Ill., v. vii. p. 136.

I have only seen one specimen, which I captured some years ago.

GENUS, **PHÆOGENES,** *Wesmael.*

MELANOGONUS, *Gmel.*

Grav., Ich. Europ., i. p. 581.

Taken by Mr. Bignell.

ISCHIOMELINUS, *Grav.*

Ich. Europ., i. 608.

Also taken by Mr. Bignell near Plymouth.

CANDIDATUS, *Grav.*

Ich. Europ., i. p. 193; *Steph.,* Ill., v. vii. p. 145.

Bred by Mr. Bignell from *Tortrix viridana.*

TREPIDUS, *Wesm.*

This is new to the British Fauna. Captured by Mr. Bignell, at Widswell Farm, in August, 1880.

GENUS, **ALOMYIA,** *Panzer.*

DEBELLATOR, *Fab.*

Grav., Ich. Europ., ii. p. 401.

Captured.

Family, CRYPTIDÆ, *Shuckard.*
GENUS, **STILPNUS**, *Gravenhorst.*

GAGATES, *Grav.*

Ich. Europ., p. 667; *Steph.*, Ill., v. vii. p. 209.

Beaten out of trees near Exeter in June; not common.

PAVONIÆ, *Scop.*

Grav., Ich. Europ., i. p. 672; *Steph.*, Ill., v. vii. p. 209.

Beaten out of oak trees in June; apparently scarce.

GENUS, **PHYGADEMON**, *Gravenhorst.*

(*Scutellum pale, abdomen red and black.*)

CINCTORIUS, *Fab.*

Grav., Ich. Europ., ii. p. 480; *Steph.*, Ill., v. vii. p. 281.

Taken in Devonshire, as recorded by Stephens.

LARVATUS, *Grav.*

Ich. Europ., ii. p. 662; *Steph.*, Ill., v. vii. p. 297.

Captured on flowers of umbelliferæ.

(*Scutellum black, abdomen red or red and black.*)

VAGANS, *Grav.*

Ich. Europ., ii. p. 758.

Taken at Plymbridge by Mr. Bignell.

BITINCTUS, *Gmel.*

Grav., Ich. Europ., ii. p. 576 (*Cryptus bitinctus*); *Steph.*, Ill., v. vii. p. 290.

ERYTHRINUS, *Grav.*

Ich. Europ., ii. p. 621; *Steph.*, Ill., v. vii. p. 294.

Apparently rare; I have seen only one specimen.

VARIABILIS, *Grav.*

Ich. Europ., ii. p. 705.

Captured at Lydford by beating hedges in June.

OVATUS, *Grav.*

Ich. Europ., ii. p. 668; *Steph.*, Ill., v. vii. p. 298.

Captured by Mr. D'Orville, probably in his garden at Alphington.

PROFLIGATOR, *Fab.*

> Grav., Ich. Europ., ii. p. 729 ; *Curtis*, Fam. Ins., p. 414 ; *Steph.*, Ill., v. vii. p. 303.

A common species. Curtis says the female deposits her eggs in the larvæ of *Depressaria daucella*, the Carrot Moth.

FUMATOR, *Grav.*

> Ich. Europ., ii. p. 687 ; *Steph.*, Ill., v. vii. p. 300.

Bred from pupæ of *Mamestra brassicæ*, the Cabbage Moth, and taken near Plymbridge.

FUMATOR, *var.*

GALACTINUS, *Grav.*

> Ich. Europ., ii. p. 682 ; *Steph.*, Ill., v. vii. p. 299.

This appears to be a rare insect with us ; taken on flowers in June.

GENUS, **CRYPTUS**, *Fabricius.*

(*Scutellum and abdomen black.*)

TARSOLEUCUS, *Schr.*

> Grav., Ich. Europ., ii. p. 447 ; *Steph.*, Ill., v. vii. p. 277.

This is a rare insect with us. Stephens says the " larva subsists on that of *Achatia juniperda*," the Pine Moth. The Pine Moth is very rare in Devonshire, so far as I have been able to ascertain.

MOSCHATOR, *Fab.*

> Grav., Ich. Europ., ii. p. 457 ; *Steph.*, Ill., v. vii. p. 277.

Rare, so far as my experience goes ; taken in July.

PORRECTORIUS, *Fab.*

> Grav., Ich. Europ., i. p. 642 (*Ischnus porrectorius*) ; *Steph.*, Ill., v. vii. p. 208.

This was bred by Mr. D'Orville from *Depressaria nervosella*, and may sometimes be taken from flowers of umbelliferæ in June.

SPIRALIS, *Fourc.*

> Grav., Ich. Europ., p. 454 ; *Steph.*, Ill., v. vii. p. 278.

Captured in August near Lydford.

LUGUBRIS, *Grav.*

> Ich. Europ., ii. p. 456.

Taken near Plymouth by Mr. Bignell.

(Scutellum spotted with white, abdomen red or red and black.)

TRICOLOR, *Grav.*

Ich. Europ., ii. p. 514 ; *Steph.,* Ill., v. vii. p. 298.

Bred by Mr. D'Orville from *Simyra venosa ;* and I have bred it from pupæ of *Pœcilocampa populi,* the Poplar Moth ; also from *Leucania.* There are several Ichneumon larvæ in the larva of the moth. Thus, in *P. populi* there were six or seven ; these, when full fed, spin a strong silken cocoon ; the silk is bound together with a white glaze ; they are placed on each side of the old skin of the caterpillar, which occupies the centre of the pupa case. The Ichneumons came out August 6th, 1867. I have also bred this insect from cocoons of *Trichiosoma leucorum,* a large Saw-fly, on Whitethorn.

ARROGANS, *Grav.*

Ich. Europ., ii. p. 494 ; *Steph.,* Ill., v. vii. p. 281.

Captured on flower heads of the umbelliferæ in July.

ALBATORIUS, *Vill.*

Grav., Ich. Europ., ii. p. 536 ; *Steph.,* Ill., v. vii., p. 285.

This appears to be a scarce species.

RUFIVENTRIS, *Grav.*

Ich. Europ., ii. p. 497 ; *Steph.,* Ill., v. vii. p. 282.

Captured by Mr. Bignell in the Plymouth district.

(Scutellum black, abdomen red or red and black.)

TITILLATOR, *Grav.*

Ich. Europ., ii. p. 564 ; *Steph.,* Ill., v. vii. p. 289.

Taken by sweeping in July.

MINATOR, *Grav.*

Ich. Europ., ii. p. 556 ; *Steph.,* Ill., v. vii. p. 288.

Not very common ; beaten from trees in July.

OBSCURUS, *Grav.*

Ich. Europ., ii. p. 548 ; *Steph.,* Ill., v. vii. p. 287.

Bred by Mr. D'Orville from *Dianthœcia capsincola.* The pupa case of this species is nearly cylindrical, with rounded ends, coriaceous, and of a dark, shining, mahogany colour. This is, perhaps, the commonest insect of all the genus.

ANALIS, *Grav.*

> Ich. Europ., ii. p. 560 ; *Steph.*, Ill., v. vii. p. 289.

Captured both by Mr. D'Orville and myself in June; taken also in the Plymouth district.

MIGRATOR, *Fab.*

> *Grav.*, Ich. Europ., ii. p. 592 ; *Steph.*, Ill., v. vii. p. 291.

Bred from *Bombyx quercus;* and Mr. Stephens says the larva feeds on that of *Spilosoma erminea;* the Oak Egger and the Ermine Moth.

PEREGRINATOR, *Linn.*

> *Grav.*, Ich. Europ., ii. p. 605 ; *Steph.*, Ill., v. vii. p. 283.

Apparently a scarce species ; taken in July.

(Abdomen with the apex entirely white.)

SIGNATORIUS, *Fab.*

> *Grav.*, Ich. Europ., p. 892.

Mr. Bignell bred this from an old bramble stem ; came out in May, 1878.

GENUS, **MESOSTENUS**, *Gravenhorst.*

OBNOXIUS, *Grav.*

> Ich. Europ., ii. p. 763.

This has been bred from *Zygœna filipendulœ*, by Mr. Bignell, Plymouth.

GENUS, **HEMITELES**, *Gravenhorst.*

(Thorax and abdomen black.)

TRISTATOR, *Grav.*

> Ich. Europ., ii. p. 787.

Taken by sweeping the banks of the South Devon Railway near Dawlish, in July and October.

SIMILIS, *Grav.*

> Ich. Europ., ii. p. 793.

Taken both by Mr. D'Orville and myself ; rather common ; generally distributed.

MELANARIUS, *Grav.*

> Ich. Europ., ii. p. 790.

Apparently scarce ; captured at Fordlands in June.

TENEBRICOSUS, *Grav.*

Ich. Europ., ii. p. 785.

Taken at Plymbridge 1880. Mr. Bignell.

(*Thorax black, abdomen red and black.*)

ÆSTIVALIS, *Grav.*

Ich. Europ., ii. p. 805.

Captured at Ide, near Exeter, in August; apparently rare.

MELANGONUS, *Grav.*

Ich. Europ., ii. p. 816.

Captured by sweeping grass in the Exeter district in the end of May.

OXYPHYMUS, *Grav.*

Ich. Europ., ii. p. 815.

I dug this species out of an old post in which were both larvæ of coleoptera and hymenoptera; which this is the parasite of I cannot say.

FLORICOLATOR, *Grav.*

Ich. Europ., ii. p. 841.

Captured by sweeping clover fields on Stokehill in May. Apparently rare.

DECIPIENS, *Grav.*

Ich. Europ., ii. p. 825.

Taken by sweeping rank hedges in the Duryard Estate, near Exeter, in August. Apparently rare.

SCRUPULOSUS, *Grav.*

Ich. Europ., ii. p. 817.

Beaten out of larch in Fordlands Wood, Ide, near Exeter, April 16, 1881; one female only.

IMBECILLUS, *Grav.*

Ich. Europ., ii. p. 813.

Beaten from oak in a field on Rollston's Farm, in May.

FORMOSUS, *Desv.*

Trans. Ent. Soc., liv. 2, v. v. p. 211.

This handsome species is figured on Plate xii. f. BB. Blackwall's British Spiders; it is parasitic on *Agelena brunnea.* I captured my specimen by sweeping in a hilly grass-field near Exwick, the end of May.

TENERRIMUS, *Grav.*

Ich. Europ., ii. p. 831.

This species, when full fed, makes a large gregarious mass of cocoons, similar to a microgaster; the mass is white, ovate, as large as a robin's egg, and attached to a blade of grass. I could not find the larvæ on which these had been. Some of the specimens were apterous, but most of them winged. Taken on Dartmoor.

CRASSICORNIS, *Grav.*

Ich. Europ., ii. p. 847.

This was taken by Mr. D'Orville, but where I do not know, probably at Alphington.

GYRINI, *Parft.*

Male. Length, 2 lines.

Head, thorax, and scutellum black; head somewhat square, wider than the thorax; mouth ferruginous; palpi pale straw-colour.

Antennæ black above, piceous beneath; the basal joint large and inflated, with a deeply impressed annulus near the apex; second joint pale yellow at the base; all densely pubescent; half the length of the abdomen.

Thorax smooth in front, the rest clothed in a yellowish pubescence.

Wings, ample, hyaline, iridescent; stigma and nerves, dark, piceous; base and scale, pale yellowish.

Legs, pale reddish straw-colour; the claws of the anterior pair, and the intermediate and posterior tarsi, dark fuscous.

Abdomen longer than the head and thorax, fusiform-clavate; peduncle very narrow, black; the first, second, and third segments red, the rest black; the first segment depressed in front, having two black dots on the dorsal surface, near the middle; inferior surface the same colour as the superior, clothed in rather a dense pale pubescence.

Female. Length, 2 lines.

Head, thorax, and scutellum, shining black; mouth black; prothorax with two deeply impressed lines ending at the base of the scutellum.

Scutellum, small cordate, with a deep impressed line running round it.

Antennæ, a *fac-simile* of the male, except that these are black, length 1¾ lines.

Wings ample, iridescent; stigma and nervures black; base pale, scale whitish.

Legs, bright red; anterior claws, middle tarsi, the base and apex of the posterior tibia, and tarsi, entirely dull black.

Abdomen, ovato-elliptical; peduncle, shining black, with two longitudinal impressed lines; the first, second, and third segments red, the latter with a black fascia; the rest black, with their extreme apices whitish.

Ovipositor ¾ line in length, black.

This distinctly marked species has been submitted to the best authorities in this country, and, so far as can be ascertained, it is undescribed; it was bred from the pupæ of *Gyrinus natator*, found by the Rev. J. Hellins attached to the tops of rushes growing by the side of the Exeter Canal, in July, 1880, and again this year at the beginning of July. The Ichneumons came out on the 20th. Three new species of the Ichneumonidæ have now been bred from these pupæ, and one hyperparasite, a species of Petromalus, apparently new.

It would be interesting to know whether the parasites attack the larva of the Gyrinus before it leaves the water, or whether the larva is attacked in ascending the rush stems, or before it has entirely covered itself in its case. The Ichneumon is provided with a sufficiently long ovipositor to reach the larva inside the case, and probably this is the mode of attack; at the same time, it is not improbable that the larvæ are attacked while still in the water. The parasite is rather thickly covered with hairs, which would entangle sufficient air to enable the insect to breathe for some little time under water. Be this as it may, the discovery of this species, and the knowledge of its habits, so far, is very interesting, and opens up a field of investigation most inviting to the entomologist.

(Thorax red and black.)

CINGULATOR, *Grav.*

Ich. Europ., ii. p. 858.

Captured by Mr. D'Orville, of Alphington, and also by Mr. Bignell, in the Plymouth district.

AREATOR, *Panz.*

Grav., Ich. Europ., ii. p. 855.

Taken both by Mr. D'Orville and myself; not common.

AREATOR, Var. i.
> Grav., Ich. Europ., ii. p. 856.

I captured this variety by sweeping clover on Stokehill, in May. The fascia on the wings are obsolete, and the base of the abdomen is black instead of red.

GENUS, ORTHOPELMA, Taschenberg.

LUTEOLATOR, *Grav.*
> Ich. Europ., ii. p. 826.

Bred from the pupa of *Rhodites rosæ*, the Rose Gall Maker. This insect varies a good deal in the colour of the abdomen, and also in the markings; sometimes these are entirely wanting.

GENUS, CREMNODES, Förster.

ATRICAPILLUS, *Grav.*
> Ich. Europ., ii. p. 888.

Captured by sweeping herbage; not common; in September. My two specimens are quite apterous.

GENUS, AGROTHEREUTES, Förster.

HOPEI, *Grav.*
> Ich. Europ. Supp., p. 715; *Curtis*, Brit. Ent. d. xxxvi.

Taken by Mr. Bignell in the Plymouth district.

GENUS, APTESIS, Förster.

NIGROCINCTA, *Grav.*
> Ich. Europ., ii. p. 880.

Taken by sweeping; July; rare.

BRACHYPTERA, *Grav.*
> Ich. Europ., ii. p. 876.

Apparently very scarce; I have seen only one specimen.

GENUS, HEMIMACHUS, Ratzeburg.

PALPATOR, *Grav.*
> Ich. Europ., ii. p. 818.

Taken in Stoke Wood by beating larch trees in October.

FASCIATUS, *Fab.*
> Grav., Ich. Europ., ii. p. 889.

I bred this from a nest of the brown spider, *Agelena brunnea;* it is one of the most common species of this group. Taken in the Plymouth district.

RUFOCINCTUS, *Grav.*

Ich. Europ., ii. p. 811, 892.

Taken by sweeping herbage on Langstone Cliff in July; not uncommon.

GENUS, **PEZOMACHUS**, *Gravenhorst.*

VAGANS, *Grav.*

Ich. Europ., ii. p. 890.

Apparently rare; taken at Dawlish in June.

NIGRICORNIS, *Först.*

Ich. Europ., ii. p. 895. *P. Agilis*, var. 2. "Antennis nigris femoribus fusco maculatis.

Not common; taken by sweeping in July.

AGILIS, *Först.*

Weigm, Arch., 1850, p. 171.

Taken by sweeping herbage near woods in July. ˙

VIDUUS, *Först.*

Grav., Ich. Europ., ii. p. 909. *P. hortensis*, var. 3. Rufofulvus, capite et antennis nigris, abdominis apice fusco aut nigro, fem.

Captured in Stoke Wood in October; not common.

VULPINUS, *Grav.*

Ich. Europ., ii. p. 914.

An uncommon species; taken by sweeping in October.

ANTHRACINUS, *Först.*

Weigm, Arch., 1850, p. 123.

Apparently rare; taken by sweeping rank herbage in August, near Exeter.

PUMILUS, *Först.*

Weigm, Arch., 1850, p. 131.

Captured running among *Formica nigra*, but not in the nest, at Dawlish, June, 1880.

MICRURUS, *Först.*

This species is new to the British list, and it is certainly one of the handsomest of the whole genus. I took it by sweeping in July, near Ide.

ZONATUS, *Forst.*

Grav., Ich. Europ., ii. p. 1096. (*P. aranearum.*)

This has been bred from spider's eggs, *Agelena brunnea*, taken in Cann Wood by Mr. Bignell.

PROCURSORIUS.

This is new to the British list; it was bred from a larva found feeding on oak in Cann Wood, by Mr. Bignell, in 1880.

RUFULUS, *Först.*

Weigm, Arch., 1850, p. 148.

Taken in the Plymouth district.

OPHIONIDES, *Holmgrén.*
GENUS, **HENICOSPILUS,** *Stephens.*

RAMIDULUS, *Linn.*

Grav., Ich. Europ., iii. p. 699; *Steph.,* Ill. Supp., pl. xl. f. 4.

Taken by Mr. Bignell in the Plymouth district.

GENUS, **OPHION,** *Fabricius.*

OBSCURUM, *Fab.*

Grav., Ich. Europ., iii. p. 689.

A common species, met with in woods, by beating trees and thick hedges, and on Exmouth Warren, in July and August.

LUTEUM, *Linn.*

Grav., Ich. Europ., iii. p. 692.

This is parasitic on the Puss Moth larva, *Cerura vinula,* and common everywhere.

VENTRICOSUM, *Grav.*

Ich. Europ., iii. p. 702; *Curtis's* Brit. Insects, pl. d., c.

Recorded by Curtis as taken in North Devon.

MINUTUM, *Kriech.*

This is new to Britain; it was captured at Laira by Mr. Bignell.

GENUS, **SCHIZOLOMA,** *Wesmael.*

AMICTA, *Fab.*

Grav., Ich. Europ., iii. p. 650; *Curtis,* Brit. Ent., d. ccxxxvi.

Bred from larvæ of *Eupithecia linariata,* taken at Laira by Mr. Bignell.

GENUS, **EXOCHILUM,** *Wesmael.*

CIRCUMFLEXUM, *Linn.*

Grav., Ich. Europ., iii. p. 643; *Donov.,* Brit. Ins., v. iii. pl. 93, f. 2.

Captured in the Plymouth district.

Genus, **ANOMALON**, *Jurine.*

XANTHOPUS, *Schr.*
>Grav., Ich. Europ., iii., p. 652.

Bred by Mr. D'Orville from pupæ of *Agrotis ripæ*. This is common on the sandhills on Exmouth Warren in July; taken also at Bickleigh.

RUFICORNE, *Grav.*
>Ich. Europ., iii. p. 655.

This has been bred by Mr. Bignell from the half-grown larvæ of the Drinker Moth, *Odonestis potatoria.*

CERINOPS, *Grav.*
>Ich. Eurep., iii. p. 658.

This has also been bred from *Agrotis ripæ*, found on Exmouth Warren.

CLANDESTINUM, *Grav.*
>Ich. Europ., iii. p. 670.

This was bred by Mr. D'Orville from larvæ of *Eupithecia albipunctata*; bred also from *Hemithea thymiaria*, by Mr. Bignell.

BELLICOSUM, *Wesm.*
>Bul. Acad., Brux, 1849, p. 124.

Taken by Mr. Bignell in the Plymouth district.

Genus, **AGRYPON**, *Förster.*

FLAVEOLATUM, *Grav.*
>Ich. Europ., iii. p. 664.

This is by no means a common species; taken in the woods at Dunsford in July.

Genus, **TRICHOMMA**, *Wesmael.*

ENECATOR, *Rossi.*
>Grav., Ich. Europ., iii. p. 641.

Taken in the Plymouth district.

Genus, **OPHELTES**, *Holmgrén.*

GLAUCOPTERUS, *Linn.*
>Grav., Ich. Europ., iii. p. 632.

Apparently very rare. I have a specimen that was presented to me by the late Mr. S. Style, from the Raddon Collection; so that it was probably taken in North Devon.

Genus, **PANISCUS**, *Schrank.*

CEPHALOTES, *Holmg.*

Taken by Mr. D'Orville and myself, but not common; also taken in the Plymouth district.

VIRGATUS, *Fourc.*

> *Grav.*, Ich. Europ., iii. p. 625; *Newport*, Trans. Linn. Society, xxi., p. 71.

This species is parasitic on the larvæ of the Broom Moth, *Mamestra pisi*, and probably on some other species, as it is rather common.

TARSATUS, *Brischke.*

New to Britain; bred from *Eupithecia abbreviata*, by Mr. Bignell.

TESTACEUS, *Grav.*

> Ich. Europ., iii. p. 626.

Bred from pupæ dug up at the roots of trees. Gravenhorst says it is parasitic on *Noctua artemisiae*. Mr. Bignell says it is parasitic on *Dicranura vinula*.

INQUINATUS (?), *Grav.*

> Ich. Europ., iii. p. 631.

Taken at Lydford.

Genus, **CAMPOPLEX**, *Gravenhorst.*

MIXTUS, *Grav.*

> Ich. Europ., iii. p. 601.

Captured in woods in August, but not common; generally distributed.

PUGILLATOR, *Linn.*

> *Grav.*, Ich. Europ., iii. 606.

One of the most frequent of all the Ichneumonidæ, on the flower heads of the umbelliferæ in July and August. Bred by Mr. Bignell from *Corycia temerata*.

ANCEPS, *Holmg.*

> *Grav.*, Ich. Europ., iii. p. 610. (*C. pugillator*, var. 6.)

Captured in Devonshire. Rev. T. A. Marshall, in Ent. Annual, 1874, p. 143.

NITIDULATOR, *Holmg.*

This little species was bred by Mr. D'Orville from pupæ of *Eupithecia venosata*.

Genus, **CASINARIA**, *Holmgrén.*

VIDUA, *Grav.*

Ich. Europ., iii. p. 532.

This has been bred from the pupæ of the Gooseberry Moth, *Abraxas grossulariata.*

TENUIVENTRIS, *Grav.*

Ich. Europ., iii. p. 482.

Bred by Mr. Bignell from *Hemithea thymiaria.*

Genus, **LIMNERIA**, *Holmgrén.*

(Abdomen and antennæ black.)

ALBIDA, *Gmel.*

Grav., Ich. Europ., iii. p. 474.

Bred from the pupæ of the Brimstone Butterfly, *Gonopteryx rhamni*, by Mr. Bignell, Plymouth, and by myself. It made a large cocoon, for the size of the insect, inside the skin of the dead caterpillar, leaving the head and tail of it free. The cocoon has a shining, whitish appearance, and set all over with minute spines, which is the old skin of the larva.

ANNULATA, *Grav.*

Ich. Europ., iii. p. 493.

Taken by sweeping long grass and nettles at Duryard, near Exeter, May 6th, 1866, male and female.

DEFICIENS, *Grav.*

Ich. Europ., iii. p. 474.

Bred from *Eupithecia pulchellata.*

DIFFORMIS, *Gmel.*

Grav., Ich. Europ., iii. p. 458.

Taken by Mr. D'Orville, on flowers; not common.

MAJALIS, *Grav.*

Ich. Europ., iii. p. 462.

Captured by beating trees in Heavitree Lane, in May, and bred by Mr. Bignell from an old oak gall.

SORDIDUS, *Grav.*

Ich. Europ., iii. p. 466.

Taken on flowers of umbelliferæ; one specimen only.

FENISTRALIS, *Holmg.*

Grav., Ich. Europ., iii. p. 464. (*C. majalis*, var. 4.)

Bred by Mr. Bignell from *Botys verticalis.*

(*Abdomen black, first joint of antennæ pale beneath.*)

FITCHII, *Bridgman.*

Catalogue British Ichneumonidæ, p. 137, fig. 13.

This was bred by Mr. Bignell from *Nola albulalis.* This does not spin a cocoon, but emerges from the long-haired, pale-coloured larva of its host.

CARBONARIA, *Brischke.*

Bred by Mr. Bignell from *Cidaria pyruliata.*

SERICEA, *Holmg.*

Grav., Ich. Europ., iii. p. 515. (*C. consumator.*)

This species makes a coriaceous cocoon, which is white on the outside, and ornamented with elongated black spots.

ERUCATOR, *Zett.*

Grav., Ich. Europ., iii. p. 458 (part.)

Taken at Lydford in June; apparently scarce.

FAUNUS, *Grav.*

Ich. Europ., iii. p. 517.

I bred this from pupæ of *Gelechia paupella.* Came out May, 1866; but it appears to be rare.

TRISTIS, *Grav.*

Ich. Europ., iii. p. 492.

This is one of the most abundant of the genus with us; it is taken by sweeping grass and clover fields in May; but up to the end of May females only have been taken. I have one small variety of this species, taken near Pinhoe; it measures only 1½ lines in length, whereas the typical ones measure 2¼ to 3 lines. The variety differs in no respect in the colouring, except that it has a narrow orange-coloured band on the apical portion of the basal segment, and the posterior legs are paler than in the larger specimens.

DUMETORUM, *Holmg.*

Captured by sweeping rank herbage at Wonford, in May.

(*Abdomen red and black, first joint of antennæ pale beneath.*)

BICINGULATA, *Grav.*

Ich. Europ., iii. p. 527.

Not common; captured by Mr. D'Orville and myself in June.

MELANOCINCTUS, *Grav.*

Ich. Europ., iii. p. 539.

Bred from the pupa case of Incurvaria (?).

ALTERNANS, *Grav.*

Ich. Europ., iii. p. 537.

Taken on heads of umbelliferæ in June.

CLAUSA, *Brischke.*

Bridgman, Catalogue, p. 161.

Bred by Mr. Bignell from *Hybernia progemmaria*.

UNICINCTUS, *Grav.*

Ich. Europ., iii. p. 529.

Bred from *Eupithecia rectangulata* and *Lomaspilis marginata*, by Mr. Bignell.

(*Abdomen red or red and black, antennæ black, rarely red beneath.*)

INSIDIATOR, *Grav.*

Ich. Europ., iii. p. 562.

Captured by sweeping in Wonford Marshes in June; apparently rare.

CRASSICORNIS, *Grav.*

Ich. Europ., iii. p. 565.

Captured on flowers in June; apparently scarce.

FLORICOLA, *Grav.*

Ich. Europ., iii. p. 600.

The commonest of all the species, on flowers, generally distributed.

MŒSTA, *Grav.*

Ich. Europ., iii. p. 599.

Bred by Mr. Bignell from *Hibernia progemmaria* and *defoliaria*.

OBSCURELLA, *Holmg.*

Bred from *Hemithea thymiaria*.

GENUS, **ATRACTODES**, *Gravenhorst*.

VESTALIS, *Hal.*
>Ann. Nat. Hist., 1839, p. 118.

This insect I bred.

GENUS, **EXOLYTUS**, *Förster*.

LÆVIGATUS, *Grav.*
>Ich. Europ., ii. p. 111.

A widely distributed species, but not common; taken in May and June.

GENUS, **MESOCHORUS**, *Gravenhorst*.

SPLENDIDULUS, *Grav.*
>Var. 1. *Grav.*, Ich. Europ., ii. p. 966.

Taken by Mr. D'Orville, probably at Alphington.

THORACICUS, *Grav.*
>Ich. Europ., ii. p, 971.

Captured by beating hedges on Red Hills, Exeter, in June.

SERICANS, *Curtis.*
>Brit. Ins., pl. 464.

This has been bred by Mr. Bignell; it is hyperparasitic on *Exorista vulgaris*, a Dipteron, out of the Gooseberry Moth larvæ.

FULGURANS, *Hali.*
>In Ann. Nat. Hist., 1839, p. 114.

Also bred by Mr. Bignell; it is hyperparasitic on *Casinaria vidua*. The Casinaria larvæ had fed on those of *Abraxas grossulariata*.

OLERUM, *Curtis.*
>Brit. Ins., p. 464; *Hal.*, Ann. Mag. Nat. Hist., 1839, p. 114.

This has been reared from *Cassinaria vidua,* and has exactly the same habits as mentioned above.

SEMIRUFUS, *Holmg.*
>So. Ak. Handl., 1850, n. s., p. 125.

Bred from *Eupithecia castigata*, by Mr. Bignell.

SYLVARUM, *Hal.*
>In Ann. Nat. Hist., 1859, p. 114.

Bred from Apenteles cocoons, out of *Vanessa atalanta*. I bred it also from *Pterophorus galactodactylus.*

ACICULATUS, *Bridgman.*
  Catalogue, p. 162, pl. viii. fig. 11.

This species is hyperparasitic on an *Apanteles*, probably *A. glomeratus.* Bred by Mr. Bignell.

GENUS, **PORIZON**, *Fallén.*

HARPURUS, *Schr.*
  Grav., Ich. Europ., iii. p. 758.

Taken by sweeping grass and nettles at Duryard, in May.

GENUS, **THERSILOCHUS**, *Holmgrén.*

SALTATOR, *Fab.*
  Grav., Ich. Europ., p. 777; Nees ab Esenb., i. p. 224.

Captured by sweeping herbage on the banks of the South Devon Railway, between Starcross and Dawlish, in August.

TRUNCORUM, *Holmg.*
  Grav., Ich. Europ., iii. p. 771. (*P. jocator*, var. 4.)

Captured by sweeping rank herbage in June; very rare.

GENUS, **COLLYRIA**, *Schiödte.*

CALCITRATOR, *Grav.*
  Ich. Europ., iii. p. 727; *Steph.*, Ill., pl. 39, f. 2.

Taken by Mr. D'Orville at Alphington. This insect is, according to Curtis, parasitic on *Cephus pygmœus*, the Corn Saw-fly, which is in some seasons very destructive to corn crops. The Collyria, therefore, should be encouraged as far as possible.

GENUS, **EXETASTES**, *Gravenhorst.*

FORNICATOR, *Fab.*
  Grav., Ich. Europ., iii. p. 402.

Not common; taken on flowers in June.

OSCULATORIUS, *Fab.*
  Grav., Ich. Europ., iii. p. 405; *E. clavator*, 473.

A frequent species on flowers of umbelliferæ; taken by Mr. D'Orville and myself. This varies a great deal both in size and colouration; in some the abdomen is quite black, and in others red; in some the scutellum is yellow or dotted with that colour, or quite black. The posterior legs also vary in the same degree. Mr. Bignell has bred it from the Cabbage Moth.

ALBITARSUS, *Grav.*

Ich. Europ., iii. p. 430.

Apparently scarce. I have only taken one specimen. It has also been taken in the Plymouth district.

CALOBATUS, *Grav.*

Ich. Europ., iii. p. 405.

Captured in the Plymouth district.

GENUS, **AROTES**, *Gravenhorst.*

ALBICINCTUS, *Grav.*

Ich. Europ., iii. p. 448 ; *Steph.*, Ill., supp., pl. 36, f. 4, p. 2.

This rare insect is said to be parasitic on *Clytus arcuatus*— a beetle, so far as I am aware, not found in Devonshire ; but an allied species, *C. arietis*, is very common, and it is probable it is parasitic on this also. I captured the only specimen I have seen near Lydford ; it is a female.

GENUS, **BANCHUS**, *Fabricius.*

PICTUS, *Fab.*

Grav., Ich. Europ., iii. p. 380 ; *Donovan*, Brit. Ins., v. xii. p. 413.

A scarce insect with us. I have a specimen from the Raddon collection ; I presume it was captured in North Devon. Mr. Bignell has bred it from *Selenia illunaria.*

FALCATOR, *Fab.*

Grav., Ich. Europ., iii. p. 385 ; *Curtis*, Brit. Ins., pl. 588.

Also scarce. I have a specimen captured a few years ago, I think, at Fordlands. It has likewise been taken near Plymouth.

VARIEGATOR, *Fab.*

Grav., Ich. Europ., iii. p. 377. (*B. compressus.*)

This pretty little species is scarce with us. Taken on flowers in June.

TRYPHONIDES, *Holmgrén.*
HOMALOPI, *Holmgrén.*
GENUS, **MESOLEPTUS**, *Gravenhorst.*

TESTACEUS, *Fab.*

Grav., Ich. Europ., ii. p. 28 ; *Steph.*, Ill., v. vii. p. 216.

Bred by Mr. Bignell from *Eupithecia castigata.*

FUGAX, *Grav.*

Ich. Europ., ii. p. 56 ; *Steph.*, Ill., v. vii. p. 220.

Apparently scarce. I have only seen one specimen.

TYPHÆ, *Grav.*

Ich. Europ., ii. p. 62 ; *Steph.*, Ill., v. vii. p. 221.

According to Stephens, this has been taken in Devonshire.

VENTRALIS, *Curtis.*

Brit. Ent., p. 644.

I bred this from a rather short oval cocoon, black, with a broad whitish band running round it. This band is ornamented near the margins, with a row of angular black spots; that is to say, the black cocoon is seen through these openings in the white band, which have the appearance of black spots.

GENUS, **CATOGLYPTUS,** *Förster.*

FORTIPES, *Grav.*

Ich. Europ., ii. p. 85 ; *Steph.*, Ill., v. vii. p. 225.

Captured by the side of the Creedy, on aquatic plants, in June. Taken also by Mr. D'Orville.

FUSCICORNIS, *Gmel.*

Grav., Ich. Europ., ii. p. 87 ; *Steph.*, Ill., v. vii. p. 226.

An uncommon insect. Stephens had it from Devon, and I have taken it.

GENUS, **EURYPROCTUS,** *Holmgrén.*

MUNDUS, *Grav.*

Ich. Europ., ii. p. 78 ; *Steph.*, Ill., v. vii. p. 224.

Stephens had this species from Devonshire, as recorded in the Illustrations. Taken in June.

GENUS, **PERILISSUS,** *Förster.*

VERNALIS, *Grav.*

Ich. Europ., ii. p. 294.

Captured by sweeping grass and clover on Stoke Hill in May.

FILICORNIS, *Grav.*

Ich. Europ., ii. p. 94.

Beaten out of hedges in various parts of the country in June.

GENUS, **ECLYTUS,** *Holmgrén.*

ORNATUS, *Holmg.*

Sv. Ak. Handl., 1855, p. 127.

Bred by Mr. Bignell from pupæ of *Tortrix heparana.*

GENUS, **MESOLEIUS**, *Holmgrén.*

HAMULUS, *Grav.*

Ich. Europ., ii. p. 322.

Captured on Maker in June, 1880, by Mr. Bignell.

MESOLEIUS BRACHYACANTHUS, *Parft.*

Length, 2¾ lines; expanse of wings, 4½ lines; antennæ, 2¼ lines.

Black; head wider than the thorax; mouth and palpi, straw-yellow; antennæ, black above, ferruginous beneath; basal joint very small; the second rather large, with an arched protuberance above.

Thorax, gibbous, smooth, shining black, very finely punctured; mesothorax with two short lateral concave spines; the metathorax with two raised lines crossing each other nearly at right angles, forming a St. Andrew's cross.

Wings, ample, with a faint smoky tinge, beautifully iridescent; stigma and nerves, testaceous, all growing paler towards the base, where they are pale straw-yellow; scale, pale yellow; cellule, 4—angular, irregular, oblique.

Legs: anterior coxa, testaceous; the trochanters of the first and second part, pale sulphur-yellow; posterior coxa, black, tipped with pale sulphur.

Anterior and median femora, testaceous yellow; posterior, piceous, with a dark stain on the inside, towards the base, where it is pale yellow.

Anterior tibia and tarsi, pale yellow; the apical joints, fuscous, or nearly black; posterior, testaceous; the apex and tarsi nearly black.

Abdomen, black, cylindrical, but growing gradually larger towards the apex; finely, but not deeply, punctured; the basal segment with two testaceous yellow spots; the rest, with their apices, pale testaceous.

BIGNELLII, *Bridgman.*

Cat., pl. 8. f. 12. p. 163.

Taken by Mr. Bignell in the Plymouth district.

GENUS, **TREMATOPYGUS**, *Holmgrén.*

VELLICANS, *Grav.*

Ich. Europ., ii. p. 263.

Captured at Widewell Farm, Tavistock Road, August, 1880, by Mr. Bignell.

I have one specimen, taken at Ide in August, 1880. This appears to be a rare insect.

GENUS, **TRYPHON**, *Fallén.*

RUTILATOR, *Linn.*

Grav., Ich. Europ., ii. p. 305 ; *Steph.*, Ill., v. vii. p. 262.

Captured near Exeter, in June. Not common.

TROCHANTERATUS, *Holmg.*

Grav., Ich. Europ., ii. p. 308 (*T. rutilator*, var. 2).

Taken at Lydford by beating hedges on the border of Dartmoor, in June.

ALBIPES, *Grav.*

Ich. Europ., ii. p. 221.

Taken by sweeping among grass and clover in May.

BRACHYACANTHUS, *Gmel.*

Grav., Ich. Europ., ii. p. 242 ; *Steph.*, Ill., v. vii. p. 250.

Not common. Taken on flowers of umbelliferæ, in June.

GENUS, **EUMESIUS**, *Westwood.*

ALBITARSUS, *Curtis.*

Brit. Ent. pl. 660.

Captured on flowers near woods in June.

GENUS, **POLYBLASTUS**, *Hastig.*

VARITARSUS, *Grav.*

Ich. Europ., ii. p. 222 ; *Steph.*, Ill. v. vii. p. 247.

Taken on flowers of umbelliferæ in June.

Var. I. Taken by sweeping herbage on Stoke Hill, in May.

HILARIS, *Holmg.*

Bred by Mr. D'Orville from pupæ of *Eupithecia succenturiata.* The pupa case of this insect is about the size of a caraway seed, and is very much like one, only this is strongly ribbed.

GENUS, **CTENISCUS**, *Haliday.*

LITURATORIUS, *Linn.*

Grav., Ich. Europ., ii. p. 149; *Steph.*, Ill., v. vii. p. 235-37.

Captured by sweeping among grass and clover on Stoke Hill, Exeter, the end of May.

GENUS, **SPHECOPHAGA**, *Westwood.*

VESPARUM, *Curtis.*

Brit. Ent., pl. 198.

I bred several of both sexes of this insect from a wasps' nest; they came out in July, 1866. It appears to be scarce, as these are the only specimens I have seen.

GENUS, **EXOCHUS**, *Gravenhorst.*

(*Anterior wings with a small cellule.*)

CURVATOR, *Fab.*

Grav., Ich. Europ., ii. p. 335; *Steph.*, Ill., v. vii. p. 265.

Taken on flowers, and by sweeping herbage in June. This has been bred by Mr. D'Orville from pupæ of *Eupithecia assimilata.*

(*Anterior wings without a cellule.*)

MANSUETOR, *Grav.*

Ich. Europ., ii. p. 339; *Steph.*, Ill., v. vii. p. 265.

Common, and generally distributed, in June and July.

GENUS, **CHORINAEUS**, *Holmgren.*

CRISTATOR, *Grav.*

Ich. Europ., ii. p. 352; *Steph.*, Ill., v. vii. p. 267.

Captured on the cliffs at Exmouth in May.

GENUS, **ORTHOCENTRUS**, *Gravenhorst.*

AFFINIS (?), *Zett.*

Insecta Lapp., p. 379.

Captured by sweeping nettles in Wonford Marshes in April; apparently rare.

SCHIZODONTES.

GENUS, **BASSUS**, *Fabricius.*

LÆTATORIUS, *Fab.*

Grav., Ich. Europ., iii. p. 358.

Not very common; taken by sweeping rank herbage, near Exeter, in July.

EXSULTANS, *Grav.*

Ich. Europ., iii. p. 328.

Frequent on flowers of umbelliferæ by wood sides in June and July; generally distributed.

FESTIVUS, *Fab.*

Grav., Ich. Europ., iii. p. 314.

Taken by Mr. Bignell near Plymouth.

ALBOSIGNATUS, *Grav.*

Ich. Europ., iii. p. 343.

Apparently rare; taken by sweeping in June.

INSIGNIS, *Grav.*

Ich. Europ., iii. p. 349.

Taken by sweeping nettles, &c., in Duryard, Exeter, in August.

LATERALIS, *Grav.*

Ich. Europ., iii. p. 342.

Beaten from a hedge at Exwick—also in hedges at Lydford, but rare—in June.

STRIGATOR, *Fab.*

Grav., Ich. Europ., iii. p. 330.

Taken by Mr. D'Orville in his garden in June.

NIGRITARSUS, *Grav.*

Ich. Europ., iii. p. 338.

Bred by Mr. Bignell from *Bombyx quercus.*

GRACILENTUS, *Holmg.*

Sv. Ak. Handl., 1855, p. 368.

Taken by Mr. D'Orville on flowers in June; rare.

DORSALIS, *Holmg.*

Desvignes, in Trans. Ent. Soc., 1862, p. 216.

Taken at Lydford in June; scarce.

CINCTUS, *Grav.*

Ich. Europ., iii. p. 327.

Taken in the Plymouth district by Mr. Bignell; I have also taken it at Lydford in June.

PICTUS, *Grav.*

Ich. Europ., iii. p. 336.

In the Plymouth district.

PULCHELLUS, *Holmg.*

Grav., Ich. Europ. iii., p. 321 (*B. sulcator*), var. 1-4.

Captured in the Plymouth district.

COGNATUS, *Holmg.*

Captured by Mr. Bignell near Plymouth.

ASPIDOPI.
GENUS, **METOPIUS**, *Panzer.*

MICRATORIUS, *Fab.*

Grav., Ich. Europ., iii. p. 299.

A scarce insect with us. Captured on flowers of umbelliferæ on wood sides in July; taken also in the Plymouth district.

DISSECTORIUS, *Panz.*

Grav., Ich. Europ., iii. p. 291.

This was captured by Mr. Curtis in North Devon.

DENTATUS, *Fab.*

> *Grav.*, Ich. Europ., iii. p. 304.

I bred this from pupæ of *Lasiocampa quercifolia.* Curtis says it is parasitic on *Bombyx trifolii.*

PIMPLIDES.

GENUS, **ACAENITUS**, *Latreille.*

FULVICORNIS, *Grav.*

> Ich. Europ., iii. p. 309.

Apparently rare ; taken by sweeping in Wonford Marshes in June.

GENUS, **RHYSSA**, *Gravenhorst.*

PERSUASORIA, *Linn.*

> *Grav.*, Ich. Europ., iii. p. 267 ; *Steph.*, Ill., vii. pl. 89, male; *Don.*, Brit. Ins., xv. p. 222.

This fine insect is not very common; it is generally met with flying round old posts or wood-ricks. It is generally distributed.

LEUCOGRAPHA, *Grav.*

> Ich. Europ., iii. p. 274.

Rare ; I have only seen one specimen, and this was given me from the Raddon collection.

GENUS, **EPHIALTES**, *Gravenhorst.*

IMPERATOR, *Kriech.*

> *Grav.*, Ich. Europ., iii. p. 232.

Not common ; taken flying round old posts and wood-ricks in July. Sparsely distributed.

REX, *Kriech.*

> *Grav.*, Ich. Europ., iii. p. 232.

The females of this are frequently met with, but I have not taken the male. The females are to be found in June.

TUBERCULATUS, *Fourc.*

> *Grav.*, Ich. Europ., iii. p. 228.

Taken by Mr. Bignell at Plymbridge.

GENUS, **PERITHOUS**, *Holmgrén.*

MEDIATOR, *Fab.*

> *Grav.*, Ich. Europ., iii. p. 256.

I bred this from bramble-sticks which were perforated by one of the small wasps.

DIVINATOR, *Rossi.*

> *Grav.*, Ich. Europ., iii. p. 252.

I bred several of this species from perforated bramble-sticks; the sticks had been bored by one of the small wasps. Came out in June, 1860.

VARIUS, *Grav.*

> Ich. Europ., iii. p. 354.

Bred from an old bramble-stem by Mr. Bignell.

GENUS, **PIMPLA**, *Fabricius.*

(*Abdomen black, or segments edged with red, scutellum black.*)

ABDOMINALIS, *Grav.*

> Ich. Europ., iii. p. 150.

Captured near Exeter, August, 1877.

(*Thorax black, scutellum spotted with white, abdomen black, banded with white or reddish-brown.*)

RUFATA, *Gmel.*

> *Grav.*, Ich. Europ., iii. p. 166, var. i.

Captured by sweeping clover when in blossom in June on Red Hills, near Whitstone.

FLAVONOTATA, *Holmg.*

> *Grav.*, Ich. Europ., iii. p. 164.

Taken by Mr. D'Orville on flowers in July. Mr. Bignell has bred this from *Tortrix viridana.*

(*Thorax, scutellum, and abdomen black, the latter with castaneous bands, posterior coxa red.*)

CALOBATA, *Grav.*

> Ich. Europ., iii. p. 176.

Taken on flowers by wood sides, June and July.

STERCORATOR, *Fab.*

> *Grav.*, Ich. Europ., iii. p. 186.

Common; taken by sweeping rank herbage in July.

TAURIONELLA, *Linn.*

> *Grav.*, Ich. Europ., iii. p. 192.

Very common; I have bred this from pupæ of *Retinia buolinana.*

(Scutellum and abdomen black, the latter sometimes with reddish bands; thorax and posterior coxa black.)

SCANICA, *Vill.*

> *Grav.*, Ich. Europ., iii. p. 204.

This has been bred from pupæ of *Hybernia progemmaria;* came out July, 1880. It is also parasitic on *Tortrix viridana.*

DIDYMA, *Grav.*

> Ich. Europ., iii. p. 172.

Captured by sweeping long grass, &c., in June.

EXAMINATOR, *Fab.*

> *Grav.*, Ich. Europ., iii. p. 207.

Taken by Mr. D'Orville and myself. Gravenhorst says this is parasitic on *Tinea 'padella*, and also in pupæ of *Bombyx fuliginosa;* and Mr. Marshall says on *Cymatophora ocularis* and *Noctua plecta.* Mr. Bignell has reared it from *Tortrix viridana.*

BREVICORNIS, *Grav.*

> Ich. Europ., iii. p. 211.

Bred by Mr. Bignell from *Eupithecia linariata.* It is also taken in the Exeter district.

INSTIGATOR, *Fab.*

> *Grav.*, Ich. Europ., iii. p. 216.

Very common everywhere. It is parasitic on the large Cabbage Butterfly, *Pieris brassicæ*, and on *Sphinx ligustri*, the Privet Hawk Moth. Mr. Marshall, in *Entomologists' Annual* (1874), p. 125, enumerates six species of butterflies and moths on which this is parasitic.

NUCUM, *Ratz.*

> *Först.*, Ichn., i. p. 115.

Taken by Mr. D'Orville at Alphington.

GENUS, ACRODACTYLA, *Haliday.*

DEGENER, *Hal.*

> In *Ann. Nat. Hist.*, 1839, p. 117.

I bred this from a reddish larva, found feeding on a small spider. The body of the spider was not large enough to contain the larva, so that part of it was exposed. The spider lived until the larva was ready to undergo its change into pupa. It then spun a cocoon, fusiform and angular, attached at both ends to the glass cover of the box, after the manner of a hammock. It remained in pupa about a fortnight, and came out September 19th, 1874.

GENUS, **CLISTOPYGA**, *Gravenhorst.*

INCITATOR, *Fab.*

Grav., Ich. Europ., iii. p. 134.

Taken in the Exeter district.

GENUS, **GLYPTA**, *Gravenhorst.*
(*Posterior coxa black.*)

TERES, *Grav.*

Ich. Europ., iii. p. 8.

Common on flowers by wood sides in July.

HÆSITATOR, *Grav.*

Ich. Europ., iii. p. 12.

Taken by Mr. D'Orville in his garden ; also captured in the Plymouth district, and at Lydford in June.

(*Posterior coxa red.*)

FRONTICORNIS, *Grav.*

Not common ; captured in the Exeter district in August.

SCALARIS, *Grav.*

Ich. Europ., iii. p. 24.

Taken by Mr. Bignell near Plymouth.

FLAVOLINEATA, *Grav.*

Ich. Europ., iii. p. 27.

Bred by Mr. D'Orville from pupæ of *Minoa euphorbiata.*

CERATITES, *Grav.*

Ich. Europ., iii. p. 18.

Taken in the Plymouth district.

GENUS, **LISSONOTA**, *Gravenhorst.*
(*Scutellum and abdomen black, the latter occasionally chestnut-coloured.*)

VARIABILIS, *Holmg.*

Grav., Ich. Europ., iii. p. 47. (*L. hortorum.*)

Taken by Mr. D'Orville and myself on flowers of um- belliferæ. It appears to be generally distributed.

BELLATOR, *Grav.*

Ich. Europ., iii. p. 106, *partim.*

Common, and generally distributed.

CONNEXA, *Grav.*

 Ich. Europ., iii. p. 106, *partim.*

Taken on flowers by wood sides; scarce.

PARALLELA, *Grav.*

 Ich. Europ., iii. p. 79.

Captured on umbelliferæ, by wood sides, in July.

CALIGATA, *Grav.*

 Ich. Europ., iii. p. 38.

Bred by Mr. Bignell from *Anticlea badiata.*

 (*Scutellum with pale spots or lines, abdomen with red or yellow bands, which are sometimes obsolete.*)

DEVERSOR, *Grav.*

 Ich. Europ., iii. p. 59.

I have a male and female I believe to be this species; captured on flowers in the Exeter district.

 (*Scutellum black, abdomen red, with the base and apex black, some of the segments banded with red.*)

CYLINDRATOR, *Vill.*

 Grav., Ich. Europ., iii. p. 102.

Taken by sweeping in clover fields in August.

GENUS, **MENISCUS**, *Schiödte.*

CATENATOR, *Panz.*

 Grav., Ich. Europ., iii. p. 45.

Rather common; taken by Mr. D'Orville and myself near Exeter in June.

IMPRESSOR, *Grav.*

 Ich. Europ., iii. p. 50.

Taken in the Exeter district.

MURINUS, *Grav.*

 Ich. Europ., iii. p. 99.

Apparently a scarce species, captured on flowers by wood sides in June.

GENUS, **PHYTODIAETUS**, *Gravenhorst.*

CORYPHÆUS, *Grav.*

 Ich. Europ., ii. p. 945.

Bred by Mr. Bignell from *Tortrix viridana.*

BRACONIDÆ.
BRACONIDES, *Westwood.*
GENUS, **BRACON**, *Fabricius.*

LARVICIDA, *Wesm.*

Nouv. Mém. Ac. Brux, 1838, p. 41, female.

Taken near Barnstaple; recorded by the Rev. T. A. Marshall in *Ent. Ann.*, 1874, p. 144.

SPATHIIDES.
GENUS, **SPATHIUS**, *Nees von Esenbeck.*

CLAVATUS, *Nees.*

Grav., Ich. Europ., iii. p. 1027.

I bred this insect from pupæ of *Anobium striatum*. It is not uncommon in old buildings in June and July. Specimens vary very much in size, especially the males, and might easily be mistaken for different species.

RHOGADIDES.
GENUS, **HETEROGAMUS**, *Wesmael.*

DISPAR, *Curtis.*

Brit. Ent., p. 512.

This appears to be a scarce species. Only one specimen has fallen to my lot, and this was taken in August, 1859.

GENUS, **RHOGAS**, *Nees von Esenbeck.*

DISSECTOR, *Nees.*

Monog. Ich. Brac., i. p. 208.

Captured by sweeping, but rare.

RETICULATOR, *Nees.*

Monog. Ich. Brac., i. p. 211.

This has been bred by Mr. Bignell and myself from young larvæ of *Odonestis potatoria*, the Drinker Moth. The larva of the parasite makes a pupa case of the skin of the victim. The latter, when about to change its skin, attaches itself to a stem of grass, by clasping it firmly with its feet. In this position I found it. The larva of the Ichneumon had finished its work of destruction, and in July the perfect insect came out.

BICOLOR, *Spin.*

Nees, Monog. Ich. Brac., i. p. 213.

I bred this from a caterpillar (?). It, like the above, uses the skin of the victim for a pupa case. When it comes out, it eats or cuts a round hole at one end, through which it makes its exit. Came out May 29th, 1866.

CIRCUMSCRIPTUS, *Nees.*

> Monog. Ich. Brac., i. p. 216.

Bred from larvæ of *Epunda viminalis*, the Osier Moth. This makes a semi-transparent oval cocoon, over which is reticulated a brownish silken thread, forming an open network.

GENICULATOR, *Nees.*

> *Nees*, Monog. Ich. Brac., i. p. 211.

Bred from a small frosted silver-white cocoon, covered with fine silk-like material. The insect escapes by cutting off one end of the case except a small portion, which is left as a hinge, on which the top falls back. I found two of these cases attached to a leaf, but do not know on what it is parasitic.

RHYSSALIDES.
GENUS, **COLASTES**, *Haladay.*

BRACONIUS, *Hal.*

> Ent. Mag., iv. p. 57.

This was bred by Mr. D'Orville from larvæ of *Lithocolletis lautella.*

SIGALPHIDES.
GENUS, **SIGALPHUS**, *Latrielle.*

CAUDATUS, *Nees.*

> Monog. Ich. Brac., i. p. 268; *Curtis*, Farm Ins., Fron. pl. H: f. 20, p. 244.

Mr. Curtis says he bred this species from pupæ of a fly which feeds on stems of barley, *Oscinis vastator*. I have taken it here, but it does not appear to be common.

AMBIGUUS, *Nees.*

> Monog. Ich. Brac., i. p. 272.

Taken by sweeping among nettles at Wonford, April 27th.

OBSCURELLUS, *Nees.*

> Monog. Ich. Brac., i. p. 270.

Captured at Exwick in August.

CHELONIDES.
GENUS, **CHELONUS**, *Jurine.*

OCULATOR, *Fab.*

> *Nees*, Monog Ich. Brac., i. p. 290.

Taken by sweeping rank herbage in August.

INANITUS, *Nees.*

Monog. Ich. Brac., i. p. 289.

Also captured by sweeping herbage in July and August; not common.

SULCATUS, *Jurine.*

Nees, Monog. Ich. Brac., i. p. 293.

Taken by sweeping on Langstone Cliff in July.

GENUS, **ASCOGASTER**, *Wesmael.*

RUFIPES, *Latr.*

Nees, Monog. Ich. Brac., i. p. 283.

Captured by sweeping herbage in June; not common.

MICROGASTERIDES.

GENUS, **APANTELES**, *Förster.*

FALCATUS, *Nees.*

Monog. Ich. Brac., i. p. 175.

I bred this from larvæ of *Eupithecia succenturiata.* The larva of the parasite, when about to undergo its transformation, eats its way out of its victim through the ninth segment of the body; it then begins to construct a cocoon for itself. The cocoons are pale brownish and shining, longitudinally eight ribbed, the ribs obtuse and paler than the rest. These cocoons are made to stand up on the plant to which they are attached; namely, the common mugwort, *Artemisia vulgaris*, on which the larva of the moth feeds, and the seeds of which these cocoons very closely resemble; sometimes they are attached to the back of their victims.

ALBIPENNIS, *Nees.*

Monog. Ich. Brac., i. p. 186.

I bred this from larvæ of *Swammerdamia griseocapitella*, var. *Pruni;* came out in August, 1858.

LACTEUS, *Nees.*

Monog. Ich. Brac., i. p. 187.

I bred this from larvæ of *Lithocolletis vacciniella*, and Mr. D'Orville has taken specimens.

JUNIPERATA, *Bouche.*

Nees, Monog. Ich. Brac., i. p. 184 (*M. Sericeus*).

Bred by Mr. D'Orville from *Melitæa artemis.*

LATERALIS, *Hal.*

In Ent. Mag., ii. p. 248.

Bred by Mr. D'Orville from larvæ of *Eupithecia assimilata.*

GLOMERATUS, *Linn.*

Westwood, in Lond. Mag., iii. p. 52, f. *a.–q.*

Bred from *Pontia brassicæ.*

RUBRIPES, *Hal.*

Curtis, Farm Ins., p. 97.

Parasitic on the larvæ of the large Cabbage Butterfly, *Pontia brassicæ.*

GENUS, **MICROPLITIS,** *Förster.*

DORSALIS, *Spin.*

Hal., Ent. Mag., ii. p. 235 (*M. mediator*).

Bred by Mr. D'Orville from larvæ of *Eupithecia subfulvata.*

SPECTABILIS, *Hal.*

Ent. Mag., ii. p. 236.

Taken by sweeping in July. Mr. D'Orville has bred it, but omitted to keep the name of the larva on which it is parasitic. It is a variable species, both in size and colour. I have four specimens, named by Mr. Marshall.

ALVEARIA, *Fab.*

Nees, Monog. Ich. Brac., i. p. 172; *West.,* Int., ii. pl. 76, fig. 17, pp. 140, 148. Mass of cocoons only.

Bred by Mr. Bignell, Mr. D'Orville, and myself from larvæ of *Boarmia rhomboidaria.* Very abundant; it has a great attachment for the twigs of jessamine, to which it fixes its masses of cocoons.

GENUS, **MICROGASTER,** *Latreille.*

NIGRICANS, *Nees.*

Monog. Ich. Brac., i. p. 167.

Apparently rare. Beaten out of bushes in Stoke Wood in July.

TIBIALIS, *Nees.*

Monog. Ich. Brac., i. p. 168; *Steph.,* Ill. Supp., t. 37, f. 2.

Taken by sweeping the railway banks between Starcross and Dawlish, in August.

NIGRIVENTRIS, *Nees.*

Monog. Ich. Brac., i. p. 178.

Taken by sweeping rank herbage in July.

GLOBATUS, *Linn.*

Nees, Monog. Ich. Brac., i. p. 163.

Taken by beating hedges in June.

SPINOLÆ, *Nees.*

Monog. Ich. Brac., i. p. 166.

Captured on a wall of the Institution in August.

DIFFICILIS, *Nees.*

Monog. Ich. Brac., i. p. 182.

Bred from a Noctua larva. From twenty to thirty of the larvæ of the parasite came out through the skin of the caterpillar of the moth; each spun a yellowish cocoon, covered with a short whitish silk. I also bred this species from the larvæ of *Lycœna alexis* in August, 1865.

POSTICUS, *Nees.*

Monog. Ich. Brac., i. p. 172.

Apparently rare. Taken in the Exeter district.

AGATHIDIDES.
GENUS, **AGATHIS,** *Latreille.*

NIGRA, *Nees.*

Monog. Ich. Brac., i. p. 128.

Taken at Plym Bridge, 5th May, by Mr. Bignell.

GENUS, **EARINUS,** *Wesmael.*

NITIDULUS, *Nees.*

. Monog. Ich. Brac., i. p. 144.

Beaten from trees in Stoke Wood, near Exeter, in May. Apparently rare.

APHIDIIDES.
GENUS, **EPHEDRUS,** *Haliday.*

PLAGIATOR, *Nees.*

Monog. Ich. Brac., i. p. 16; *Curtis,* Farm Ins., p. 290, woodcut, f. 14.

This is one of the useful insects to the farmer, as it is parasitic on the aphis of the wheat, and consequently destroys great numbers of this pest.

GENUS, **APHIDIUS,** *Nees von Esenbeck.*

PICIPES, *Nees.*

Monog. Ich. Brac., i. p. 18; *Curtis,* Farm Ins., p. 290, woodcut 39, f. 12.

This insect was bred by Mr. Curtis from *Aphis avenæ,* on which it is parasitic.

ROSARUM, *Nees.*

Monog. Ich. Brac., i. p. 19.

I bred this insect from the aphis of the rose; it came out June 12, 1880.

PARCICORNIS, *var.* B, *Nees.*

Monog. Ich. Brac. i. p. 16.

Taken by sweeping on Red-hills in April.

GENUS, **LYSIPHLEBUS**, *Förster.*

DISSOLUTUS, *Nees.*

Monog. Ich. Brac., i. p. 23.

Taken by sweeping herbage on Red-hills in May.

EUPHORIDES.

GENUS, **WESMAELIA**, *Förster.*

CREMASTA, *Marsh.*

In Ent. Mon. Mag., viii. p. 257.

Mr. Marshall captured a female of this species in a wood in North Devon; and he remarks that the English insect is more highly coloured than the one from the Spanish Pyrenees.

PERILITIDES.

GENUS, **ZEMIOTES**, *Förster.*

ALBIDITARSUS, *Curtis.*

Brit. Ent., pl. 415; *Nees*, Monog. Ich. Brac., i. p. 34.

Taken by Mr. D'Orville and myself in May; by no means common.

GENUS, **PERILITUS**, *Nees von Esenbeck.*

PENDULATOR, *Lat.*

Nees, Monog. Ich. Brac., i. p. 38; *Curtis*, Brit. Ent., p. 415.

Taken by Mr. D'Orville in his garden at Alphington.

ATRATOR, *Curtis.*

Brit. Ent., p. 415.

Taken in the Plymouth district.

MEDIANUS.

Bred by Mr. Bignell from *Agrotis tritici*. I have taken a specimen in this neighbourhood. This is new to Britain.

GENUS, **HOMOLOBUS**.

DISCOLOR, *Wesm.*

Mr. Bignell bred this new British insect from *Cabera pusaria*, 24th September, 1880.

MACROCENTRIDES.
Genus, ZELE, Curtis.
TESTACEATOR, *Curtis.*

Brit. Ent., p. 415; *Nees*, Monog. Ich. Brac., i. p. 201.

Taken occasionally in woods. It is by no means common.

Genus, MACROCENTRUS, Curtis.
LINEARIS, *Nees.*

Monog. Ich. Brac., i. p. 200 (*Rogas linearis*).

This has been bred by Mr. Bignell from pupæ of *Botys verticalis*, Plymouth. I have taken it. Not uncommon in the Exeter district.

THORACICUS, *Nees.*

Monog. Ich. Brac., i. p. 204.

Taken both by Mr. D'Orville and myself.

OPIIDES.
Genus, OPIUS, Wesmael.
APICULATOR (?), *Nees.*

Monog. Ich. Brac., i. p. 56.

Captured by sweeping in Stoke Wood, near Exeter, in July.

TACITUS, *Hal.*

Nees, Monog. Ich. Brac., i. p. 54 (*B. circulator ?*).

I bred this from some Dipterous larvæ feeding on boletus, September 22nd, 1867.

ALYSIIDES.
Genus, CHASMODON, Haliday.
APTERUS, *Nees.*

Monog. Ich. Brac., i. p. 264; *Curtis*, Brit. Ent., p. 289.

Apparently rare; I have only seen one specimen, taken by myself, in sweeping herbage.

Genus, GONIARCHA, Förster.
TIPULA, *Scop.*

Nees, Monog. Ich. Brac., i. p. 245.

Captured by sweeping hedges at Exwick, near Exeter, in July.

TRUNCATOR, *Nees.*

Monog. Ich. Brac., i. p. 245.

This does not appear to be a common insect with us. Taken by sweeping in July.

MANDIBULATOR, *Nees.*

Monog. Ich. Brac., i. p. 242.

Beaten from hedges at Lydford, on the border of the Moor, June.

GENUS, **ALYSIA,** *Latrielle.*

CINGULATOR, *Nees.*

Mouog. Ich. Brac., i. p. 259.

I bred this from holly leaves, in which had been feeding the larvæ of a small Dipteron. This came out in June, 1865.

MANDUCATOR, *Panz.*

Nees, Monog. Ich. Brac., i. p. 239 ; *Curtis,* Farm Ins., p. 144.

Captured in the north of Devon by Mr. W. C. Woollcombe.

GENUS, **DAPSILARTHRA,** *Förster.*

APII, *Curtis.*

Brit. Ent., pl. 141.

Common ; taken by sweeping rank herbage, from May to July.

DACNUSIDES.

GENUS, **SYNALDIS,** *Förster.*

CONCOLOR, *Nees.*

Monog. Ich. Brac., i. p. 254.

Taken in Stoke Wood, near Exeter, in April and September.

GENUS, **SYMPHA,** *Förster.*

HIANS, *Nees.*

Monog. Ich. Brac., i. p. 273.

Captured by sweeping coarse herbage, in May and July.

GENUS, **CŒLINIUS,** *Nees von Esenbeck.*

NIGER, *Nees.*

Monog. Ich. Brac., i. ; *Curtis,* Farm Ins., woodcut 34, f. 8, p. 234.

I bred this from pupæ of *Chlorops tæniopus,* August, 1865. The larvæ of the fly live in and are destructive to barley, causing what is called gout in the stems. They also attack the wheat plant, causing in some seasons great destruction to the crop of plants. The parasite, therefore, is of great benefit in keeping in check this destructive little fly.

T 2

GENUS, **RHIZARCHA**, *Förster.*

AREOLARIS, *Nees.*

Monog. Ich. Brac., i. p. 262.

An abundant species on flowers of grasses and carices in July and August; generally distributed.

EVANIIDÆ.
EVANIIDES.
GENUS, **HYPTIA**, *Illiger.*

MINUTA, *Fab.*

Nees, Monog. Ich. Brac., i. p. 312; *Steph.*, Ill., vii. p. 119; *Curtis*, Brit. Ent., pl. 257.

Very scarce; I have only seen one specimen, which I took several years ago.

GENUS, **FŒNUS**, *Fabricius.*

JACULATOR, *Linn.*

Steph., Ill., vii. p. 120; *Nees*, Monog. Ich. Brac., i. p. 307.

A very uncommon insect with us.

ASSECTATOR, *Linn.*

Nees, Monog. Ich. Brac., i. p. 308; *Curtis*, Brit. Ent., pl. 423; *Steph.*, Ill. vii. p. 121.

Taken in Devon, on the authority of Stephens, in *Illustrations.*

ON THE OCCURRENCE OF UPPER DEVONIAN FOSSILS IN THE COMPONENT FRAGMENTS OF THE TRIAS NEAR TIVERTON.

BY THE REV. W. DOWNES, B.A., F.G.S.

(Read at Dawlish, July, 1881.)

FOR some years past there has been exhibited, in the Albert Memorial Museum at Exeter, a specimen of Palæozoic grit, brought, as the label attests, from the Trias "near Tiverton," and containing the well-known and characteristic Upper Devonian fossil, *Strophalosia caperata* (Sow.)*

Although the words "near Tiverton" are somewhat indeterminate as to locality, it may be safely assumed that the place in which this fragment was found must have been many miles to the southward of any exposure of Upper Devonian beds. Tiverton lies very near to the junction of the Trias with the Culm measures, some eight miles (superficies) of the latter separating the Trias from the nearest Upper Devonian beds. I have heard this specimen adduced as evidence of Triassic currents having set from north to south, in opposition to the contrary evidence very prevalent elsewhere. But this supposition will presently appear to be inadmissible.

Again, in the autumn of last year I was invited by the Rev. C. S. Bere, rector of Uploman, to inspect some specimens of a similar character found in his parish, very near to his house. The specimens had been sent to Mr. Etheridge, who had reported the included fossils to be *Strophalosia caperata* (Sow.), *Spirifera disjuncta* (Sow.), *Rhynconella pleurodon* (Phillips), *Actinocrinus* (?) sp., *Cucullella* (?) sp., *Retepora* (?) sp. Another fragment from the same locality (one which had not been sent to Jermyn Street) contained, I believe, *Streptorhynchus crenistria* (Phillips).

* Syn. *Strophalosia productoides*, *Leptæna productoides*.

The character of the Trias in which these fossils were found, as exhibited in a pit upwards of thirty feet in depth, is a loose rubbly aggregation of angular and subangular fragments of grit of all sizes confusely intermixed in a sandy matrix. The whole mantles round the Palæozoic slopes, and gives the impression that the component fragments have been derived from adjacent rocks. That they have not travelled far is attested by the absence of complete attrition, as well as by the non-separation of coarse and fine material.

If we analyse the above list of fossils, it will be found that *Strophalosia caperata* (Sow.) and *Spirifera disjuncta* (Sow.) are regarded as characteristically Upper Devonian.

Rhynconella pleurodon (Phillips) and *Streptorhynchus crenistria* (Phillips) are Devonian and Carboniferous. The latter especially has a very wide range.* But in Devonshire neither have been, so far as I can discover, hitherto referred to any but Devonian and " passage " beds.

The remainder, not being specifically determinable, may be disregarded. The whole, however, has a decidedly Devonian *facies*.

It was certainly not a thing to be expected that fossils characteristically Devonian, whose *in situ* localities are " Baggy," " Marwood," " Pilton," " Petherwin," " Torquay," and " Druid, near Ashburton," should be found in the Tiverton Trias, adjoining the heart of the Culm measures, in a comparatively untravelled state.

My own first impulse naturally was to picture to myself some hypothetical fold in the rocks, which by repetition should invert the beds, and bring the earlier beds locally nearer to the surface than the later ones. The same idea seems to have occurred to Mr. Etheridge, who sketched upon his letter to Mr. Bere a rough diagram illustrative of such an hypothetical fold.

I scarcely imagine, however, that Mr. Etheridge, or any other competent authority, would, after an examination of the locality, seriously and deliberately advocate the theory of a fold as a *vera causa* for the fossils. The area which it would underlie, if anything adequate be supposed, is of such extent as to demand a great regional disturbance extending over many miles; the out-crop of the nearest Devonian beds being fully eight miles to the northward. To postulate a fold of this extent in the entire absence of evidence would be to assume a good deal.

My next hypothesis was, palæontologically speaking, rather

* BAILY's *Characteristic British Fossils*, vol. i. p. 111.

a revolutionary one. *Rhynconella pleurodon* and *Strepto-rhynchus crenistria* have elsewhere an extended range; and though their presence may not have been hitherto detected in the Carboniferous rocks of Devonshire, there is (I argued) nothing improbable in the idea that they might be found in them. Nay, more, in spite of the text books, why (I asked) might not even *Spirifera disjuncta* and *Strophalosia caperata* range into the Culm measures? If it were so, and if the fact could be attested by confirmatory evidence *in situ*, it would be a palæontological discovery of no little importance. No such evidence, however, was forthcoming, and, as the sequel will show, it was not needed.

I further took into consideration the present drainage system of the locality, which (being from north to south) might be supposed capable of bringing down southward fragments of parent rocks situated far to the northward. But independently of the subangular form of the fragments, clearly distinguishable from the more rounded river pebbles, they were found not in alluvium nor in a river terrace, but in a deep pit near the top of a hill, where recent drainage could have in no way affected them.

Subsequently I paid several visits to the new railway now in the course of construction between Tiverton and Dulverton, and in the cuttings between Tiverton and the hamlet of Bolham, about two miles to the north of the town, I found, I believe, the solution to the problem.

On the first visit which I paid to these cuttings I was accompanied by Mr. Spring,* of Tiverton, when we began by going through the customary formula of questioning the workmen. This we did in the first cutting going northward from Tiverton, where a gang of men happened to be working, and in reply to our enquiry whether any fossils had been found, or anything else in any way remarkable, we received the unpromising reply, "No; it is just the same kind o' dirt all along."

We resolved, however, to see the "dirt" for ourselves, and as the result of this and of some subsequent visits to the five short cuttings between Tiverton and the hamlet of Bolham, two miles to the north of the town, the following description may be offered.

Cutting No. 1.—Nearest cutting to Tiverton. Maximum depth about nine feet. Sand rock, with partings of chocolate marl, and with a shallow capping of drift and soil.

* The same gentleman afterwards went with me over the ground between Bolham and Washfield.

Cutting No. 2.—At the southern end this is of a similar character to the above, but merges gradually northward into an aggregation of small angular and subangular fragments of grit. The change is more apparent than real; for at a little distance it is difficult to distinguish the cuboidal weathering of the marl from grit fragments; but the grit fragments are present nevertheless, and increase in number northward. Maximum depth about fourteen feet.

Cutting No. 3.—Maximum depth about twenty-five feet. The small fragments of grit, such as those above mentioned, occur again, and increase in size northward very perceptibly. They are confusely mixed in a sandy or marly matrix, without regard to the relative size of the fragments.

Cutting No. 4.—Maximum depth about twenty feet. Of the same character as the last, but fragments still increasing in size northward. Near the bottom of this cutting I found a subangular piece of trap, about eight inches along the major axis, similar in character to the trap *in situ* at Washfield, about a mile distant in a westerly direction. Here also are a few lumps of a soft brown substance, appropriately termed "rotten stone" by the navvies, and prized by them as serviceable for burnishing the brass on the harness of their horses.

Cutting No. 5.—Close to Bolham. Maximum depth about twenty-five feet. Fragments still increasing in size northward; many might rather be described as boulders. "Rotten stone" plentiful, and in larger pieces, but unaltered grit still predominant. The steady increase in the size of the fragments clearly indicates an approach to an old shore line, while the confused, unstratified conditions of deposit, no less than the subangular character of the fragments, exclude the idea of distant travel.

I have above used the one term "rotten stone" for the soft brown substance found in this place; but there can, I think, be little doubt but that there are two kinds of it—the one probably of directly igneous origin, a very light pumiceous substance, which I have found on comparison to agree pretty closely with some specimens *in situ* at Washfield; the other unquestionably altered Palæozoic grit, of indirectly igneous origin. The former only would be available for burnishing. The latter is found under various degrees of alteration, and I even saw a boulder of which one half was grey and hard, and the other half brown and "rotten." Fossiliferous fragments either were exceptional or the fossils in most cases had been destroyed. Nearly the first fragment, however, which I attacked with my hammer showed abundant organic matter. As may be supposed, the fossils were not in a good state of preservation, and from their soft friable nature required very delicate handling. Some pieces forcibly reminded me of the altered Silurian shale at Tortworth, in Gloucestershire, found in contact with the greenstone of Damory Bridge.

The fossils are encrinites, three species of Brachiopoda, and a spiral univalve. Among the Brachiopoda *Spirifera disjuncta* and *Strophalosia caperata* are unmistakably and numerously present. The third brachiopod is most probably *Productus prælongus* (Sow.). The univalve might be one of the species of *Loxonema* figured by Phillips, but with the distinctive striæ obliterated.

Here then again occur Devonian fossils in the Trias of this district, increasingly associated with igneous traces as we approach the igneous outburst at Washfield. That igneous disturbance will account for everything. The subjacent rocks must have been bent and shifted by its deep-seated forces, which would have brought deep-seated rocks to the surface, at least in a fragmentary condition. It is worthy of note that while the undisturbed Palæozoic rocks are seen just north of Lythe Court, dipping about 35° E.S.E., the next exposure in the direction of Washfield, the last exposure visible, shows them in a vertical position. To my mind no other hypothesis is needed to account for the presence of Devonian fossils in the Trias of this district than that of which we have clear, ocular, and tangible confirmation; viz., an active volcano upon the coast of the early Triassic sea.

P.S.—Since writing the above I have learned that fragments containing *Rhynconella pleurodon* have been found in the Trias at Silverton, at a considerable distance from the above-mentioned localities, but upon the same line of igneous disturbance.

WELL-SECTION AT STONEHOUSE, PLYMOUTH.

BY W. WHITAKER, B.A., F.G.S.

(Read at Dawlish, July, 1881.)

The following account of the section given by the sinking of a well, lately finished, at the Anchor Brewery, Stonehouse, may be of interest to the Association. The well was made for Mr. A. H. Butcher by Messrs. Legrand and Sutcliff, of London, who have kindly given me the particulars. The water-level is 7½ feet below the surface of the ground, and the yield is 12 gallons a minute.

I should much like to see other records of this character in the *Transactions* of the Association, the fit publication for the notice of such local matters.

		Feet.
[Surface-deposits, 13¼ feet.]	Stony Clay	10¾
	Black Pebbles	2½
[Middle Devonian. Limestone, with occasional layers of Shale, 98¾ feet.]	Rock	½
	Shaly stone	7
	Hard black stone	3
	Hard shaly stone	4
	Grey stone	2½
	Shaly rock	8½
	Hard blue shale-stone	5½
	Clay	¾
	Blue shaly stone	½
	Hard blue stone	5½
	Clay	½
	Hard blue stone	5
	Clay	½
	Hard blue stone and white spar	1½
	Clay	1
	Hard blue stone and white spar	45
	Shaly blue clay	7½
	Total	112

NOTES ON SLIPS CONNECTED WITH DEVONSHIRE.

BY W. PENGELLY, F.R.S., F.G.S., ETC.

PART IV.

(Read at Dawlish, July, 1881.)

THIS, fourth, batch of *Slips connected with Devonshire*, has been culled from my Memoranda of Slips noted during the two years since the last batch was read.

I. ASHBURTON GROWYTTE KEVE, 1533-4.

A Pamphlet, of 50 octavo pages, entitled "The | Parish of Ashburton | in the | 15th and 16th Centuries ; | as it appears from | Extracts | from the | Churchwardens' Accounts, A.D. (1479–1580) | With Notes and Comments. | Published by Request. | London : | Printed by Yates and Alexander, Symonds Inn, | Chancery Lane. | 1870," contains the following statement, under the heading "Expenses," during the year "1533-4":—

"vi⁸ for a growytte (great) keve (key) made by John Aysshetrege."

The two words "(great)" and "(key)" which, in parentheses, follow respectively "growytte" and "keve" are, no doubt, interpolations by the anonymous editor, and intended to signify that the passage, put into nineteenth century English, would read thus :—

"Six shillings for a great key made by John Aysshetrege."

I venture to believe that the editor *slipped* into an error in each case.

Six shillings make a suspiciously large sum to be paid for even a "great key" in the sixteenth century, especially when the same "Accounts" contain the following entries :—

"1532–3 . . . . iiii^d for a loke and corde for churche yette."

"1536–7 . . . . vi^d for lokyn of the stocke to make Saynt Cristoffer."

"1548–9 . . . . ii^s for a new lock and key for the poor mens' box."

"1563–4 . viii^d to Ryxtaylle for ii Keys."

Should it be asked "If a *keve* be not a *key*, what is it? I would reply that, though the word does not occur in JOHNSON (ed. 1784) or WALKER (ed. 1833), every native of the four south-western counties ought to know that a KIEVE is a large wooden tub, and that in the local Glossaries it is thus defined:—

BARNES:—*Dorset Dialect*, 1863:—"KEEVE, or KIVE. (A.S. cyf, *a vat*.) A large tub, used for the wort to work in at brewing."

JENNINGS:—*Dialect of West of England, particularly Somerset*, 1869. "KEEVE. A large tub or vessel used in brewing. A mashing-tub is sometimes called a *keeve*." "To KEEVE. To put the wort in a keeve for some time to ferment."

PALMER:—*Glossary to Dialogue in Devonshire Dialect*, 1837. "KEIVE or KEEVE. The mashing tub or vat used in brewing."

PULMAN:—*Rustic Sketches in the Dialect of S. W. Somerset, West Dorset, and E. Devon*, 1817. "KEEVE. A tub used for fermenting beer."

ROCK:—*Jim and Nell. Dialect of N. Devon*, 1867. "KIEVE. A large tub used for fermenting beer."

WILLIAMS AND JONES:—*Dialect of Somersetshire*, 1873. "KEEVE, or KIVE. A large tub used in brewing or cider making." To KEEVE or KIVE. "To put the wort or cider in a keeve to ferment."

The word does not occur in any Cornish or S.W. Devonshire Glossary which I have seen; nevertheless I was perfectly familiar with its use in S.E. Cornwall in my boyhood, and were I to see such a tub anywhere I should certainly call it a *Kieve*.

The late Mr. R. J. King (*Murray's Handbook for Travellers in Devon and Cornwall*, ed. 1872), when describing the waterfall known as St. Knighton's Keive, near Boscastle, N. Cornwall, says, "The stream is hurried to a fall, and tumbles about 30 feet into a circular basin, or *Keive*."

HALLIWELL, (ed. 1874), has "KEEVE. A large tub or vessel used in brewing. *West*."

WEBSTER, 1864, has "KEEVE. A large vessel for fermenting liquors; a beer tub; a mashing-tub." "To KEEVE. To set in a keeve or tub, for fermentation." "KEEVER. The same as keeve." "KIVE. A mashing vat; a keeve. *Obs.*"

The word does not occur in NARES (ed. 1876), or in BAILEY (ed. 1726); but the latter has "KEEVER. A Brewing Vessel for the Drink to work in before it is tunn'd;" and HALLIWELL has "KEEVER. A tub. *MS. Lansd.* 1033."

As defined above, a *Keeve* seems to be used for no other purpose than that of making fermented liquor, but in S.E. Cornwall its use was by no means restricted to any definite purpose.

I have no doubt that the *Keve* mentioned in the *Ashburton Accounts*, in 1533–4, and for making which John Aysshetrege was paid vi⁵, was a large wooden tub, and not a *Key*.

Turning now to *Growytte*, which the editor supposes to signify *Great*, but is probably neither more nor less than the *Grout* of English Dictionaries and Glossaries, and defined as follows:—

JOHNSON (ed. 1784) "*Grout.* (1) Coarse meal; pollard.
(2). That which purges off.
(3). A kind of wild apple."

BAILEY (ed. 1726) "*Grout.* (1) The great of, or large Oatmeal.
(2). Wort of the last running, new Ale. N.C."
[= North Country.]

WEBSTER (ed. 1864). "GROUT (1) Coarse meal; pollard.
(2) Liquor with malt infused for ale or beer before it is fully boiled; a kind of thick ale.
(3) Lees; grounds; dregs; sediment.
(4) A thin, coarse mortar, used for pouring into the joints of masonry and brick-work; also a finer material, used in finishing the best ceilings.
(5) A kind of wild apple."

WALKER (ed. 1833) "*Grout.* Coarse meal, pollard; that which purges off; a kind of wild apple."

HALLIWELL (1874). "*Grout* (1) Ground malt. Ray explains it, wort of the last running, and Pegge adds that it is drunk only by poor people, who are on that account called *grouters*. Kennet says, 'In Leicestershire, the liquor with malt infused for ale or beer, before it is fully boiled, is called *grout*, and before it is tunned up in the vessel is called wort. They have in the west a thick sort

of fat ale which they call *grout-ale!* The grout-
ale is sweet and medicated with eggs. In Dean
Milles MS. Glossary, p. 136, in my possession, is
given the best account of grout-ale,—'a kind of
ale different from white ale, known only to the
people about Newton Bussel' [*sic*] 'who keep the
method of preparing it as a secret; it is of a
brownish colour. However, I am informed by a
physician, a native of that place, that the preparation is made of malt almost burnt in an iron
pot, mixed with some of the barm which rises on
the first working in the Keeve, a small quantity
of which invigorates the whole mass, and makes
it very heady.'

" (2) A masonic process of filling up the interstices between bricks or stones, by pouring fluid
mortar, which is the grout, over each course or
two to saturation. Hence jocularly applied to
one who may happen to take anything fluid late
in a meal. *Var. dial.*

" (3) To bore with the snout, or dig up like a
hog. *Yorksh.*

" GROUTS. Dregs; lees; *Var. dial.* Thick muddy
liquor is *grouty.*"

It may be well to add that KENNETT, quoted by Mr. Halliwell, was White Kennett; born in Kent in 1660; bishop of
Peterborough from 1718 to 1728, when he died; author of
several works, including *Parochial Antiquities*, having a useful Glossary. (*Pen. Cyclo.* xiii. 180.)

Dean Milles, also quoted by Halliwell, was born in 1714;
Dean of Exeter from 1762 to 1782, when he died. Whilst
Dean, he is said to have formed a large collection of materials
for a *History of Devonshire (Ibid.* xv. 224–5.)

The "physician a native of" Newton Bussell, or Bushel
(for the name appears to have been written anciently either
way; after the family of Bussell or Bushell to whom the
town belonged in the 13th and 14th centuries. See *Morris
and Co.'s Directory,* 1870) was perhaps Hugh Downman,
M.D., who was born in 1740, in or about that town as some
say (*Stirling's Hist. of Newton,* 1830, p. 63); or at Alphington, according to Dr. Oliver, or at Newton St. Cyres, according
to the Lysonses. He was physician of the Devon and Exeter
Hospital, whilst Dr. Milles was Dean. (See *Trans. Devon.
Assoc.* xi. 114.)

Though the word *Grout* does not occur in any South-western Glossary known to me, there appears to be little or no doubt that the *Keve* paid for by the Ashburton Church-wardens in 1533-4 was for the reception of one or other of the substances known by that name; that is to say, Coarse meal; or pollard; or wild apples; or Some kind of fermented liquor; or lees; grounds; dregs; sediment; or a liquid preparation used by builders; and as we learn from Dean Milles that a beverage known as *Grout-Ale* was a popular drink within seven miles of Ashburton, and that *White ale*, (well known at later times at Ashburton I am told) in which Grout was an indispensable ingredient, was at least equally popular in most of the South Hams, I have no hesitation in expressing the belief that the *Growytte Keve* which John Aysshetregge made, was not a *Great Key*, but a large wooden vessel, or tub, or vat, to be used in brewing *Grout ale*, or *White ale*, or both.

It is, perhaps, worthy of note that Dean Milles in his description speaks of the Grout-ale working, that is fermenting, in the *Keeve*.

Those who are familiar with old parish accounts will not be surprised to find that such a payment had been made by the Churchwardens. The *Accounts* now under notice prove that ale of some kind was regularly brewed in the "Church house," and sold for the benefit of the church, or some of its officers; that wardens were annually appointed for this work; that private persons, on making suitable payment, might brew their own ale in the said house, or might hire, at least, some of the brewing utensils, and especially the chetell, or cauldron, or cacabus. Thus, we find the following entries, amongst many others of the same kind:

1482-3   "v^{li} xiii iiii^d received for ale of the aforesaid parishioners" [of the Parish Church of Aysberton] "sold by the hands of William Halewyll, John Ferreys, John Ollysbrome, and Thomas Perry this year.

           "For mending the chetell of the said church iiii^d."

1489-90 "xxi^d received for sale of ale and brewing in the house of the church."

1495-6   "iiii^s viii^d from different men for the church chetell and brewing in the church house."

1501-2   "x^d from Thomas Cole because he did not assist the brewers for the brewing when they were elected."

1505-6   " iii^s iiii^d received for the chetell."

1524-5   "xii^d for one cleansing sieve for the ale."

It will scarcely be thought foreign to the object of this *Note* to remark that, whilst, according to his interesting paper on White Ale (*Trans. Devon. Assoc.* ix. 188–197), Mr. Karkeek is of opinion that Grout Ale is the same as White Ale, "from the fact that grout is still the name for the ferment used in its manufacture" (*Ibid.* pp. 191–2), Dean Milles, in the passage quoted by Halliwell, and reproduced above, states distinctly that it was "a kind of ale different from white ale, known only to the people about Newton Bussell, who keep the method of preparing it a secret;" and he adds "it is of a brownish colour."

II. PRINTING AT TORQUAY, Mr. R. N. Worth on the HISTORY OF.   1879.

Mr. R. N. Worth says, in his *Notes on the History of Printing in Devon*, read to the Devonshire Association, July 1879, and printed in the *Transactions* of that body (xi. 497–515), "Printing was introduced into Torquay by an amateur. The Rev. Mr. Fayle, incumbent of Trinity Church, brought from Somerset a schoolmaster named Lane, and he was the first who practised the printing art within the rising watering place. Not only did he print, but he tried his hand at casting types, though his efforts in that direction were not marked by any great success. The earliest professional printers in Torquay were Messrs. Cockrem and Elliott, who established an office there about 1834. Mr. Cockrem had served his time at Totnes, with Mr. Hannaford; and Mr. Elliott his at Plymouth Dock (Devonport) with Mr. Congdon." pp. 513–4.

The passage just quoted, appears calculated, if not intended, to convey, explicitly or implicitly, the following propositions:—

1. That the Rev. Mr. Fayle, or Mr. Lane the schoolmaster, or both, came from *Somersetshire* to Torquay.

2. That Mr. Lane was the first who practised the art of printing at Torquay.

3. That Messrs. Cockrem and Elliott were partners, as printers, at Torquay.

4. That neither Mr. Cockrem, nor Mr. Elliott, had begun business as a printer, at Torquay, before 1834.

5. That Mr. Cockrem, or Mr. Elliott, or both as partners, opened the first professional printing office at Torquay.

On reading the quotation I felt very sceptical about each

of the propositions; and investigation has shown that they are all incorrect.

1. Through the kindness of a member of his family, I am able to state that the late Rev. R. Fayle, as well as the late Mr. Lane, the schoolmaster, resided not in Somersetshire, but at Wareham in Dorsetshire, of which parish Mr. Fayle was Rector; and that they left Wareham for Torquay.

Mr. Fayle bought Trinity Church, Torquay, in 1837, but did not resign the living of Wareham, nor settle permanently at Torquay, before 1840, probably not before 1841.

Mr. Lane, a Serjeant retired from the army, had been the schoolmaster at Wareham; and after his Rector left, he requested that he might follow him; and this being consented to, he became Master of the school connected with Trinity Church, Torquay, where he arrived, it is believed, in 1841, but certainly not before 1840.

2. It is obvious, therefore, that even if Mr. Cockrem's office was not opened until 1834, as Mr. Worth states, Mr. Lane could not have been the first who practised the art of printing at Torquay.

3. Mr. Elliott, on whom I called on 22nd September 1880, authorized me to state that he was never in partnership with Mr. Cockrem, either as a printer or in any other business; that he began business at Torquay, as Bookseller, Stationer, and Librarian, in 1837, but as a printer not before 1839; and that Mr. Cockrem was in business as a Bookseller, Stationer, and Printer, at Torquay, some years before the earlier date.

4. It is certain, however, that Mr. Cockrem had established a printing office at Torquay before 1834; certain that he had established it in 1829; and eminently probable that it was as early as 1828.

Mr. John L. Narracott, now in business as a Bookseller, Stationer, and Bookbinder, at Torre, Torquay, on whom I called, on 27th September 1880, informed me that Mr. Cockrem, on the expiration of his apprenticeship at Totnes, came to Torquay as an assistant to Mrs. Cole, who was in business there as a Bookseller, Stationer, and Librarian, but never engaged in Printing; that in 1829, he—Mr. Narracott —was apprenticed to Mr. Cockrem at Torquay; that, according to his Indenture, dated 21st June 1829, which he submitted to my inspection, he was " to be instructed in the Art Trade or mystery of a Stationer Bookbinder and Printer in all its branches ;" that Mr. Cockrem, whilst in Mrs. Cole's employ, commenced business as a printer, "in a small way," on his own account, in what was then called Mill Street, Torquay, where he had taken two rooms; that he did what printing came in his way "before hours in the morning and after hours in the evening;" that before he, Mr. Narracott, was apprenticed to Mr. Cockrem, he was with Mr. T. N. Hayward, grocer at Totnes, with a view to learning that business; and that he remembered distinctly that, not later than 1828, Mr. Cockrem, then at Torquay, printed "trade lists" for the said Mr. Hayward.

That Mr. Cockrem's printing business soon became a thriving one is indicated by the fact that, to say nothing of Hand-bills, circulars, &c., he printed, at least, four books in 1830. One of these was an octavo pamphlet of 48 pages, of which through the Author's kindness, I possess a copy. Omitting two poetical quotations, the title-page runs thus :—

"The | Swallow's Repast, | A | Series of Poems. | By H. Dart, | Torquay : | Printed and Published for the Author, | By E. Cockrem, | and sold by all other Booksellers. | 1830 : "

Mr. Dart, who is still residing at Torquay, informs me that his Poems were printed in August 1830; that in the same year, but in an earlier part of it, Mr. Cockrem printed, first, a small volume of Poems for Mrs. Emery, wife of Captain Emery, then resident at Torquay ; and, next, a volume of Poems for Mrs. Isaac S. Prowse, wife of a Torquay merchant.

I have not seen a copy of Mrs. Emery's work ; but Mr. S. H. Slade, of Torquay, has recently presented a copy of Mrs. Prowse's book to the Torquay Natural History Society. It is an octavo volume of 184 pages, entitled "Poems by Mrs. I. S. Prowse," dated MDCCCXX, and having at the bottom of the last page the words "Cockrem, Printer Torquay."

The fourth work which, as already stated, Mr. Cockrem printed in 1830, was the First Edition of the *Panorama of Torquay*, by Mr. Octavian Blewitt; who, writing me on 1st October 1880, said "It was a small 12mo of less than 100 pages, 'printed by Edward Cockrem for the Author,' and published in 1830." I have not seen a copy of this edition. The second and larger edition of *The Panorama*, of which I have a copy, was printed in 1832, by Mr. Cockrem.

Mr. Narracott informed me that Mr. Cockrem's business in 1830 required him to keep a journeyman, as well as an apprentice ; and he directed my attention to the fact that the "List of Subscribers" at the end of Mr. Dart's volume contained the names of "Mr. J. L. Narracott, Mr. E. Cockrem, and Mr. J. W. Taylor," or, as he told me, first the apprentice, then the master, and last of all the journeyman. This was confirmed by Mr. Dart.

5. There seems to be satisfactory evidence that Mr. Cockrem was not the first professional printer in Torquay. I remember perfectly being told in 1836 that a Mr. Luscombe,. whom I knew by sight, had come from Newton to Torquay, where he endeavoured to establish himself as a printer before Mr. Cockrem opened his office there, but was unsuccessful. This was recently confirmed to me by Mr. J. L. Narracott, already mentioned, who added that, according to a tradition in Mr. Cockrem's office, Mr. Luscombe was wont to express the opinion that he, rather than Mr. Cockrem, should have become the Torquay printer, as he was in the field before him.[*]

Some of the older inhabitants of the town not only confirm the priority of Luscombe's attempt, but add that the late Mr. Thomas Pitts, who became a Yorkshire Rector, was a still earlier Torquay printer, and that he disposed of his business, as such, to Luscombe before proceeding to Cambridge preparatory to entering the Church.

The only definite information I have been able to obtain on the matter was kindly furnished by Mr. Charles Way, the well-known Artist and Drawing Master at Torquay, who, writing me on 13th October 1880, stated that he began residence at Torquay in 1827; that at that time Mr. Thomas Pitts and his father were in business there as printers; that soon after that, and before Mr. Cockrem arrived, Mr. Luscombe opened his printing office there; that he was unable to say whether or not the latter "took to" Mr. Pitts's business; and that he knew nothing of any Torquay printer earlier than the Messrs. Pitts.

Mr. Luscombe's printing business was apparently not very long-lived, for in "Cockrem's Directory of Tradesmen at Torquay and Tor," appended to the second edition of Mr. Blewitt's *Panorama of Torquay*, published in 1832, the names of four "Booksellers and Stationers" are given— "Luscombe, R." being one of them; and it is added of "Cockrem, E."—another of the four—but not of any of the others, that he was also a "Printer."

---

[*] Since this Paper was read, Mr. J. T. White, of Torquay, has shown me a copy of a printed placard, announcing a Sale, dated "February 11, 1829," and having at the foot "Luscombe, Printer, Binder, &c. Torquay." This, however, does not prove priority to Mr. Cockrem.

I have not been able to ascertain whether Mr. Pitts was the first Torquay printer, or when his business was established; but there is reason to believe that there was no printer in the town in 1810, for Mr. G. E. Hearder has kindly lent me a printed sermon, of which the following is a copy of the title page:—

"A | Sermon, | preached | in the Parish Church of Tor, | on Thursday the 13th day of September, 1810, A.L. 5810. | On the Consecrating the Lodge of | St. John, No. 216, at Torquay. | By the Rev^d· William Cockburn, M.A. | Late Fellow of St. John's College, Cambridge. | Published at the particular Request of | the Brethren of the Lodge of St. John; | and of the neighbouring Lodges. | Dartmouth : | Printed by J. Salter. | 1810."

It can scarcely be supposed that a Sermon preached at Torquay, would have been sent elsewhere to be printed, had there been a printer there at the time.

I have reason to believe that for several years after 1810 inhabitants of Torquay, having no one in the trade in their own town, were wont to employ a printer, named Bowden, resident at Paignton, and that this was the practice as late as 1819.

III.   RALEIGH, Sir Walter, Birthplace of.

The Monthly Magazine, or *British Register*, for 1st August 1804 (xviii. 44), contains a copy of a letter addressed by "Sir W. Raleigh" to "Mr. Duke." There is nothing in the Magazine to show where, when, or how the Editor obtained the copy, what was the Christian name of Mr. Duke, or where he resided. The letter, however, if trustworthy, settles completely the somewhat disputed question of Sir Walter's birth place.

A paper by the Rev. H. G. J. Clements, M.A., F.R.G.S., of Sidmouth, in the *Transactions of the Devonshire Association* (1873, vi. 225), contains a copy of the same letter; but as the two copies are not identical, there are clearly *Slips* somewhere.

Mr. Clements has been so good as to inform me that the letter, as printed in his Paper, was copied from *The Life of Sir Walter Raleigh*. By Edward Edwards, (*Macmillan*, 1868) II. 26; and Mr. R. W. Cotton, of Newton Abbot, having kindly favoured me with the loan of the said "Life," I find that Mr. Clements's copy differs from that in Edwards in the following particulars only :—

1. Mr. Clements substitutes "than" for "then" in one instance.

2. He introduces italics, whilst there are none in Edwards; —this was done, he says, "merely to illustrate the orthography."

3. He dispenses with capitals, in one or two cases, where they are used by Edwards.

4. He omits two brief foot-notes.

The two copies are printed below, side by side, precisely as they appear in the *Life* and in the *Magazine* already mentioned, in order that the *Slips*, by whomsoever made, may be seen at a glance.

Mr. Edwards's Copy:

" To MR. RICHARD DUKE OF OTTERTON, IN DEVONSHIRE.

" As transcribed from the original by JOHN AUBREY. MS. Aubrey iv. f. 47. (Bodleian Library, Oxford.)

" The original letter was, for a time, kept at Hayes, and was shown to visitors. Its present abode is not known.

" MR. DUKE
          " I WROTE to MR. PRIDEAUX to move yow touchinge the purchase of a farme[1] sometime in my Fathers posession. I will most willingly give whatsoever in your conscience you shall deeme it worth; and if at any time you shall have occasion to use me yow shall fynd me a thankefull frind to yow and yours.

" I am resolved, if I cannot entreat yow, to build at Colliton. But for the naturall disposition I have

Monthly Magazine Copy:

" MR. DUKE,
" I wrote to Mr. Prideaux to move you for the purchase of Hayes, a farm sometime in my father's possession. I will most willingly give you what soever in your conscience you shall deem it worth; and if you shall, at any time, have occasion to use me, you shall find me a thankfull friend to you and yours. I am resolved, if I cannot intreat you, to build at Colliton; but for the naturall disposition I have to that place, being born in

" [1] Hayes Barton, in the parish of East Budleigh, Devonshire. See vol. i, chap. 1."

to that place,[2] being borne in that house, I had rather seate my sealf there then any where els. So I take my leve, readie to counter-vaile all your courtesies to the uttermost of my power. From the Court, the xxvi of July, 1584.

"Your very willing frind in all I shalbe able

"W. Ralegh."

that house, I had rather seat myself there than any where else. I take my leave, resting ready to countervaile all your cour-teseyes to the utter of my power.

"Court, the xxvi of July, 1584.

"Your very willing friend, in all I shall be able.

"WALTER RALEIGH."

"[2] Namely, Hayes."

The differences in the two copies, though, perhaps, not very considerable at first sight, are by no means unimportant. The foot-notes given, or quoted, by Edwards can scarcely be re-garded as part of the original, but must, in all probability, be looked upon as originating with Aubrey or some later copyist. It is obvious, however, that without them there is nothing in Edwards's copy to identify the "farme" with "Hayes," or to suggest where it lay; nothing, in short, beyond the simple implication that it was, at the time, the property of Mr. Duke, and was not at "Colliton."

On the other hand, the *Monthly Magazine* copy explicitly states that the property was "Hayes, a farm;" and thus, if it be trustworthy, settles the entire question of the birthplace, which the other copy fails to touch.

John Aubrey, whose copy, printed by Edwards, was "trans-cribed from the original" by himself, was born in Wiltshire, on 12th March 1625–6, as some say, but on the 3rd of the following November, according to others. In other words, he could have had no personal knowledge of Ralegh, who was beheaded at least seven years before Aubrey was born.

The original letter cannot, unfortunately, be appealed to, for, though Mr. Clements spoke of it as "in existence" (See *Trans. Devon. Assoc.*, vi. 224) in 1873, the statement in Edwards, quoted above, that "its present abode is not known," showed that in 1868 there was no evidence of its existence. We are therefore reduced to speculation on the relative trustworthiness of the two copies under notice.

The *Monthly Magazine* copy has clearly been "doctored" or "improved," for, 1st, the orthography of the text has been modernized, in most instances; the copyist being apparently vain enough to believe that his readers were less capable than himself to understand English words in a sixteenth century dress.

2nd. The signature "Walter Raleigh" looks also suspiciously modern. Considerable license was, no doubt, used during Sir Walter's lifetime, in spelling his surname. Thus Manningham, his contemporary, has in his *Diary* (1602–3), "Rawley" (p. 33), "Rhaleigh" (p. 58), "Rhaley" (p. 109), and "Rhaly" (p. 174). (See also *Trans. Devon. Assoc.* vii. 385–6); nevertheless, Sir Walter, as well as other members of his family, wrote "Ralegh," at least occasionally; for an acknowledgment of receipt of money, dated 1616, and signed by Sir Walter, his lady, and their son, bears the names

"W. Ralegh

E. Ralegh

W. Ralegh."

(See *Notes and Queries*, 1st S. xi. 262; or *Trans. Devon. Assoc.* viii. 733.) That is to say, the knight's signature differs from that in the *Monthly Magazine*, but is in every particular identical with that in Edwards. It is " W.," not " Walter ; " and " Ralegh," not "Raleigh."

Being ignorant as to who he was, we cannot appeal to the character of the *Magazine* copyist, and it is to be feared that Aubrey's character, as sketched by his contemporary and co-worker, Anthony à Wood, is not calculated to inspire much confidence. " He was," says Wood, " a shiftless person, roving and magotie-headed, and sometimes little better than crased : and being exceedingly credulous, would stuff his many letters sent to A. W. with folliries " [*sic*] " and misinformations which sometimes would guide him into the paths of error." The writer of the article " AUBREY, JOHN," in the *Penny Cyclopædia* (III. 75), whence the foregoing quotation has been copied, says he was "certainly a man of good natural parts, considerable learning, and indefatigable application—a great lover of, and diligent searcher into, antiquities. He . . . was considered one of the best naturalists of the day, though credulous (as Wood has remarked) and very strongly tinctured with superstition."

If it be allowable to venture so far, I would express the *feeling*—scarcely amounting to *belief*—that the copy of the letter in Edwards is more trustworthy than that in the *Monthly Magazine ;* but it must not be forgotten that this view deprives the letter of any value as evidence that Sir Walter Ralegh was born at Hayes, in the parish of East Budlegh. It proves that he was born in a farm house that was the property of Mr. Duke in 1584, and was not at

Colliton; but it does not prove or indicate what was the name of the house, or in what parish it stood.

In this *Note* we have encountered numerous *Slips*, but by whom they were made, or what was their precise character, there is nothing to show.

IV. REGNAL YEARS OF KING JOHN OF ENGLAND.

In his *Historical Sketch of Totnes (Trans. Devon. Assoc.* xii. 159–178) Mr. E. Windeatt says "King John, in the seventeenth year of his reign, 10th May, 1215 (some authorities say seventh year of his reign, and which is correct cannot be determined), granted to the borough its earliest known charter." p. 163.

The passage just quoted is not free from ambiguity, as it does not clearly show what was the exact point on which the "authorities" differed. In any case, however, there is a *Slip* somewhere. Assuming that the point which "cannot be determined" is whether the date of the year was 1215 or 1205, it is certain that the 10th of May in 1205 was not in the "seventh" year of John's reign, and equally certain that the 10th May 1215 was not in his "seventeenth" year. Or assuming that the undeterminable point is whether the event was on the 10th of May in the seventeenth, or in the seventh, year of John's reign, then it is certain that it was neither in 1215, nor in 1205.

Richard I. died on 6th April 1199, but John's reign did not begin until the 27th of May; in other words, England was without a recognized king for 51 days. The legal maxim that "the king never dies" did not exist in England until the death of Henry VIII. From the Conqueror to Henry III. inclusive, each king began his reign on the day of his coronation—not on the day of his predecessor's decease ; and it will be found that the intervals between two consecutive reigns varied from 59 days between Henry II. and Richard I., to 3 days between William II. and Henry I., and averaged 31½ days.

There is, however, a further noteworthy fact in the case of John's reign. He was crowned, as already stated, on 27th May, 1199, which being Ascension day, the years of his reign were calculated, not from 27th May to 27th May, but from Ascension day to Ascension day—a moveable feast. The result was that his Regnal years began not only on different days in May, but in one instance in June; they fluctuated, in fact, from 3rd May, in 1201 and 1212, to 3rd June, in 1204. His "seventh" year, instead of including the 10th May 1205, began on the 19th of that month and ended on 10th May 1206. Nor did his "seventeenth" year include 10th May 1215, for it began on the 28th of that month and ended on the 18th May 1216.

The fact that the custom of dating public instruments in the year of the king's reign—not in the year of our Lord —was in existence in John's time, is sufficient to protect this Note from the charge of Chronological trifling.

Those desirous of pursuing the subject will find much valuable and interesting information in Sir Harris Nicolas's *Chronology of History* (*Cab. Cyclo.*), to which I was much indebted when preparing this Note.

V. "RENDYVOO" AS AN ENGLISH WORD. The *Saturday Review* on. 1879.

An article in the *Saturday Review* for 22nd November 1879 (No. 1256. vol. 48, pp. 627–8), entitled *Devonshire Provincialisms*, contains the following paragraph:—

"We do not know whether in former Reports" [*i.e.* prior to vol. xi.] "of the Devonshire Association, any one has taken the trouble to collect the words and phrases which survive as relics of the time when the French prisoners of war were kept at Princetown. It is still not uncommon to hear one village child, threatening another, say, 'I'll make 'ee holloa out *morblew*;' and '*a proper rendyvoo*' is used to express a gathering of people." p. 628.

The article was anonymous, and I have no intention of attempting to name the author, which it would probably be easy to do. I gather from the paragraph, quoted above, however, that he believes the word *rendyvoo* was first brought into England by the Frenchmen who, as prisoners of war, were kept at Princetown, on Dartmoor. In this belief he has certainly made a remarkable *Slip*.

As Princetown prison was erected in 1809 for the reception of French prisoners (Murray's *Handbook for Travellers in Devon and Cornwall*, 8th ed., 1872, p. 216), it would seem that England must have been quite in need of the word, and adopted it instantly, inasmuch as it was in common use in my native Cornish village, 30 miles from the prison, as long ago as my memory takes me; that is to say, within a very few years of the arrival of the first French captives on Dartmoor.

If, however, the author had only consulted his dictionaries he would have found it not only in WEBSTER (ed. 1864) and WALKER (ed. 1833), but in JOHNSON (ed. 1784) and in BAILEY (ed. 1726). Johnson, moreover, would have told him that the word was not only a recognized member of spoken and written English, but that it had at least three distinct shades of meaning as a noun (besides being used as a verb), one of which may now be regarded as obsolete; and, further, that it had been used in the Elizabethan era, by some of the writers who have shed a lustre on our literature.

The following is a verbatim copy of all that Johnson says on the word:—

"RENDEZVOÚS. *n. s.* [*rendez vous*, Fr.]

"1. Assembly; meeting appointed.

"2. A sign that draws men together.

"The philosophers-stone and a holy war are but the rendez-vous of cracked brains, that wear their feather in their head instead of their hat. *Bacon*" [1561–1626.]

"3. Place appointed for assembly.

"A commander of many ships should rather keep his fleet together, than have it severed far asunder; for the attendance of meeting them again at the next rendezvous would consume time and victual. *Raleigh's Apology*" [1552–1618].

"The king appointed his whole army to be drawn together to a rendevouz at Marlborough. *Clarendon*" [1608–1674].

"This was the general rendezvous which they all go to, and, mingling more and more with that oily liquor, they sucked it all up. *Burnet's Theory of the Earth*" [1691].

"*To* RENDEZVOUS. v. n. [from the noun] to meet at a place appointed."

If the Saturday Reviewer, moreover, had taken the trouble to refer to *Notes and Queries*, he would have found, in the following Notes, further examples of the early English use of the word:—

"Rendez-vous . . . appears to have been a very favourite expression of Oliver Cromwell's. In one of his earliest letters, dated 3rd May, 1643, and addressed to 'The Honourable the Committee at Lincoln,' I find it used no less than four times, and in the later part of his correspondence it frequently occurs. R. PASSINGHAM."

5th S. II., Aug. 29, '74. p. 169.

Again: "I do not find an instance of this word older than Hakluyt" [1553–1616] "(*Voyages*, II. 285).

CHARLES F. S. WARREN, M.A."

Ibid, Sept. 26, '74. p. 255.

Further:—" . . . It will be found four times in the plays" [of Shakspere]. "1 *Henry IV.* Act iv. sc. 1, line 57; *Henry V.* Act ii. sc. 1, line 15, and Act v. sc. 1, line 76; *Hamlet*, Act iv. sc. 4, line 4.

"Several examples of the use of the word could be given from other plays; for instance Chapman's" [1557–1634], "Jonson's" [1574–1637], "and Marston's" [1575?–1634?], "Eastward Hoe" [1599], "opens thus:—*Touchstone.* And whether with you now? what loose actiō are you bound for? Come what cōrades are you to meete withal? whers the supper? wheres the randeuous?—Edition 1605.

SPARKES HENDERSON WILLIAMS,
Kensington Crescent."
Ibid, Decr. 5th, '74· p. 458."

The following are the passages in Shakspere mentioned by Mr. Williams, taken in the order in which he gives them :—

> "A comfort of retirement lives in this.
> A *rendezvous*, a home to fly unto."

> "And when I cannot live any longer, I will do as I may: that is my rest, that is the *rendezvous* of it."

> "News have I that my Nell is dead i' the spital
> Of malady of France;
> And there my *rendezvous* is quite cut off."

> "Go, captain, from me greet the Danish king;
> Tell him, that by his licence, Fortinbras
> Claims the conveyance of a promis'd march
> Over his kingdom. You know the *rendezvous*."

To the foregoing examples of the use of the word I may add the following from the *Survey of Cornwall.* By Richard Carew, of Antonie, which, though in Cornwall, may almost be called a Suburb of Devonshire :—

Speaking of Plymouth, Carew says, "Here, mostly, have the troops of aduenturers, made their *Rendez vous*, for attempting newe discoueries or inhabitances." Ed. 1769. p. 114. (1st Ed. in 1602.)

Again, speaking of Bodmin, the same writer says, "*Perkyn Warbecke*, after his landing in the West parts of *Cornwall*, made this towne the *Rendez vous* of his assembling forces." *Ibid*, p. 124.

It is obvious, therefore, that "*Rendyvoo*," instead of being a "relic of the time when the French prisoners of war were kept 'at Princetown," from 60 to 70 years ago, has been a recognized English word for at least 300 years.

But if the naturalization of the word had been much less ancient, the long continued and active smuggling intercourse between France and Devonshire, as well as Cornwall, would have fully explained its prevalence in the current speech of the people of the two counties. Indeed, "Randyvoo," "Morbleu," "Parlyvoo," and sundry other such words, were recognized parts of the language spoken around me as long ago as I remember; that is to say, at a period too early to allow me to believe that the French prisoners on Dartmoor had anything to do with their introduction.

P.S.: Since the "Proof" of this paper was corrected, Mr. Blewitt has kindly presented me with a copy of the first edition (1830) of his *Panorama of Torquay*, mentioned on page 306 above. It must be needless to say that it confirms Mr. Blewitt's statement respecting its date, as well as the place in which it was printed, and the printer by whom the work was done. W. P.

CLOUTED CREAM.

BY REV. TREASURER HAWKER, M.A.

(Read at Dawlish, July, 1881).

IT is, I know, a vexed question whether Devon or Cornwall ought to have the high honour of originating clouted or clotted cream. They are by some supposed to be the same words; by others not; the latter deriving "clouted or clowted" from its being spread over the milk like a "clout" or piece over the sole of a shoe, whence "clouted shoon." In the *Shepherd's Calendar* Spenser says "clouted"—

> "Ne would she scorn the simple shepherd swain,
> For she would call him often heam,
> And give him curds and clouted cream."

Devonians occasionally have flung at their heads the Phœnicians as its introducers into the West Country, when they visited for tin the Cassiterides or Scilly Islands.

I am disposed to reply, as the master of my old college (Balliol) did, when inconveniently pressed for his authority, after a bold ecclesiastical assertion, "Tradition, Ward, tradition."

For myself, I am content to rest upon Fuller's old maxim, "Non ubi nascor, sed ubi pascor;" and I take it that far more of the cream consumed is from Devon than from Cornwall.

Besides, I conclude that Cornwall has virtually given up the article by its proverb, "Cream upon pilchards;" meaning that cream has no business, and is an incongruity, on tables where such food as pilchards are common, as they once were in Cornwall.

But it is altogether a mistake to suppose that any county is debarred by soil or otherwise from making clouted cream. It is merely a question of the way in which the richness of the milk is separated from it.

I have eaten it frequently in Hampshire at a friend's house, whose cook understood the Devonshire fashion. There, however, it was served up with a becoming reverence, as sufficient for itself, in a side dish.*

The manner of producing clouted cream is as follows : The milk is strained into shallow pans, each containing about half-a-pint of water to prevent the milk from adhering to the sides. In these it is allowed to remain undisturbed for twelve or twenty-four hours, according to the weather. It is then scalded, and often in Devonshire farmhouses by a wood fire (which gives the butter made from it the smoky taste that some like and some dislike), or better, according to modern usage, by warm water. In the former case it is moved slowly towards the fire so as to become gradually heated, and in about forty or fifty minutes the cream is formed. This is indicated by bubbles, and takes place at a temperature of 180° Fahrenheit. The milk is then removed from the fire, and skimmed from twelve to thirty-six hours afterwards.

Now, indeed, there is a machine for dividing cream from milk, invented by a Mr. Lamm, a Swede, which claims to separate the milk and cream far more speedily and perfectly than the natural rising of the substance. It runs, so it is said, 6,000 revolutions in a minute, and will separate thirty-two Imperial quarts of fresh milk and cream per hour.

"The creameries of Northern Illinois and Iowa," again, "set in very cold water, often using ice," and they get in America the highest market quotations.

There are sundry derivations of the word. I do not quite know where I found cream derived from the Greek χρῆμα, kreima, "cream of the thing," with the quotation from Keats's Endymion, perverted or parodied thus—.

> "A thing of cream, sir, is a joy for ever."

That derivation sounds a little fanciful and forced. Richardson, in his dictionary, says, French, "crème ;" Italian, " creme ;" Anglo-Saxon, "ream ;" Dutch, "room ;" German, "ram or rahm ;" all, says Skinner, from the Latin "cremor," the thick juice proceeding from corn when pressed, so that, supplying "lactis" to "cremor," it would be the thick juice of milk.

* In the *Heart of Midlothian* the Duke of Argyll is, so Jeannie Deans writes her father, "enamoured of Devonshire kye ;" and Mrs. Dolly Dutton's passage across the Frith of Clyde, to her new home and dairy at Roseneath, is a scene of delightful humour.

And Vossius derives " cremor " from " cern-ere," because it is that fatness which is separated (*secernitur*) from the milk.

Scaliger thinks " cremor " to be an old French word, signifying the juice expressed from any grain or seed.*

In Devon, as Lye says, " ream " is still used for the rich part of milk, not clotted; and Anglo-Saxon " hrim " is " pruina," superficial hoar-frost.

Under " Verbal Provincialisms of South-West Devonshire," in vol. vii. pp. 530–31 of the *Reports of the Devonshire Association*, A.D. 1875, under the initials of W. P., from *Notes and Queries*, there is a dissertation on raw milk, raw cream, raw milk.

But it is not material from what the name is derived so long as we possess the thing itself; any more than it is of importance from what particular breed of cows the delicious substance proceeds, if it is ours, and we have enough of it.

Dr. Johnson is said to have complained once that he had never had enough of wall-fruit; and if we judged of the antiquity of clotted cream by the infinitesimal quantity some people give one, it would be a young discovery indeed from being, as Foote said of his small glass of old Curaçoa, so little of its age.

I should hold that the Channel Islands' cows give the best cream, from the superior richness of their milk; at least, that is my experience; and the yellow tinge they impart is thought by dairy-keepers a recommendation, although it is not the colour Shakspere was thinking of when he makes Macbeth say—

> " Thou cream-fac'd loon,
> Where got'st thou that goose look ? "

and yet I am not sure whether he did not mean something more than white in the scolding Rosalind gives to Phœbe in *As you like it*.

> " 'Tis not your inky brows, your black silk hair,
> Your bugle eyeballs, nor your cheek of *cream*,
> That can entame my spirits to your worship."

But, as I have said, it is not of much consequence from what the name " cream " is derived if we have the thing itself.

I remember how in my boyhood all the previous materials of a feast—the soup, the fish, the roast and boiled—were

---

* One of the most beautiful of our provincialisms is " reaming out one's heart to another," as if the heart was being strained or torn asunder to bring to the surface some deeply-seated inner feeling.

nought, even as derivations or any other uninteresting pre-
liminaries, whilst I waited impatiently, hardly restrained by
parental presence from violent clamour, until the apple, or
currant, or cherry-pie arrived with its accompaniment of
thick cream, the better half indeed.

And how we children hated that imaginary cat, who was
threatened as a demolisher of that unmannerly morsel, which
we slily kept in one corner of our plates for the last luscious
mouthful.

Perhaps Shakspere had reminiscences of a like early date
when he put into Falstaff's mouth—

> " I am as vigilant as a cat to steal cream."

Some not unworthy verses in praise of this admirable
creature have been written by a remarkable man, Wm. Barry
Peacock. He was, my friend, the late Professor Hodgson,
our exceeding loss, told me, a tailor and clothier in Manchester. Professor Hodgson gave me the verses, an eulogy
on a can of cream sent by a lady to Peacock from Exeter. I
have since seen them in print in the *North Devon Journal* of
September 4th, 1879. They express alike the sentiments of
my youth, mid-life, and old age. The writer having declared
that—

> " Nothing on earth or in poet's dream
> Is so rich and rare as your Devonshire cream,"

proceeds to describe it to perfection :

> " Its orient tinge, like spring-time morn,
> Or baby-buttercups newly-born ;
> Its balmy perfume, delicate pulp,
> One longs to swallow it all at a gulp,
> Sure man had ne'er such gifts or theme
> As your melt-in-mouthy Devonshire cream."

The audacity of the new coinage, " melt-in-mouthy," is, I
think I may say, justified by the facts of the case : nothing
succeeds like success. He goes on with a recital of its
properties, which, although I have eaten a good quantity of
it, I cannot absolutely vouch for in my own person—

> "Oh, it makes me fat and it makes me fair,
> And were I not bald, it would curl my hair !
> It makes me sleek and soft and slippery ;
> It turns my thoughts from French-cook frippery ;
> It rises daily in my esteem,
> Though sinking fast is this Devonshire cream."

From the date of the poem, 1853, the author having died
only in 1878, he must have been far from an old man when

he wrote it, and his adoration is certainly that of a young man in his first love, like Florizel's burst of admiration for Perdita in the *Winter's Tale*—

> "Good sooth, she is
> The queen of curds and cream."

Charles Lamb has hardly written more ardently of the delights of a sucking-pig in his charming essay.

I pass over some gibes at the clergy of old time, although Wordsworth's description of a clerical fop in the pulpit might have been drawn from his having seen the effect on the palate of a first taste of cream—

> "And, winding up his mouth,
> From time to time, into an orifice
> Most delicate, a lurking eyelet, small,
> And only not invisible, again
> Opens it out, diffusing thence a smile
> Of rapt irradiation exquisite."

I prefer to take the testimony of the well-known "Red Lions" of the British Association, who from their scientific and pre-historic tastes are better judges even than the clergy of what is good and pleasant.

The verses, of which I quote the first stanza, smack of the racy style of a distinguished member of the company, whose roar is not unknown to our Devonshire Association, and, I may add, is always welcome.

The title is "The Red Lions in the West in 1877"—

> "The lions went to the west countree,
> The land of the clotted cream,
> Where they found a home in a spacious cave,
> Very near the Tamar stream,
> When they saw the cave they wagged their tails,
> And they roared with might and main ;
> They buried their whiskers in the cream,
> And they wagged and roared again."

Let us hope that when they return, which they certainly will ; for after they had dipped their mouths in the cream—

> "They recorded a vow with a mighty roar
> That they'd visit the West again,"

the manufacture of the delicious substance may still be going on in increasing quantities under the care of many a fair dairymaid or comely matron, even if their resources are not so large as those of the lady of whom the song says—

> "Dame Durden has three serving-men
> To follow the milking pail."

Then, when

> "Steep'd grain and curdlet milk with dulcet cream,
>   Soft temper'd in full merriment they quaff,

they may echo the not extravagant rhapsody of the same
poet from whom I have quoted—

> "Talk not of 'worlds of chrysolite,
>   Talk not of 'seas of sapphire' bright;
>   I don't desire on *such* to float,
>   The boat I seek is a butter-boat;
>   In this let me launch on an ocean stream—
>   A mighty sea of Devonshire cream.
>
> "It matters not, then, if I sink or swim;
>   It matters not what may be my whim;
>   Whether I float on the buoyant wave,
>   Or in its deeps my limbs do lave:
>   For oh! what a sensuous joy supreme
>   Would *drowning* be in this Devonshire cream."

I am not so sure that I agree with this last stanza, remembering, as I do, the sensation of sinking in a Dartmoor
mire. No doubt it is preferable to perish in an agreeable
substance rather than the reverse. Clarence certainly
showed his taste by choosing a butt of malmsey for his
drowning instead of muddy beer; but *ne quid nimis.* You
may have too much of a good thing, and the idea of being
suffocated in Devonshire cream rather chokes one. Indeed
its delights are, I contend, better elucidated by contrasts, as
people are said to marry their opposites; by being used with
fruit or wedded to its connection, if not close relation,
junket, than when it is taken pure and simple.

Nor am I quite sure that a full diet of perpetual cream
would produce so many good results, mental and physical, as
the poet asserts.

Visions of biliousness pass before one's eyes, although I
remember hearing of an old lady with a fair complexion, a
plump figure, and a youthful elasticity, being asked by what
means she had preserved her freshness so well, and replying
with Demosthenic brevity, "Butter, butter, butter."

It is said also that clouted cream has all the health-giving
properties of codliver oil, with the difference of taste thrown
in; and a dear friend of mine, who came to Ilfracombe for
his health, told me that his London doctor, in sending him
there for the winter, said, "And fill up your tea or coffee-cup,
whenever you can, with their thick cream so that your spoon
will stand upright in it."

However, I will give the stanza, which states the writer's theory—

> "But still, whilst my pen runs on so swift,
> Let me think of the *giver*, as well as the *gift*.
> There's a smile in her eye would make any man sigh,
> A place in her heart where all good things lie;
> And gentle and pleasant her thoughts do seem,
> For hasn't she lived on Devonshire cream?"

Certainly if Devonshire cream will give us smiles, and make our thoughts gentle and pleasant, the sooner we begin to order up some buckets of it, the better for ourselves and our neighbours.

Climate, however, I believe, has as much or more to do with longevity than cream, and self-restraint will do more for people's tempers than diet.

Nevertheless, I so thoroughly share in the writer's eulogium about the donors and manufacturers of cream, that I perfectly echo his concluding wish, and will say the same of anyone who will favour me with a can.

> "May she still go on lapping, still go on napping;
> Like Sterne's kindly soul the flies 'only flapping,"
> Years fall like dew on her heart and her head
> 'Till the fruit shall have ripened, the last leaf be shed,
> Then with 'folding of hands' may her spirit-dream
> Be soft and sweet as her Devonshire cream."

ON THE DEVONSHIRE PRONOUN MIN, OR MUN = THEM.

BY FREDERIC THOMAS ELWORTHY,

Member of Council of the Philological Society.

(Read at Dawlish, July, 1881.)

ONE of our Devonshire provincialisms has hitherto been an unsolved problem to philologists. Being a pronoun, and thus entering into the very construction and grammar of the language, it has had great attention paid to it—far more than would have been given to a mere word, expressing the name or quality of something, or implying some action.

The form of pronoun I allude to is well known throughout this county, and in the middle as well as in the northern part it is the regular objective case plural, and occasionally in the singular also.

All modern writers in the Devonshire dialect use it, and it was common in its present form early in the last century. How much earlier it was so used, or when the present form was first spoken, is not yet known, though, as we shall see, modern inquisitiveness and research may yet unearth some documents to make this certain.

The *Exmoor Scolding* and *Courtship* is, so far as is known at present, the earliest piece of writing in which the word is found, as spoken now. There it is spelt both *mun* and *min*. Wilmot, in twitting her sister about saying her prayers, says: "And whan tha dest zay mun, tis bet whilst tha art scrubbing, hewstring, and rittling abed. And nif by gurt hap tha dest zay mun at oll, thy marrabones shan't kneelee." In the *Courtship*, Andrew says of his property at Parracomb Down: "Tes wor twenty Nobles a year and a Puss to put min in."

See also *mun* in the Report of Provincialisms by your committee this year.

Nathan Hogg spells the word *min*, and uses it very frequently. In "Mal Brown's Crinalin" he says: "Hur pitch'd irt inter min, an pummild tha lot" (of boys). I need not quote instances of its use. The word must be well known to every Devonshire man; but out of this county it is not heard at all, unless spoken by Devonshire men. Hitherto its history has been a great puzzle. The first editor of the *Exmoor Scolding*, in 1771, about 30 years after the dialogue first appeared, was evidently quite ignorant, though he was beating about for a meaning, for he mentions it in his Glossary in the same paragraph with *mun*, the common form of *man*, (as in the every-day expression, "A'll tell thee what, mun!") and learnedly tells us that "it seems rather to mean *mannus*, for which the Saxon word was also man."

Being so obviously a pronominal form, it has hitherto been considered to represent the German indefinite pronoun *man*, but how it represents it, or how it got to its present form, or how it so entirely changed its meaning from the indefinite to the definite, no one has, so far, done more than make the merest guesses. It is a usual thing, when there is a similarity in the sound, or an approach in the spelling, of two words, to connect them in meaning. I remember a gentleman, who has much reputation for learning, asking me if I knew the origin of the word *sheriff*. I replied that I had understood it to mean *shire-reeve*. "Nothing of the sort," was the confident reply; "it is an Arabic word; '*shereef*' is the headman." On another occasion, by another gentleman, I was asked if I knew our common word *soce*, and what it came from. Upon giving the explanation which seemed to me most probable, I was in this case also most confidently contradicted, and was told by the gentleman that his uncle was a great scholar, and that "he always said that *soce* came from the Greek *zoos*." Again, a well-known writer once pointed out to a friend of mine that YARROW was a frequent name for river; "doubtless," as he said, "from the Anglo-Saxon *earewe*, an arrow, because they run straight and fast." "Thus," said he, "we have the *Yarrow* in Scotland, the *Yarra* in Africa, the *Yarra-yarra* in Australia!" How Anglo-Saxons could have gone and induced negroes and New Hollanders to give to their rivers the Anglo-Saxon name for an *arrow* he had never considered, nor did he seem to think that it was of any practical moment. He was not the only man who treats words and names as if they were fungus spores, or cholera germs, travelling about in the air and fixing themselves on to congenial subjects without human intervention!

To what absurdities a *little* knowledge may lead us! But many of our etymological problems are at present in the process of solution. The great Dictionary of the English Language now in course of preparation, under the auspices of the Philological Society and the University of Oxford, through the Clarendon Press, has acquired such a mass of information as never before was got together; so that in the end, by means of quotations from the writings of authors, beginning at the early days of the language, down to our own time, we shall see at a glance all the *history* of every word in it; how the word was first used, how it developed in both its pronunciation and in its meaning, until it finally dropped out of use, or, on the other hand, became part of our modern vocabulary. Dr. Murray, the editor of this great work, whose name will, without doubt, be much more of a household word among our children than that of either Dr. Johnson, Walker, Webster, or of any other lexicographer, has ever been among us, says, in a letter to the *Academy*, December 24, 1880:—"I am sure that if literary men and students of English in any department had the faintest conception of the amazing and enormous light which the dictionary is going to throw upon the history of words and idioms, they would work with enthusiasm to hasten its appearance. To myself, I may say, the handling of the materials—the two and a-half million quotations which the labours of more than a thousand readers and nearly a quarter of a century have amassed—afford an endless succession of surprises; every day I learn therefrom things which I had never dreamed of, and of which I know nobody else has dreamed. I never turn over the pages of *Notes and Queries* without finding men laboriously elucidating, or partially elucidating, points of which the full explanation lies ready in our pigeon-holes, waiting to be edited and published. Will not more scholars help us to hasten this coming illumination by each thinking of the dictionary in his daily reading and research, and sending us notes of *every* point likely to conduce to its completeness, of *every* isolated fact which will combine with other facts already in our hands into perfect wholes of word history? No single student can hope, even in the case of a single word, to glean all the facts which a thousand readers and a quarter of a century's work have brought together; but every student may swell the store which we are eager to lay open to all. We are doing for England and the English tongue a work which will be built upon and extended and completed, but will itself never grow old; generations of Englishmen will rejoice in our light, and bless the workers who gave the light in which men shall see to do better work; will not more deserve the blessing?"

Among the books read for the purposes of this great work is one which has but lately come to the light of day. It is one of the publications of the Early English Text Society, printed for the first time in 1879, from a MS. in the Bodleian Library. The book is a translation into English of an old French romance, and is entitled *Sir Ferumbras*. It is, in fact, one of the old Charlemagne romances, chiefly about the doings of the famous Roland and Oliver, and was translated about the year 1380. Apart from the main point on which I now bring it before you—that is, the light it throws on our modern dialect *mun*, and to which I shall return—the work is of great interest locally, and I cannot do better than quote to you Mr. Black's account of the Ashmole MS., 33 in his catalogue—*i.e. Sir Ferumbras :*—

"The book is not more curious than its antient covers, which are now preserved in a case with it. They are a triple invelope of parchment flapping over the right-hand cover, and consist of 2 sheets. The outer one is a letter executory of a bull of pope Innocent VI. for the presentation of Thomas de Silton to the vicarage of Culompton, in the diocese of Exeter, then vacant by the death of Peter Moleyns; which bull, being addressed to the Abbots of Schirbourne and Cerne, and to John de Silvis, dean of S. Agricola at Avignon, was executed (by the last named) in the present letter addressed to the Bishop of Exeter. The foot containing the date is cut off; but the bull is dated at Villa-Nova, 3*id Maij, anno* 5, which is 1357.

"The inner cover is a very long and imperfect (Latin) instrument, stating that before mass on the 7th Sunday after Trinity, in 1377, in the chapel of Holne, in the diocese of Exeter, Roger Langeman, rector of Lydelynche (dioc. Schirb.), publicly read and expounded an instrument which cites the proceedings and final sentence in the Court of Rome, in consequence of the consecration of a burial ground adjoining the said chapel, which was prejudicial to the rights of John Bryge, the vicar of Buckfastleigh, to whose parish church the right of burial belonged, the said chapel being a member thereof. [But] these covers are most remarkable for having preserved a curiosity not equalled in any collection of MSS., and that for antiquity is unique of its kind, namely, a part of the author's original corrected draught of this poem [of

'Ferumbras'] written on the back of the documents already described."

Black concludes that "the author was a clergyman, lived in the diocese of Exeter (probably in that city), and composed his work shortly after 1377, or early in the reign of Richard II."

There is no doubt whatever that the poem was written by a Devonshire man, in his own native tongue; but, at the same time, it is evident that he had, either by travel or, more likely, by long residence, become so familiar with, and so practised in the use of, Northern forms of speech, that he even uses both Northern and Southern typical forms in one and the same line; for example, in ll. 1976-7—

> " & er *sche* cam strau3t in-to halle! neuere *heo* ne stente,
> & forp *sche* praste among hem alle! & to her fader ri3t *heo* wente."

For all this the man wrote mainly in his native speech, and that clearly was Devonshire.

Inasmuch as the poem is metrical throughout, and in rhyme, we are much helped towards the correct pronunciation, and especially the correct accentuation, which, as we shall see further on, is of the greatest importance to our present purpose.

In spelling he was, as was usual in his day, on the whole phonetic. The pronunciation was by no means fixed, and hence we find him spelling the same word in three or four different ways.

We find the author of *Sir Ferumbras* constantly and very frequently writing *a* for he, as in ll. 126-8—

> " panne pe kyng gan waxe wrop! & aboute him gan beholde,
> & by seynt dynys a swer is op! pat after pat tyme a nolde
> Ete ne drynke no more pat day! for none kynnes pynge."

Compare this with l. 210 of the *Exmoor Scolding*—

> " Tha hast no Stroil nor Docity, no Vittiness in enny keendest thing;"

also l. 293.

A, spelt *ha* (ll. 159, 167), is used for *he* in the *Scolding*, and we all know how common it is now in Devonshire speech.

Again he uses *to* for *at* with the word to play, at any kind of games, as in the following: ll. 2224-5—

> " po pat williep to leue at hame! pleyep to pe eschekkere,
> & somme of hem to iew-de-dame! & somme to tablere."

In this example we note the word *live* is spelt *leue*, which both the spelling and the metre show must have been pronounced *leev*. A modern Devonshire man still says:—"I do leev to Beesh-Nymp'm hon I be hom."

Further, our author repeatedly drops the *e* in the inflection *eth*, in such words as *comth, bringth, fallth* or *valth* :—

"God him spede for his mi3t! now he takp ys waye," l. 252

"Wan he saw erld Olyuer ; a tornp him pat oper side." l. 348

"& hef vp ys swerd, & til him a gop! & smot to Olyuore." l. 621

So we find also *þynkþ, kepþ, calþ, gifþ*, and probably many others.

It would be easy to multiply quotations to any extent, but the instances I have given are enough to prove that none but a Devonshire man could have written the poem, inasmuch as they are still the true marks to know him by, and because they are found nowhere east of this county, either in modern speech or, I believe, in mediæval writings. Besides these typical forms, there are very numerous peculiarities, all pointing in the same direction, such as the invariable use of *ago* for *gone*, *bame* for *balm*, *be* for *been*, *dude* for *did*, *he* for *it*; as in l. 4309

"Mantrible pe Citee ys y-called! Wyp marbre fyn ys he walled."

Thus making the modern description of us true for 500 years *agone;* viz., that "everything is *he* excepting a Tom Cat, and that is a *she*."

Moreover, we find *vores* for *furrows*, *thuse* for *those*, *op* for *up*, and a vast number of other forms written in the fourteenth century, which are still quite familiar to West Country ears. Having, then, proved to demonstration that the poem is Devonshire, the remainder of our task is easy.

The author uses five forms to express the plural pronoun THEM; viz., hymen, hymyn or hemen, hyme, hem, em, and þaym or þeym. For the last I am indebted to the editor, as I cannot find it after reading the poem over very carefully. Of these forms, *hymen* and *hem* are the most frequent, and it is with the former of these that we have now to do. The word *hymen*, meaning *them*, occurs not less than 96 times in the poem, and probably much oftener. The rhythm shows, as we shall see later on, that the first syllable was not accented, while in many cases the line will not scan unless the syllable is dropped altogether.

By the kindness of my good friend, Dr. Murray, who has lent me the MS. of his article for the new Dictionary on this pronoun *hymen*, together with those on *Him, Hin, Hi, Hem*, and *Em*, I shall be able to clear up in the most conclusive manner the vexed problem of the Devonshire *min* or *mun*.

And here I may state that I have his permission to quote "in part or in full." I have, of course, chosen the latter, and in doing so, have to congratulate this Society in being able to present to the world not only the solution of this most interesting question, now first worked out by Dr. Murray, but also on being first to give the public a fair sample of the grand work now in progress, thereby forestalling by some two or three years the regular appearance of the article in its proper place.

I have further to congratulate this Society upon the subject matter of these articles, inasmuch as they will be the first to publish such a piece of compressed essence of word-history as has never before been worked out—such word-history as only the mass of information collected by the Philological Society, and by Dr. Murray's 750 special volunteer readers, could have made possible, and such as, perhaps, no other man than the editor would have so digested and compressed. I may add that reading and re-reading will be necessary to the mastery of these articles, and that finally, when they see daylight in their perfect shape, they will be supplemented by apt quotations to illustrate each historical period referred to under the different divisions. Thus: the figures 1–4 represent centuries, dropping the thousand, as in Italian—1 = 11th century, 2 = 12, and so on; 1–4 = 11th to 14th century.

I give here the articles on *Him*, &c., leaving that on *hymen* for convenience till last.

Him (*him*) *pers. pron.* 3 sing. m. dat.-acc.   Forms :—

[1. Orig. dat. sing. masc. and neut. of HE, IT; cogn. with O. Fris. *him*, (?) O. Sax. *imu, imo*, (?) O. H. G. *im* (mod. Germ. *ihm*, mod. Du. *hem*), (?) Goth. *imma.* 2. In 10th c. *him* began to be used for the *acc.* HINE in midl. dial.; by 1150 *him* had entirely supplanted *hine* in midl., and was encroaching on it in the south, in which, however, *hin* was still written in 15th c.; it is still, as '*n*, *en*, *un*, the regular form in southern dialect speech, as *we twold-en*, 'we told him.' 3. While *him* thus became both dat. and accus. in the masculine, in the neuter the dative *him* was disused, and its place taken by the accus. *hit, it*, as in 'give it a push.' Thus from being originally dative masc. and neut., *him* is now dat. and accus. masculine, having received extension in case, restriction in gender. Cf. mod. Germ. restriction of *ihm* to living beings.]

Hin, hine, *pers. pron.* 3 sing. acc. m.   Obs. or dial.   Forms : 1 (*i.e.* 11th century), hiene; 1–2, hyne; 1–4, hine; 2–3, hin; 4, hen; 5, hyn; 9, dial. en, un.

[The original acc. sing. masc. of HE; cogn. with O. Fries. *hine,* *hini,* Norse *hann,* O. Sax. and Goth. *ina,* O. H. G. *in, inan* (mod. G. *ihn*). Already before 1000 the midl. dial. had begun to substitute the dat. *him* for the acc. *hine,* and before 1150 *hine* was quite lost in the north and midl. It was still common in Kentish in 1340, but is rare in literature after 1400, though still the ordinary form in S.W. dialects, as *We zeed 'n gwayn,* 'We saw him going.' See Elworthy, *W. Som. Gram.* p. 36.]

Hi, *pers. pron.* 3 pl. *n.* and *acc.* Obs. Forms: 1, hia, hiæ; 1–3, hie, hea, hio, hiȝ; 1–5, hi, hy; 1–4, heo; 2, hyo, y, i; 2–3, ho; 2–4, ha; 2–5, he; 3–4, hii, hue; 4, hiu; 3–5, hee, a.

[1. The original pl. nom. and acc. in all genders of HE, q.v.; cogn. with O. Fris. *hia,* (?) Goth. *ei-s, ijo-s, ŷ-a* (obs. in O. Sax. and O. H. G., and replaced by the corresponding case (*sia*) of the demonst. SE, q.v.). 2. In 10th c. the *accus. hi* began to be supplanted by the dat. *heom, hem,* q.v., in the midl. dial., and became obs. before 1150; it was retained in south. dial. till 1330, but was obs. in 1350. 3. Already in 950 the north. dial. had begun to use, as equivalent to *hi,* the demonstrative *tha, þa,* plur. of *that;* before 1200 the cognate form *þeȝȝ, they,* adopted from Norse, had quite displaced *hi,* nom., in N. midland; by 1300 *thei, they,* had become the only form in the midl. generally; by 1400 *thei, thai,* was used along with *hi* even in S.W., and after 1450 *hi* disappears from literature. One of its latest forms, *ă,* still lingers in S.W. dial. speech. 4. Thus the *accus. hi* was supplanted between 10th and 14th c. by the dative *hem,* which was in turn supplanted between 12th and 16th by the demonstrative *them;* the *nominative hi* was superseded between the 12th and 15th c. by the demonst. *they.*]

Hem, 'em ('em), *pers. pron.* 3 *pl. dat.-acc.* Forms: 1–3 (*i.e.* 11th to 13th cent.), him, hem; 1–2, hym; 2–5, hom, ham; 2–7, hem; 3–4, -m, -em; 3–4, am; 4, hyme; 6–9, 'em.

[1. Orig. dat. pl. all genders of HE; cogn. with O. Fris. *him, hiam,* (?) O. Sax. and Goth. *im,* (?) O. H. G. *im, in* (mod. Ger. *ihn-en,* mod. Du. *hen, hun*). 2. In 10th c. it began in midl. dial. to be substituted for the *accus.* pl. HI, *heo,* &c.; by 1150 *hem* had quite supplanted *hi* in midl., and was encroaching on it in the southern; and by 1350 it entirely superseded *hi* in southern also, the dat. and accus. becoming alike *hem.* (Cf. the history of HIM, ME.) 3. In 10th c. *thœm,* dat. pl. of the demonst. THE, THAT, often took the place of *hem, heom* in the north (perhaps as more emphatic); before 1200 we find *theym, þeȝm* (Norse form of *thoem*), used for *hem* in north midl., and *thaim* as the only northern form; in 15th c. *them* and *hem* are used together by Caxton, as more and less emphatic.   After 1500 *them* is the recognized form, *hem* surviving only (written *'em*) as a subordinate form, chiefly conversational, in which capacity it is still used.   As early as 3 *hem* was combined as *-m* with other pronouns, as *him* = *hi'm*, i.e. *hi-hem;* and in 4, appended as *-m, -em*, to verbs, as *sendem*, which is identical with modern *send 'em*.   In some S.W. dialects *them* has not yet encroached upon *hem, em;* but in the north no trace of *hem* has been left for 700 years.   In the form *hym, him*, this word was identical with the dative (and subsequently accus.) sing., a confusion which was curiously remedied in S.W. dialect in 4 by making the pl. *hym-en, hem-en*, whence the *min, mun* = *them*, now used in Devonshire.]

Em, 'em ('em), *pers. pron.* 3 pl. dat.-acc.

[A contracted form of the M. E. Hem, already in 14th c. added enclitically to verbs, and still used in speech and familiar writing as *'em*, which spelling may have originated in the opinion that it was a contraction of THEM, the pronoun which has superseded *hem.* Cf. *it* for *hit.*]

= THEM.

Hymen, hymyn, hemen, 3 *pers. pron. pl. dat.* and *acc.*

[An interesting S.W. form found in end of 14th c. (as yet only in *Sir Ferumbras*, see *infra.*) alongside of *hym(e), hem, em*, as a more distinctive *plural;* the dat.-acc. sing. being also *him, hym, hem, 'em*, the plural forms were specialized by an affixed *-en*, a plural ending common to nouns and verbs, in some of which it is moreover, as in *hym-en*, so far as form goes, a pleonastic or additional affix.   Cf. *childr-en, brethr-en, ky-en*, later plurals for earlier *childre, brether, ky*, O. E. *cildru, breðer, cý;* also O. E. *sind-on, bið-on*, 'are,' formed for greater distinction on *sind, bið;* and especially Mid. and Mod. High Ger. *in-en, ihn-en*, 'to them.'   O. H. G. *im, in*, where the pl. affix *-en* has been similarly added to distinguish it from acc. sing. *ihn.*   *Hym-en* is thus an almost exact analogue of *ihn-en*.   It is the original of the still common Devonian *min, mŭn*, 'them, to them;' the enclytic *hymyn, hemen*, having become *myn, men*, just as *hine, hin*, has become *en, 'n*, and the ordinary pl. *hem* has become *em, 'm.*]

= THEM, TO THEM.

Sir Ferumbras:

Line 1893—

> " Wan pay had ete & dronke ynow⁏ þe bord sche het arere,
> Ryche garnymentȝ forþ sche drow⁏ & by-tok hymen for to were."

Line 1559—

> " Hit semeþ sarasyns as þe siȝte⁏ þat prikeaþ as wynd & rayn ;
> Willeþ we wiþ hymen mete & fiȝte⁏ oþer ȝe wollaþ turne agayn ⁈"

Line 1567—

> " Wan pey come to-gadre ne3 ! & Moradas pe kyng hem mette ;
>   A cryede to hymen welan he3 ! & pus he hymen grette :"

Line 1963—

> " & so pou schalt hemen alle schewe ! pat pay bup al mys-went."

Line 2526—

> " pan spak Florippe pat burde bri3t ! to hymyn enerechone :"

Line 3542—

> " And had ordeynt him per to lyn Wip xxx^d pousant of Sara3yn
>   To holde hymen po with-inne."

Line 5048—

> " y-come sche ys a3en wel sone, & afforn hem per sche hit hap oundone
>   & schewed hymen Aparenly."

At line 3022 we find the most interesting and probably conclusive illustration of all : "Ac hymen douste don on þe fon ;" *i.e.*, "But they threw them(selves) down on the foe." Here we have our Devonshire pronoun almost in its modern form written quite 500 years ago. It is well known that contractions in pronouns were common in the South for 150 years before our pronoun was written. Such as *he* and *hem* became *hem ; he* and *him* became *him.* Just as now we contract *they-am* into *they-m, they-have* into *they-ve,* so in the text it would have been, if not so contracted, "Ac hy hymen douste ;" but, dropping the unaccented syllable, we have " Ac hy 'men douste don on þe fon," which might have been written by Nathan Hogg or any modern Devonshire poet. We find that in another place our author wrote :—

> " So harde hy hem panne qua3te ! fleoying toward hure host,
>   pat pe most part of hem hy ca3te ! and sone abatede hure bost."
>   (l. 2981-2.)

Here we have precisely the same grammatical construction, only that he uses *hem* instead of *'men* for his accusative case.

These examples, which might be multiplied more than twelve-fold from the poem, are quite sufficient for our purpose, and we see from them, especially from the two first and two last, that even at the date when they were written the word was beginning to lose its first syllable, and to be sounded much as it now is, *m'n.* We see this, because if we distinctly pronounce the syllable, we destroy the rhythm ; while in the two last examples, which occur in the second part of the poem, and after a change in the metre, we find that we must drop the *hy* altogether, or else the metre, which otherwise is smooth and flowing, becomes halting at once.

A very curious circumstance about the pronouns in this poem is that the sing. *hin* or *'en* (*i.e.* him), is not once used by

the author. We see by Dr. Murray's history of *hin*, that before
his day it had disappeared from Northern speech, and we can
only account for his (a Devon man) not using it by presuming
that he had acquired the Northern form so entirely as to dis-
place his native speech in that particular, so far as writing it
went; while, as we all know, the former remains still in
common use in our South-west country spoken tongue, as in
the common sentence, " I told 'n to be sure and take care
o' un;" or, as in the *Exmoor Scolding* (l. 219), where Wilmot
is speaking of the " Natted Yeo," and says to her sister:
" Rather than tha wudst ha enny more Champ, and Hoster,
and Tanbast wi' un, tha tokst en and dest wetherly bost
tha neck o' en." This form is so thoroughly familiar that
I need not quote further. It is one of our West Country
provincialisms which is usually set down to bad grammar,
but which Dr. Murray now proves to be the true descendant
of good old English, thus adding one more proof to my
contention before you last year, that Devonshire speech is
the true classic English.* This fact of the author of *Sir
Ferumbras* not using it is the more curious, inasmuch as from
beginning to end the poem is so bristling with Devonshire-
isms that no one who knew West Country talk could fail to
claim the author as a neighbour.

In conclusion, I would repeat that in the fourteenth century, when this poem was written, the usual form in the
northern and midland districts for dat. acc. sing. was, as now
in literary English, *him ;* while in the plural the dative and
accusative were *hem* and *heom.* It was only our forefathers
who then in the south-west confounded both singular and
plural in the same word, *him ;* hence they only needed to
make a distinction, and so added *en* to form a plural, thus
developing the *hymen* of *Sir Ferumbras*, which, as we have
seen by Dr. Murray's history and analogy, lost the *hy*, and
has curiously come down to us in the unique Devonshire
pronoun *men* or *m'n.*

There is so much of interest in *Sir Ferumbras* that, unless
you are already tired of " him," I shall hope to have something further to say on the subject when we meet again.

* See *Trans. Devon. Assoc.* 1880.

NOTES FROM THE AUTOBIOGRAPHY OF DR. JAMES YONGE, F.R.S.

BY R. N. WORTH, F.G.S.

(Read at Dawlish, July, 1881.)

THE Library of the Plymouth Institution contains a manuscript autobiography by Dr. James Yonge, the ancestor of the Yonges of Puslinch, written in the closing years of the seventeenth and the opening years of the eighteenth centuries. Amidst much matter that is purely of personal, and more that is of strictly local interest, there are scattered frequent topographical and other references to matters affecting the county at large. The more important of these I propose to extract; but a brief biography of the writer, a Devonshire celebrity in his day of some little note, and one of the early members of the Royal Society, may fittingly be prefaced.

James Yonge was born at Plymouth, February 27th, 1647, and after a couple of years at the Grammar School was bound by his father, who practised medicine, "for eight yeares to Mr. Silvester Richmond, chyrurgeon of the *Constant Warwick.*" This was on the 14th February, 1657, and three days afterwards he sailed on his first voyage. In May, 1660, he became surgeon's assistant on board the *Montague,* and took part in the expedition to Algiers. A few graphic touches depict the miseries of the young naval surgeon in those days; for he states that the whole drudgery of attending to the injured men fell upon his hands, "besides often emptying the bucketts they went to stool in—a nasty and mean employment, but such as usually chyrurgeons mates formerly did in y⁰ navy." On the return of the *Montague* he was discharged at Portsmouth with five shillings in his pocket, walked to London, and acted for some time as assistant to an apothecary named Clark.

When he returned to Plymouth, his father bound him apprentice to himself for seven years more, the former indentures, of which five years were expired, being given up. His next trip was to Newfoundland in the *Reformation;* and subsequently he went voyages in the *Robart Bonadventure,* of the captain whereof he says : " Hee was a quaker that had been a ranter, and soe high that hee had lost his nose . . . . . —a froward, cross, ill-conditioned fellow as ever lived." In May, 1666, this vessel was captured by a Dutch vessel, and Yonge carried prisoner to Holland. Here he remained, finding the Dutch " damnably insulting," part of the time on parole, until exchanged in March, 1667.

Returning to Plymouth, and picking up some little practice, he took two voyages with the fishing fleet to Newfoundland. In his first he was the only surgeon in the fleet except Edward Cape, of Dartmouth, who, being a very " mean " one, and having no business of his own, was compelled to accept £12 to be assistant to Yonge, the latter clearing altogether about £100. This was in 1668 ; in 1669 he again sailed the Newfoundland voyage. It was so cold, that he entered in his journal : " I am resolved It shall be the last time I will hazard being frozen to death on ye sea ; " but he follows this up with the naïve admission that at " Bay Bulls " he lived a " jolly life with Mr. Richd Munyon, R^d Avent, Caleb Hall, and Mr. Hingston, all chyrurg^o of plym^o, and in o^r mutual caressings spent all o^r liquor and good things designed for the whole voyage." As the fleet was attacked by the small-pox, this voyage proved well-nigh as profitable as that of the preceding year. Nevertheless it was, as he had resolved, his last.

Once more in Plymouth, he married in 1671 an old flame, Jane Crampporne (whose only fault was that she " went to conventicles "), and fought his way into practice, notwithstanding the " private arts " of his rivals. When war broke out with the Dutch, he became surgeon of the hospital established at Plymouth. This was a very profitable post while it lasted. He had 5s. a day, 3s. for each man for medicine, and 2s. 6d. a day for each mate. One mate being allowed to every thirty men, sometimes he drew pay for four, and only kept one ! while there was a good profit also out of the capitation allowance, some of the men running away as soon as they came, and the " scurvy cases " costing little ! When the war ended the hospital was given up ; but it was not long ere Yonge was appointed deputy to the surgeon-general of the navy—James Pearse—whom he had obliged with credit, the pay being 6s. 8d. a man, and 1s. a day for victuals. When, in August, 1677, Charles II. came to Plymouth, and touched for the evil in St. Andrew Church, Yonge by that and "other business recomended to me by y⁰ serjeant [Knight, the king's surgeon] ... gott above 50 lb besides some secrets in chirurgery."

Not long after this—1678—Yonge went to London, being six days on the road, his coach fare from Exeter costing him 30s. At this date there was no stage-coach, apparently, below the western city. Three years later he took his wife to London—she in a coach, and he riding a "Goonhilly" pony— and amusingly records how at Windsor he saw the Duchess of Portsmouth ushered by a French "abbot"—his rendering of *abbè*. "She seems an elegant lady, round face, but noe great beauty." He ungallantly adds: "The Queen came wadling like a duck."

Year by year Yonge's practice grew, and he did some notable cures. Thus in November, 1684, he "was sent for to Sʳ Arthur Harris, whoe had run his man thro' the body with a rapier, which God be praised I cured." In 1685 he became surgeon of a regiment of militia raised by the Earl of Bath. Four years later he gave up the surgeoncy of the hospital; but when the Dockyard was established at Devonport (Dock), he obtained the surgeon's place there. It was not until then that he obtained a diploma at Surgeons' Hall— "free gratis, and without examination, which was never granted to any one before." He did not become a Licentiate of the College of Physicians until 1703. He had written several medical works, of interest and value for their day, but when it was suggested that he should be made a licentiate, rejoined that he was licensed already by the Bishop (!); that it would only be a feather in his cap that would cost more than it was worth; and that he was too old to be catechised. However, being told—reasonably enough—that the Bishop's license was nothing without the College's, that the catechising should be *plain* and the fees *low*, he consented, and paid in all £11 15s. 6d. In November of the same year he was made a fellow of the Royal Society.

Yonge's practice was not only very extensive, covering great part of the Two Counties, but highly remunerative, and he records fees ranging up to a hundred guineas! He amassed a good estate, filled the chief public offices in his native town, including that of Mayor; but finally fell upon evil days. Death removed nearly all his relatives and friends. In 1708, which he calls *Annus tenebrosus*, he lost his only grandson, his daughter-in-law, and his wife. In the previous year he lost a son-in-law and brother; and he had lost sons and daughters previously. With the notice of the deaths of several other dear friends the manuscript closes abruptly:

"How it will end God knows. I am not Fancyfull nor have I any opinion of these critical times [it was his grand climacteric] as some men have, but Its remarkable that this yeare hath proved a troublesome one to me to this 23rd Aug."

He died July 25th, 1721, aged 75.

It only remains to add that Yonge was a sturdy Church and King man, and a sound hater. His opinion of those who differed from him is recorded in such terms as these— "crafty spightfull"—"peevish, talkative Idiot"—"fopp"— "fanatick"—"meer merchant"—"shuffler"—"k—— and hypocrite"—"tool and fool." When Cromwell passes away he "goes to the divell in a tempest." Judge Jeffries is "famously loyal;" and when the Sir Francis Drake of that day dies "a Lingering and tormenting death," Yonge piously adds: "I wish he be not punished worse in yᵉ other life."

I first proceed with the Topographical notes.

Lundy.—"Lunday is a very high smooth Iland, good pasturage, many wild fowle and Rabbets. Its inaccessible but one way, and that narrow and in some places wynding, soe as one man could keep out 1000. It had only a pretty strong house like a Castle, wherein lived a gentleman that retyred from England on accᵒ of Loyalty." [1659.]

Torrington.—"Its a fyne country town, built on a hill stands high, and is mayntayned cheifly by the woole trade."

Barnstaple.—"An ancient corporation lying on a fyne River of late somewhat choaked. Its one of the pleasants towns I ever saw being round on a plaine fayr, streight broad streets and many good houses of old fashion. It was lately a place of very great Trade and hath now many rich men In It, but Bideford hath stoln It all away since the river hath grown shallow, yᵗ ships cannot well come up. theyre is a fine bridge passeth over the River, and cooms to yᵉ town." [1674.]

Hatherleigh.—"A small country town or village."

Bideford.—"Its a narrow Creek, hath a deep River and very rapid, and a good strong Bridge. yᵉ town lyeth on yᵉ side of a Hill is a place of great trade, hath many ships of good bignes and force from 16 to 24 guns. they trade mostly to Newfoundland, thence to Portugall and the Streights. they send a few to Virginia, Newengland, W. India, Ireland, many to Wales and Bristoll; which are theyre great marketts." [1674.]

Lydford.—"A small town where is an old Castle, wch In the late Rebellion was made a prison, but a sad one, God wott; many men perishing there. the people are Rude and ill bread. formerly it was a burrough, sent members to parliament and kept court, but after such a prejudicial way, as it became a saying, *like Lydford law, hang first and judge him afterwards.*"

Brent Tor [Tarr].—"Its a church on a very High hill I beleeve nearest heaven of any church in England. the people are very rude and brutish, though not so Ill as fame and Dr. *Fuller* (English worthyes) makes them viz that they are savage, go naked, lye in vaults on straw, promiscuously like Hoggs, &c."

Nutwell Court.—"Nutwell Sr Henry Fords house, a large stately one a fayre chapell. Its situate on ye River Ex about 2 myle below Topsham."

Topsham.—"A fyne little town pleasant and ye place where ships and goods are generally embarqued or unladen for or from Exon."

Torquay.—Riding to "Tarr Key" between Newton Bushell and Haldon "we ryde over ye Longest bridge in England. Its called Tynebridge, and Is above halfe a myle long."
In a map of Torbay "Tarr" is shown as consisting of a row of five houses. "Tarrkey" has a little pier close by, with two houses adjoining. The pier is directed across the bay.

Paignton.—"Paynton a town on the bottom of Tarrbay was anciently a Borrough town, and as Is sayd held her charter by a whitepot (whence Devonshire men are soe called) which was to be 7 yeares making, 7 baking, and 7 eating."

Totnes.—"A fyne town seated on a Hill by a River hath a fayre delicate church, and a pretty small library of old bookes."

Honiton.—" A fyne country town, sends burgesses, hath a great trade in making lace." Passing through Honiton, April 23rd, 1702, he " saw a very pretty procession of 3 hundred women and girles In good order 2 and two march with three women drummers beating, and a guard of 20 young men on horseback. each of yᵉ females had a white Rod in her hand on the tipp of wᶜʰ was Tossil made of white and blew Ribband (wᶜʰ they said was the Queenes colours) and bone lace the great manufacture of the town. thus they had marched In and about the town from ten in the morning [it was then 8 in the evening] Huzzaing every now and then, and then weaving their Rodds. then they returned at 9 and then break up very weary and hungary." This was on the Coronation day of Queen Anne, and in celebration thereof.

Stowe.—" I waited on my Lord of Bathe to his delicious house *Stowe.* It lyeth on yᵉ ledge of yᵉ north sea of Devon, a most curious fabrick beyond all description."

Axminster.—" A fyne kinde of village pleasantly scittuate on a hill."

Some of Yonge's most interesting notes are connected with the old Newfoundland fish trade, of which Devonshire in his days enjoyed a practical monopoly, and of which he gives us the best description now extant. His first voyage was in 1663, in the *Reformation.* In 22 days they reached the "false bank," and saw many icebergs. He describes a "pretty way" of catching "noddys." " They take a round peece of corke as bigg as a trencher and fasten a peece of lead to Itt and with a fishing lyne let it swim off; to the edges of this cork are fastned divers small hookes with some bayt, as pork flesh &c. this the noddyes swallow and are drawn in. they are good meat and eat but a little fishy."

Monday morning, April 3rd, saw the land, and made for Renoose harbour.

" Found noe ship there, but divers possessors ; we presently hyred a sloop from a planter, and sent the mate with divers men, along shore, to get possessions, (as they call It) the manner is thus. they put a man on shore at every harbour, and at last according to theyre turnes, they take the best place they can of all theyre possessions ; there were 4 at Renoose befor us. only one stuck theyre wᶜʰ was mʳ thomas

Waymouth of Dartmouth, whoe kept 18 boats, In the *Dorcas*, soe o^r master resolved to be his vice admiral, besides us there fished m^r thomas Hammett of Barnstaple, with 12 boats, m^r frances martyn of plym° 4 boats, m^r Scott of barnstaple 6 boats." The planters had 9 boats.

The admiral always wore a flagstaff, Sundays a flag, and was called " my lord;" the vice admiral " my lady."

" Those vessels that had no surgeon agreed with me and gaue 1-6^d 20^d or 2/ a man for the season, which the master paid in fish at the end of the summer." Yonge agreed to share with Cutt, Weymouth's surgeon; and not only arranged for Renoose, but with seven Barnstaple men at Firmoose, four miles off, who had no surgeon, at 2s. a man, to visit twice a week, Wednesdays and Sundays. If any great occasion arose, the men were to be sent to them. The two went alternately. Yonge had a bottle of brandy hid behind a tree, which he marked, and took a dram on his way.

The Barnstaple men preferred Renoose above any other harbour.

" As soon as wee resolved to fish here, ye ship is all un-rigged, and in the snow and cold all ye men goe into the woods, to cutt timber (firr spruce birch being here plentiful) with this they build stages flakes cookeroome and houses. the houses are made of a frythe of Bowes, ceeled inside with rindes, wch look like planed deales, and covered with the same, and turfs of earth upon to keep the sun from Raning them. the stages are begun on the edge of the shore, and built out Into ye sea, a floor of round timbers supported with posts and shores of great timber. ye boates lye at ye head of y^m as at a key, and throw up theyre fish, wch is splitt salted &c, they throw away the heads and sound bone."

Boats had five men, three to catch fish, and two to save them. Boats of three to four tons would carry 1000 or 1200 cod. The master of the boat rowed at the stem against the other two, not only rowing, but steering; and thus the three would row the boat a long way. The masters generally were able men, the midship and foreship men striplings. When they came to the stage head, the foreshipman went to boil their kettle, the other two threw up the fish to the stage with " pews." A pew was a staff with a prong of iron. When thrown up, a boy laid the fish on a table, and they were thus treated :

"On one side of wch stands a header, whoe opens the belly, takes out the Liver and twines off ye head and gutts (wch fall thorough ye stage in to ye sea) with notable dexterity and suddenness. the liver runes thorough a hole in ye table, into a coale or great tubb, wch is thrown into the trayn fatt. This is a great square chest the corners of which are frythed athwart through this the oil soaks and is by tapps drawn out into casks."

The "header" having done, pushed the fish across the table to the "splitter," who with a strong knife split the fish abroad, and with a back stroke cut off the bone, which fell into the sea through a hole. Some would split twenty-four score in half an hour (!) As the fish were split they fell into a "drooge barrow," which when full was drawn to one side of the stage. Here boys piled the fish, and they were salted in heaps three feet high—the salter being a "skilful officer." The fish so lay two or three days; if bad weather, sometimes eight or ten; then they were washed by the boys in salt or fresh water, and laid by them in piles skin upwards on a platt of beach stones, which was called a "horse." After a day or thereabout the fish were next laid on "flakes"— boughs thinly placed on a frame like that of a table. Here they dried. By night or in wet weather they were put up in "faggots"—four or five fishes with the skin upwards, and a broad fish on top. When well dried, the fish were made up into "press pile," where the salt sweated out, and "kerning" made them look white. Next they were dried one day on the ground, and put up in "dry pile," three times as big as the "press pile." Thus they lay until shipped off, when they were dried part of a day, weighed, carried on board, laid and pressed snug with great stones.

The men had no fixed wages, but the owners of the ship had two-thirds, and the men one-third of the proceeds, which was divided into shares according to the men in the ship. Some men had money above the share from the master, but others had much less.

"Soe y^t I beleive in o^r ship, ye master might have 9 shares cleare, the mate 2 shares, and 40^s; spilters [or splitters] 1 share & 3 or 4 lb., header 1 share 20/ salter 5 pounds, sometymes less boats master 1 share and 6 or 7 lb. midshipman share and twenty or 30^s foreshippman 3 lb. or half a share and tenn shillings. boyes Lurgins and such 20^s 30^s or 40^s. the manner of paving ye chyrurgeon is the owners give 5 6 7 or 9 pounds in ye hand towards the chest, the master giveth him a share, and every man giveth half a crown out

of his share, besides which he hath one hundred of poore
Jack from y° whole."

Breaking out of the " arm wrists," coughs, colds, and scurvy
were the chief diseases.   Dry scurvy was often mortal ; acute
scurvy was soon caught, and soon cured by a " few vegitives " of
the country.   It was caused partly by the great mutation of
the weather, which when they came was very cold, and in
July intolerably hot, partly from " aqueous and crude nourishment, colds after hard labour, but mostly from the crude and
foggy air."   Eating the livers of the cods, which were very
delicious, produced bleeding at the nose.   It is quite clear
that Yonge attached no medicinal value to cod liver oil.

In July " y° muscetoes (a litle biting fly) and garnippers
(a larger one) will much vex us sometymes the boyes soe
tyred with labour will steale off, and hide under y° flakes, or
get into the woodes, and sleep 3 or 4 hours soe hearty that
they feel not y° muscatoes, when by y° tyme hee wakes,
shall have swoln him blind and y^n hee knowes not how to
get out."

" When the fishermen lade Its hard work for the shoremen
who rest not above 2 hours a night."   Nor were the fishermen
better off ; they rowed hard, and fished all day, and every
second night took nets and drove to catch herrings for bait.
The first bait was mussels, then herrings, which generally
lasted all the year ; at the middle or end of June they had
capling ; then squid.

In the winter the planters [*i.e.* the residents] got fish,
sawed deal boards, made oars, caught beavers, and fowled.

Such was the way in which Devonshire men fished for cod
at Newfoundland a couple of centuries since.

ON EXPOSURES OF THE SUBMERGED FOREST CLAYS AT PAIGNTON AND BLACKPOOL BEACHES IN APRIL, 1881.

BY ARTHUR ROOPE HUNT, M.A., F.G.S.

(Read at Dawlish, July, 1881.)

THE beach at Blackpool, near Dartmouth, has been the subject of more than one paper read to this Association, descriptive of the gold coins found there some years ago, and of the submerged forest that has been from time to time laid bare when the sands have been removed by violent gales.

So far as I am aware, the portion of the submerged forest that has hitherto come under notice has been confined to the western end only. In his paper on the subject, Mr. Pengelly expressly states that "it (the forest clay) occupied a rectangular area, extending from the small river or stream at the western end of the inlet, about one furlong eastward."* Quite recently, for the first time in my life, I have had an opportunity of seeing the eastern end of the beach denuded of its covering of sand, and exposing what I believe to be the eastern limit of the forest beds, about midway between the extreme points of the beach; and though very unwilling to burden the Transactions of this Association with an unnecessary communication, I have with some hesitation come to the conclusion that the exposure of the Blackpool forest in 1881 should be recorded. On the 19th April, 1881, in company with Mr. G. F. Whidborne, F.G.S., I visited the beach, approaching it by the regular road that terminates in a slipway about midway between the headlands that bound the sands on the east and west. The tide was about half ebb, and the sea, moderately rough, was dashing up against the eastern sea-wall, and further on against the cliffs themselves, rendering it quite impossible to move more than a few yards

* *Trans. Devon. Assoc.* vol. iii. p. 128.

1

SAND of PRESENT BEACH

GREY CLAY

THE FOREST BED

RED SHALY CLAY WITH STONES

SAND of PRESENT BEACH

At Blackpool

2

RED MARL

CLAY

RED BRECCIA

At Preston Lane
Thornton

from the slipway in that direction. This fact alone will be sufficient to prove to anyone acquainted with the locality what an enormous amount of sand had been removed from that quarter. For my own part, I have known Blackpool for at least a quarter of a century, and had never supposed that such a vast expanse of sand could be anything but practically permanent, or that a time would come when the eastern half of the strand would be impassable at half tide, as was now the case.

Now as to the amount of temporary denudation. The wall alluded to, running from the slipway eastwards, is fourteen feet high; a few weeks previously a lady could easily step off the top on to the beach, now it was laid bare to the foundations, breached in two places, and damaged throughout. Owing to the state of the tide, I could see little of the strand to the eastward, but in the extreme eastern corner I could distinguish a patch of sand high up among the rocks, a remnant of an old high level of the beach, but now appearing to have as little to do with the then present strand as though it had been an ancient raised beach. According to one of the local coastguardsmen, the sand from the eastern end had been piled up at the western end, and distributed in the little coves beyond; and we agreed that the enhanced height, when we stood at the western end not far from ordinary low-water mark, was at least sixteen feet; but this is a guess, and a guess only.

Let us now turn to the forest beds exposed on this occasion. The exposure commenced a few yards to the westward of the slipway, and this seems to be the eastern limit of the Blackpool submerged forest. In a well-defined section, projecting from under the sands of the beach, about a foot of fine grey clay rested on a similar thickness of the forest bed, emerging from the sand, and both these beds abutted against, and to a certain extent rested on, a mass of red shaly clay. In this particular section the grey clay had scattered throughout it much carbonaceous matter; but so far as I could judge, composed entirely of grass. In the peaty clay of the section there was a good-sized branch of a tree, but the vegetable *débris* seemed, if I may use the term, to be much muddled together, though lower down on the beach, close at hand, was the stump of a tree, standing as it grew. (See sketch No. 1.) In portions of the forest deposits further west, the verging clay sometimes contained the carbonized grass, and sometimes did not.

The overlying clay was sometimes buff, and sometimes grey, difference so far as I could judge, of colour only, and not of age, though on this point I cannot be positive.   The carbonized grass occurred in the grey clay only, and not in the buff.   The section seems to me an important one, as affording proof positive that the forest beds containing remains of trees are occasionally overlaid by clays of a different age not containing such remains, a fact difficult to prove ; for when deposits of various characters occur at different points in a beach, it is quite impossible to be sure as to their relative positions, or to judge of the beds at one point by the sections found at another.

In 1869 Mr. Pengelly observed that "the lower or seaward portion of the forest area, occupying about two-thirds of its entire breadth, consisted of a brownish drab-coloured clay, which was crowded with vegetable *débris*, such as small twigs, leaves, and nuts.   There were also numerous prostrate trunks and branches of trees lying partly imbedded in the clay, without anything like a prevalent direction." " Towards the uppermost or landward margin of the area, the clay was of a bluish lead-colour. . . . . If a conjecture may be hazarded on this point, I would suggest that the blue clay is perhaps the substratum on which the brown clay lies, and that the latter with its vegetable débris has been stripped off the landward belt of the old forest ground."[*]   This was written in 1869 of a western exposure of the beds, and there is no certainty that either of the beds mentioned could be corre-lated with the 1881 section.

Here may be introduced a note, made on the 19th of February, 1873, when I visited Blackpool, for the purpose of enquiring if any more coins had been found than to examine the beach.

" West (Mr. Newman's gardener) tells me that the beach up to the last gales was uncovered much more than in 1869, so much so that it was bare from the lane to the sands up to the west end.   Under the leaf-bed, which was about two feet thick, was a layer of sand a few inches thick, under which lay the clay of unknown depth.   The sea undermining the sand destroyed the leaf-bed to a considerable extent.   Ever since November the sea has been gradually carrying off the sand, so that latterly, as stated above, half the beach was bare.   The gales of February 1st and 2nd brought it nearly all back.   Previous to that the clay had been more or less exposed for nearly three months.   No coins turned up. To-day many logs of wood, upwards of nine feet in length, were lying under the cliffs, and pieces of the leaf-bed more than I could lift. West said cartloads of wood had been carried away."

[*] *Loc. cit.* p. 129.

Now in this note we have an account of the following series of beds at Blackpool: (1) Clay of unknown depth; (2) a few inches of sand; (3) two feet of leaf-bed. This leaf-bed was very remarkable, and from the large masses scattered about I think West's explanation of the way the sea removed it, by eating away the underlying sand, very probable. To the best of my recollection it was of a light-brown colour, and looked much more modern than the forest peat. Any attempt to correlate the four beds here recorded, and the two observed by Mr. Pengelly, must from the slender evidence at our disposal be unsatisfactory; but it would seem quite clear that we cannot dismiss the Blackpool submerged forest as nothing more than a deposit of clay, containing vegetable remains overlying a clay destitute of such remains; but that there are at least two different deposits of vegetable *débris*; viz., the leaf-bed, and the clay with remains of trees; and that there are at least two other deposits to be accounted for; viz., the overlying grey clay of my 1881 section, and the sand bed mentioned by West. None of the facts observed are inconsistent with the following ascending order; viz., (1) the forest clay with trees; (2) the clay with or without carbonized grass; (3) West's sand bed; and (4) the leaf-bed.

The apparent termination of the forest deposits coincides with the spot where the cliffs begin to rise towards the east. From the nature of the case the forest could not be looked for beyond this point, unless it were possible that there had been no retrogression of the coast-line since the forest era, and it is not possible, as the work is even now in progress. The forest deposits coincide with the embouchure of Blackpool vale; and the rocky platform that forms the base of the eastern part of Blackpool beach is more modern than the forest deposits.

Mr. F. Teage informed me that the sand, a few days before my visit, had been completely removed from the eastern end of the beach, leaving bare a strand of stones and loose rocks, but no "living" rock. Nothing could be more decisive as to the entire denudation of the sand; but what Mr. Teage said was in singular contrast with a piece of information given me by the coastguardsman; viz., that during the past winter so *much* sand was accumulated at the eastern end that he could walk right out to the point. In so short a time had this portion of the beach passed from a state of extreme accumulation to one of perfect denudation, so far as the sand was concerned.

The week after my visit to Blackpool, observing from the sea that the late gales had extensively breached the sea-wall under Redcliff House, I landed for the purpose of examining the submerged forest beds at Paignton Sands, in the hope that some section similar to that at Blackpool might be found to settle the question as to the relative positions of the clays containing remains of trees, and the barren clay occasionally exposed close to the field between Preston Lane and Redcliff House. In 1873 I described an exposure of this bed in a paper to the Torquay Natural History Society. In 1878 Mr. Pengelly and Mr. Ussher referred to it in papers read to this Association. There were three possible opinions on the subject; viz., that the peaty clay rested on the barren clay; that the barren clay rested on the peaty clay; and lastly, that there was no evidence as to their relative positions. These three opinions were expressed respectively by Mr. Pengelly, Mr. Ussher (as I understand him), and myself. As these beds are being rapidly destroyed, and observations are becoming yearly more difficult, I will quote what I wrote of the good exposure visible on the 4th February, 1873: "Under the Red House the sea had to a considerable extent washed away the sand, and laid bare a broad shelf of red sandstone. The north-eastern end of this shelf, that towards Hollowcombe, was covered with a grey tenacious clay, alternating with a blue-black clay, containing remains of trees, as at Torre Abbey. The latter in one place unquestionably rested immediately on the rock, but I could not distinguish any decided superposition between the grey and blue clays relative to each other. Out of the blue clay here I took several angular flints. From the Red House, towards Hollowcombe, the grey clay bed occupied the extreme left, close up to the margin of the fields, whilst the blue was exposed lower down the beach, and soon disappeared beneath the sand. The grey, on the contrary, could be traced continuously to the south-western bank of Preston Lane, where it terminated in a bank about four inches thick. About two-thirds of the distance between the Red House and the lane, the breadth of this bed from the field to the sands was about twelve yards. Further on towards its termination it rises from the level of the sands, and is well seen in a low bluff a few yards from the said lane. Here the bed seems to lie on a red Triassic breccia,* and has over it about two feet and a half of red earth. Near this spot I extracted from it two

---

* This is an error. Mr. Pengelly has since pointed out the nature of this breccia. (*Trans. Devon. Assoc.* vol. x. p. 201.)

pieces of flint and a small pebble, seemingly composed of felspar and quartz crystals." (See sketch No. 2.)

Mr. Pengelly refers in 1878 to this clay and its dip as follows (*Trans. Devon. Assoc.* vol. x. p. 201): " . . . At about 100 feet south of the lane this dip has carried the clay down to the level of the tidal strand, as well as the bed of stones below it. . . . Though the clay becomes gradually thicker, its character is not strongly pronounced until at and beyond 40 feet south of its first appearance at Preston Lane end. . . . From about 100 feet to upwards of 380 feet south of Preston Lane, the clay forms the landward margin of the tidal strand, with a covering of sand and shingle at intervals; but at the distance just mentioned a peaty bed is found overlying the clay. That this bed of vegetable matter extends continuously beneath the sand and shingle, to at least low-water line, and for considerable distances southward, has been placed beyond any doubt, not only by exposures after heavy gales, but also by excavations made by workmen at various times. . . ." On the following page Mr. Pengelly tells us that "on the 24th September, 1877, he was shown an excavation 4 feet deep immediately north of Redcliff Tower in which the bed of peat, 2·75 feet thick, was lying on the characteristic clay."

Mr. W. A. E. Ussher, F.G.S., in a paper immediately following Mr. Pengelly's, speaks of the same locality as follows: "The Pleistocene deposits" (of Paignton) . . . "consist of (*a*) old fluviatile deposits capping the low cliffs between Livermead and Preston Sands; of (*b*) peat, with traces of a submerged forest associated with bluish clay which is exposed on Preston Sands. The peaty matter slopes seaward from under the recent alluvial deposits of Paignton Marsh."

I gather from this description that in Mr. Ussher's opinion the blue clay and peat slopes seaward from under the grey clay, which is alluvial, instead of the grey clay being under the peat; but as he does not specify the exact locality of the alluvial deposits referred to, I may be putting a wrong construction on his words.

On the occasion of my examination of Paignton beach, on the 28th April, 1881, it was in a totally different condition from that obtaining in 1873. The heavy seas that at Blackpool had swept the sands clean away had at Paignton removed them from the lower levels only. The sand was washed high up, leaving the strand at and above low-water mark comparatively level. Thus the higher beds exposed in 1873 were now covered up, whereas the lower portion of

the beach, then covered with sand, was now laid bare. I was
again unable to satisfy myself as to the relative ages of the
true forest clays and the bed of angular stones that caps the
Trias at Preston Lane, and to the northward thereof, and on
which, as already stated, rests the doubtful grey clay.

From the Red House to Preston Lane the red Triassic rocks
were exposed here and there for the whole distance. At places
the forest clays were exposed, but seemed much worn away.
In our place clay with organic remains might be seen over
what appeared to be a small patch of the stone bed, and at
others under it. The clays exposed were red, blue, and grey,
and it was difficult to distinguish their relations to each other.
In no case was there anything like so good a section visible
as the one seen at Blackpool.

There is a singular coincidence between the eastern extremity of the forest beds at Blackpool and of those at
Preston. In each case the beds are observed at a point where
the land on which they lie rises from under them to much
higher levels. At Blackpool the beds in the section observed lie
on the eastern side of an old valley of unknown depth, against
one of whose rapidly rising sides they rest. At Preston also
they lie in a depression, though a shallow one, abutting
against its north-eastern side as it rises toward Hollowcombe
Point. In each case the beds on which they immediately
rest consist of unrolled stones in a red and more or less
clayey matrix, beds in all probability of like character. The
highest bed observed at Blackpool, abutting against the
rising ground, is a nearly barren grey clay; the only bed so
observed at Preston is of a similar character. I cannot help
thinking that this bed at Preston bears the same relation to
the peat as does the similar one at Blackpool; and that it is
of more recent origin than the peat. In this case the clay observed by Mr. Pengelly in the excavation near the Red House
must have been a different bed altogether, and older than either
the peat or the grey clay under consideration. That this is
possible, I gather both from my own observation, and from
the fact that Mr. Pengelly distinctly states that at the time
he saw the exposure he describes, the clay forming the landward margin of the tidal strand was overlaid " with a covering
of sand and shingle at intervals," which sand and shingle
would render it quite impossible for two clays similar in
colour to be distinguished from each other in the absence
of a section in which both could be seen together.

ON GLACIAL CONDITIONS IN DEVON.

BY R. N. WORTH, F.G.S.

(Read at Dawlish, July, 1881.)

OF late years the current of geological enquiry and research has run strongly in the direction of the more recent formations, stimulated largely by the interest which attaches to everything associated with the question of the antiquity of man. Apart from this special connection, no period of recent geology has attracted so much attention as that which is commonly known as the glacial. The relation of Devonshire to this period, or rather the conditions contemporary in Devon with the glacial era of Britain generally, have had their share of notice, but without leading to any very definite conclusions. There appears indeed to be a general agreement that neither in Devon nor in Cornwall are the more pronounced marks of the glacial era to be found. We have, so far as known, no distinctly identifiable scratched or *moutonnees* rocks, no unquestionable moraines, no certain boulder clays; and therefore it is generally assumed that, during the glacial epoch, the conditions of our land surface were not such as to favour the formation of glaciers. This, however, is a very different thing from assuming that we have no evidence of the existence here of glacial climate; and I wish to bring together what seem to me to be abundant proofs of glacial conditions in this county, quite apart from the more marked phenomena of glaciation, which may, or with greater likelihood, may not, exist. There are two ways of accounting for this absence of striæ, moraines, and boulder clays. First, the non-existence of a mountain range of sufficient magnitude to develope a glacier system; second, the submergence of what is now Devon during the glacial epoch. The latter hypothesis is untenable for two reasons. First, because there are, as I hope to show, proofs of glacial conditions inconsistent with the idea of submergence. Second, since in the case of submergence we should hardly fail to have had a number of erratics scattered over the county, whereas only in the North of Devon, in the neighbourhood of Barnstaple, is there any erratic block which can be conclusively attributed to the agency of floating ice.

The class of phenomena to which my attention has chiefly been directed as affording proof of former glacial conditions in Devon, is that connected with certain terminal curvatures of our slate rocks. There are many places in the south of Devon (to which these observations specially apply), and particularly in the neighbourhood of Plymouth, in which the slates are seen to be bent over in the opposite direction to their dip, for two or three feet, and sometimes more, from their upper edges, preserving at the same time in many instances so much cohesion and regularity, that if the upper part of the section only were visible, the rocks would be read in reverse order. This is no merely isolated phenomenon, but one which occurs at frequent intervals over a large area, and generally under closely allied conditions. The best examples I have seen are on the slopes of hills (where our deep sunken Devonshire lanes afford excellent opportunities of observing surface sections), the slates dipping with the hill, and having their edges turned forward, as if by the action of a force which was exerted down the slope, and yet was modified so far—so slow and steady in its operation—that the laminæ were simply curved, rarely broken, and left pretty much in *situ* instead of being carried to the hill-foot.

That such an effect could not be produced by any violent, still less by any cataclysmal action was evident; and this at once disposed of the idea that there had been any torrential rush of water. Such a rush would not have simply curved and then passed over the laminæ, but would have swept the surface smooth and clear of all loosened portions. Moreover, the main pressure of the water would be exerted down the valleys—along the axes—and not transversely, towards them. Much the same reasoning would apply to what is commonly understood as glacial action. The pressure of a glacier would also be chiefly exerted in the line of the valley, but its force would be such that instead of merely bending or breaking the slaty laminæ, it would crush and grind them into mud. Neither to the action of water, nor to that of ice, in its more usual form, can this phenomenon be attributed.

So far back as 1867, Mr. D. Mackintosh, F.G.S., called the attention of the Geological Society to "some striking instances of Terminal Curvature in West Somerset." In his paper he pointed out that among the Quantocks and upon Exmoor he had found numerous instances in which "the laminæ of the ... slate" were "very regularly and distinctly curved backwards;" the most important fact in connection with these sections being : "The bending and curving-back over extensive areas has taken place on perfectly level ground, with a depression instead of an elevation on the side whence the movement must have come. There are indeed instances in which the curving-back has been forced up a slight acclivity." Mr. Mackintosh traced this phenomena "to a powerful and uniformly operating cause," but did not indicate his opinion as to the actual nature of that cause beyond the statement : "It is sometimes difficult to resist the impression that a great weight of *solid* matter, powerfully propelled in a southerly direction, must have curved back the slaty laminæ, and, with an almost geometrical exactness, rounded the forms of the limestone and other eminences of the South-West of England." The natural inference is that the word "solid" points to a preference in Mr. Mackintosh's mind for some form of ice action. The progression southward was deduced by him from the fact that he only found the phenomenon affecting summit levels or southern declivities. He suggested also that the "uniform curving-back would only occur when the laminæ leaned toward the moving agent (or at least did not lean away from it), so as to afford a certain degree of resistance to its action. In other places the planing-off of the edges of the laminæ would either leave them cleanly cut or very irregularly shattered."

In a paper on "The Evidences of Glacial Action in South Devon," read at the Honiton meeting of this Association, Mr. E. Vivian, reasoning on the same lines, cited in evidence "a section of the Devonian slate near Torquay, with the deposits in the Torwood valley;" and also "the condition of the stalagmitic floor and successive fillings in Kent's Cavern." The section was in the Torwood valley. In a deep excavation for buildings "on the summit the laminæ are curved over to the uniform depth of about six feet, in the line of least resistance. . . . This has been assigned by Mr. Godwin-Austen, and other writers, to the action of ice during the last glacial period." The deposits in Kent's Cavern Mr. Vivian suggested had been acted upon by flood water, "on the breaking up of the last glacial period, when the valley . . . . was filled with a glacier or compact snow, the water being derived from the bursting of debacles or ice lakes, and heavy rains at higher levels." * I think, however, the evidence of torrential glacial action in Devon generally of a doubtful character; at all events so far as South Devon is concerned.

The arguments of Mr. Mackintosh were examined by Mr. Ussher, in a paper read before the Geological Society in 1877,† in which, accepting the evident leaning of Mr. Mackintosh towards a land-ice theory, Mr. Ussher assailed it on three principal grounds. First, because the hypothesis ignored the great Pleistocene surface waste of the South-West; second, because instances of terminal curvature occurred in situations which during the glacial epoch must have been too far removed from the suppositional ice bed to have sensibly felt its pressure; third, because the survival of glaciated shales would be inconsistent with the absence of hard rocks presenting *moutonnees* or striated surfaces.

Nevertheless, Mr. Ussher was "inclined to think, that the absence of deposits commensurate with the great Pleistocene denudation experienced by the South-Western Counties may be due in the first place to some powerful denuding agent in the form of a local ice sheet or glacier system, and, in the second, to the great force and volume of surface water likely to be liberated at a close of Arctic severity."

It seems to me that in these suggestions Mr. Ussher himself thus admits the possible existence of sufficient glacial conditions for the production of the phenomenon under review. I agree with him in believing that the glacial epoch in Devon was not one of total submergence.‡ Indeed if it had been, as already noted, we should have had no terminal curvature, assuming that curvature in any way to be due to land ice action.

I agree with Mr. Ussher, too, in rejecting the idea that this phenomena was produced by any oceanic current, water-rush or land slips; for reasons which have been already stated.

Mr. Ussher's own hypotheses of the origin of terminal curvature are three in number.

First he instances "the great and oft-repeated internal movements to which the Palæozoic rocks were subjected." The cause is adequate to produce the most gigantic distortions; but the peculiarly exterior character of terminal curvature, its regularity, and its general correspondence

---

* *Trans. Devon. Assoc.* vol. ii. pp. 357–60.
† *Quarterly Journal Geo. Soc.* xxxiv. pp. 49–55.
‡ The granite boulder at Saunton and its neighbours prove the submergence in glacial time of part of North Devon; but the absence of similar erratics elsewhere in the district is good negative evidence that this submergence was not general.

with contour, point to a less deeply-seated and less remote origin.

The second cause assigned is "the intrusion of wedging frosts between the laminæ of shales, leaving earthy matter filling up the gaps between them, on the approach of summer."

The third "the intrusion of roots acting as wedges."

As I believe the first of these three causes to be too remote; so I must consider the second and third inadequate to account for a phenomenon of such a persistent and extensive kind. They are too partial and irregular in their operation to explain physical changes so extensive and so consistent. I accept Mr. Ussher's arguments against floating ice, ocean current, or cataclysmic action as conclusive. There is left, therefore, only the "land ice" theory; and as Mr. Ussher does not "deny its applicability to some instances of terminal curvature within three or four feet of the surface in glaciated districts," its adequacy is admitted. His objections to its wider acceptance seem to me rather to rest upon a tacit assumption that glacial phenomena invariably proceed in sequence or companionship; and in part may be met by chronological considerations. The relation of terminal curvature to Pleistocene waste depends very much upon the portion of the glacial epoch to which it belongs.

While I use the phrase "land ice theory," it is in a certain modified sense. Many of the objections which apply to the attribution of "terminal curvature" to bodies so ponderous as glaciers, apply also to "ice caps" as usually understood. They do not seem, however, to militate against the operation of a consolidated snow cap slowly moving down the faces of the hills, as the climate of the glacial period gradually ameliorated. I am, therefore, disposed to find in "terminal curvature" a phenomenon allied to some described by Dr. Geikie in his *Prehistoric Europe.*[*] Noting the fact that "sheets of coarse gravel and detritus .... spread often continuously over wide districts in Southern England," with little or no relation to present drainage systems, "frequently very coarse and rudely bedded ... confused and troubled," he quotes the suggestion of Mr. Darwin, that during the commencement and height of the glacial period, great beds of frozen snow accumulated, and that during the summer gravel and stones were washed from the higher land over its surface, and in superficial channels, the larger streams cutting through the snow, and leaving their gravel in lines. Each autumn

* pp. 140, 141.

z 2

the lines of drainage would be filled up, and it would be a mere chance whether the next deposit would follow the same course. Thus, he proceeds, "alternate layers of frozen snow and drift in sheets and lines would ultimately have covered the country to a great thickness, with lines of drift probably deposited in various directions at the bottom of the larger streams." These beds would melt slowly, and the elongated pebbles arrange themselves more or less vertically, and the drift "be deposited almost irrespective of the outline of the underlying land."

I am not at all sure that I have not seen deposits on certain South Devon hill sides—somewhat akin to, but differing from, that commonly known as "head"—in which clayey loam is thickly interspersed with angular fragments of slate, which might, with great probability, be attributed to some such process as this. Be that as it may, I believe that in such a consolidated snow cap we have the true cause of the disputed phenomenon of terminal curvature.

May we not find in the same direction a sufficient explanation of the presumably transported blocks of South Devon, to which attention has been directed by Mr. Pengelly, at Waddeton, Englebourne,* Druid, East Leigh,† Diptford, Morleigh, and Tamerton Foliott ‡; of the boulders in the Dawlish and Ashcombe valleys noted by Mr. Pycroft §; and of similar blocks observable elsewhere?

That the granite boulder at Saunton, on the shore of of Barnstaple Bay, dealt with by Mr. Pengelly in our *Transactions* ‖ was carried by floating ice there is now no question; and Mr. T. M. Hall has shown the existence of other granite boulders, leading to a similar conclusion, at Bickington ¶; but these I think belong to quite another division of the glacial epoch from that with which we have now to deal. Mr. Pengelly has proved ** that the Saunton block is older than the raised beach, which is itself older than our submerged forests, and the accumulation known as "head." The glacial epoch represented by the Saunton boulder is, therefore, separated from the present day by an enormous interval of time, characterised in part by inter-glacial conditions. The relations of terminal curvature to present surface contour, and more recent deposits, forbid our carrying back its origin to so remote a date. Are there then any indications of an Arctic climate in this county, apart

---

* *Trans. Devon. Assoc.* vii. pp. 154–161.   † *Ibid.* ix. pp. 177–183.
‡ *Ibid.* xii. pp. 304–11.   § *Ibid.* v. pp. 75–81.   ‖ *Ibid.* vi. pp. 211-222.
¶ *Ibid.* xi. pp. 428–9.   ** *Loc. cit.*

from the phenomenon under consideration, more recent than the North Devon boulders, to which also terminal curvature may be assigned? We shall find that there are.

The deposit known as "head," to which reference has already been made, and which has been the subject of lengthened investigation by Mr. Godwin-Austen, has long been recognized as indicating "a period of great subærial waste, a more rigid climate," which Mr. Ussher, in his *Cornish Post-Tertiary Geology*, correlates with the second glacial period, and characterises with "considerable snowfall and penetrating frosts,"* the elevation of the land "perhaps culminating in continental conditions"—a state of affairs closely approximating to that which he suggests as the introduction of the glacial period proper, when there were "great quantities of snow accumulating on the highlands (possibly giving rise to a local glacier system)"; the two periods being separated by an epoch of subsidence. To me it seems clear that while the Saunton boulder dates from the older glacial era, probably from its close; terminal curvature with the "head" belongs to the later, possibly originating when the glacial conditions were beginning to lessen in severity.

The "head" of the Bovey Heathfield deposits has distinct Arctic if not precisely glacial characteristics. In association with it, there have been found remains of leaves "from which the dwarf birch (*Betula Nana*) and three species of willow (*Salix cinerea, S. repens,* and *S. amygdalina*) have been determined. These plants betoken a climate much colder than that which at present obtains in Devonshire. Indeed, the little birch is an Arctic plant, which has at present no British habitat south of Scotland," and takes us back "apparently quite to the modern verge of the glacial era."†

We have then absolute and not merely inferential proof, of the existence of an Arctic climate here during the formation of the "head." To the same period I assign the older "clitters" of the Dartmoor Tors—a true "head," peculiar indeed in form, but not in cause, nor essentially in character.

Mr. C. Spence Bate has expressed the opinion that the "clitter" "is formed of masses of granite that have been rent by the action of frost from the surface of the Tor;" and that the peculiar distribution of the blocks of the "clitter" "heaped one upon another, or lodged in the side of the valley at various distances from the Tor," is due to the action of ice "of a character somewhat peculiar to Dartmoor, and of a

* p. 50.
† Mr. Pengelly's Presidential Address, *Trans. Devon. Assoc.* vol. ii. pp. 24-5.

sub-glacial character"—ice coating of the kind known as Hamel or Ammil, enabling the riven blocks to glide "more or less rapidly down the side of the hills until, meeting with an obstruction, many of them were gathered together." *

The "snow-cap" to which reference has been made would, however, supply all the required conditions for the distribution of the "clitters"; and I have seen quite recent instances on the Moor of the rending asunder of granite blocks by the wedging influence of ice between the weathered joint faces. If modern winters can produce these results, those under which the "head" accumulated must have been far more potent; yet, if not in the "clitters," they have left little other trace behind.

There are still two further indices of Arctic conditions in Devon, both associated with our cavern phenomena. Dr. Geikie holds that "the cavern breccia and the numerous large limestone blocks, which overlie the Pleistocene fossiliferous strata in many caves, owe their origin in chief measure to the action of severe frost, and pertain for the most part to the close of the Pleistocene."† Beyond this we have the presence in our cave fauna of such undoubted northern forms as the reindeer, glutton, and cave pika, with the mammoth and woolly rhinoceros.

The evidence as to the condition of Devon during the first glacial period is not as yet very clear; we have proof of partial submergence in the Saunton boulder, but none of general submergence on the one hand, or of the existence of a glacier system on the other. With regard to the second glacial period, however, I think we have proof in the phenomena recited, and particularly in the terminal curvatures of our slate rocks, not indeed of glaciers, but of the existence of a "snow-cap" of great density spreading over the whole surface of the country, and presenting an appearance akin to that of the northern portions of the Hudson's Bay Territory bordering upon the Arctic Circle.

I have been induced to lay this stress upon facts which, to a certain extent, are not only familiar but accepted, because I think that the common incredulity concerning the glacial period in Devon has arisen from too exclusive regard being paid to the more pronounced phenomena, the existence of which in this district has never yet been proved. That the "snow-cap" may have developed in specially favourable localities into small local glaciers is indeed possible, but unlikely.

* *Trans. Devon. Assoc.* iv. pp. 518–19.   † *Prehistoric Europe*, p. 543.

NOTES ON RECENT NOTICES OF THE GEOLOGY AND PALÆONTOLOGY OF DEVONSHIRE.

PART VIII.

BY W. PENGELLY, F.R.S., F.G.S.

(Read at Dawlish, July, 1881.)

THIS, the Eighth, set of *Notes on Notices of the Geology and Palæontology of Devonshire* will be found to traverse—in many cases very briefly—almost all the deposits of the county, from the *Devonian System* to the *Submerged Forests* on our tidal strands.

I. HANDBOOK OF DEVONSHIRE (*Murray's, 9th Edition*, 1879) ON THE GEOLOGY OF DEVON.

It is, no doubt, generally well known that, at least, the seventh and eighth editions of *Murray's Hand Book for Travellers in Devon and Cornwall* were prepared for the press by a late President of the *Devonshire Association,* whose loss we all deplore. He appears to have been strongly impressed with the feeling that, notwithstanding all his care, the book might not be quite accurate, and he requested earnestly that those who might detect errors or omissions would send notes of them to the care of the publisher. (See *Introductory Notice* to 8th edition, 1872.) In a conversation with him soon after the 8th edition appeared, I directed his attention to certain geological statements which appeared to be certainly or probably inaccurate; and it was arranged between us that, instead of preparing *Notes* on them, as on the present occasion, I should give him my opinion on the said statements when he prepared the next edition.

A ninth edition, devoted to Devonshire exclusively, was published in 1879. Whether it was prepared by him I am

not aware; but as the passages referred to remain unchanged,
I propose to take each of them as it occurs in the volume,
together with subsequent passages to the same effect, and,
having offered a few remarks, to proceed thus to the end.   It
is not my intention to comment on passages which do not
strictly relate to Devonshire.

Should it be suggested that it is scarcely necessary to
correct errors on scientific questions in a work of a professedly
popular character, and intended for the million, I would reply,
firstly, that whatever is worth doing is worth doing well, and
that such books should either be silent on such topics, or
should be accurate; secondly, that errors of this kind are
most likely to be harmful when they occur in popular books,
the majority of their readers being at the mercy of the editor
or compiler, whilst most readers of works on special branches
of science are able to take care of themselves; thirdly, that
in correcting these errors I am, under the circumstances,
doing my best to carry out the wishes of my departed friend,
the editor; fourthly and lastly, that in making these corrections I am discharging a duty to myself, inasmuch as the
editor stated that to my *Address on the Geology of Devonshire,*
delivered in 1867, his notice of the geology of the county was
largely indebted. (See *Hand Book,* 9th ed., 1879, p. xxvi.)

The Metamorphic Schists of South Devon.

QUOTATION I.   A.:—"The metamorphic schists forming
the southern angle of Devonshire, the Prawle and the Bolt.
These, which consist of mica and chlorite slates, belong most
probably to the *Cambrian* series; the most ancient sedimental rocks which exist.   Rocks of the same series are
found at the Lizard in Cornwall, at St. David's Head in S.
Wales, in parts of N. Wales, and forming the Longmynd
hills in Shropshire." p. xxvi.

B. "The Cambrian rocks of the Prawle and the Bolt form
. . . . a singularly wild and romantic coast line, and abut, at
no great distance inland, on the Devonian rocks.   *Gneiss is
chiefly noticeable near the Prawle, and mica-slate near the Bolt
Head.*" p. xxvii.

C. "The Prawle is principally composed of gneiss rock."
p. 172.

(The passage I have italicised in Quot. I. B. is almost
identical with one in the 1st ed.—Mr. Paris's—of the *Handbook,* 1850, p. vii.; and Quot. I. C. was copied by the editor
verbatim from that edition.)

There are in the foregoing passages three topics on which remark seems called for :—(*a*) The age of the Metamorphic Schists forming the southern angle of Devonshire.

(*b*) The place of the Cambrian series amongst Sedimentary Rocks.

(*c*) The alleged occurrence of Gneiss at, and near, the Prawle Point.

(*a*) *The Age of the Metamorphic Schists forming the southern angle of Devonshire :*—Three distinct hypotheses on this question have been submitted to geologists:—1st, That which may be conveniently and, so far as I am aware, justly ascribed to Sir H. De la Beche, who, in his *Report on the Geology of Cornwall, Devon, and West Somerset* (1839), says, in his Chapter (II.) on *Mica Slate, Hornblende Slate, and Associated Rocks,* " If we consider our planet as a cooling mass of matter, the present condition of its surface being chiefly due to such a loss of its original heat by long-continued radiation into the surrounding space, that, from having been wholly gaseous, then fluid and gaseous, and subsequently solid, fluid, and gaseous, the surface at last became so reduced in temperature, and so little affected by the remaining internal heat, as to have its temperature chiefly regulated by the sun, there must have been a time when solid rock was first formed, and also a time when heated fluids rested upon it. The latter would be conditions highly favourable to the production of crystalline substances. . . . . We could scarcely expect that there would not be a mass of crystalline rocks produced at first, which, however they may vary in minor points, should still preserve a general character and aspect, the result of the first changes of fluid into solid matter, crystalline and sub-crystalline substances prevailing, intermingled with detrital portions of the same substances, abraded by the movements of the heated and first-formed aqueous fluids.

" In the gneiss, mica slate, chlorite slates, and other rocks of the same kind associated together in great masses, and covering large areas in various parts of the world, we seem to have those mineral bodies which were first formed supporting others in some localities . . . . which contain, as far as we yet know, the remains of animals and plants created when the surface of our planet was first fitted for their existence." p. 33.

The author, without pretending to ignore the hypothesis of metamorphosis, concludes thus :—

" In the absence of any contradictory evidence, it would appear fair to infer that these rocks" [*i.e.* the Schists of the

Prawle and other southern headlands of Devon] "belong to that class which is more ancient than the grauwacke series" [*i.e.* the Silurian and Cambrian]; "and though the mica and chloritic slates of the district may be associated with rocks possessing an arenaceous aspect, even supposing they may be detrital, that they form no part of that series which adjoins them on the north." p. 36.

Whatever may be the value of Sir Henry's cosmological views, it is scarcely necessary to say that, so far as the Schists in question are concerned, his hypothesis finds very few supporters in the present day, and the Editor of the *Handbook* was certainly not one of them.

2. The second hypothesis was, that instead of being in the condition in which they existed at the beginning, the Schists under consideration have undergone metamorphosis; and, though, therefore, of less antiquity than De la Beche supposed, they were of Lower Silurian age, and, perhaps, contained primarily organic remains, all traces of which had been obliterated in the transformation. So far as I am aware, this hypothetical chronology originated with me in 1864. No longer ago than 1877 I sketched briefly the hypothesis, and recorded the fact that I had abandoned it. (See *Trans. Devon. Assoc.* ix. 410.) This, no doubt, is the hypothesis adopted by the Editor of the *Handbook*, who, however, uses the phrase Lower Silurian as equivalent to Cambrian, which, as is well known, some writers are wont to do.

3. The third, and last, hypothesis, was, it is believed, first proposed by Dr. Harvey Holl, and the late Mr. J. Beete Jukes, independently, but almost simultaneously, in 1868. (See *Trans. Devon. Assoc.* ix. 411.) It adopts Metamorphism; but makes the Crystalline Schists of the same age as the Slates, Limestones, and Grits immediately on their north and elsewhere in Devonshire, and which, whilst they belong to the Devonian System of most geologists, are of Carboniferous age according to Jukes. Waiving this question of classification, I have no doubt that this is the true solution of the problem. "About the headland, to the westward of Start Point," says Jukes, "the dark grey or black slate was to all appearance the ordinary Carboniferous (or Devonian) slate of the country. . . . We had not time to visit Prawle Head, but felt certain, from what we saw of the cliffs stretching towards it, that the mica-schist could be nothing more than metamorphosed (Devonian or) Carboniferous slate, as we afterwards found Bolt Head to be." (*Notes on Parts of South Devon and Cornwall*, 1868, p. 44.)

(b) *The Place of the Cambrian Series among Sedimentary Rocks:*—The Editor of the *Handbook* pronounces "The Cambrian Series the most ancient sedimental rocks which exist;" and, in doing so, either forgets the Laurentian Series altogether, or denies their sedimentary character. I venture to assume that it was a case of forgetfulness. The Laurentian System, however, is a good deal to forget. In America, it lies north of the river St. Lawrence; consists of crystalline rocks of gneiss, mica-schist, quartzite, and limestone; is divisible into an Upper and a Lower Series, of which the Upper is more than 10,000 feet thick, and the Lower about 20,000 feet; it covers 200,000 square miles—or more than three times the area of Great Britain; and, beginning at the Cambrian era—the Editor's most ancient sedimentary era—stretches, it is believed, backwards into antiquity almost, if not quite, as far as the Cambrian system does from the present day. Upper Laurentians occur in the Hebrides; but there is no known British equivalent of the Lower Series.

(c) *The alleged occurrence of Gneiss at, and near the Prawle Point:*—There can be little doubt that the Editor of the *Handbook* borrowed the statements that "Gneiss is chiefly noticeable near the Prawle," and that "the Prawle is principally composed of Gneiss rock," from Sir H. De la Beche. I had occasion to call attention to this statement in 1879, and to remark that no one else appeared to have detected it there. (*Trans. Devon. Assoc.* x. 322.) The late Mr. John Prideaux, so far from believing in the gneissoid character of the Prawle, observed, when speaking of the Eddystone reef, "One rock, on which the light-house stands, and that one only, is gneiss; . . . this single rock of gneiss being the only one I have heard of in England." (*Trans. Plym. Inst.* 1830, p. 40).

Mr. Worth, writing on this question in 1880, said "Although Mr. Prideaux was mistaken in supposing that the gneiss of the Eddystone was the only gneiss in England, it has usually been regarded as the only occurrence of that rock in the West of England. I have recently ascertained, however, through the fortunate preservation of portions of the rock removed from the Shovel Reef when the Breakwater Fort was built [immediately within the Plymouth Breakwater], that the rocks there are gneissic also." (*Trans. Roy. Geol. Soc. Cornw.* x. 104.)

The Polperro Fossil Fish.

QUOTATION II.:—"The so-called 'Polperro fossils,' which

were long held to be sponges, have been shown by **Mr.** Pengelly himself to be true fish ('*Trans. Devon. Assoc.*,' 1868)," p. xxviii.

The credit of showing that the "Polperro fossils" were not sponges, but true fish, does not, as the Editor supposes, belong to me; but to the Rev. W. S. Symonds, F.G.S., of Pendock, Herefordshire. I told the story of this determination as long ago as 1868 (*Trans. Devon. Assoc.* ii. 423–442), and have now nothing to add but the expression of regret that arrangements made in 1869 for figuring and describing the numerous specimens in my private collection, have up to the present time produced no result.

The Minor Patches of Granite.

QUOTATION III.:—"Granite occurs in Devonshire and Cornwall in six distinct patches. . . . These six principal bosses are connected with smaller patches, apparently outlying fragments, or links which unite the great bosses. . . . These minor patches are all marked by ruggedness and elevation above the neighbouring slate, and form the eminences of Boringdon Park near Plymouth, Kit Hill and Hingston Down near Callington," &c. &c., p. xxx.

The Editor is undoubtedly in error, (*a*) in speaking of the "smaller patches" of granite as "outlying fragments;" and

(*b*), probably also, in stating that granite forms the eminence of Boringdon Park.

(*a*). An "outlier" is a portion of rock lying, *in situ*, detached, or out, from the main body of the same character and age; to which it belongs; with which it was primarily connected in unbroken continuity; but from which it has become separated through the removal, by denudation, of the portion which once covered the entire intermediate space. The term is only applicable to rocks *formed on the surface*, such as strata, and overflows of lava; and cannot be applied, under any circumstances, to granite, or any other *nether-formed* rock.

If, as the Editor states, and no doubt quite correctly, the smaller patches of granite are links which unite the great bosses of the same kind of rock, the union, though subterranean, is actual, and still as existent as it ever was; and would be laid bare by the denudation of the overlying beds in the interjacent country. In fact, such denudation, were it completed, would destroy the *isolation*, but not the previously *isolated mass*.

Small visible portions of nether-formed rocks may be termed *exposures* or *inliers*, not *outliers*.

(*b*) The Editor, in the passage quoted above, places one of his minor patches of granite in Boringdon Park, in the parish of Plympton St. Mary, about 4·5 miles N.E. from Plymouth harbour, but omits to state on what authority he does so. Sir H. De la Beche (*Report on Cornwall, Devon, and W. Somerset,* 1839), Mr. John Prideaux (*Geol. Surv. of some parts of the Country near Plymo.*, 1830), and Mr. J. C. Bellamy (*Nat. Hist. S. Devon,* 1839), are all silent as to the occurrence of granite there, and nothing of the kind is figured on the Map of the Geological Survey. The statement occurs in the first edition (Mr. Paris's, 1850) and still retains its place, but there can be no doubt that it needs confirmation.

Since this Paper was read, I have been confidently assured by a gentleman living near Boringdon Park, and well acquainted with, at least, its economic geology, that there is no granite rock there.

The Granites of Dartmoor.

QUOTATION IV.:—"There are . . . three distinct kinds of granite found on Dartmoor alone; and these three are by no means contemporaries. It has been conclusively shown that the order in which these granites were projected is: 1, the Schorlaceous Variety; 2, the Porphyritic; and 3, the Elvan. The Porphyritic granite cuts through the Schorlaceous in dyke-like forms, and is itself similarly traversed by the Elvan," p. xxxi.

There is no doubt that the passage quoted above was compiled—almost copied—from me (*Trans. Devon. Assoc.* ii. 16). In 1877 I reopened the question; stated the circumstances under which I had been led to believe in the threefold age of the Granites of Dartmoor; read my recantation; and concluded with the remark, "So far, therefore, as I am aware, the evidence justifies the statement, not that 'the Dartmoor granites are of *three* periods,' but of two periods. The Elvan is undoubtedly more modern than the common granitoid rock of Dartmoor, whether the latter be schorlaceous, or porphyritic, or both." (*Ibid.* ix. 412.)

Fragments of Granite near Crediton.

QUOTATION V.:—A. "The" [New] "Red rocks are more modern than the era of the disturbance of the Carboniferous deposits. This disturbance is generally attributed, and with reason, to the intrusion of the granite. In 1861 Mr. Vicary (whose paper on the subject will be found in 'Trans. Devon. Assoc.' for 1862) detected pebbles of each of the three kinds of granite in the Red Conglomerate at the base of Haldon. They have been found elsewhere in the New Red rocks, especially near Crediton." p. xxxi.

B. "The New Red sandstone in the neighbourhood of Crediton contains numerous boulders and fragments of granite slightly changed." p. 212.

Though not prepared to say whether or not boulders of granite may be found in the New Red Sandstone near Crediton, I am not aware on whose authority the assertion was made, and cannot but express the opinion that it needs confirmation.

The New Red Rocks of Devonshire.

QUOTATION VI.:—"Mr. Pengelly considers that the New Red rocks of Devonshire belong to the Triassic series, and to the Keuper, or uppermost group of the Trias." p. xxxiii.

This passage is not quite a correct rendering of my published opinion, which may be briefly stated thus:—The typical Triassic System, of Continental Europe, is divisible into three sub-systems—*Keuper* or uppermost, the *Muschelkalk*, and the *Bunter* or lowermost. Britain is supposed to have no representative of the Muschelkalk. The Upper New Red rocks of Devon, between the Otter and Dorsetshire, are undoubtedly Keuper; and as there appears to be no physical break in the entire series of Red rocks so largely developed on the coast of south-eastern Devonshire, from Torbay to the confines of Dorset, I incline to the opinion that our Red rocks taken as a whole belong to the Keuper; or, if not, that all three sub-systems of the Trias are represented in Devon. Such was my opinion in 1867, and such it remains. (*Trans. Devon. Assoc.* ii. 21.)

Devonshire Lias.

QUOTATION VII.:—A. "The *Lias* found at the base of the cliff E. from Axmouth . . . but not really occurring in Devonshire or Cornwall." p. xxvi.

B. "The *Lias* . . . is not, in fact, found in Devonshire." p. xxxiv.

The Editor was no doubt in error here, as Lias really occurs in Devonshire; being not only found *in situ* on the tidal strand immediately east of the mouth of the Axe, but yielding fine characteristic fossils. I have little or no doubt of a great "fault," more or less parallel with the existing line of cliff, which has let down the Lias sea-ward there.

Greensand Outliers.

QUOTATION VIII. :—A. "Outlying patches" [of Greensand] "cover the eminences of Haldon and the lower grounds between Chudleigh and Newton, and a small patch occurs on the Black Hill near Exmouth, and another of a few acres near Bideford." p. xxxiv.

B. At "Orleigh Court" [near Bideford, there are] "a few isolated acres of *greensand.*" p. 253.

The first of the foregoing quotations is a verbatim copy of a passage in the 1st edition of the *Handbook* (p. xiv.), and the second is almost identical with another (p. 99).

The Greensands of the Haldons, and of Milber Down between Torquay and Newton Abbot, are well known; but I venture to repeat what I said in 1867 :—" It may be doubted whether all the localities so represented in the Map of the Geological Survey are really true Greensand localities. For example, it is, at least, difficult to find any beds of this age or character at Woodbury Common, near Exmouth, or at Orleigh Court, near Bideford. In each of these districts there is a Supracretaceous gravel, rich in flint and other Cretaceous debris, but probably nothing more." (*Trans. Devon. Assoc.* ii. 22.) I subsequently came to the same conclusion respecting the so-called Greensand "outliers" S. and W. of Newton Abbot, and am not surprised to find Mr. H. B. Woodward of that opinion. (*Geol. of Eng. and Wales.* Foot-note, p. 236.)

The Lignite Formation of Bovey Tracey.

QUOTATION IX. :—" The *Bovey Deposit* is very remarkable and interesting. It belongs to the *Lower Miocene* Series, which, before Mr. Pengelly had determined the age of the Bovey formation, was believed to be unrepresented in England." p. xxxiv.

Here, again, I must disclaim the credit which the Editor gives me. The determination of the age of the Bovey formation was achieved by the Rev. Professor Heer, of Zurich, not by me. The investigation carried on at Bovey Tracey in 1860 may be said to consist of two parts — Geological and Palæophytological; the first was mine, the second, Professor Heer's. He identified the fossils, and by them was enabled to say that the deposit was on the same geological horizon as certain well-known Continental deposits, usually ascribed to the Lower Miocene era. (See *Trans. Devon. Assoc.* i. 29–39, ii. 21.) The decision arrived at by Heer as to the horizon to which the Bovey Lignites and their Continental contemporaries should be referred has recently been questioned, and may be said to be at present before the Courts. (See *Geol. Mag.* April, 1879, New Series, Dec. ii. vol. vi. pp. 152–153; also *The British Eocene Flora.* By John Starkie Gardner, F.G.S., M.G.S. France, &c., and Constantin Baron Ettinghausen, PH.D. Parts I. and II. *Pal. Soc.* 1879, 1880.)

? *Contorted Limestone Strata near Exminster.*

QUOTATION X.: — Mr. Paris said, in the first edition of the *Handbook*, "*Exminster.* In this neighbourhood are stone quarries, and contortions of the strata, which may be observed in the cuttings of the road," pp. 25–6.

In the fifth edition (1865) the words "limestone quarries" are substituted for "stone quarries," and the whole passage, without further change, is repeated (p. 53); and in this "amended" form it reappears in the ninth edition, p. 77.

The passage had escaped me until the autumn of 1880, when my attention was directed to it by a gentleman long and intimately acquainted with the district, and who stated, what I knew very well, and what the map of the Geological Survey confirmed, that there was no limestone in the locality.

To remove the possibility of doubt, Mr. Vicary of Exeter and I made a visit of inspection on 28th of April, when we proceeded to all the quarries and road-cuttings at and near Exminster, Kenn, and Kennford, and found, as we expected, the entire district occupied with the Sandstones and "Conglomerates" of the Triassic System, without a trace of a limestone bed anywhere.

There were no such things, moreover, as "contortions of the strata" to be found. The writer was probably misled by thin layers of "Pan," or concreted sand and iron, which occur in the fine road-sections near the entrance of the asylum at Exminster; but even these could boast of nothing more than a few diminutive plaits, and were provokingly free from the grotesque foldings often seen near Dawlish, and in other Triassic localities, but never to be mistaken for "contortions of the strata."

Kent's Cavern.

QUOTATION XI.:—"Permission to view it" [Kent's Cavern] "must be obtained at No. 1, Victoria Cottages, Abbey Road" [Torquay], "and a guide with a torch will be required. (The charge is 3s., and visitors who desire a good light should provide their own.) . . . There are two entrances to the cavern. . . . The whole may be explored for a distance of 650 ft., when it terminates in a pool of water. The inner chambers are reached by a squeeze through the *Great* and *Little Oven*. The floor . . . was covered with stalagmite about 3 in. thick. . . . In 1864 the British Association appointed a committee to make a thorough and systematic exploration of the cavern. This committee . . . will probably continue their work until the cavern is quite emptied of its contents. . . . *Above* the stalagmite is a surface of black mould, containing relics of human art, ranging through the Roman and pre-Roman periods to a date which corresponds with the earlier state of civilization in the Swiss lake-dwellings—spindle whorls, bone combs, amber beads, and lumps of native copper being common to both. The floor of stalagmite varies from a few inches to 3 ft. in thickness. *Under* the stalagmite is a depth of red clay. . . . In this clay the bones of the following animals have been found—great horse-shoe bat (the only bat which now frequents the cavern), shrew, bear (ursus priscus and ursus-spelæus), badger, stoat, wolf, fox, hyæna (spelæa), cave-tiger (there is some doubt whether this *Felis spelæa* was a lion or a tiger), wild cat, *Machairodus latidens,* a very large and destructive feline animal, 3 voles, hare, rabbit (*Lagomys spelæus*), mammoth, rhinoceros (tichorhinus), fossil-horse, hippopotamus (major), great Irish deer, gigantic round-antlered deer, and red-deer. Of these the remains of bears and hyænas are most numerous, and a quantity of fæcal remains . . . besides marks of gnawing on many of the bones indicate that the cave was frequented at one time, perhaps, by bears, and at another by hyænas. . . . Arrow heads and knives of flint (all of the palæozoic type) occur in all parts of the cave, and throughout the entire thickness of the clay. In what was called the *Vestibule,* near one of the external entrances, occurs (under the stalagmite) a layer of black soil . . . called the *Black band.* In this have been found more than 326 flint implements, chips, and bone tools. . . . The whole of the relics, human and animal, belong to the Post-pleiocene period." pp. 155–157.

The somewhat lengthy quotation just given incites me to offer a few remarks on the following topics :—

(*a*) Permission to view the Cavern.
(*b*) The Cavern Entrances.
(*c*) The Extent of the Cavern.
(*d*) The Pool of Water.
(*e*) The Ovens.
(*f*) The Extent of the Researches by the Kent's Cavern Committee appointed by the British Association.
(*g*) The Civilization denoted by certain relics found in the Cavern, compared with that indicated by objects found in the Swiss Lake-dwellings.
(*h*) " Native Copper."
(*i*) The Cavern Deposits.
(*j*) Animal Remains in the Cave Earth.
(*k*) The most prevalent Animals.
(*l*) Occupancy of the Cavern by Bears and Hyænas.
(*m*) Flint Implements.
(*n*) Implements in the "Black Band."

(*a.*) *Permission to View Kent's Cavern:*—The history of guide-book information to those desirous of "permission to view the Cavern" is not a little amusing. In 1846, the late Sir L. V. Palk gave, and restricted, to the Torquay Natural History Society, during their brief exploration of it, power of granting permission to view Kent's Hole. This was duly announced in the local newspaper, and finally, after the power had ceased, found its way into the guide-books, and remains in the latest editions of some of them to this day. Indeed, guide-book-instructed visitors apply still, and in no inconsiderable numbers, at the Society's rooms, for "permission to view," though the power to grant it expired in 1846.

A very efficient guide was appointed many years ago, who lived at No. 1 Victoria Cottages, Torquay. He died, however, as long ago as 1871, and since that date no one dwelling at the address just given has had any thing whatever to do with the Cavern. Nevertheless, the latest edition of the *Handbook* under notice, published no longer ago than 1879, continues to send would-be visitors to No. 1 Victoria Cottages.

Without pursuing this subject further, it may be of service to state that the existing arrangement (1881) is this :—Kent's Cavern may be seen on applying at the Cavern itself any time between 10 and 5 o'clock, daily. The guide, who is in constant attendance, will provide lights. Arrangements for visits before or after these hours, can be made with the guide, George Smerdon, 2 Happaway Place, Torquay. Mr. Smerdon was for many years the foreman of the labourers who, under the Committee, explored the Cavern.

(b) *The Cavern Entrances :*—The Cavern was always known to have two entrances, both of them on the eastern side of the Cavern-hill, not far apart, and both available. During the researches by the Exploring Committee appointed by the British Association, three additional entrances were discovered and reported in 1871 (See *Rep. Brit. Assoc.* 1871, p. 7), and in 1879 two others were discovered and reported (See *Rep. Brit. Assoc.* 1879, p. 145). The five thus newly-discovered are all closed with rubbish, so that practically it is still the fact that there are two, and only two, available Entrances to the Cavern.

(c) *The Extent of the Cavern :*—The statement that "the whole may be explored for a distance of 650 feet" may be taken as a rough estimate if the principal Chambers and Galleries only are contemplated. 650 feet, however, will fall very far short of the truth if all the off-shoots and ramifications—some of them of great importance and interest—are included.

(d) *The Pool of Water :*—The *Handbook* makes the Cavern terminate in a pool of water, but why the said pool should be supposed to be the termination it is not easy to make out, as a chamber at some distance from it is certainly further from the Entrances, and more decidedly on the opposite side of the hill. The pool, it may be added, ceased to exist as long ago as February, 1869, as was duly reported (See *Rep. Brit. Assoc.* 1869, pp. 196–9).

(e) *The Ovens :*—Instead of "The inner chambers *are* reached by a squeeze through the Great and Little Oven," the *Handbook* might have said The inner chambers *may be* reached by a squeeze through the Great and Little Oven. There never was the least occasion to go through the Ovens. Not one out of every five visitors ever went through either of them probably, and certainly not one out of fifty went through the Little one. One of the results of the recent exploration, however, is to render it eminently improbable that one out of ten thousand will go through either of them in future.

(*f*) *The Extent of the Researches by the Kent's Cavern Committee appointed by the British Association:*—When the Exploring Committee began their researches it was hoped that they would be able to continue their work until the Cavern was quite emptied of its contents. This hope, however, was based on the assumptions that the extent of the Cavern was less, and that the deposits were not so deep, as they proved to be. On the 19th June, 1880, after the continuous daily labour of nearly sixteen years, and the expenditure of very nearly £2,000, the work was discontinued, not because the Cavern was quite emptied of its contents— for to do this would probably require another period of sixteen years, as well as £2,000 more—but because it was feared there would be a difficulty in raising funds ; and also because the low-lying deposits yielded but few specimens of any kind.

(*g*) *The Civilization denoted by certain relics found in the Cavern, compared with that indicated by objects found in the Swiss Lake-dwellings:*—According to the *Handbook* some of the articles found in the Black Mould above the Stalagmite belong " to a date which corresponds with the earlier state of civilization in the Swiss Lake-dwellings—spindle whorls, bone combs, amber beads, and lumps of native copper being common to both." I have met with this conclusion elsewhere, but it has always appeared to me that it was not borne out by the evidence. When it is remembered that at the date of the Swiss Lake-dwellings, intercourse between different parts of Europe must have been more difficult and less frequent than between the antipodes in the present day, that the comparatively high civilization of Greece and Italy coexisted with gross barbarism on their very borders, that, as beads and in other forms, amber has not yet ceased to be used for ornamental purposes, that, without entering at present into the question whether anything of the kind was ever found in Kent's Cavern, native copper would be gladly used by existing British coppersmiths, and that spindle whorls were used in the British Isles up to a late period of the last century, if not in the present, it seems most unsafe to infer contemporaneity from the presence of such articles in Switzerland and in Devonshire. In fact the arguments, if "trusted home," might awkwardly prove the Swiss Lake-dwellers contemporaries of savages in various parts of the world in the present day. Be all this as it may, it must not be forgotten that the spindle-whorls and other articles mentioned in the *Handbook* belonged to the most modern deposit in the Cavern, and did not extend back to the times of extinct mammals.

(*h*) "*Native Copper*":—It is, no doubt, true that Mr. Mac Enery, the early and famous explorer of Kent's Hole, says, "In the same stuff" [= the *Black Mould*] was picked up a lump of copper ore much oxydised which the late Mr. P" [hilips] "analyzed and found to be pure virgin ore." (*Trans. Devon. Assoc.* iii. 220.)

Again, he says "2 lumps of virgin copper ore were pressed together into a cake on a large flat stone." (*Ibid.* 296.)

Again, the Cavern Committee appointed by the British Association, speaking of objects they had met with in the Black Mould, say in their First Report, "In this connection may be mentioned a lump of metal which, from its general appearance, would be termed copper ore, but from its interior, a small portion of which has been exposed accidentally, it is probably native copper, or a mass of metal which has been smelted." (*Rep. Brit. Assoc.* 1865, p. 20.)

There is probably little or no doubt that the lumps of copper mentioned by Mr. Mac Enery were of the same character as that found by the Committee. Nevertheless, I am satisfied that they were not native, but smelted, copper. It will be observed that the Committee speak of their "find" doubtfully. After the Report just quoted was published, they submitted their specimen to experts, who at once pronounced it to be smelted; and when recapitulating the substance of their First Report, the following year, the Committee speak of it as "a large fragment of a plate of smelted copper." (*Ibid.* 1866, p. 2.) A smaller specimen was subsequently found.

(*i*) *The Cavern Deposits*:—According to the *Handbook* the Cavern Deposits were, in descending order, Black Mould, Stalagmite, and Red Clay (= Cave-earth). These were, no doubt, the only Deposits known in the Cavern for some time after the late exploration was begun; but as long ago as 1868 the Committee reported the existence of two lower and older Deposits—a Crystalline Stalagmite underlying the Cave-earth, and a mechanical accumulation, to which they gave the name of Breccia, which in its turn underlay the Crystalline Stalagmite. (*Rep. Brit. Assoc.* 1868, p. 51.) These older beds disclosed a more ancient Fauna of which Man was also a member, but, judging from his Industrial Remains, a Man ruder far than his descendants or successors, as the case may be, of the Cave-earth.

(*j*) *Animal Remains in the Cave Earth:*—The list of animals, of which relics were found in the Cave-earth, given in the *Handbook*, includes those mentioned by Professor Owen (*Hist. Brit. Foss. Mam.* 1846), and was obviously copied by the editor from a list I compiled thence in 1868. (*Trans. Devon. Assoc.* ii. 502–3.) So far as is known, however, no relics of the Great Horse-shoe Bat, the Shrew, the Stoat, the Rabbit, or the Hippopotamus were found in the recent exploration. It is not intended to cast any doubt on any of the foregoing forms, with the exception of the Hippopotamus, which I believe may be safely stated not to have belonged to the Cavern fauna. Indeed, it is, to say the least, very doubtful whether there is satisfactory evidence that remains of *Hippopotamus major* have been found anywhere in Devonshire. (*Ibid.* iii. 485–6.)

With regard to the Bat, Col. Montagu was of opinion that there were two species of Horse-shoe Bat—the Larger and the Lesser; and that *both* occurred in considerable abundance in Kent's Hole, which the Colonel spoke of as a "dark and frightful region." (*Ibid.* ii. 475.)

Few palæontologists, it is believed, would say, with the *Handbook*, that "there is some doubt whether . . . Felis spelæa was a lion or a tiger," or hesitate to pronounce it a lion; indeed, there is great reluctance to admit that it differed specifically from the existing *Felis leo.*

Current opinion sets also against the idea that the so-called Fossil horse was separated by any sharp line from the existing horse, *Equus caballus.*

The *Handbook* list is also defective. It was known as long ago as 1869, that remains of Glutton, Brown Bear, Wild Bull, Bison, Reindeer, and Beaver had also been met with in the Cave-earth.

(*k*) *The most prevalent Animals:*—The statement of the *Handbook* that "the remains of bears and hyænas are most numerous," requires amplification to be made true. When corrected it would stand thus:—The remains of Bears were most numerous in the Breccia—the most ancient of the Cavern deposits with which we are acquainted; but the remains of Hyænas were most prevalent in the Cave-earth. In fact, no traces of Hyæna occurred in the older deposit.

(*l*) *Occupancy of the Cavern by Bears and Hyænas:*—Taken in the sense stated in the immediately preceding Note it is true, no doubt, "that the cave was frequented at one time . . . by bears, and at another by hyænas;" but this was not the sense intended by the *Handbook*, the editor of which appears to have had the idea that during the Cave-earth era the Bear and Hyæna took "turn and turn about" in their Cavern home. It cannot be doubted that the Cavern was the home of Hyænas during the Cave-earth period; that, with the exception of Man, no other large animal occupied it during any part of that time; that when Man left it he took possession, and was expelled whenever the Human occupant returned. (*Trans. Devon. Assoc.* xii. 641–2.)

(*m*) *Flint Implements:* — According to the *Handbook*, "Arrow heads and knives of flint (all of the palæozoic type) occur in all parts of the cave, and throughout the entire thickness of the clay." This statement contains an incautious expression and a positive blunder. It may be very much doubted whether a single flint "arrow-head" was found in the Cave-earth. "Flint tool," or "Flint implement" is a safer term, and is amply sufficient as evidence of Human Antiquity. Moreover, the "Arrow-head" assumes the existence of contemporary bows and arrows.

The *blunder* spoken of is the word "palæozoic," which was no doubt a slip of the pen, being written where the writer meant "palæolithic." Yet this slip has appeared in at least two editions.

(*n.*) *Implements in the Black Band:*—"In this" [the Black Band], says the *Handbook*, "have been found more than 326 flint implements, chips, and bone tools." The truth is, however, in the *Black Band* were found 366 flint and chert implements, chips, and cores; and 3 bone tools.

Windmill Hill Cavern, at Brixham.

QUOTATION XII.:—"The results" [of the exploration of Windmill Hill Cavern, at Brixham] "no doubt prove the very high antiquity of the human race in this district—flint implements, similar to those found in the drift, having been discovered in the loam at the lowest levels, associated with the remains of hippopotamus, cave lion, hyæna, and other subtropical animals. Deeply imbedded in the stalagmitic floor was found a fine pair of antlers of the reindeer, showing a vast change in the climate between these periods. . . . The external entrances are high above the present bottom of these" [adjacent] "valleys; but there is little doubt that the valleys, when the wild animals and as wild 'cave men' frequented the district, were filled to a considerable height by a blue clay, in which grew a forest, affording shelter and protection. The specimens found in this cavern are at present in the apartments of the Geological Society, London." p. 163.

The foregoing quotation invites remark on—
(a) The Flint Implements;
(b) The Hippopotamus;
(c) The Cave Lion and Hyæna;
(d) The Reindeer Antlers;
(e) The Blue Clay and the Forest; and
(f) The Present Whereabouts of the Specimens.

(a) *The Flint Implements:*—With one probable exception, the flint implements found in the Brixham Cavern were *not*, as the Editor says, similar to those found in the drift. They were *flake*-implements, not *nodule*-implements, and, though as certainly palæolithic, were somewhat less ancient than the drift specimens.

The excepted tool belonged primarily, it is believed, to the oldest of the Cavern beds—known as the Gravel bed, or Fourth bed—and had been dislodged and redeposited in the less ancient bed—known as the Third bed—in which, with this exception, all the tools were flake-tools. (See *Trans. Devon. Assoc.* vi. 833, 849. Nos. 6 and 8.)

(b) *The Hippopotamus:*—No trace of Hippopotamus was found in the Brixham Cavern. Nor did the labour of almost sixteen years disclose any relic of it in Kent's Cavern. Indeed, it must be admitted that there is at present no satisfactory evidence that this great Pachyderm ever existed in Devonshire. (*Ibid.* iii. 485–6.)

(c) *The Cave Lion and Hyæna:*—Though both the Cave Lion and the Cave Hyæna were met with in the Brixham Cavern neither of them occurred "at the lowest levels," that is, as I understand the phrase, in the lowest of the Cavern beds—known as the *Gravel bed*, or *Fourth bed*. The bones found in this lowest bed were exclusively those of Bear, Horse, Ox, and Mammoth. (*Ibid.* vi. 814.)

The Hippopotamus would, no doubt, be good evidence of a subtropical climate, but in his absence, the species that were actually represented cannot be held to betoken necessarily a climate warmer than that which obtains at present in Devonshire ; and it may be doubted whether they are inconsistent with a colder one, especially as the Reindeer and Grizzly Bear were amongst them. (*Ibid.* vi. 828).

(*d.*) *The Reindeer Antlers :*—When the *Handbook* spoke of "a fine pair of antlers" it doubled the truth. It was not a *pair* of antlers, but *one* antler only ; no doubt a "fine" one.

Again, it was *not* deeply imbedded in the stalagmite, but, to repeat the description I gave of it in 1874, "it was found lying *on* the Stalagmite, firmly attached to, but not embedded in, it ; indeed, some portions of it were completely free from more than the slightest incrustation." (*Ibid.* 809.)

(*e*) *The Blue Clay and the Forest :*—The speculations that the Brixham Valleys in the era of the Cave men were filled to a considerable height ; that Blue Clay was subsequently deposited in, at least, the principal—"the east-and-west"—valley ; and that a Forest once grew in this Blue Clay, as a soil, in the said principal valley, are, I believe, exclusively mine ; but the *Handbook* has distorted my views ; as it makes the Forest, the Blue Clay, and the Cave Men all belong to one and the same period, whereas the Forest was certainly, and the lodgement of the Blue Clay probably, not only subsqeuent to the era of the Cave men, but subsequent to the excavation, or, probably, re-excavation of the valleys. Perhaps, I cannot set forth my opinion better than by repeating the words which, according to the shorthand writer, I employed in a lecture at Manchester in 1875, in an attempt to take the audience, by successive steps, back into antiquity from the present day:—"At least two thousand years ago the relative level of sea and land in Britain was the same as now. Prior to that was a period during which the whole of Western Europe subsided, at least, sixty-seven" [I can now say seventy-five] "feet—even supposing that trees grew at high-water level. Prior to that was the growth of the forest. Prior to that was possibly—but I will not insist on this" [order]—"the era of the deposition of the blue clay in which the forest grew. Prior to that was the period of the re-excavation of the valleys to a depth of from seventy to a hundred feet lower than it was when the Cave earth " [= *Third bed*] " was carried into the Cavern. Prior to the commencement of this excavation men were living in Devonshire. That is, step by step, the conclusion to which I have come respecting the changes in the *local* geography since the Cave men of Devonshire lived." (*Science Lecture delivered in Manchester. Seventh Series*, p. 155.)

(*f*) *The Present Whereabouts of the Specimens:* — The specimens—both archæological and palæontological—found in the Brixham Cavern, were lodged "in the apartments of the Geological Society, London," as soon as the exploration was finished, that is to say in the summer of 1859. There they remained until 1872, when the Report of the Cavern Committee was read to the Royal Society, after which, but how long after I cannot definitely state, the osseous remains were sent to the British Museum; and the Human Industrial remains, to the "Christy Museum," 103, Victoria Street, Westminster. Those at the British Museum were temporarily lodged in an underground cellar, where I saw them in January, 1875. What has been their subsequent history I am unable to state; but I have no doubt that they are still at the Museum, and not in the apartments of the Geological Society.

Since this Paper was read, I have seen many of the bones, well-displayed for public investigation, in the New Museum, South Kensington.

The Ash Hole, near Brixham.

QUOTATION XIII. :—"Nearer the old barracks" [on Berry Head, South Devon] "is the cavern called the *Ash Hole* . . . Below the stalagmite here the bones of hyænas and other animals have been discovered." p. 163.

Having transcribed and reprinted every thing, so far as I am aware, that has been written on the Ash Hole (*Trans. Devon. Assoc.* iv. 73–77) I feel assured that the Editor slipped into an error when he assigned hyænas to that Cavern. The only mammals represented by the bones found in it appear to be Man, Mammoth, Badger, Pole-Cat, Stoat, Water Vole, Rabbit, and Reindeer.

QUOTATION XIV.:—"The " [Submerged] "forest and the " [Raised] "beaches " [of Barnstaple Bay] "indicate that there have been two distinct movements of the coast—a subsidence, and an upheaval. It seems probable that the elevation preceded the depression; but this is not quite certain." p. 256.

In various papers I have discussed the question of the relative ages of the Raised Beaches and Submerged Forests of Devonshire, and as long ago as 1865 expressed the belief that the Beaches were the older, stating at the same time the grounds on which the belief rested (*Trans. Devon. Assoc.* i. pt. iv. 33.) Still, it remained to be no more than a *belief* until 1878, when I produced what was regarded as "*proof* of what had previously been considered *probable* by most, that in Devonshire the Submerged Forests are more recent than the Raised Beaches." (*Ibid.* x. 202.) It must be admitted that the proof applied strictly to Torbay only, but on the assumptions that all the Raised Beaches in Devonshire are of one and the same age, and all the Submerged Forests of the county are also of one and the same age—and the organic remains found in them respectively are in harmony with this—it may now be said that it is certain that the last elevation preceded the last depression.

II. NEWTON, Mr. E. T., on BRITISH GLUTTONS (=*Gulo luscus*). 1880.

In a Paper entitled *Notes on the Vertebrata of the Pre-Glacial Forest Bed Series of the East of England.* By E. T. Newton, F.G.S., *Part II. Carnivora*, in the *Geological Magazine* for September 1880, Decade II. Vol. vii., pp. 424-7, the author remarks, "The occurrence of the Glutton in Britain was first intimated by MM. Boyd Dawkins and Sanford in the year 1866 (Pal. Soc.), but it was not until 1871 (*Q. J. G. S.* vol. xxvii. p. 406) that the former gentleman described the lower jaw of this species, which had been obtained by M. M. Hughes and Heaton from the cave at Plas Heaton. Prof. Busk subsequently recognised the remains of the Glutton among the bones found by the Rev. J. M. Mello in the Cresswell Crag Caves (*Q. J. G. S.* vol. xxxi. 1875, p. 687)," pp. 424-5.

The following is the passage by MM. Boyd Dawkins and Ayshford Sanford to which Mr. Newton, no doubt, refers:—
"Genus *Gulo*. Species *Gulo luscus*, Linn.—The wolverine or glutton (*Gulo luscus*), the great pest of the fur-hunters of North America and Siberia, has left traces of its presence in

Britain in Banwell and Bleadon Caverns " [in Somersetshire],
"and also in a cavern at Gower" [in Glamorganshire].
British Pleistocene Mammalia.   Part I. (Pal. Soc.) pp. xxi-
xxii. 1866.

It will be seen, therefore, that this intimation of the
Glutton in Britain, which Mr. Newton believed to be the
"first," points to the Mendips and to South Wales as the
localities in which the "finds" were met with.   There was,
however, an earlier intimation of a British Glutton; and it
was made by a native of Devon, and of a Devonshire fossil,
as I propose now to show :—

The Natural History of South Devon, by J. C. Bellamy,
Surgeon, 1839, contains a description of the famous Ossiferous Cavern at Yealm Bridge, about seven miles E.S.E. from
Plymouth, and not more than one mile from Mr. Bellamy's
residence at Yealmpton.   "In the summer of 1835," says
Mr. Bellamy, "having casually heard of certain bones, met
with in the progress of working a limestone quarry at Yealm
Bridge, I undertook to investigate their value, and the circumstances under which they occurred." p. 86.

When it is remembered that the author was not only
describing his own observations and discoveries, but that he
was a surgeon and a practised naturalist, it will be seen that
his statements have more than ordinary value.

When enumerating the various kinds of animals represented by the relics he investigated, he says, "Next in
frequency of occurrence to the bones of the *hyæna* and *fox*
were those of the *horse, ox, deer, sheep, and rabbit.*   After
these ranks the *rhinoceros*, whilst the bones of the *elephant,
wolf, pig, glutton, bear*, and *duck* were extremely rare." p. 89.

Again, when writing of the bones of *mice* amongst the
remains, he remarks, "Looking also to the wise provisions of
Nature in regard of food, we see that these small creatures
would hold a decided relation to the predaceous habits of
the animal I have ventured to designate glutton, from its
evident similarity to our *mustelo gulo*" [= *Gulo luscus*]. p. 94.

Finally, in his *Catalogue*, he places the *Glutton* amongst
the *Carnivora* of the cavern. p. 102.

Mr. J. C. Bellamy, M.R.C.S., was born at Plymouth in 1812,
and died 1854 (Mr. Worth, in *Trans. Plym. Inst.* iv. 294);
and, so far as I am aware, was the first to identify, as well as
to announce, the remains of *Glutton* amongst British fossils.

The cavern at Yealm Bridge, it may be added, is not the

only one in Devonshire which has yielded a relic of the *Glutton*, as is shown by the following passage in the Report, in 1869, by MM. Boyd Dawkins and Ayshford Sanford, on the animals found in Kent's Hole, by the Committee to whom the exploration of that famous mausoleum was entrusted. Speaking of *Gulo luscus*, the authors just named remark, "A single os innominatum of a nearly full-grown Glutton indicates the presence of this rare mammal in the Cave-earth. Although it belonged to an animal not quite adult, it agrees almost exactly in size with that of a fully-grown male from Sweden." (*Rep. Brit. Assoc.* 1869, p. 207.)

This statement was not so early by three years as that by the same authors, mentioned by Mr. Newton, and quoted already; but it was earlier, by two years, than the announcement of the discovery of relics of Glutton in the cave at Plas Heaton, near St. Asaph, North Wales.

It must not be supposed that the whole, or anything like a tithe, of the Kent's Hole relics have been finally examined. It is, therefore, possible that the os innominatum may not be the only indication of Glutton amongst them.

III. GEIKIE (*Dr. James*) ON KENT'S CAVERN, 1881.

Prehistoric Europe, A Geological Sketch, by James Geikie, LL.D., F.R.S., 1881, contains a few brief Notices of Kent's Cavern, some of which invite *Quotations* and *Notes*.

A Bone Pin.

Quotation I :—" A bone pin (3¾ inches long), which was found in Kent's Cave, is supposed by Dr. Evans to have been employed as a fastener of the dress. It bears a high polish, he says, as if from constant use." p. 17.

The description of the pin alluded to by Dr. Geikie will be found, with a good figure of the specimen, in Dr. J. Evans's *Ancient Stone Implements, Weapons, and Ornaments of Great Britain*, p. 460 (1872). Dr. Evans, however, compiled it, no doubt, from the following passage in the *Third Report of the Committee for Exploring Kent's Cavern, Devonshire*, which I drew in 1867 : " The second bone-tool from the Cave-earth is a well-finished pin, 3¼ inches in length. It was found on the 3rd of January, 1867. The pin is well made, almost perfectly round, tapers uniformly from the head to the point, and has a considerable polish. It is, perhaps, more than probable that it was an article of the toilet, and hence the polish it

bears, instead of having been designed, may have been the
result of the constant use to which it was put. It may probably be said of its original possessor, as it has been said of
a more modern savage,

> 'The shaggy wolfish skin he wore,
> Pinned by a polished bone before.'"

(*Rep. Brit. Assoc.* 1867, p. 31.)

In copying from Dr. Evans, Dr. Geikie slipped into a little
error; the pin, as stated in the Report, as well as by Dr.
Evans, was 3¼, not "3¾" inches long.

The Main Result of the Recent Exploration of Kent's Hole.

Quotation II.:—"After such caves as that at Brixham
(Torbay), and the still more famous cavern near Torquay,
called Kent's Hole, had been subjected to long and careful
examination under the auspices of the Royal and Geological
Societies, and the British Association, even the most sceptical
hammerer threw aside his doubts. But while giving all due
credit to the Exploration Committees for their admirable and
exhaustive work, we must not forget that the main result of
their labours has been merely to verify and confirm the conclusions arrived at by the earlier investigators. It is needless to say that those who have taken the most active share
in cave-exploring are the readiest to admit this; and none
more willingly than Mr. Pengelly, who has personally super-
intended the investigations carried on in the two famous
Devonshire Caves." pp. 76–77.

Dr. Geikie says in effect, in the passage just cited, "that
those who have taken the most active share in Cavern
exploring are the readiest to admit" that "the main results
of their labours has been merely to verify and confirm the
conclusions arrived at by the earlier investigators." If by
"the conclusions arrived at" he mean the simple proposition
that man dwelt in Britain, and in Western Europe generally,
at the same time as the Mammoth and his extinct contemporaries, I, for one, am amongst "the readiest to admit
this;" but if he mean that during the recent exploration of
Kent's Hole no new facts were discovered which of necessity
enhanced the value of human antiquity as inferred from any
previous exploration of that Cavern, or, indeed, of any other
in Devonshire, I not only decline "to admit this," but feel
called on to show that it is incorrect.

At the beginning of the exploration in 1865, it was
neither known nor suspected that there was any deposit in

the Cavern of greater antiquity than that termed the *Cave-earth*, which was everywhere rich in remains of Mammals—some extinct and others not—the Hyæna being the most prevalent form; and that with them were found flint implements and other relics of human industry. In 1868, however, the explorers began a series of discoveries which ultimately disclosed a much earlier chapter of the Cavern history, and enabled them to announce—

1. That underlying the Cave-earth was a very thick sheet of stalagmite, which from its peculiar structure was termed *The Crystalline Stalagmite.*

2. That underneath this again was an older Cave-earth, to which the name of *The Breccia* was given.

3. That these previously unknown and unsuspected deposits—and especially the Breccia—contained remains of mammals, almost exclusively Bears, but without any trace or indication of Hyænas.

4. That in this pre-hyænine Breccia there were undoubted flint implements, but comparatively rude, massive, and unsymmetrical, and unaccompanied by any other indication of man.

In short, the recent exploration of Kent's Hole informed the world that men vastly more ancient than those known to the most advanced of "the earlier investigators" of the Devonshire caverns had lived in that region; and that, judging from the facts, they were much ruder, and belonged to an earlier British fauna.

Duration of Rev. J. Mac Enery's Kent's Cavern Researches.

QUOTATION III :—" The Rev. J. Mac Enery, who between the years 1825 to 1841, seems to have explored Kent's Cavern with great assiduity." p. 77.

We learn from Mr. Mac Enery's MSS. that his first visit to the Cavern was made "in the summer of 1825" (*Trans. Devon. Assoc.* iii. 208), and that he began his systematic researches "towards the close of 1825." (*Ibid.* 444.) It was unfortunately not his practice to date his visits, memoranda, or discoveries; but he did record a visit "On the 14 Augt. 1829." (*Ibid.* 295.) There is reason for believing that all his important discoveries were made considerably before that date. His "Plate F" states that the famous canines of *Machairodus latidens* were found "Jany. 1826 in diluvial Mud mix'd with Teeth and gnaw'd Bones of Rhinoceros,

Elephant, Horse, Ox, Elk, and Deer with Teeth and Bones of Hyænas, Bears, Wolves, Foxes, &c."

The following brief summary of facts compiled from the *Literature of the Cavern*, shows not only the progress of the work in 1826, but that during that year Mr. Mac Enery made presents of specimens with a liberality which necessarily betokened very numerous discoveries:—

Amongst the papers of the late Sir (then Mr.) W. C. Trevelyan, the following two memoranda occur:—"Torquay, 27th February, 1826. Saw Mrs. Cazalet's collection of bones from Kent's Hole. Very fine. Bear, Tiger, Wolf, Hyæna, Elk, Ox, Horse, Elephant, Rhinoceros, Flint Knives. Mr. Mac Enery's bones. Very fine. Horse and Rhinoceros numerous. . . ."

" 28th. Spent 7 hours in Kent's Hole with four men, and found bones and teeth of Bear, Tiger, Rhinoceros, Elephant, Hyæna, Horse, Deer, Elk, and Flint Knives, under Tufa; *i.e.* Stalagmite from the side or wall of Cavern." (*Trans. Devon. Assoc.* x. 146.)

Mrs. Cazalet, mentioned above, was a co-religionist and friend of Mr. Mac Enery; and her fine collection is known to have been made up, at least, very largely of the presents he made her from time to time.

The Baron Cuvier, writing Mr. Mac Enery, on 6th March 1826, said "My co-worker, Dr. Buckland" [then in Paris] " has remitted to me the fossil bones from Kent's Cavern that you have much wished to send me." (*Ibid.* iv. 475–6.)

Later in the same month, Dr. Buckland, writing from Paris, said, " I have sent the gnawed fragments you gave me to Scotland." (*Ibid.* iv. 475.)

In May 1826, Mr. Mac Enery presented a series of the Cavern specimens to the Yorkshire Philosophical Society, and in a letter addressed to the President, on the 3rd of that month, he said "similar collections to the one now forwarded have been transmitted to Cuvier for the Paris Museum, to Professor Buckland for the London G " [eological] " Society, and to Bristol." (*Ibid.* iv. 472–5.)

Writing Sir W. C. Trevelyan, on " 19 June 1826," he said, " I have found, ten feet below the surface, a perfect skull, with teeth entire, processes perfect, of a full grown Hyæna. . . .

" I have added considerably to my Elephants, Rhinoceros, Elks, Deer, and Bears. I have some teeth of the last of great size. A large Tiger's, perhaps Lion's, jaw now embellishes my collection.

"The open chamber, where you excavated so successfully, has long been exhausted. In my Idol Cave" [which he called sometimes the Wolf's Cave] "I have made the most important discoveries, which I am daily following up with ardour.

"Some plain account I intend to publish when the Professor" [Buckland] "returns. Mrs. Buckland proposes doing us the honour of a visit, when I hope to have collected abundant materials for her pencil." (*Ibid.* x. 144.)

On "December 6th, 1826," Dr. Beeke, the Dean of Bristol, who resided frequently at Torquay, wrote Sir W. C. Trevelyan as follows:

"Mr. Mac Enery has arranged his Kent's Hole collection very neatly. . . . He appeared to think that very little remains worth digging for. He has prepared the materials for an account of the Cave, so far as his own observations extend, but waits for Dr. Buckland's advice and assistance, and no drawings have yet been made of the most important bones." (*Ibid.* x. 145.)

Mr. Mac Enery issued a circular announcing his intention to publish his *Cavern Researches*, in one volume quarto, to be illustrated with thirty plates; and he stated that specimens of the plates might be seen at Cole's Library, Torquay. This circular is unfortunately not dated; but Mr. Northmore, writing on "4th June, 1832," mentioned a prospectus which Mr. Mac Enery had circulated "about five years since," thus giving 1827 as, at least, its approximate date. (See Blewitt's *Panorama of Torquay*, 2nd ed., 1832, p. 110, or *Trans. Devon. Assoc.* ii. 480.) This harmonizes with the previous statements and dates, and the whole appear to leave little room to doubt that the bulk of Mr. Mac Enery's Kent's Cavern work was done, and all his important discoveries were made, by the end of 1826. That he visited the Cavern occasionally, perhaps not unfrequently, after that date there can scarcely be a doubt. Many an uncertain point would require verification or reconsideration; and he might be not disinclined to treat his friends to a day's digging, as he probably did "on the 14th August, 1829," when he "visited the cave accompanied by Master Aliffe." He may even from time to time have devoted a few consecutive days to small recesses overlooked here and there, but I am strongly of opinion that after 1826 such labours as he undertook in the Cavern were of a very desultory character.

Be all this as it may, I am confident that when I visited Kent's Hole first, about Midsummer, 1834, his researches had been for some time abandoned. Mr. Mac Enery died on 18th February, 1841, and I venture to suggest that in the quotation from Dr. Geikie which I have placed at the head of this Note, the words "between the autumn of 1825 and the end of 1833" may with safety and advantage be substituted for the words "between the years 1825 to 1841."

The first discovery of Flint Implements associated with extinct Mammals in Caverns.

Quotation IV.—" It was in . . . Kent's Hole that the first discovery in cave deposits of the association of human implements with the remains of the extinct Mammalia was made. This important 'find' occurred to the Rev. J. Mac Enery." p. 77.

The following is Mr. Mac Enery's statement respecting the first "flint blade" he found in Kent's Hole: "In the summer of 1825 Dr. Buckland, accompanied by Mr. Northmore of Cleve [near Exeter] visited the Cave of Kent's Hole in search of bones. I attended them. Nothing remarkable was discovered that day excepting the tooth of a Rhin" [oceros] "and a flint blade. This was the first instance of the occurrence of British relics being noticed in this or I believe any other cave; both these relics 'twas my good fortune to find, but it was not the first case of the discovery of organic remains. . . . I am assured that at a still earlier period Mr. N" [orthmore] "had collected some single teeth of Hyæna. To this ardent inquirer therefore the priority of discovery belongs. . . Dr. Buckland had also on two former occasions made a search there, but owing to the want of leisure for pushing his inquiries, nothing new was developed." (*Trans. Devon. Assoc.* iii. 441. See also p. 443.)

Mr. Northmore states that the first discovery of Mammalian remains in Kent's Cavern—that to which Mr. Mac Enery refers—was made by him on "21st of September, A.D. 1824" (see Blewitt's *Panorama of Torquay,* 2nd ed. 1832, p. 116; or *Trans. Dev. Assoc.* ii. 482); and he adds soon after, "I should mention that Professor Buckland some short time afterwards (for I immediately communicated to him my discovery) continued the search in the same spot, and found a British flint-knife, and some bones and teeth, if I recollect right, of the bear and rhinoceros."

In the absence of further evidence, it might be concluded .that the flint which, as we have seen, Mac Enery claims to have found, and that which, according to Mr. Northmore, Dr. Buckland discovered, were, perhaps, one and the same. The following fact, however, shows that they were distinct "finds," and that Dr. Buckland's was the earlier. There is in the *Monthly Magazine*, or *British Register*, for March, 1825, under the heading of *Provincial Occurrences, Devonshire*, an article entitled, *Organic Remains in Kent's Hole and Chudleigh Cave*, in which the following statements occur: "Mr. Buckland has been on a visit to Lord Clifford, in company with Sir Thomas Acland, and has examined the cave at Chudleigh. . . . The Professor has also visited Kent's Hole, and commenced his operations in the two caves where Mr. Northmore had made his original discoveries; among other treasures we hear that Mr. Buckland discovered the blade of a knife belonging to the ancient Britons, made of flint, about two inches and a half long, and half an inch broad." (*Op. cit.* lix. 190–1; see also *Trans. Dev. Assoc.* iii. 194.)

This, no doubt, was the "British flint knife" which, according to Mr. Northmore, in the passage cited from him above, was found by Dr. Buckland. Indeed, I am not without strong suspicions that Mr. Northmore was the writer or inspirer of the article in the *Monthly Magazine*. As the *Magazine* was published on the first of each month, it is clear that Dr. Buckland's "flint knife" was found in February, 1825, or earlier, and could not have been the "blade" mentioned by Mr. MacEnery, as he states that his first visit to Kent's Hole was made in the "summer of 1825" (*Trans. Dev. Assoc.* iii. 208), and he adds that it was his "first visit to a scene of this nature."

It is clear therefore that he was in error in supposing that his "flint blade" was the first instance of the occurrence of what he called "British relics being noticed in" any cave; Dr. Buckland had certainly anticipated him.

All this, however, may be utterly foreign to Dr. Geikie's idea; for, returning to the first passage quoted above from Mr. MacEnery, it will be observed that it does not state in what deposit the "flint blade" was found, or whether or not it was met with beneath a sheet of stalagmite, or whether or not it was found lying with, or near, or under the same conditions as, the tooth of rhinoceros found during the same visit. In short, the statement under notice does not justify the assertion that it was a "discovery in cave deposits of the association of human implements with the remains of the extinct mammalia," and the "find" may not be that to which Dr. Geikie alluded.

That Mr. Mac Enery met with flint implements soon after beginning his systematic researches, "towards the close of 1825," may be inferred from Sir Walter C. Trevelyan's Memorandum of 27th Feb., 1826 (quoted on page 384 above), where "flint knives" are mentioned as forming part of Mrs. Cazalet's collection, and which had, no doubt, been given to her by Mr. Mac Enery. Sir Walter's Memorandum of the following day shows, 1st, that he also found flint knives during his seven hours' work; and, 2nd, that they occurred under the stalagmite. All this, however, does not necessarily imply an "association of human implements with the remains of extinct mammalia," and I am by no means convinced that Mr. Mac Enery was himself a believer in such an association as I understand Dr. Geikie to mean.

His mention of flint implements is frequent, but it is not always easy to determine his exact meaning. The following is at once his fullest and clearest statement on the question :

" I first discovered them " [the flint implements], he says, " mixed with Human bones in loose carbonaceous mould within half foot of the surface near the mouth—the crust " [of stalagmite] "had been broken up and its remains were visible in flakes scattered through the mould—When we descended about three feet the loose black mould gave place to a firm bed of a dirty red color the surface of which displayed the singular phenomenon of flint instruments intermingled with fossil bones !—About 1 foot lower down they disappeared, but the fossil bones continued constant to the red marl " [= Cave-earth]. " Thus far their existence in the present state of the cavern was determined—Still the difficulty remained unsolved—viz. whether the flint did actually occur under the unbroken floor of stalagmite—and whether they originally co-existed before their position was invaded. In this spot the crust " [of stalagmite] " was confessedly disturbed and removed, and in the other localities, tho there was no doubt of their existence under the crust and touching the mud " [=Cave-earth], "there was still a doubt whether the crust had been dug thro for ovens and pits, the stalagmite in those places assuming rather the character of a conglomerate, than a regularly stratified bed; but now there is no longer a question of their actual presence under the stratified unbroken floor of stalagmite. All along the lobby-like passage it has been already remarked that they abounded, but under ambiguous circumstances; it now became imperative to continue on excavating towards the end till we should fall in with the crust at its undisturbed point, and we succeeded

. . . Having cleared away on all sides the loose mould and all suspicious appearances, I dug under the regular crust—and flints presented themselves to my hand—this electrified me. I called the attention of my fellow laborers (Master Aliffe) and in his presence extracted from the red marl" [=Cave-earth] "arrow and lance heads. I instantly proceeded to the excavation inside, which was only a few feet distant in the same continuous line, and formed part of the same plate" [of stalagmite]; "the crust is about 2 ft. thick steady, the clay" [= Cave-earth] "rather a light red, about 3 in" [ches] "below the crust the tooth of an ox met my eye—I called the people to witness the fact—which I extracted before M. Aliffe—and not knowing the chance of finding flints, I then proceeded to dig under it, and at about a foot I dug out a flint arrow head. This confirmation I confess it startled me. I dug again, and behold a second, of the same size and color (black). I struck my hammer into the earth a third time, and a third arrow head (but white) answered to the blow. This was evidence beyond all question. I then desisted, not wishing to exhaust the bed, but in case of cavil leaving others an opportunity of verifying my statements . . . This is the region of the flints—Here they were deposited before the addition of the plate" [of stalagmite] "above." (*Trans. Devon. Assoc.* iii. 328–330.)

There can be no doubt that Mac Enery had fairly satisfied himself that the flint implements occurred below the sheet of stalagmite. The following passages from him will show what was his opinion respecting their depth in the Cave-earth immediately underlying.

"The crust" [of stalagmite], he says, "is thickest in the middle; towards the sides it thins away. For opening the excavation the same means were employed as to break up a mass of ancient masonry. Flint blades were detected in it at all depths even so low as to come in contact with the fossil bones and their earthly matrix" [= Cave-earth] "but never below them." (*Ibid.* p. 247.)

Again, "Having described the form of these singular flints . . . it is our next duty to state the position they occupied in the caves under consideration. Excepting the solitary instance of their occurrence in the disturbed shingly covering of the loam" [= Cave-earth] . . . "their uniform situation is intermediate between the bottom of the stalagmite and the upper surface of the loam" [= Cave-earth] "forming a connecting link between both; one extremity has been generally found inserted in the loam, the other protruding upwards into the

stalagmite above. . . . They have likewise been found, tho
rarely, at a still lower depth dispersed irregularly thro the
loam promiscuously with the other relics . . . but the greatest
depth that I have been able to trace them down has been no
more than a few inches below the surface of the mud "
[= Cave-earth] thro which while it was yet in a state of
fluidity they sank down." (*Ibid.* 326–7.)

Again, "Dr. Buckland is inclined to attribute these flints
to a more modern date, by supposing that the anc[t]. Britons
had scooped out ovens in the stalagmite, and that through
them the knives got admission to the diluvium " [= Cave-
earth] " . . . Without stopping to dwell on the difficulty of
ripping up a solid floor, which, notwithstanding the advantage
of undermining and the exposure of its edges, still defies all
our efforts, tho commanding the apparatus of the quarry, I
am bold to say that in no instance have I discovered evidence
of breaches or ovens in the floor, but one continuous plate of
stalagmite diffused uniformly over the loam " [=Cave-earth].
(*Ibid.* p. 334.)

Finally, Mr. Mac Enery, in the following citation, closes
what he had to say respecting the Flints:—"Thus have I
given the result of long and anxious investigation of the
circumstances of these curious relics.   It cannot be urged
that I have been from the commencement indifferent or in-
attentive to their localities; the circumstance of my discovering one on the occasion of my first visit with Dr. B.
and Mr. Northmore " [See p. 386 above] "forcibly called my
attention, and ever afterwards directed it to the examination
of their situation in the ground.   Nor can it be with justice
objected that in my present explication of this anomaly I
have been influenced by a desire to advance or support a
favorite Theory.   Those from whom I have the misfortune to
dissent on this subject are aware of my reserve and re-
puguance I long showd to admit their artificial origin; the
clearest evidence exhibited by the uniformity of their shape
and fracture, and thus differing from natural flints, and their
I had almost said identity with the Mexican and Druidical
Reliques determined my assent.   From this period more
especially, March 1827, I attached still greater importance to
their presence, carefully, cautiously, and deliberately scru-
tinized and noted their localities, and looked for fixed and
settled grounds for building my opinion upon, but this
evidence is not perhaps yet complete; future inquirers may
hereafter light on some more decided document to define
their epoch." (*Ibid.* p. 339.)

I believe the following to be a fair and correct summary of Mr. Mac Enery's opinion respecting the various points in the history of the Cavern from the time of the extinct mammals whose relics were found in it, down to the close of the formation of the sheet of stalagmite. It is not necessary for me to say here whether I believe the said opinion to be correct:—

1. That the Cavern was tenanted by various species of carnivorous mammals, some of which are now extinct.

2. That bones of the said mammals, as well as of others taken in by the tenants, lay strewed on the Cavern floor, which consisted of the limestone rock *in situ*, with accumulations, here and there, of fallen fragments of the same rock.

3. That the waters of the Noachic Deluge rushed into the Cavern, carrying with it a vast quantity of mud and stones, in which the bones already mentioned, as well as the bodies of the living animals it surprised in the Cavern, were confusedly entombed.

4. That there was but one such rush of water.

5. That after the waters had abated, men, who made and used flint implements, entered the Cavern, leaving some of the said implements here and there, almost all of which lay on the surface of the mud, whilst a very few sank below the surface, but never to a depth exceeding one foot, and rarely more than three inches.

6. That after this, came a period during which man, as well infra-human animals, rarely entered the Cavern, and a sheet of Stalagmite was formed, covering up the mud with the bones lodged throughout its entire depth, and the flints lying on, or but little below, the surface.

7. That no remains of extinct mammals occurred in the Stalagmite.

If this summary be accepted, it will follow that, as hinted already, Mr. Mac Enery did not believe in such an "association of human implements with the remains of extinct mammalia" as implied the contemporaneity of man and the said mammalia. According to his view, the mammals were antediluvian, the men were postdiluvian, and the association, if such it can be called, of the bones of the one with the tools of the other was very partial and merely accidental.

The first to announce explicitly the thorough inosculation of Human Industrial Remains with the bones of extinct mammals in Kent's Cavern, was Mr. Godwin-Austen, so far as I am aware.   He had made some independent researches in the Cavern, and states that they "were constantly conducted in parts of the cave which had never been disturbed." In a Paper *On the Bone Caves of Devonshire*, read to the Geological Society of London in 1840, and incorporated subsequently in his *Geology of the South-east of Devonshire*, he says, "Human remains and works of art, such as arrowheads and knives of flint, occur in all parts of the cave and throughout the entire thickness of the clay; and no distinction founded on condition, distribution, or relative position can be observed, whereby the human can be separated from the other reliquiæ.

"The obvious inference from this fact is at variance with the opinions generally received . . . there is not a single appearance which can suggest that the cave has been used as a place of sepulture."   (*Trans. Geol. Soc. Lond.* 2nd Ser. Vol. vi. Part 2, p. 444; or *Trans. Devon. Assoc.* ii. 498.)

The Amount of Time represented by the Stalagmites of Kent's Cavern..

Quotation V :—When speculating on the amount of time represented by the Stalagmites of Kent's Cavern, Dr. Geikie says, "At present the rainfall near Torquay is about 35 inches, but in former times it may have been three or four times as much, or even greater still.   With a rainfall of 140 inches the stalagmites would accrete, other things being equal, four times as rapidly." p. 82.

Dr. Geikie has somewhat understated the present rainfall at Torquay.   My rain-gauge, kept ever since 1st January, 1864, has been examined daily at 9 a.m., the rain it contained has been carefully measured and registered, and the annual aggregate has averaged 38·55 inches.

But let this pass; and let us, without discussion, accept the hypothesis that in former times the Torquay rainfall may have been four times greater than it is now.   The conclusion Dr. Geikie arrives at thence, presupposes,

1st. That the rainfall being four times greater the water entering the Cavern would also be four times greater.

2nd. That four times as much Cavern-water would precipitate four times as much carbonate of lime.

I demur to each of these propositions, and for the following reasons :—

1. The annual number of "wet-days" at Torquay ever since 1st January, 1864, has averaged 189, or more than half the number of days in the year. It is obvious, therefore, that the hypothetical four-fold increase in the amount of rain could not be attended by even a *two-fold* increase in the number of wet days; hence the mean wet-day rate of rain would be greatly increased, and, instead of being ·20 inch as at present, could not under any circumstances be less than ·41 inch, and would probably be much more than that; in other words, the rains would be much more violent than at present.

Meteorologists will, I believe, endorse the proposition that, all other things being the same, gentle rains have a much greater power of penetrating the earth than those of a comparatively violent character. I visited Kent's Cavern almost every day during nearly sixteen years, and the ample opportunities there afforded of testing it satisfied me that this principle is perfectly trustworthy. One example, however, must suffice at present. In 1875 there was a very wet period, extending from 16th September to 18th November, with very few rainless days. Before October began the ground was thoroughly saturated with water, and there was a considerable drip into the Cavern. On the 19th of that month the rainfall was no less than 1·78 inch, a very heavy fall for the district, but especially noteworthy from the fact that it all fell in two hours; yet this fall produced no appreciable effect on the amount of water which entered the Cavern. It happened, however, that on the 26th of the same month there was almost as great a fall—one amounting to 1·67 inch—but it differed from the former in that it occupied the entire twenty-four hours, falling all the time at a sensibly-uniform rate. The augmentation of the quantity of water entering the Cavern in this case was very marked. The violent rain of the 19th did *external* work, its principal effect being to furrow the surface; the gentler rain of the 26th scarcely affected the exterior, it penetrated the soil and did *internal* work. With such facts before me I must decline to admit that if the rainfall were four times greater the water entering the Cavern would be anything like four times greater, especially as, from the configuration of the surrounding country, the Cavern water must be entirely supplied by the small Cavern hill.

2. But if four times as much water *did* enter the Cavern, would it necessarily or probably precipitate four times as much stalagmite? Before attempting to answer this question,

consideration must be given to the character of the water, and its behaviour after its ingress; and to these ends I venture to submit the following propositions, which, it is believed, will be at once admitted :

1. That the water entering the Cavern takes in the carbonate of lime, of which, at least mainly, the stalagmite is formed.

2. That the water obtains the carbonate of lime from the roof and walls of the Cavern whilst passing through them.

3. That the water holds the carbonate of lime in *solution*, not in *suspension*.

4. That pure water is practically incapable of dissolving carbonate of lime.

5. That a definite volume of water can hold in solution only a definite limited quantity of carbonic acid.

6. That this power of dissolving acid increases with an increase of the pressure to which the water is subjected, but that the operation of pressure need not be regarded in the case of Kent's Cavern.

7. That the power of dissolving acid decreases with an increase of the temperature to which the water is exposed.

8. That a definite volume of acidulated water can hold only a definite limited quantity of carbonate of lime in solution, which quantity is a maximum when the water is saturated with the acid.

9. That acidulated water saturated with carbonate of lime passes into a supersaturated state on exposure to heat, or a dry current of air, or both.

10. That rain water acquires carbonic acid from the atmosphere, and from decomposing vegetable matter on or in the soil.

11. That at the moment of entering the Cavern the water is not supersaturated with carbonate of lime.

12. That whilst *within* the Cavern the water, in order to form stalagmite, must become supersaturated with carbonate of lime.

13. That the stalagmite is formed exclusively of the supersaturating surplus of carbonate of lime, which is precipitated in various solid forms.

14. That all the water entering the Cavern finally leaves it again.

15. That the escaping water carries out of the Cavern all the carbonate of lime it is capable of holding in solution.

16. That water holding carbonate of lime in solution, but

not in sufficient quantity to cause saturation, may pass through a Cavern without precipitating any stalagmite.

17. That water saturated with carbonate of lime on entering a Cavern, would pass through it without precipitating any stalagmite, provided the internal atmosphere were humid, and also colder than that of the exterior.

To the foregoing propositions I venture to add the following, for which my own long-continued observations and experiments enable me to vouch :—

18. That the temperature of Kent's Cavern remains constant through day and night, summer and winter, from year to year, and stands at 51°5 Fahr. the mean annual temperature of the exterior.

19. That there is not at present, nor was there during the formation of the less ancient, or the more ancient, Stalagmite, any current of air passing through the Cavern.

20. That the atmosphere of the Cavern is always humid; the most careful observations with the most delicate thermometers having always failed to disclose the least difference between the wet and dry bulbs.

But now to return. Four times as much water, all other things being the same, would require for saturation four times as much carbonic acid; and without this the water might enter the Cavern and escape from it without precipitating *any* carbonate of lime. It is necessary, therefore, to show that the requisite amount of carbonic acid was, at least, probably forthcoming during the hypothetical *pluvial* period, and this, so far as I am aware, has not been done or attempted.

But apart from this; four times the quantity of water entering the Cavern would probably, at times, cause a stream to flow through it, and thus a great portion of the carbonate of lime, even if sufficient for saturation, would be carried out just as fast as it was taken in.

If, however, the water were never sufficiently abundant to form such a stream, it would rarely succeed in being so small in amount as to allow of that slow and intermittent drip which is essential to the formation of the sub-conical bosses—to say nothing of the long thin pillars, and thinner " paps "—which, both in the more ancient or Crystalline, as well as in the less ancient or Granular, Stalagmite, is so marked a feature in Kent's Cavern. The ingress of so much water would compel any stalagmite which might be precipitated to take the form of approximately horizontal sheets.

In short, I decline to admit that a fourfold rainfall would

send four times more water into the Cavern; or to admit
that four times as much Cavern-water would precipitate four
times as much stalagmite.

If my readers are not tired with reading it, it may be well
to repeat here what I have often said and written elsewhere;
viz., "I have always abstained from, and cautioned others
against, insisting that the thickness of the stalagmite is a
trustworthy chronometer."

It will be seen from the 20th proposition, enunciated
above, that there can be no evaporation of water in Kent's
Cavern, except in the chambers into which the external
entrances open; and yet this is commonly regarded as, at
least, the principal cause of the formation of stalagmite.
Thus, Professor Tyndall, in the first of his Course of Six
Lectures "On Water and Air," delivered at the Royal
Institution, at Christmas, 1879, says, "If you wander, as I
have done, in limestone caves, you will usually find in each
cave a stream of water which has washed out the limestone
and produced the cavern; and sometimes you see from the
roofs of those caverns .... stalactites hanging down. These
are due to the water which has entered into the fissures in
the roof above, and percolated through the roof and dissolved
some of the limestone, and made its way into the cavern,
where the water is in part evaporated; and in consequence
of the evaporation, the solid matter has been deposited, and
you find that, as it evaporates, these beautiful stalactites
grow longer and longer from the roof towards the floor.
Then drops of water fall from the end of the stalactites
upon the floor, and there the water is still further evaporated,
and a heap is produced called a stalagmite." (*Journ. of Science.*
Third Series, ii. 51, 1880.) This is, of course, strictly
applicable to all caverns through which a current of air
passes, but it is not applicable to Kent's Hole, where there is
no such current, and the air is always humid.

Unless I have misread the phenomena, the formation of
stalagmite is there confined mainly, if not exclusively, to the
winter months, when the Cavern temperature being above
that of the exterior, the expulsion of carbonic acid gas from
the water which enters is the result; and this, in its turn,
causes the precipitation of the carbonate of lime.

*A Recent Cake of Stalagmite in Kent's Hole, six inches in
thickness.*

Quotation VI.:—[In Kent's Cavern], "overlying a superficial layer containing remains of Romano-Saxon times, we

find a thin interrupted cake of stalagmite which nowhere exceeds six inches in thickness and is generally much thinner, or absent altogether." p. 82.

Suspecting that Dr. Geikie had quoted from memory when he wrote the words just cited, I directed his attention to the passage, and requested to be informed whence it was taken. In his reply, dated "19th April, 1881," he stated that, being away from his books and papers, he could not at that time say what authority he had for the statement.

The only explanation that occurs to me is that he had, when writing, allowed his memory to mix a passage from the *First Report* by the Cavern Committee with one from their *Third Report*. The following are the passages alluded to :— " Even of those " [blocks of limestone which have fallen from the roof, and] " which lie on the surface, there is conclusive evidence that in some cases a considerable interval of time must have elapsed between the fall of two blocks lying one on the other—an interval sufficiently great for the formation of the cake of stalagmite between them, and which is sometimes fully 6 inches thick." (*Rep. Brit. Assoc.* 1865, p. 19.)

Again, after describing several objects of interest, and especially a bone comb, the Third Report says, " This interesting object, the two fragments of combs, the grit spindle-whorl previously mentioned, a cockle shell, several potsherds, and a bone cut with some keen edged tool, were found in the south-eastern portion of the Great Chamber, where the overlying Black Mould was itself overlaid by a cake of stalagmite, which was attached to the wall of the cavern, from 1 to 2 inches thick, and which measured 7 feet from north to south, by 6 from east to west. In many instances stalagmite, fully as thick, had been found on the large blocks of limestone lying on the Black Mould ; but this was the first, and, indeed, is at present the only example of such a cake formed immediately on the Black deposit itself." (*Ibid.* 1867, p. 28.)

The " cake of stalagmite " mentioned in the passage just quoted from the " Third Report " was the only one found in the Cavern overlying the " Black Mould," that is the only deposit containing comparatively recent objects ; and was, therefore, presumably the " cake " to which Dr. Geikie alluded. He, however, spoke of the objects found immediately beneath it as " remains of Romano-Saxon times." This he did, I believe, on his own responsibility, no one else having so characterized them, so far as I am aware.

The noteworthy point in Quotation VI., however, is the

statement to the effect that the cake of stalagmite was occasionally "six inches in thickness," whilst the passage quoted from the Third Report makes it "from 1 to 2 inches thick." The fact is it was nowhere so much as two inches. The "six inches," I suspect, really belonged to the cake mentioned in the First Report, which cake is not spoken of as having any artifical or other objects of interest beneath it, and had nothing whatever to do with the "cake" of the Third Report. This is the supposed *mixing* which not improbably took place in the author's memory.

The error—for such I must regard it—though not important in itself, is made to be so by Dr. Geikie, who bases on the alleged "*six* inches" a calculation as to the possible amount of time represented by the Cavern Stalagmites. I have elsewhere, and frequently, expressed my belief that such calculations were not very trustworthy, but, allowing that to pass, it will be seen that the rate of accretion being taken at six, instead of two, inches in 2,000 years, as Dr. Geikie supposes, the time arrived at must be three times too small.

Cause of the fall of Fragments from Cavern Roof and Walls.

Quotation VII.—"Throughout all the cave deposits occur, more or less frequently, large and small angular fragments of limestone that have evidently fallen from the sides and roof. Sometimes these are scattered pretty equally through the floor accumulations, at other times they are perhaps more numerous at some levels than at others. They seem also to be present most abundantly in the chambers or galleries that open directly to the day, or which can be shown to have formerly had some direct connection with the external atmosphere . . . . .

"The fragments may have been detached from the roof in various ways. It cannot be doubted that, as Mr. Pengelly has pointed out (*Trans. Devon. Assoc.* vol. vii., 1875, p. 315), the gradual widening of the joints in limestone by the corrosive action of percolating water must occasionally loosen large blocks, and allow these to fall away; and as percolation is always going on, such accidents as the sudden dislodgment of fragments may take place at any moment, in any part of a cave, and under any condition of climate. Again, it is not improbable, as some have suggested, that the tremor of the ground during an earthquake might shake down many half-loosened blocks and fragments. But such will hardly account for all or even for any great proportion of the scattered blocks and thick aggregations of limestone *débris* that are met with in so many caves. I am inclined to believe that very many of these fragments may have been dislodged by the action of frost, which at some epochs during the Pleistocene Period was certainly more intense in our latitude than it is now. This would account for the more abundant presence of fallen blocks and *débris* at and near the entrances of caves, for in the deeper recesses the cold would necessarily be less intense, and less capable therefore of rupturing the limestone and detaching angular fragments. If the dislodgment of all these fragments had been due solely to the corrosive action of percolating water or to the vibrations of earthquakes, we should be at a loss to understand why the greatest falls should have so frequently taken place in those portions of the caves that are most accessible to the influence of the external atmosphere." pp. 85–6.

The foregoing somewhat lengthy quotation contains two statements to which it seems desirable to call attention :

1. That angular fragments of limestone that have fallen from the roof seem "to be present most abundantly in the chambers or galleries that open directly to the day, or which can be shown to have formerly had some direct connection with the external atmosphere."

2. That very many of the fragments were dislodged by frost during periods of greater cold than is now experienced in Devonshire.

1. With regard to the first, I can only say that the statement does not apply to Kent's Hole, nor to any Devonshire Cavern I have studied. Whilst it is true that blocks were numerous and large in "The Great Chamber" and "The Vestibule," into which the two entrances to Kent's Hole open respectively, it is equally true that they were still more numerous and, at least, equally large, in Chambers far in the interior; and there is not the shadow of a doubt that that part of "The Long Arcade," whence "Underhay's Gallery" and "The Labyrinth" branch off—that is to say the most central portion of the Cavern—surpassed all other parts in the number and the size of the blocks it contained. "The Labyrinth itself was also crowded with them; indeed, it took its name from the difficulty which visitors had in finding their way between them. Further, were I asked to name the mass in the Cavern which is at present most likely to fall, it would certainly be that which divides partially "The Laby-

rinth" from "The Long Arcade," where there never could have been any "direct connection with the external atmosphere."

Again, there is adjacent to the churchyard at Buckfastleigh, a large disused quarry termed "Baker's Pits," where, many years ago, the workmen, having removed many thousand tons of limestone, broke into a large cavern.   I visited it on 22nd April, 1859, and amongst my memoranda, made at the time, the following occurs :—"Huge masses of limestone, which had fallen from the roof, lay in the wildest confusion" (see *Trans. Devon. Assoc.* vi. 72). Here, again, there certainly never had been any "direct communication with the external atmosphere."

2. The temperature of Kent's Hole is at present, as stated already, invariable throughout the year, and from one year to another, and stands at 51·°5 Fahr.—the existing mean annual temperature of the surrounding district.   The visitor steps into a hot or a cold bath—and that within five feet of the entrance—according as his visit is made in the depth of winter or in the height of summer.   It need not be said that this is precisely what everyone would expect who has paid attention to the question of underground temperature.   It would be absurd to doubt that during certain geological times the mean annual temperature of Devonshire has been lower, and at others higher, than at present; but whatever it may have been, that was, for that time, the minimum invariable temperature of Kent's Hole.   I say the minimum because if, since that time, the Cavern Hill has lost any considerable portion of its summit, the Cavern temperature, though invariable for the period, would exceed the mean annual temperature of the immediate exterior—the excess being in proportion to the depth below the surface in the ratio of 1° Fahr. for every (say) 60 feet.

In order, therefore, for frost to have existed in the interior of Kent's Hole the Torquay district must have been on the isotherm of 32° Fahr., or on a still lower one; that is to say it must have had a mean annual temperature at least 20° Fahr. below that which obtains at present.   According to Johnston's *Physical Atlas* the isotherm of 32° Fahr. passes, at present, through the White Sea, a very little south of the North Cape, along the north coast of Iceland, a very little south of Cape Farewell, through mid Labrador and Hudson's Bay.   It is for the student of Geological Climatology to say whether he is prepared to assign such a climate to the shores of Torbay.

It must be borne in mind that frost does the work of breaking up rocks largely through the action of successively and frequently freezing and thawing, owing to frequent, perhaps diurnal, fluctuations of temperature; but that in the Cavern the condition would be "once a frost always a frost" until a sufficient rise took place in the mean annual temperature of the district, when the Cavern frost would cease for ever. I am somewhat doubtful whether we are well acquainted with the physical action of ice under such conditions, and whether it would be disintegrating.

Before closing this Note, I will add that there can be no doubt that some of the large blocks of limestone found in Kent's Hole fell within historic times, when ice must have been as unknown there, even at a yard within the entrance, as it is at present.

I cannot take leave of Dr. Geikie's work without thanking him very cordially for so valuable a contribution to Geological Literature.

IV. CARTER, Mr. H. J., on the BUDLEIGH SALTERTON TRIASSIC PEBBLES. 1881.

Mr. Davidson, F.R.S., F.L.S., F.G.S., &c. in his *Monograph of the British Fossil Brachiopoda,* Vol. iv., Part iv., published by the *Palæontographical Society* in 1881, quotes an interesting statement prepared by Mr. H. J. Carter, F.R.S., of Budleigh Salterton, in which the following paragraph occurs :—

"The Cove of Budleigh Salterton is about two and a half miles long, confronted by a narrow pebble beach, bordered by the sea on one side, and for the most part by high cliffs of the New Red Sandstone series, capped by a thin detrital layer of the flinty remains of the Cretaceous, which formerly overlaid it, on the other. The pebbles of this beach, which are derived from the sources just mentioned, are of all sizes below a foot in diameter; and from the prevalence of the south-west wind on this coast, they are chiefly gathered together at its eastern end, *although kept from extending further on either side by the presence of reefs of New Red Sandstone conglomerate projecting into the sea."* p. 317.

There appears to be no room to doubt that, by the words I have italicised in the foregoing quotation, Mr. Carter intended to state that the famous Budleigh Salterton pebbles are not transported beyond Otterton Head on the east, or beyond the Straight Point on the west.

It is well known that there is a famous bed of pebbles, chiefly quartzites, and some of them fossiliferous, in the Triassic, or New Red Sandstone, cliff immediately west of the village of Budleigh Salterton. The attention of the scientific world was first directed to them, I believe, by Mr. W. Vicary, F.G.S., of Exeter, who, in 1863, read a paper on them to the Geological Society of London. (See *Quart. Journ. Geol. Soc.* xx. 283.) It can scarcely be doubted that others had previously observed that the pebbles yielded occasional fossils, but, so far as I know, the observations, if made, were barren.

Mr. Vicary and I had, from time to time during some years, traversed systematically all the beaches from the mouth of the Exe eastward to the confines of Dorsetshire, and in a paper read to the Devonshire Association in 1864, I stated that the said quartzite pebbles of Budleigh Salterton were " easily detected at Sidmouth, Branscombe, Seaton, and Charton and Pinney Bays," a distance of fully eighteen miles eastward. (See *Trans. Devon. Assoc.* vol. i. part iii. pp. 52, 53.)

As long ago as 1849, however, Mr. Godwin Austen had announced that pebbles " derived from the older rocks of South Devon " might be collected on the Chesil Bank or Beach connecting the Isle of Portland with the mainland of Dorsetshire, and therefore farther eastward still (see *Quart. Journ. Geol. Soc.* vi. 73); whilst in 1853 Mr. J. Coode, M.I.C.E., had pointed explicitly to Budleigh Salterton as the source whence some of the Chesil Bank pebbles had travelled. (See *Min. of Proc. of Inst. of C. Engineers*, xii. 520–546.)

In 1870 Mr. Vicary and I made a careful study of the Chesil Beach in order to satisfy ourselves on this point, and were rewarded by finding at least one undoubted Budleigh Salterton quartzite pebble in every square yard of beach, and sometimes as many as three per square yard. Our search ended with Portland, but I have little doubt that pebbles of the same kind are to be met with on still more easterly beaches. (See *Trans. Devon. Assoc.* iv. 195–205.)

Proceeding now to the coast west of Budleigh Salterton, I am not prepared to say whether or not the quartzite pebbles are to be found on the strand immediately west of Straight Point; but Mr. Vicary writes me that on the left bank of the Exe, between Topsham and Exmouth, and also on the banks of the Clyst, a tributary of the Exe, they occur in great numbers.

LIST OF MEMBERS.

Year of
Election.

1879*ACLAND, H. W. D., M.A., M.D., LL.D., F.R.S., F.R.G.S., Broad
Street, Oxford.

1880 Acland, Rev. Preb., M.A., Broadclyst, Exeter.

1875 Adams, James, M.D., Ashburton.

1877 Adams, James, jun., Kingsbridge.

1872†Adams, John Couch, M.A., D.C.L., F.R.S., F.R.A.S, Director of
Observatory and Lowndean Professor of Astronomy and
Geometry in the University of Cambridge, The Obser-
vatory, Cambridge.

1880 Adams, S. P., Bridgetown, Totnes.

1878 Alexander, James, M.D., Paignton.

1874 Alsop, R., Teignmouth Bank, Teignmouth.

1877 Amery, Jasper, Glena, Kingsbridge.

1869 AMERY, J. S., Druid, Ashburton.

1869 AMERY, P. F. S., Druid, Ashburton.

1875*Andrew, T., F.G.S., Southernhay, Exeter.

1877 Andrews, R., Modbury.

1880 Anthony, Rev. F. Evans, Woodland Terrace, Plymouth.

1863 APPLETON, EDWARD, F.R.I.B.A., 1, Vaughan Parade, Torquay.

1880 Armstrong, L., St. Bernard's, Newton Abbot.

1870 Arnold, G., Dolton.

1877 Arthur, Edward, Mounts, R.S.O., South Devon.

1868 Ashley, J., Honiton.

1874 Ayerst, J. S. A., M.D , 2, Belgrave Terrace, Torquay.

1881 Baillie, Rev. J., 20, Upper Camden Place, Bath.

1881 Baker, A., M.D., 31, High Street, Dawlish.

1880 BAKER, A. DE WINTER, L.R.C.P., M.R.C.S. (HON. LOCAL
TREASURER), 2, Lawn Terrace, Dawlish.

1877 Balkwill, B., Devon and Cornwall Bank, Kingsbridge.
1871 Bangham, Joseph, Torrington.
1881 Barham, Rev. R. H. D., B.A., 11, West Cliff, Dawlish, President Teign Naturalists' Field Club.
1878 Baring-Gould, Rev. S., M.A., Lew Trenchard, Lewdown.
1862 Barnes, Rev. Preb., M.A., The Vicarage, Heavitree, Exeter.
1879 BARNETT, C. G., Ilfracombe.
1879 Baron, Rev. J., D.D., F.S.A., Rectory, Upton Scudamore, Warminster, Wilts.
1877 Bartlett, Rev. J. M., Manor House, Ludbrooke, Modbury, Ivybridge.
1876 Bastard, B. J. P., Kitley, Yealmpton, South Devon.
1862 BATE, C. SPENCE, F.R.S., &c., 8, Mulgrave Place, Plymouth.
1872 Bate, James, J. R., Bampton Street, Tiverton.
1873 Batten, J. Hallett, F.R.G.S., M.R.A.S., 2, Manston Terrace, Exeter.
1866 Bayly, John, Seven Trees, Plymouth.
1871*Bayly, Robert, Torr Grove, Plymouth.
1876 Beatty, W., Buckfastleigh.
1875 Bedford, Admiral E. I., R.N., Fairlawn, Paignton.
1878 Benbow, V., Torbay Mount, Paignton.
1875 Bennett, C., 5, Victoria Terrace, Mount Radford, Exeter.
1877 Bennett, E. Gasking, 10, Woodland Terrace, Plymouth.
1877 Berry, J., 18, Belgrave Terrace, Torquay.
1879 Berthon, Miss, Southcombe, Paignton.
1876 Bickford, J., Bank, Ashburton.
1880 Birch, Rev. W. M., M.A., Vicarage, Ashburton.
1879 Birkmyer, J., 13, Lower Terrace, Mount Radford, Exeter.
1876 Bishop, E., 4, Lancaster Terrace, Regent's Park, London, N.W.
1878 Blackmore, Rev. R., M.A., Probus, Cornwall.
1872 Borlase, W. C., F.S.A., M.P., Laregan, Penzance.
1876 Bovey, Edward, Baddaford, Staverton, Buckfastleigh.
1873 Bowring, L. B., C.S.I., Lavrockbeare, Torquay.
1874 Bowring, Lady, 7, Baring Crescent, Exeter.
1876†Bray, Mrs., 40, Brompton Crescent, South Kensington.
1869 Brendon, William, George Street, Plymouth.
1872 Brent, F., 19, Clarendon Place, Plymouth.
1873 Brewin, R., Bearsden, Ide, Exeter.
1872 Bridges, W. T., D.C.L., Torwood, Torquay.
1878 Bridgman, G. Soudon, Brampton, Torquay.
1870 Briggs, T. R. A., F.L.S., 4, Richmond Villas, Saltash Road, Plymouth.
1872 Brodrick, W., B.A., Littlehill, Chudleigh.
1879 Brown, D., M.D., Pen y Graig, Kingskerswell.
1878 Brown, H., Greystone, Teignmouth.
1878 Brown, James, Goodrington House, Paignton.
1876 Brown, M. G., Stanmore House, Dawlish.
1881*Bryant, Wilberforce, Southbank, Surbiton, Surrey.

1879*Bryce, J. B., Bystock, Exmouth.
1872 Buckingham, W., 12, Southernhay, Exeter.
1874 Bulteel, C., F.R.C S., Durnford Street, Stonehouse.
1871 Burch, Arthur, 5, Baring Crescent, Exeter.
1873*Burdett-Coutts, Right Hon. Baroness, 1, Stratton Street, Piccadilly, London.
1879 Butcher, L. G., Manor House, Ilfracombe.

1881 Cann, F. M., M.R.C.S., L.S.A., Sefton House, Dawlish.
1874 Carew, W. H. Pole, Antony, Torpoint.
1866*Carpenter-Garnier, J., M.P., Mount Tavy, Tavistock.
1880 Carter, S. S., Noland Park, South Brent, Ivybridge.
1881 Cartwright, H. A., Heavitree, Exeter.
1878 Cary, R. S. S., Tor Abbey, Torquay.
1880 Cary, Stanley E., J.P., Follaton House, Totnes.
1879 Cater, S., North Devon Place, Tavistock Road, Plymouth.
1866*CHAMPERNOWNE, A., M.A., F.G.S., Dartington House, Totnes.
1876 Champernowne, Rev. R., M.A., Dartington, Totnes.
1866 CHANTER, J. R., Fort Hill, Barnstaple.
1877 Chaplin, R. P., Earlham, Torquay.
1881 CHAPMAN, Rev. Professor, M.A. (PRESIDENT), Western College, Mannamead, Plymouth.
1871 Charlewood, Admiral E. P., R.N., Porthill, Northam, Bideford.
1876*Chatto, W. P., The Daison, St. Mary Church, Torquay.
1881 Clare, Capt., A.B., R.N., St. James's Square, London, S.W.
1869*Clark, R. A., Wentworth, Torquay.
1871 Clements, Rev. H. G. J., M.A., Vicarage, Sidmouth.
1872 Clifford, Col. Morgan, St. Ronan's, Torquay.
1881 Clifford, Right Hon. Lord, Ugbrooke, Chudleigh.
1875 Clinton, Right Hon. Lord, Heanton Satchville, Beaford.
1874 Coffin, J. R. Pine, Portledge, Bideford.
1870 Coffin, T., 81, Queen's Crescent, Haverstock Hill, London, N.W.
1868*COLERIDGE, Right Hon. Lord, M.A., 1, Sussex Square, London.
1873 Coleridge, W. R., Salston, Ottery St. Mary.
1879 Collier, Arthur Bevan, Carthamartha, Callington.
1876 COLLIER, Right Hon. Sir R , M.A., Bigod's Hall, Dunmow, Essex.
1866 COLLIER, W. F., Woodtown, Horrabridge.
1871 Cook, Rev. Precentor, M.A., The Close, Exeter.
1879 Cooke, L. R., Lauriston Hall, Torquay.
1880 Cornish-Bowden, F. J., Blackhall House, Ivybridge, S. Devon.
1877 Cornish, J. F., Stancombe, Kingsbridge.
1881*Cornish, Rev. J. F., Christ's Hospital, London, E.C.
1867 COTTON, R. W., Woodleigh, Newton Abbot.
1866 COTTON, W., F.S.A., The Close, Exeter.
1878 Cranford, R., *Directory Office*, Dartmouth.
1877 Crimp, W. A., Kingsbridge.
1880 CROFT, C. W., Devon and Cornwall Bank, Totnes.

1881 Crossing, W., Splatton, South Brent, Devon.
1877 Cubitt, W., J.P., Fallapit, Mounts, R.S.O., South Devon.

1881 Darbyshire, C., Riversdale, Ilfracombe.
1875 David, Rev. W., Colleton Crescent, Exeter.
1875 DAVIDSON, J. B., Secktor House, Axminster.
1877 Davies, W., Kingsbridge.
1881 Davies, F., Dawlish.
1878 Davson, F. A., M.D., Dartmouth.
1878 Davy, A. J., Fleet Street, Torquay.
1880 Dawkins, Admiral, Maisonette, Stoke Gabriel, Totnes.
1870 De Larue, P. F., M.R.C.S., 40, Ker Street, Devonport.
1879 Dennis, J. C., Ilfracombe.
1873 DEVON, Right Hon. the Earl of, Powderham Castle, Exeter.
1881 Discombe, W., The Strand, Dawlish.
1862 Divett, John, M.A., Bovey Tracey.
1867 DOE, G., Castle Street, Great Torrington.
1869*Douglas, Rev. R., M.A., Manaton, Moretonhampstead.
1873*Dowie, J. M., Wetstones, West Kirby, Birkenhead.
1876 DOWNES, Rev. W., B.A., F.G.S., Kentisbeare, Collumpton.
1880 Drake, Sir W. R., 12, Prince's Gardens, South Kensington,
     London.
1878 Dredge, Rev. J. Ingle, Buckland Brewer, Bideford.
1877 Dumbleton, Rev. E. N., M.A., St. James's Rectory, Exeter.
1879 Dymond, A. H., Castle Chambers, Exeter.
1871 Dymond, F. W., 3, Manston Terrace, Exeter.
1872 DYMOND, R., F.S.A., Bampfylde House, Exeter.

1877 Eady, Mrs., Coombe Royal, Kingsbridge.
1881 Eales, C., J.P., Eastdon, Starcross.
1876 EARLE, Venerable Archdeacon, West Alvington, Kingsbridge.
1878 Edgelow, F., Hermosa, Teignmouth.
1880 Edmonds, T. H., Bridgetown, Totnes.
1879 Edmonds, Rev. W. J., M.A., High Bray Rectory, Southmolton.
1873 Ellacombe, Rev. H. T., F.S.A., M.A., Clyst St. George.
1877 Elliot, J., Tresillian, Kingsbridge.
1877 Elliot, R. L., Tresillian, Kingsbridge.
1878 ELWORTHY, F. T., Foxdown, Wellington, Somersetshire.
1881 Ermen, P. A., Ermenville, Dawlish.
1869*Evans, J., D.C.L., LL.D., F.R.S., F.S.A., F.G.S., Nash Mills, Hemel
     Hempstead, Herts.
1877 Evans, J. L., Moreton House, Tyndall's Park, Bristol.
1880 Evans, Parker N., 23, Pembroke Road, Clifton, Bristol.
1880 Everett, Rev. A. J., M.A., Berry Pomeroy, Totnes.
1871*EXETER, Right Rev. the Lord Bishop of, The Palace, Exeter.

1869*Farley, H. W., C.E., Devon County Surveyor's Office, Post
     Office Chambers, Queen Street, Exeter.

1879 Featherstone, Rev. S., M.A., Whitchurch Vicarage, Tavistock.
1864 Finch, T., M.D., F.R.A.S., Westville, St. Mary Church, Torquay.
1875 FIRTH, F. H., Cator Court, Ashburton.
1873 Fisher, Edward, Blackmore Hall, Sidmouth.
1875 Fisher, G., High Street, Torrington.
1876 Fisher, Thomas, M.D.,
1880 Fixsen, Rev. J. F., M.A., Ugborough Vicarage, Ivybridge.
1876 Fleming, J., Bigadon, Buckfastleigh.
1876 Foaden, J. H., Ashburton.
1867 Fortescue, Right Hon. Earl, Castle Hill, Southmolton.
1867*Foster, Rev. J. P., M.A., The Vicarage, Mirfield, Normanton, Yorkshire.
1878 Foster, Samuel, Abergeldie, Torquay.
1876 Fouracre, J. T., Chapel Street, Stonehouse, Plymouth.
1875 Fowler, C., Villa Mentone, Torre, Torquay.
1876*Fowler, Rev. W. W., Repton, Burton-on-Trent.
1876 Fox, Charles, Kingsbridge.
1877 Fox, George, Kingsbridge.
1863 Fox, S. B., 7, Southernhay, Exeter.
1880 French, W., North Tawton.
1881 FRIEND, Rev. Hilderic, 3, Alma Terrace, Newton Abbot.
1881 Friend, H. L., Dawlish.
1874†Froude, J. A., M.A., 5, Onslow Gardens, London.
1876 Fulford, F. D., Exmouth.
1880 Furneaux, J., Hill Crest, Buckfastleigh.

1872 Galton, J. C., M.A., F.L.S., New University Club, St. James's Street, London, W.
1862 GAMLEN, W. H., Brampford Speke, Exeter.
1881 Garland, T. G. T., 2, Stafford Villas, Heavitree, Exeter.
1881 Gastrell, Major-General, 7, Lansdown Place, Wimbledon, Surrey,
1876*Gaye, Henry S., M.D., 3, Courtenay Terrace, Newton Abbot.
1872*Geare, J. G., Exeter.
1881 Germon, Col., Gortlee, Dawlish.
1871*GERVIS, W. S., M.D., F.G.S., Ashburton.
1872 Gidley, Bartholomew C., M.A., Hoopern House, Exeter.
1865 GILL, H. S., J.P., Tiverton.
1881 Gill, W., 1, West Street, Tavistock.
1875 Glubb, P. B., Potacre Street, Torrington.
1877*Glyde, E. E., F.M.S., Kirkham, Babbacombe, Torquay.
1868*Goldsmid, Sir Julian, Bart., M.A., M.P., 105, Piccadilly, London, W.
1880 Gosset, F., Lieut., R.E., 9, Molesworth Terrace, Stoke, Devonport.
1876 Goodrick, G., 11, George Road, Edgbaston, Birmingham.

1878 GREGORY, A., Bank, Paignton.
1878 Gregory, Rev. E. L., M.A., Halberton Vicarage, Tiverton.
1881 Gregory, A. T., Gold Street, Tiverton.
1877 Gretton, Rev. W. H., M.A., Alvanley, Torquay.
1875 Groser, A., North Hill Villa, Plymouth.
1873 Grundy, T., Beetlands, Sidmouth.
1878 Grundy, Rev. T. R., Elbury Lodge, Newton Abbot.
1876 Guenett, Rev. J. F., Point-in-View, Lympstone, Exeter.
1875 Guille, Rev. G. de Carteret, Rectory, Little Torrington.
1874 Gulson, J. R., East Cliff, Teignmouth.
1873*Guyer, J. B., F.C.S, 1, Lisburne Cottages, Torquay.

1880 Hacker, S., Newton Abbot.
1870 Haddy, Rev. J. P., 61, Chapel Street, Devonport.
1880 Hains, J., J.P., Bridgetown, Totnes.
1862 Haldon, Right Hon. Lord, Haldon House, Exeter.
1867*HALL, TOWNSEND M., F.G.S., Pilton, Barnstaple.
1873*Halliday, W. H., M.A., J.P., Glenthorn, Lynmouth, Barnstaple.
1862 HAMILTON, A. H. A., M.A., Fairfield Lodge, Exeter.
1880 Hamlyn, James, Bossell Park, Buckfastleigh.
1880 Hamlyn, John, Toll Marsh, Buckfastleigh.
1880 Hamlyn, Joseph, Park View, Buckfastleigh.
1880 Hamlyn, W., Croppin's Park, Buckfastleigh.
1878 Hamlyn, W. B., 4, Abbey Crescent, Torquay.
1873*Hanbury, S., Bishopstowe, Torquay.
1868 Harper, J., L.R.C.P., Bear Street, Barnstaple.
1874 Harpley, R. B., West Hartlepool.
1862 HARPLEY, Rev. W., M A., F.C.P.S. (HON. GENERAL SECRETARY),
     Clayhanger Rectory, Tiverton.
1878 Harris, Rev. E., M.A., Grammar School, Exeter.
1877 Harris, Rev. S. G., M.A., Highweek, Newton Abbot.
1873*Harvey, J. T., Aberfeldie, Torquay.
1881 Hatcher, W., Dawlish.
1875*Hatt-Cook, Herbert, Hartford Hall, Cheshire.
1869 HAWKER, Rev. Treasurer, M.A., Berrynarbor Rectory, Ilfra-
     combe.
1869*Hayne, C. Seale, Kingswear Castle, Dartmouth.
1872 Hayward, P., Cathedral Yard, Exeter.
1862 Hearder, G. E., Chelston Cottage, Cockington, Torquay.
1865 Hearder, W., Rocombe, Torquay.
1868*Heberden, Rev. W., M.A., 14, Gloucester Place, Portman
     Square, London.
1875 Hedgeland, Rev. Preb., M.A., Penzance.
1871 Heineken, N. S., Sidmouth.
1880 Hewetson, T., Wear, Staverton, Buckfastleigh.
1876 Hill, H. S., *Cornish Telegraph*, Penzance.
1872 Hill, J., J.P., Pitt House, Moretonhampstead, Exeter.
1862 Hine, J., F.R.I.B.A., 7, Mulgrave Place, Plymouth.

1869 Hingston, R., Dartmouth.
1873 Hodge, B. T., M.D., High Street, Sidmouth.
1881 Hodgson, Mrs., Bonaly Tower, Colinton, Scotland.
1880 Holman, W., Bridgetown, Totnes.
1877 Holt, Major, Ogbeare Hall, Holsworthy, Devon.
1872 Hooper, B., Bournbrook, Torquay.
1878 Hooper, J., Kingsbridge.
1879 Hooper, S., Hatherleigh.
1872 Horniman, W. H., Coombe Cliff House, Croydon, Surrey.
1871 Hounsell, H. S., M.D., Woodlands, Torquay.
1868*HUNT, A. R., M.A., F.G.S., Southwood, Torquay.
1878 Hunton, T., B.A., Bronshill, Torquay.
1877 Hurrell, A. W., B.A., The Knowle, Kingsbridge.
1877 Hurrell, Henry, LL.B., 1, New Court, Middle Temple,
　　　　London.
1876 Hurrell, J. S., Buttville, Kingsbridge.
1876 Hurrell, R., The Knowle, Kingsbridge.
1873 Hutchings, Rev. H., M.A., The Clintons, Teignmouth.
1868 HUTCHINSON, P. O., Sidmouth.

1877 Ilbert, Rev. P. A., M.A., Thurlestone Rectory, Kingsbridge.
1877 Ilbert, W. R., Bowringsleigh, Kingsbridge.
1869 Inskip, Rev. R. M., M.A., R.N., C.B., 1, Houndiscombe Place,
　　　　Plymouth.

1877 Jackson, G., F.R.C.S., St. George's Terrace, Plymouth.
1877 Jane, Rev. J., Upton Pyne Rectory, Exeter.
1862 JONES, WINSLOW, Office of Messrs. Follett and Co., Cathedral
　　　　Close, Exeter.
1871 JORDAN, W. R. H., Bitton Street, Teignmouth.

1874 KARKEEK, P. Q., 1, Matlock Terrace, Torquay.
1880*Keeling, F., F.R.G.S., St. Mary's Terrace, Colchester.
1879*Kelland, W. H., 110, Jermyn St., Piccadilly, London, S.W.
1877*Kellock, T. C., Totnes.
1872*Kennaway, Sir John H., Bart., M.A., M.P., Escot, Ottery St. Mary.
1880 King, C. R. B., 35, Oakley Square, London, N.W.
1878 Kitson, R., M.A., Hengrave, Torquay.
1865*Kitson, W. H., Hemsworth, Barton Road, Torre, Torquay.
1880 Knight, S., F.R.I.B.A., Cornhill Chambers, 62, Cornhill,
　　　　London, E.C.

1869*Laidley, Rev. W., M.A., Ware.
1879 Lake, R., Chairman of Local Board of Health, Ilfracombe.
1871 LAKE, W. C., M.D., F.M.S., 2, West Cliff Terrace, Teignmouth.
1881 Lane, John, 2, Bannercross, Abbey Road, Torquay.
1873 Lavers, W., President Torquay Natural History Society,
　　　　Upton Leigh, Torre, Torquay.

1871 Lee, Godfrey Robert, Timaru Cottage, Teignmouth.
1881 Lee, F., Chairman of the Local Board of Health, Dawlish.
1872 LEE, J. E., F.G.S., F.S.A., Villa Syracusa, Torquay.
1873 Lethaby, R., Market Place, Sidmouth.
1878 Lewis, J., Winner Street, Paington.
1877 Lidstone, J., Kingsbridge.
1880 Lilly, Rev. P., Collaton Vicarage, Paignton.
1872 Linford, W., Elstow, Old Tiverton Road, Exeter.
1879 Loosemore, R. F., Tiverton.
1873 Loveband, M. R., Torrington.
1879 Loveband, Rev. W. C., M.A., West Down Vicarage, Ilfracombe.
1877 Luscombe, John, Alvington, Torquay.
1877 Luskey, J., Vine Terrace, Kingsbridge.
1869 Luttrell, G. F., Dunster Castle, Somerset.
1881 Luxton, G. H., Queen Street, Dawlish.
1863*Lyte, F. Maxwell, F.C.S., Cotford, Oak-hill Road, Putney, London.

1881 McCasland, A., Stonelands, Dawlish.
1865 Mackenzie, F., F.R.C.S., Tiverton.
1877 Mallock, R., Cockington Court, Torquay.
1881 Manley, Rev. O., B.A., Vicarage, Dawlish.
1873 Marsh Dunn, R. M., Carlton Lodge, Teignmouth.
1881 Marshall, H. W., Reed Vale, Teignmouth.
1879 Marshall, Miss S. (Care of Mrs. Miller, 30, Girdler Road, Brook Green, London).
1871 Marshall, W., 12, Cornwall Street, Plymouth.
1871*MARTIN, JOHN MAY, C.E., F.M.S., Bradninch House, Exeter.
1870 May, J., M.R.C.S., J.P., 1, Nelson Villas, Stoke, Devonport.
1867*Merrifield, J., LL.D., F.R.A.S., Gascoigne Place, Plymouth.
1880 Michelmore, H., 11, Higher Summerlands, Exeter.
1880 Michelmore, J., Berry House, Totnes.
1879 Milligan, J., The Library, Ilfracombe.
1870 Mogg, W., Stafford's Hill, Devonport.
1873 Mogridge, Robert Palk, Withycombe House, Wiveliscombe, Somerset.
1862 Moore, W. F., The Friary, Plymouth.
1872 Mortimer, W., 14, Bedford Circus, Exeter.
1881 Moss, H., Bellevue, Dawlish.
1874*Mount Edgcumbe, Right Hon. Earl of, Mount Edgcumbe, Devonport.

1881 Nankivell, C., M.D., Layton House, Torquay.
1880 Newton, H. Cecil, 24, Finborough Road, London, S.W.
1876 Nosworthy, W., Ford, Manaton, Moretonhampstead.

1862 ORMEROD, G. W., M.A, F.G.S., F.M.S., Woodway, Teignmouth.

1872 Paige-Browne, J. B., M.A., Great Englebourne, Harberton, South Devon.
1869*Pannell, C., Walton Lodge, Torquay.
1862 PARFITT, EDWARD, Devon and Exeter Institution, Exeter.
1872 Parker, C. E., 13, Scarborough Terrace, Torquay.
1872‡Peach Charles, W., A.S.L., 30, Haddington Place, Leith Walk, Edinburgh.
1877 Pearce, F. D., Brook House, Kingsbridge.
1876 Pearse, W. E. G., M.D., 24, Bessborough Gardens, London, S.W.
1874 Pearse, W. H., M.D., 1, Alfred Place, Plymouth.
1872*Peek, Sir H. W., Bart., M.P., Rousdon, Lyme, Dorset.
1862 PENGELLY, W., F.R.S., F.G.S., &c., Lamorna, Torquay.
1872 Pershouse, F., jun., Tor Mohun House, Newton Road, Torquay.
1879 Petherick, W. J., 8, Southernhay, Exeter.
1864 PHILLIPS, J., Moor Park, near Newton Abbot.
1867 Pick, Joseph Peyton, Castle Street, Barnstaple.
1876 Pitt-Lewis, G., 1, Elm Court, Temple, London, E.C.
1881 Plumptre, R. C. E., Darlington Street, Wolverhampton.
1879 Plymouth Free Library.
1880 Pode, T. D., Slade, Ivybridge.
1862 Pollard, W., M.R.C.S., Southland House, Torquay.
1868 Porter, W., M.A., Hembury Fort, Honiton.
1878*Powell, W., M.B., F.R.C.S., Hill Garden, Torquay.
1876 Power, Rev. J., M.A., Altarnun Vicarage, Launceston.
1876 Powning, Rev. J., B.D., Totnes.
1879 Price, Right Rev. Bishop, M.A., Hoone Villa, Ilfracombe.
1875 Price, W. E., South Street, Torrington.
1878 Pring, James H., M.D., Elmfield, Taunton.
1874 Proctor, W., Elmhurst, Torquay.
1867 Prowse, A. P., Horrabridge.
1878 Pulliblank, Rev. J., M.A., St. Mary's Lane, Walton-on-the-Hill, Liverpool.
1880 Punchard, W. H., Springville, Totnes.
1862 PYCROFT, G., M.R.C.S., F.G.S., Kenton, Exeter.

1869*Radford, I. C.
1868*Radford, W. T., M.B., F.R.A.S., Sidmount, Sidmouth.
1876 Radford, Rev. W. T. A., Down St. Mary Rectory, Bow, North Devon.
1872 Ramsay, H., M.D., Duncan House, Torquay.
1873*Rathbone, T., M.A., Backwood, Neston, Cheshire.
1877 Rayer, W. C., J.P., Holcombe Court, Wellington, Somerset.
1880 Reed, T. C., Clifton Villa, Launceston, Cornwall.
1872 Reichel, Rev. Oswald J., B.C.L., Sparsholt, Wantage, Berks.
1873 Remfry, G. F., Firsleigh, Torquay.
1869 Ridgway, Colonel, Sheplegh Court, Blackawton, South Devon.
1862 RISK, Rev. J. E., M.A., St. Andrew's Chapelry, Plymouth.

1879 Robbins, W. M., High Street, Ilfracombe.
1877 Roberts, I., F.G.S., Kennessee, Maghull, Lancashire.
1867 Rock, W. F., Hyde Cliff, Wellington Grove, Blackheath.
1870 Rolston, G. T., M.R.C.S., Stoke, Devonport.
1878 Rooker, W. S., Bideford.
1872 Rossall, J. H., M.A., Norwood, Torquay.
1865 Row, W. N., J.P., Cove, Tiverton.
1862 ROWE, J. BROOKING, F.S.A., F.L.S. (PRESIDENT ELECT), Plymouth.
1866 Russell, Lord Arthur J. E., M.P., 10, South Audley Street, London.
1869*Ryder, J. W. W., J.P., 5, Tamar Terrace, Stoke, Devonport.

1869 Sanford, W. A., F.G.S., Nynehead Court, Wellington, Somerset.
1881*Saunders, E. Symes, Devon County Asylum, Exminster.
1877*Saunders, J. Symes, M.B., Devon County Asylum, Exminster.
1880 Saunders, W. S., 3, Rougemont Terrace, Exeter.
1881 Savile, Lieut.-Colonel, J.P., Langdon, Dawlish.
1876 Scott, T. A. Sommers, Reay Cottage, Reigate, Surrey.
1865 Scott, W. B., Chudleigh.
1876 Sharman, Rev. W., F.G.S., 20, Headland Park, Plymouth.
1881 Sharp, Rev. G. W., Plantation House, Dawlish.
1879 Shelly, J., 20, Princess Square, Plymouth.
1868 Sidmouth, Right Hon. Viscount, Upottery Manor, Honiton.
1876 Sinclair, J. B., 13, Park Road, Southborough, Tunbridge Wells.
1869*Sivewright, J., The Grove, Torquay.
1878 Slade, S. H., Simla, Goodrington, Paignton.
1878 SLADE-KING, E. J., M.D., L. San. Sc., Croft Side, Ilfracombe.
1879 SLADE-KING, Mrs., Croft Side, Ilfracombe.
1874 Smith, E., F.C.S., Strand, Torquay.
1879 SMITH, Rev. Preb., M.A. (HON. LOCAL SECRETARY ELECT), Crediton.
1873*Sole, Major W. H., Hareston, Torquay.
1874*Somerset, His Grace the Duke of, Stover, Newton Bushel.
1879 Spencer, Rev. T., The Presbytery, Ilfracombe.
1864*Spragge, F. H., The Quarry, Paignton.
1874*Spragge, F. P., The Quarry, Paignton.
1877 Square, J. Harris, Barnfield, Kingsbridge.
1878 Square, W., F.R.C.S., Plymouth.
1874 Standerwick, R., Chagford.
1868 Stebbing, Rev. T. R. R., M.A., Kensington House, Calverley Park, Tunbridge Wells, Kent.
1876 Stevens, H., Hazeldene, Ashburton.
1876 Stentiford, C. D., *Western Morning News* Office, Plymouth.
1872*Stewart-Savile, Rev. F. A., M.A., Kilmorie, Torquay.
1880 Stockdale, W. Colebrooke, Bridgetown, Totnes.
1876*Stone, J., Leusdon Lodge, Ashburton.
1879 Stoneham, P., F.R.C.S., Ilfracombe.

1875 Strangways, Rev. H. Fox, Silverton Rectory, Collumpton.
1869 Studdy, H., Waddeton Court, Brixham.
1875*Sulivan, Miss, Broom House, Fulham.

1876 Tanner, E. Fearnley, Hawson Court, Buckfastleigh.
1881 Tapper, W., Dawlish.
1877 Taylor, H., M.D., Ellerton, Torre, Torquay.
1880 Taylor, R. W., M.A., Kelly College, Tavistock.
1881 Tebbitt, W., Brooklands, Dawlish.
1876*Templer, J. G. J., M.A., Lindridge, Teignmouth.
1877 Thomas, Henry Drew, Dix's Field, Exeter.
1872 Thomas, J. L., New Hayes, St. Thomas, Exeter.
1872 Thomson, Spencer, M.D., Ashton, Torquay.
1868 Thornton, Rev. J. H., B.A., North Bovey Rectory, Moreton-
            hampstead.
1878 Tippetts, G. E., The Mount, Mannamead, Plymouth.
1878 Tomlinson, Rev. J. P., Rooklands, Torquay.
1869*Tothill, W., Stoke Bishop, Bristol.
1872 Tozer, Henry, Ashburton.
1876 Tozer, J., Ashburton.
1876 Tozer, Solomon, East Street, Ashburton.
1876 Trehane, James, Wanbro', Torquay.
1880 Trehane, John, St. David's Hill, Exeter.
1876 Tucker, Edwin, Ashburton.
1876 TUCKER, R. C., Ashburton.
1878 TUCKER, W. EDWARD, Paignton.
1872 Turnbull, Lieut.-Col. J. R., The Priory, Torquay.
1877 Turner, Miss E., Coombe Royal, Kingsbridge.
1880 Turner, T., J.P., F.M.S., Cullompton.

1876 Ubsdell, H., Buckfastleigh.
1875 USSHER, W. A. E., F.G.S., 28, Jermyn Street, London, S.W.

1870 Vallack, C., 5, St. Michael's Terrace, Stoke, Devonport.
1881 Varwell, H. B., Melrose, Exeter.
1872 VARWELL, P., Melrose, Exeter.
1881 Veysey, Rev. J., 3, Plantation Terrace, Dawlish.
1862*Vicary, W., F.G.S., The Priory, Colleton Crescent, Exeter.
1862 VIVIAN, E., M.A. (GENERAL TREASURER), Woodfield, Torquay.

1881 Wade, C. J., J.P., Knowle, Dawlish.
1879 Wainwright, T., Grammar School, Barnstaple.
1880 Walker, W. H., Princess Place, Plymouth.
1880 Walrond, H., Dulford House, Cullompton.
1878 Warner, Rev. G. T., M.A., The College, Newton Abbot.
1878 Watkins, Rev. W., Bridgetown, Totnes.
1880 Watts, F., Newton Abbot.

1864 Weeks, C., 83, Union Street, Torquay.
1877 Were, H. B., Woodland Vicarage, Ashburton.
1870*Were, T. K., M.A., Cotlands, Sidmouth.
1866*Weymouth, R. F., D. LIT., M.A., Mill Hill, Middlesex, N.W.
1877 Weymouth, T. W., Woolston House, Kingsbridge.
1878 Whidborne, G. F., M.A., F.G.S., Charante, Torquay.
1880 WHIDBORNE, J. S., (HON. LOCAL SECRETARY), 1, Cleveland
     Terrace, Dawlish.
1881 Whidborne, J., Gorway, Teignmouth.
1872‡Whitaker, W., B.A., F.G.S., Geological Survey Office, 28,
     Jerymn Street, London, S.W.
1880 White, Rev. F. Gilbert, Leusdon Vicarage, Ashburton.
1876 White, G. T., Glenthorne, St. Mary Church, Torquay.
1864 White, J. T., Myrtle Villa, Torquay.
1867 White, Richard, Instow, Barnstaple.
1875 White-Thomson, Col., Broomford Manor, Exbourne, North
     Devon.
1871 Whiteway, J. H., Brookfield, Teignmouth.
1870 Whitley, N., Penarth, Truro.
1872 Wilcocks, H., Spurbarne, St. Leonard's, Exeter.
1878 Wilks, G. F. A., M.D., Stanbury, Torquay.
1876 Willan, L., M.D., The Library, Penzance.
1881 Willcocks, F., M.D., King's College Hospital, Lincoln's Inn
     Fields, London, W.C.
1877*Willcocks, Rev. E. J., M.A., The School House, Warrington,
     Lancashire [Teignmouth].
1877*Willcocks, G. W., A.I.C.E., 34, Great George Street, West-
     minster [Teignmouth].
1877*Willcocks, R. H., LL.B., 34, Great George Street, West-
     minster [Teignmouth].
1876*Willcocks, W. K., M.A., 52, Scarsdale Villas, Kensington,
     London. W. [Teignmouth].
1871 Willett, J. S., Monkleigh, Torrington.
1871 Wills, Joseph, Haven Bank House, St. Thomas, Exeter.
1881 Wills, Rev. J., 21, Grayland Villa, Stony Lane, Catford, S.E.
1875 Wiltshire, Rev. T., M.A., F.G.S., F.L.S., F.R.A.S., Hon. Sec.
     Palæontological and Ray Societies, 25, Granville Park,
     Lewisham, London. S.W.
1875 WINDEATT, EDWARD, Totnes.
1866 Windeatt, John, Woodland House, Plymouth.
1872 WINDEATT, T. W., Totnes.
1872*Winwood, Rev. H. H., M.A., F.G.S., 11, Cavendish Crescent,
     Bath.
1878 Wolfe, Rev. Preb., M.A., Arthington, Torquay.
1880 Wolfe, J. E., Arthington, Torquay.
1881 Wood, Charles William, B.A., Q.C., Gerston House, Paignton.
1872 WORTH, R. N., F.G.S., President Plymouth Institution,
     4, Seaton Avenue, Plymouth.

1876 WORTHY, Charles, 17, Ryecroft Terrace, Ryecroft Road, Lewisham, London. E.C.
1870 Wren, A.B., Lenwood, Bideford.
1881 Wright, Miss F. C., Beaconsfield, Exmouth.
1876 Wright, W. H. K., 7, Headlands Park, Plymouth.

1880 Yonge, Rev. Duke, M.A., Puslinch, Yealmpton, S. Devon.

The following Table shows the progress and present state of the Association with respect to the number of Members.

	Honorary.	Corresponding.	Life.	Annual.	Total.
July 27th, 1880 ..	3	2	61	442	508
Since elected......	...	...	9	46	55
Since deceased	...	...	...	4	4
Since withdrawn ..	...	...	...	65	65
Since erased	...	...	...	11	11
July 28th, 1881	3	2	70	408	483

INDEX

TO

THIRTEENTH VOLUME OF THE TRANSACTIONS OF THE DEVONSHIRE ASSOCIATION
FOR THE ADVANCEMENT OF SCIENCE, LITERATURE, AND ART.

LIST OF CORRECTIONS REQUIRED IN "TRANSACTIONS OF THE DEVONSHIRE ASSOCIATION," VOL. XIII., 1881.

Page   5, insert "SMITH, PREB.," and "WHITE, J. T.," in the List of the Council.

"   23, line 7, omit the word "enrolled."

"   29   "   36, for "£61 19s." read "£64 1s."

"   "   "   37, for "£18 7s. 6d." read "£22 1s."

"   77   "   7, for "Geological" read "Geographical."

" 100   "   29, for "this" read "that."

" 103   "   2, for "masts" read "mast."

"   "   "   13, for "Cautelhoe" read "Cantelhoe."

" 126, last line, for "1073" read "1072."

"   " 3rd note, cancel first sentence.

"   " 3rd note, line 7 from bottom, for "1073" read "1072."

" 150, line 17, for "Austin" read "Austen."

Pages 161 and 162, *passim* for "Exe" read "Ex."

Page 195, line 11, for "Swifts" read "Twists."

"   "   "   14, for "Sarcross" read "Tarcross."

"   "   "   39, for "Bogams" read "Bogans."

" 196   "   25, for "Selling" read "felling."

" 197   "   46, for "swifts" read "Twists."

" 200   "   22, for "mopp" read "mapp."

" 222   "   24, for "Dartmouth" read "Totnes."

" 306   "   32, for "MDCCCXX." read "MDCCCXXX."

" 350   "   9, for "our" read "one."

THE ANNUAL MEETING IN 1882.

THE ANNUAL MEETING AT CREDITON

WILL COMMENCE

ON TUESDAY, JULY 25TH, 1882.

Lightning Source UK Ltd.
Milton Keynes UK
UKHW012024111218
333851UK00015B/872/P

9 780282 258054